Golden Harvest
or Hearts of Gold?

Golden Harvest or Hearts of Gold?
Studies on the Wartime Fate of Poles and Jews

Edited by

Marek Jan Chodakiewicz
Wojciech Jerzy Muszyński
and
Paweł Styrna

Copyright © 2012 by Leopolis Press

All rights reserved. No part of this publication may be reproduced or transmitted in any fashion or manner without written permission from the publisher, except by a reviewer to quote brief passages in connection with a literary or scholarly review, or by independent scholars under "fair use" rules.

Cataloguing-in-Publication data on file with the Library of Congress

ISBN-10: 0982488815
ISBN-13: 978-0-9824888-1-2

Published in the United States by

Leopolis Press
1521 16th Street NW
Washington, DC 20036

www.leopolispress.com

Cover art: A typical Polish peasant farmhouse, similar to those whose families provided refuge for Jews escaping the Nazis.

"Anyone who fosters hatred for the Polish people is committing a sin! We must do the opposite. Against the background of anti-Semitism and general apathy, these people are glorious. There was great danger in helping us, mortal danger, not only for them but also for their families, sometimes for the entire courtyard they lived in. …

I repeat it today: to cause the death of one hundred Jews, all you needed was one Polish denouncer; to save one Jew, it sometimes took the help of ten decent Poles, the help of an entire Polish family; even if they did it for money. Some gave their apartment, and others made identity cards. Even passive help deserves appreciation. The baker who didn't denounce, for instance. It was a problem for a Polish family of four who suddenly had to start buying double quantities of rolls or meat. And what a bother it was to go far away to buy in order to support the family hiding with them. … And I argue that it doesn't matter if they took money; life wasn't easy for Poles either; and there wasn't any way to make a living. There were widows and officials who earned their few złotys by helping. And there were all kinds of people who helped."

Yitzhak Zuckerman "Antek"
A Surplus of Memory: Chronicle of the Warsaw Ghetto Uprising
(Berkeley: University of California Press, 1993), 461.

"You are Jews. If they find you they will kill you, and they will kill me, my wife, and daughters. I have a commitment to G-d Almighty to save the suffering Jew, but I do not know if I am right to do this… I go to church. I cry to G-d. He does not tell me. So I decide to save you. If G-d protects you to come from the ghetto to here and the Germans couldn't find you, I will help you."

Dr. Antoni Docha to Fania Frank Lubich and Helena Bibliowicz in the little town of Żukiewicze near Grodno in 1942. Dr. Docha of the underground Home Army and his wife Janina were recognized as Righteous Gentiles by Yad Vashem in 1979.

Shalomis Koffler Weinreb
"'I Shall Not Die But Live':
The Miracle Journey of Helena Bibliowicz," May 2009

Table of Contents

Acknowledgements   9

Introduction   11

Part I - Facts and Polemics

1. Reflections: A New Work, but the Same Old Method
– *Marek Jan Chodakiewicz*   21

2. Insults Instead of Facts: Notes on the Recent Debate
on Poles and Jews – *Peter Stachura*   64

3. "If the Facts Are Against Us, Too Bad for the Facts":
On Jan Tomasz Gross's Scholarly Method in *Golden Harvest*
– *Piotr Gontarczyk*   70

4. The Attitude of the Polish Population Towards Jewish
Escapees from the Treblinka, Sobibór, and Bełżec Death
Camps in Light of Jewish and Polish Testimonies
– *Teresa Preker*   97

5. The Rescue of Jewish Escapees from the Treblinka
Death Camp – *Mark Paul*   117

6. The Tale of Two Hamlets: The Cases of Wólka-Okrąglik
and Gniewczyna – *Paweł Styrna*   138

7. Collective Rescue Efforts by Poles on Behalf of Jews in the
German-Occupied Polish Countryside – *Ryszard Tyndorf*   153

8. Looting as a Case Against Racial Determinism
– *Bethany M. Paluk*   201

Part II - Methodology

1. Moral Dilemmas in Turbulent Times
   – *Prof. Fr. Waldemar Chrostowski* — 217

2. Whose Tenements? A Legal Analysis of the Status of Former Jewish Property in Light of Postwar Polish Law
   – *Barbara Gorczycka-Muszyńska* — 223

3. Jan T. Gross's Methodology in *Golden Harvest* From the Perspective of Sociology – *Tomasz Sommer* — 232

4. The Neo-Stalinist Discourse in Polish Historical Studies in the United States – *John Radziłowski* — 239

Part III - Comparative History

1. Poles and Jews in Poland's Eastern Borderlands in September 1939 – *Mark Paul* — 257

2. The Polish Nationalists: A Mainly Theoretical Anti-Jewishness – *Wojciech Jerzy Muszyński* — 294

3. The Polish Nationalists and the Jews: Everyday Practice During the German Occupation, and the Case of the National Armed Forces (NSZ) – *Sebastian Bojemski* — 325

Synopses of Chapters — 349

About the Authors — 361

Index of Geographic Names — 363

Index of Proper Names — 365

About Leopolis Press — 369

Acknowledgements

The editors of this book wish to express their great gratitude to everyone who has made its publication a possibility. First of all, we wish to thank the great Mrs. Molly Ulam of Leopolis Press.

We also must acknowledge our debt and thank Mr. Frank Spula (Polish National Alliance) and our benefactors at the Polish Army Veterans Association of America (PAVA) representing the organization's National Headquarters: Mr. Vincent Knapczyk (National Commander); Mr. Anthony Domino (First Vice-President); Mr. Marian Dorr-Dorynek (Treasurer); Mr. Krzysztof Olechowski (Adjutant General). We must also thank the generous representatives of PAVA's District II: Mr. Anton Chrościelewski (District Commander); Mr. Jerzy Włodarczyk (First Vice-President); Dr. Teofil Lachowicz (Recording Secretary/PAVA Archivist); Sylvia Pełka (Financial Secretary); and, last but not least, Dr. Magda Kapuścińska (Piłsudski Institute of America, New York, NY).

In addition, we are extremely grateful to the following individuals for all of their assistance and support: Dr. Maria Michejda (North Potomac, MD); Lady Blanka Rosenstiel (Miami Beach, FL); Mrs. Ava Polansky-Bąk and Mr. Adam Bąk (New York, NY) Mr. Jan Małek (Rancho Palos Verdes, CA); Mr. Zbigniew Styrna (Hoffman Estates, IL); Mr. John Niemczyk (Mountainside, NJ); Mrs. Zofia and Mr. Zdzisław Zakrzewski (Hayward, CA); Capt. Stefan Komar (Bellerose, NY); Mr. Klaudiusz Wesołek (Gdańsk, Poland); Mrs. Krystyna and Mr. Szymon Apanowicz (Calgary, Canada); Mrs. Zofia Braun and Prof. Kazimierz Braun (Getzville, NY); Mr. Andrzej Skulski (Ottawa, Canada); Mrs. Anna Gwarnicki (Hoffman Estates, IL); Dr. Magdalena and Prof. Iwo Cyprian Pogonowski (Sarasota, FL); Dr. Janusz Subczyński (Marco Island, FL); Mrs. Anna Chodakiewicz Wellisz (Kensington, MD); Mrs. Lidia and Mr. Władysław Poncet de la Riviere (Nokomis, FL); Dr. Marian Pośpieszalski (Charlottesville, VA); and Mrs. Wanda and Mr. Paweł Woś (Sarasota, FL).

We also are grateful to our colleagues at the Institute of World Politics, the graduate school in Washington, DC, that houses the Kościuszko Chair in Polish Studies, which publishes Leopolis Press. Those colleagues include Dr. John Lenczowski, the founder of IWP;

Gen. Walter Jajko USAF (Ret.), Mrs. Mallorie Marino, Dr. Juliana Geran Pilon, and Dr. J. Michael Waller.

Finally, we wish to thank Dr. Tania Mastrapa for her collaboration with us at various stages, including post-prototype copyediting and suggestions for stylistic changes; and Dr. Danusha V. Goska for her diligent fact-checking and proofreading of the prototype edition of this book. Dr. Goska painstakingly detailed several typographical errors in her spirited Red Team approach to this volume. We are delighted that she found no substantive factual errors in our critique of the neo-Stalinist narrative.

INTRODUCTION

Marek Jan Chodakiewicz and Wojciech Jerzy Muszyński

Golden Harvest or Hearts of Gold? is a collection of essays on Polish-Jewish relations during the Second World War. In search of the much-debated truths about those times, the authors present the results of their historical research and analyses based on forensic evidence, primary sources, and testimonials. Throughout the volume, the writers reject as extreme and indefensibly reductive two of the most popular – and contradictory – interpretations of the relations between Poles and Jews. The authors refer to these interpretations as the "black legend" and the "heroic mythology."

The black legend, dominant in the West, reduces all Poles to the Nazis' godless, cowardly, and cynical henchmen, and accuses them of collective complicity in the crime of the Holocaust for material gain. The heroic mythology, still prevalent in Poland, portrays the Polish population exclusively in a positive light, as never wavering in its commitment to the Golden Rule in relations with the Jewish neighbors facing the Shoah.

Although both views are a part of popular culture, unchallenged and unencumbered by the demands of rigorous historical research, the black legend made a successful bid for the scientific status of its theories – largely thanks to the murky standards of identity politics frameworks thriving within post-modernist academia.

Our collection offers a corrective to the false and extreme portrayals of Polish-Jewish relations. The authors' approach is not the result of an all-too-popular style of circular argument wherein an opinion becomes a truth, propped up *post-factum* with a combination of conjecture and a carefully edited list of isolated incidents. Instead, the writers of these essays have been engaged in rigorous research, based on traditional, logocentric, and empirical constraints that scientific methodology requires; all available evidence is evaluated as it supports or disproves the varied hypotheses and, by extension, allows for the drawing of logical conclusions.

From the point of view of gaining knowledge and understanding, this moderate method of enquiry seems to convincingly offer the reader an exhaustive and multifaceted portrayal of relations between the Christian majority and Jewish minority in wartime Poland, with all the complexity the unprecedented historical context deserves.

The fashionable approach promoting the "black legend" focuses exclusively on instances of social pathology and outright criminal behavior, defining both as national characteristics, a "natiopathic norm," as it were. Apart from constituting an implicit collective *ad hominem* attack, such thinking seems to be a logical fallacy. For pathology may only be considered a norm among sociopaths, though even in such a group, one would argue, there must exist different degrees of degeneration.

The black legend's polar opposite, the "heroic mythology," suffers from a similar logical flaw. Focusing exclusively on instances of heroism, it misrepresents reality by suggesting that heroic behavior was dominant or that it constituted a behavioral average among Polish Christians; it ignores the fact that heroism is the *norm* only among heroes. Therefore, both the "black" and the "heroic" interpretations contain a contradiction: exceptional behavior, by definition, cannot represent any society's statistical average.

The heroic mythology of collective Polish help for Jewish victims of the Holocaust dates back to the Communist period of the Polish People's Republic. Based on shreds of individual memories and family histories, an informal stereotype coalesced into a myth, and functioned as a subconscious self-defense reflex, a psychological self-preservation mechanism of a nation humiliated under totalitarian rule. It constituted an important element of the national legend, sustaining the Poles' sense of dignity; by force of inertia, the myth took root in the so-called Third Polish Republic. Yet, unexamined by self-reflection or serious local research, the heroic myth was at best a starting point to introductory studies of Polish-Jewish relations during the Second World War.

Unbeknownst to the Poles cordoned off behind the Iron Curtain, the "black legend" of Polish collective complicity in Nazi crimes emerged and started spreading in the West unhindered; despite the freedom of speech, there simply was no competing narrative offered in the Western marketplace of ideas.

This monopolistic narrative did not appear by accident. The legend of the Polish anti-Semite owes its historiosophical foundations to the Stalinist propaganda machine. His moral capital strengthened by the Soviet liberation of the Auschwitz Death Camp in January 1945, Stalin was eager to exploit the Holocaust with a deviousness not fully appreciated in the West at least until the 1950's. The deliberate fashioning of a "Pole-Fascist," whose anti-Semitic impulses must be revealed and stamped out, suddenly lent the unpopular Soviet occupation of Poland a nearly humanitarian dimension. This narrative thread bestowed upon Communist Russia a new moral legitimacy in the eyes of Western scholars, scientists, pundits, entertainers, and the general public; it managed to elicit Western antipathy towards the Polish people, still prevalent among intellectuals today.

The black legend resonated with the Western Powers in the wake of the war's end as well, discomfort with the Soviet expansionism notwithstanding, because it offered the leaders of the free world a moral alibi in the eyes of Western public opinion and eased their post-Yalta pangs of conscience. It allowed them to explain to the electorate, whose fathers, brothers, and sons fought side by side with Polish soldiers on the fronts of the Second World War, the rationale for the handing over of a stalwart ally to Stalin at the February 1945 Allied Heads of State Crimea Conference, effectively letting the Iron Curtain drop, and setting the stage for the Cold War. Even though Stalin's cynicism and the Soviet Union's hostility towards the Jews are now well known, the black legend served its political purpose – and, as stories often do, far outlasted its creator.

Because of Poland's isolation and the Polish scholars' complete absence from the Western scholarly exchanges and intellectual debates, the historical discourse concerning Polish-Jewish relations originated in the West in 1945, and has been dominated since, by Jewish voices, naturally driven to know and understand the greatest historical calamity that ever befell their people.

The absence of Polish voices was hardly surprising for a variety of reasons. First of all, disorganized and lacking in material resources and knowledge, the Polish Diaspora in the US was entirely unequipped to participate effectively in a modern historical debate. Moreover, Poland remained under Soviet occupation for fifty years; as may be expected, there were no research results or documents being exchanged between the Polish *émigrés* and scholars left behind the Iron Curtain – not to mention the limitations put on "scholarship" by travel restrictions, censorship, and the thought police of the totalitarian state.

However, a crucial factor contributing to the imbalances in the debate that shaped the historical interpretation of Polish-Jewish relations is the rise in the American academia of identity politics with its assumption that the moral right is always on the side of the minority. Consequently, in the context of the Holocaust debate, any attempt at a nuanced analysis of the individual behavior of all actors involved runs the risk of being branded as "anti-Semitic" and dismissed without serious consideration of its merits and implications. Within the confines of a mental shorthand focused on the simplistic labeling of victims and perpetrators, any attempt to research and discuss exhaustively Poles and Jews during the Second World War as individuals who observe, experience, react, and interact with all the complexity afforded a human being – precisely the category the Nazis sought to deny their victims – is automatically found guilty of constituting an apologia for anti-Semitism.

The arrival of this new cultural climate in the West coincided with mass Jewish emigration from Communist Poland to America. In 1968, the U.S. received the victims of anti-Semitic purges from within the higher echelons of the Communist Party and the regime's intellectual elites, orchestrated by the Soviet satellite government of the Polish People's Republic. It is hardly surprising that some *émigrés* from Poland at the time, and their children, joined the Polish-Jewish relations debate. They must have felt that their own personal experience fit perfectly with the Stalinist black legend.

In an intellectual environment in which the interpretation of history is governed by the victim-perpetrator dichotomy, few – if any – western researchers venture into the orthodox narrative of Polish-Jewish relations to apply Socratic logic and empirical research methodologies, no matter how much light its rigorous examination may shed on the understanding of the Second World War or the reasons for the Cold War. We shall not dwell on the fact that most scholars currently active in the field, regrettably, form and express opinions about the Holocaust, Poles, and Jews without the knowledge of local languages.

With few exceptions, they write deprived of direct access to primary sources at the site of the genocide or the tools necessary to conduct meaningful field research and case studies, which could then serve as a basis for formulating more reliable theories – and for drawing more sound conclusions. They rely instead almost exclusively on primary and secondary sources available in English (and German, albeit to a lesser extent), effectively limiting their scholarly contribution to the intellectual equivalent of the mechanical reproduction of existing monographs.

The reticence of many scholars about entering the debate, combined with the uniform repetitiveness of the works by those participating in it, is bound to skew the historical interpretive trajectory of the field and shape the perception of Polish-Jewish relations in accordance with the dominant – indeed, uncontested in the West – narrative of the black legend.

The authors of the present collection seek to restore proper balance to the subject and the debate that surrounds it. This debate has not only a scholarly dimension, but also an important cultural, ethical, and moral aspect. In the end, a discussion about genocide is ultimately about good and evil, but it is also about the integrity of a historical fact and the notion of truth, the respect for which the authors of *Golden Harvest or Hearts of Gold?* share. The writers of the present essays strive to discuss the past with the utmost factual and scholarly accuracy possible and to offer intellectual counterweight to the thrust of the dominant narrative of Polish-Jewish relations, according to which the Polish Christians allegedly took part in the extermination of their Jewish neighbors. Unlike the black legend, the authors of this collection do not demonize or incriminate the Polish population *en masse*; nor do they eschew a scholarly analysis of both Jewish and Polish actions.

The essays are divided into three parts. *Facts and Polemics,* the first and longest section in the collection, contains eight texts engaging in the discussion of the most recent publications on Christian-Jewish relations during the Second World War. Each individual essay is based on a combination of micro-studies and case studies, archival research, and a thorough review of primary and secondary sources, solidly anchoring the texts in the realities of the era, and not in anachronistic theoretical speculations.

Marek Jan Chodakiewicz opens this section with an exposition of the many levels on which the current writings about the alleged Polish role in the extermination of the Jews take place – from the symbolic aspect of the events, to the local and international context, to the issues of propaganda, and to contemporary references. The author emphasizes the exceptional demands the seriousness of the subject matter places on a scholar: the imperative to precede all theses and conclusions with multifaceted, thorough, and exhaustive archival research and in-depth local case studies is the only guide to reconstructing and describing the past in all its complexity, unwarped by biases resulting from any single author's anachronisms.

Peter Stachura and Piotr Gontarczyk's essays follow, contributing to the collection their analyses of *Golden Harvest*, the most recent publication in the black legend tradition by an American sociologist, Jan T. Gross of Princeton University. While the authors appreciate the ease with which the book's popularizing language may be digested, they question the volume's scholarly merit, its disappointing lack of intellectual rigor, and visibly tendentious inclination to cite facts selectively and outside of the historical context. As deeply held as Gross's convictions appear, the resulting circular argument is as unsatisfying as it seems dishonest, and it suggests an attempt to further a preconceived – if unproven – notion. Moreover, both Stachura and Gontarczyk note that despite the book's learned appearance, the author, surprisingly, does not reference a single piece of research he conducted in relation to the events covered in his publication.

The present collection devotes considerable attention to the issue of Polish help for the Jews trying to escape Nazi extermination. We reprint in its entirety a little known, but important 1993 article by the late historian Teresa Preker on the treatment by the Christian majority of Jews who escaped from the Treblinka II Death Camp. As a corollary to her text, Ryszard Tyndorf and Mark Paul discuss more than 200 specific accounts of Jews rescued by Polish Christians in two essays based on their regional studies and examination of predominantly Jewish sources. The analysis of the behavior of the Poles compelled to live in the immediate vicinity of death camps established by the Nazis is the subject of an essay by Paweł Styrna. He addresses the question of how the tragic impotence of those in forced proximity to death – who could see it, hear it, and smell it – affected their lives and moral choices. Bethany M. Pałuk's essay concludes the *Facts and Polemics* part of the volume with a discussion of looting – a human phenomenon, Pałuk finds, rather than an alleged national characteristic that would set Poland and its people morally apart from other nations.

The second section in the present collection, *Methodology*, belongs to a group of experts in ethics, law, sociology, and history. One by one, they undertook specialized analyses of various aspects of Polish-Jewish relations during the Nazi occupation of Poland or its immediate aftermath.

The first essay, by Fr. Waldemar Chrostowski, examines an array of behavioral patterns among the Poles from the point of view of theology and ethics, focusing on the unprecedented complexity of the times on the one hand, and on the seductiveness of easy moral judgments on the other.

Barbara Gorczycka-Muszyńska shares her legal expertise to shed light on the status of Jewish property and property restitution in postwar Poland in view of the Soviet-imposed law and jurisprudence. Analyzing Communist-era court rulings, she draws attention to the privileged treatment, seemingly unusual for a Communist state such as post-Yalta Poland, afforded after the war to a select group of owners of property confiscated by the German occupiers. The judgments included, in large part, the restitution of Jewish property, while, by contrast, Polish landowners and industrialists generally lost their property and holdings, without compensation, under nationalization decrees, or state sponsored larceny – a trend consistent with the brand of justice implicitly promised by Soviet propaganda.

Tomasz Sommer adds his sociological expertise to this section of the volume with an analysis of the methodology employed by the sociologist Gross in *Golden Harvest*, which inspired the title of our response to his approach. Sommer demonstrates the consistency with which *Golden Harvest* fails to uphold the classical scholarly standards generally expected of a professional researcher in the field.

John Radziłowski concludes the *Methodology* section with an essay on the neo-Stalinist school of historical thought, to which Gross's writings belong. In his analysis of the works by some historians of Jewish-Polish relations, Radziłowski explains the logic behind the absence of rigorous scholarly method: the scientific veneer of these scholars' output appears to be but a camouflage for a historiosophical vision rooted in Soviet propaganda of the 1940's; their mission seems to be not so much finding the historical truth as bringing about a *sui generis* "awakening" of conscience and "change" in the world.

Comparative History represents the third and final section in the present volume. The three essays within it focus on the context of Polish-Jewish relations during the Soviet and Nazi occupations and their immediate aftermath.

Mark Paul opens this section with a richly researched text on the Jewish community's reaction to the war of the Poles against the Nazis and Communists in September 1939; he discusses the Jewish attitude towards the pre-war Polish state apparatus, the Jewish community's response to the Soviet attack after 17 September, and the internal relations within this diverse community. Paul also talks about scantly researched, but surprisingly numerous, instances of crimes – both of opportunity and ideology – committed by groups of Jewish Communists on their Polish neighbors in the Soviet-occupied eastern provinces of the country.

The last two essays in the collection offer a close look at the heretofore mythologized, rather than researched by contemporary scholarship, issue of the anti-Jewishness of the Polish nationalist camp.

Wojciech Jerzy Muszyński elucidates the discussions of the Jewish minority in the nationalist propaganda in Poland and the forms that those discussions took, both before the war, and during the German occupation. Based on thorough archival research, he points out the political and cultural, as opposed to racial, nature of the Polish-Jewish debates within nationalist circles. Any attempt to merge pre-war speeches and publications aimed at an electorate of a peaceful and diverse state with the racist and genocidal Nazi program of exterminating a people based on a genetic formula, Muszyński argues, not only defies logic but also falsifies historical truth. His examination of the wartime *Endecja* (National Democratic Party) records and underground pamphlets demonstrates that the *Endecja* as a whole not only rejected the anti-Semitic policies of the German occupiers on moral grounds, but also actively opposed them, documenting the Nazi crimes against the Jews years before the West gave their reports any credence.

Details and specific examples of the nationalists' opposition to extermination of Polish Jews can be found in Sebastian Bojemski's essay on the best known and often perceived as an anti-Semitic nationalist organization, the National Armed Forces (NSZ). Bojemski cites many examples of direct help offered to the Jews by the NSZ underground soldiers; he also highlights the presence of Poles of Jewish descent in the ranks of that organization, both as privates and leaders. His analysis points not to race, but to political and cultural ideology, and a sense of national belonging, as the key to understanding Polish-Jewish relations from the perspective of the nationalist camp.

The following is an English-language version of the book, which appeared originally in Polish in March of 2011. The editors of the former have taken into account the cultural differences between the two target audiences. Hence, the tone and timbre of the English version differs slightly from the Polish original. Nevertheless, the essence of both editions remains unaltered.

Part I: Facts and Polemics

REFLECTIONS:
A NEW WORK BUT THE SAME OLD METHOD[1]

Marek Jan Chodakiewicz

In *Golden Harvest*, a book on Polish-Jewish relations in the wake of the Second World War, Princeton University Professor Jan T. Gross once again misses the mark – if the work's objective was serious scholarship.

Instead of analyzing case studies or providing a research-based synthesis, Gross offers a collection of defamatory stereotypes and continues to demonize the Poles *en masse*, ignoring, as he did in his earlier *Neighbors* and *Fear*, virtually all empirical and scholarly evidence that contradicts his theories. His prejudices aside, we shall primarily focus on Gross' rejection of the scientific method or logocentric reasoning in favor of fallacy as methodology. Instead of focusing on every single cherry-picked and carefully edited anecdote Gross cites, we shall address the intellectual structure of the *Golden Harvest* as a whole.

The late eminent historian Teresa Preker had been one of the most formidable moral and scholarly authorities of the so-called progressive intelligentsia in Poland in regards to the study of the Jewish history in general and the Holocaust in particular. Her arguments are of course logocentric and grounded in empirical research.[2] Gross negated her

---

[1] Jan Tomasz Gross and Irena Grudzińska-Gross, *Złote żniwa: Rzecz o tym co się działo na obrzeżach zagłady Żydów* [Golden Harvest: On the peripheries of the Holocaust] (Kraków: Znak, 2011). It is forthcoming in English from Oxford University Press as *Golden Harvest: Reflections about Events at the Periphery of the Holocaust*. All quotes and statistics are from our works listed below. The footnotes have been kept at the minimum because many problems mentioned in passing in our essay have been addressed in detail by other scholars in the present work, which first appeared in Polish as *Złote serca czy złote żniwa: Studia nad wojennymi losami Polaków i Żydów* [Hearts of Gold or a Golden Harvest? Studies on the Wartime Fate of Poles and Jews] (Warsaw: The Facto, 2011).

[2] Teresa Prekerowa, "Stosunek ludności polskiej do żydowskich uciekinierów z obozów zagłady w Treblince, Sobiborze i Bełżcu w świetle relacji żydowskich i polskich [The Attitude of the Polish Population Towards the Jewish Escapees from the Death Camps in Treblinka, Sobibór, and Bełżec in Light of Jewish and Polish

conclusions and disregarded both her factography and methodology. He substituted her traditional historiographical approach with moral relativism and the viewing of history through the discriminating – and discriminatory – prism of identity politics that has informed his intellectual output since 1998.[3]

Reflection 1: The symbol

A symbol tends to bypass our intellect and appeal directly to our feelings. Whether visual, aural, or other, its role is to stir emotions, to soothe, rally, move, or shock us. Jan T. Gross visibly appreciates both the power and usefulness of symbols, and he does not shrink from fashioning them outright to bolster his argument. The photograph on the cover of Gross's *Golden Harvest* is a case in point. The image itself is innocuous enough: a group of simple-looking men, leaning on shovels, loose soil underfoot. But in Gross's telling, the photograph becomes Exhibit A, depicting a sinister band of Polish looters in search of "Jewish gold" on the outskirts of the Treblinka death camp. Seen in this light, the photo would be chilling indeed – *if* the image represented what Gross alleges it does.

An idea of criminals photographing themselves in the act is not unheard of; neither is the police documenting a successful raid with a camera. But there have certainly been some horrific mistakes,[4] and an

---

Testimonies]," *Biuletyn Głównej Komisji Badania Zbrodni przeciwko Narodowi Polskiemu—Instytutu Pamięci Narodowej* [The Bulletin of the Head Commission to Investigate Crimes Against the Polish Nation – The Institute of National Memory], vol. 35 (1993): 100–114, which is translated and included in the present collection of essays below.

[3] See his four brief works: *Upiorna dekada: trzy eseje o stereotypach na temat Żydów, Polaków, Niemców i komunistów: 1939-1948* [A Terrifying Decade: Three Essays on Stereotypes Regarding Jews, Poles, Germans, and Communists, 1939-1948] (Kraków: Universitas, 1998); *Sąsiedzi: Historia zagłady żydowskiego miasteczka* [Neighbors: The Story of the Destruction of a Shtetl] (Sejny: Pogranicze, 2000); *Strach: Antysemityzm w Polsce tuż po wojnie. Historia moralnej zapaści* [Fear: Anti-Semitism in Poland Right After the War, the History of Moral Downfall] (Kraków: Znak, 2008); and *Złote żniwa* (Kraków: Znak, 2011).

[4] One immediately recalls the macabre photograph of dead children, apparently strung to a tree with barbed wire. For years, this image functioned widely in the public sphere as a symbolic indictment of the Ukrainian nationalist underground which, allegedly, perpetrated the crime against the Christian Polish innocents sometime in the mid-1940s. Lately, however, scholars have discovered that the children were victims of a heinous common crime committed in the 1920s. Namely, they were killed by their own insane mother. The Ukrainian Insurgent Army had nothing to do with the gruesome deed. Further, the victims were Roma, not Poles. The truth was obtained only through a critical, scholarly approach to the photograph, which had emotionally seized the

interpretation of an old, undated, and heretofore unattributed image requires diligence – especially if the picture is submitted as damning evidence, a smoking gun around which the prosecutorial narrative may be constructed. It is therefore hardly surprising that Gross's interpretation of the cover photograph, which serves as a point of departure – indeed, as both a thesis and a conclusion – for his controversial *Golden Harvest*, has not been unquestioningly accepted by scholars.

Some have pointed out that it depicts persons on an exhumation project, cleaning and organizing graves of the victims of the Second World War, which was a common endeavor in the post-war era. Displaying personal effects found in unmarked graves was a common practice, often enabling identification of the remains. Investigative journalists from Poland's most respected daily, *Rzeczpospolita* [The Republic], also examined the photograph. They, too, have reasons to believe that the picture has been mislabeled. Documentary evidence does confirm that a police action against diggers at Treblinka did indeed take place in the frigid weather of Poland's early March 1946. However, neither the anonymous persons leisurely looking into the camera lens nor their light, harvest-time attire – nor, for that matter, the location, which does not match any part of the camp surroundings – fit Gross's grisly description or the circumstances of a police raid.

The source of the photograph is also suspect. It came from a local activist who said he received the photo, along with the "gold digging" explanation, from someone else, who has since passed away and, therefore, cannot verify the narrative. The image was then acquired by Gross's long-time champion and a stalwart promoter of his books, the Polish daily *Gazeta Wyborcza* [Electoral Gazette].

It was *Gazeta Wyborcza* that brought the photograph to Gross's attention; Gross decided to use it, along with the unverified golden narrative, as a point of departure for his new book. The local activist, meanwhile, when interviewed by the *Rzeczpospolita* investigative team, changed his explanation: he now claimed that the photograph

---

popular imagination and through the gripping power of its shocking symbol prevented any serious examination and alternative interpretation for decades. There were even plans to build a monument replicating the picture to commemorate the victims of the Volhynian genocide of the Poles by the Ukrainian nationalists. Thus, a real atrocity would have been commemorated through a false symbol. See Ada Rutkowska and Dariusz Stola, „Fałszywy opis, prawdziwe zbrodnie [Real Crimes, Incorrect Caption]," *Rzeczpospolita*, 19-20 May 2007; Piotr Głuchowski and Marcin Kowalski, „Podobno była piękna [They Say She Was Beautiful]," *Gazeta Wyborcza*, 17 July 2007, http://wyborcza.pl/1,76842,4314383.html.

depicted grave cleaners and not, as he earlier told *Gazeta*, grave robbers. Not only do the location, date, and circumstances captured in the photograph remain unsubstantiated, but no one so far has been able to identify any of the purportedly local people in the picture.[5] Gross's embrace of the image as he wants it to be perceived, and his interpretation of it as a symbol of Polish looting of Jewish remains, expose his uncritical approach to sources as deeply biased and unscholarly at best.

In an even greater challenge for Gross, the reporters from *Gazeta Wyborcza* who brought forth the photo and the false explanation, as we shall see later in this volume, have since backed away from their claim, and the paper removed the untruthful caption. And yet Oxford University Press offers the following unquestioning description of its English language publication of *Golden Harvest*:

> The starting point of Jan Gross's *Golden Harvest*, this haunting photograph in fact depicts a group of peasants – 'diggers' atop a mountain of ashes at Treblinka, where some 800,000 Jews were gassed and cremated. The diggers are hoping to find gold and precious stones that Nazi executioners may have overlooked. The story captured in this grainy black-and-white photograph symbolizes the vast, continent-wide plunder of Jewish wealth. [...] The theft of this wealth was not limited to conquering armies, leading banks, and museums, but to local populations such as those pictured in the photograph.[6]

And so a false symbol has been created and validated, without proof, even before the book and its notorious cover reach the hands of the readers.

Reflection 2: Methodology

Gross's preferred methodology – in logical terms, a combination of several popular fallacies, including *argumentum ad nauseam*, or proof by repetition, begging the question, and circular logic – dates back to his 1998 publication of *Horrific Decade*. He develops his method

---

[5] Michał Majewski and Paweł Reszka, „Zagadka starego zdjęcia [The Mystery of an Old Photograph]," *Rzeczpospolita*, 21 January 2011, posted at http://www.rp.pl/artykul/598065.html. Even the *Gazeta Wyborcza* has disavowed the photograph now. The question of the photograph is discussed comprehensively by Piotr Gontarczyk below.

[6] As posted on 4 June 2011 at Oxford University Press's official web site at http://www.oup.com/us/catalog/general/subject/HistoryWorld/European/EasternEurope/?view=usa&ci=9780199731671#.

further in *Neighbors* and *Fear*, and the approach remains essentially unchanged in *Golden Harvest*. In his introduction, instead of a hypothesis or any premise to be proven true, the author presents the reader with a conclusion, unsubstantiated by serious research but propped up instead with a carefully selected, decontextualized, and heavily redacted list of examples. Then, reaching beyond language and eschewing any critical instinct, the author unveils a macabre image-symbol.

In Gross's latest work, it is the picture of the alleged Polish hunters for Jewish golden teeth; in *Neighbors*, it was a horror story – fabricated but effective – about the Polish Christians of Jedwabne playing soccer with a Jewish head. The author then uncritically invokes unverified testimonies of real and alleged eyewitnesses, including those obtained through torture by the Stalinist police in the course of infamously brutal, sometimes deadly interrogations during the cruel early years of the Soviet occupation. Gross carefully picks only the material that supports his conclusion-thesis and bolsters his circular argument.

Instead of citing his own research, Gross relies heavily on secondary sources. It is hard to determine how diligently he familiarizes himself with scholarly publications by his peers since he does not acknowledge accounts that contradict his narrative.[7] He also rejects primary sources that fail to tally with his opinions. The narrative itself is suffused with emotive prose, occasionally verging on history.

While such methodology may be acceptable in literary criticism, it does not satisfy a historian, interested in reconstructing the past – in good faith and as best he or she can – based on all the available evidence at the scholar's disposal. After all, without commitment to truth, in the absence of facts, reliable evidence, or documents, what can a writer contribute to discussions about the past? What is the value of a book that claims to represent the past with a symbol, reflect on it at length, and offer a moral judgment – inductively, as it were – if the representation itself is untrue; if it proves to be a misrepresentation? What then is the value of *Golden Harvest*?

---

[7] See, for example, Mariusz Bechta, *Między Bolszewią a Niemcami: Konspiracja polityczna i wojskowa Polskiego Obozu Narodowego na Podlasiu w latach 1939–1952* [Between the Bolsheviks and the Germans: The Political and Military Underground of the Polish Nationalist Camp in the Podlasie Region, 1939-1952] (Warsaw: Oficyna Wydawnicza RYTM, 2009). Bechta's conclusions have been confirmed by other scholars, including Ryszard Tyndorf below.

Reflection 3: Golden teeth for everyone

Does the misattributed photograph on the book's cover mean that the stories about the search for golden teeth – in Poland or elsewhere – are false? Unfortunately not.[8] Documented instances of looting human remains, often horrific beyond imagination, took place during the war in Europe, Asia, and elsewhere, and this form of theft was not confined to any national group. Recalling his wartime service in the Pacific, Charles Lindbergh gives a rare and chilling account of the American troops brutally robbing the Japanese dead.[9]

A Nazi concentration camp survivor, Iwo Pogonowski, writes about a gang of "gold diggers" in Sachsenhausen, where bodies, stripped of anything deemed valuable as part of the camp's official operations, were additionally targeted by an underground theft-and-commerce chain that cut across virtually all the strata of the camp life, from the most vulnerable to the most powerful. It started with the Jewish prisoners of the *Sonderkommando*, whose official task was cremating the dead and searching for valuables for the treasury of the Third Reich; the gold they managed to hide passed through other prisoners of various nationalities and religions, only to reach the bosses of the "enterprise," the SS camp guards.[10]

The Sachsenhausen scheme is far from being an isolated incident involving human gold. The Archive of New Records (AAN) in Warsaw contains, among many other Second World War documents, a report about the so-called Pinkert men (Pinkertowcy), the Jewish employees of the Pinkert funeral home in the Warsaw Ghetto. They were known, in addition to their regular duties, for robbing the ghetto dead of their golden teeth. They were universally scorned within and without the ghetto walls as "the cemetery hyenas."

When the Holocaust intensified, the underground Polish Workers' Party promised the gang protection in exchange for the looted gold. They smuggled the Pinkert men out of the ghetto and guided them to the Wyszków Forest on the outskirts of Warsaw. There, the gang was summarily executed by members of the Communist People's Guard (GL) and the Jewish Fighting Organization (ŻOB). The Communists

---

[8] Marek Jan Chodakiewicz, „Złoto ze zwłok: O manipulacjach Grossa," [The cadaver gold: About the manipulations of Gross] *Uważam Rze: Inaczej Pisane* [Tygodnik Rzeczpospolitej, Warsaw] 20 February 2011.
[9] A. Scott Berg, *Lindbergh* (New York: G.P. Putnam's Sons, 1998), 490, 506.
[10] Iwo Cyprian Pogonowski, *Handel złotymi zębami w obozie w Sachsenhausen* [The Trade in Golden Teeth in the Camp at Sachsenhausen], 11 January 2011, http://www.pogonowski.com/?p=2396.

wanted the gold; the Jewish underground sought justice for the desecration of the ghetto dead.

Searching through the AAN archives yielded more clues to crimes involving "Jewish gold" in Poland, including the evidence of a multiple murder of Jews by the Communist People's Guard (GL) unit of Grzegorz Korczyński in the Kraśnik area in the winter of 1942/1943.[11] The incident started with a quarrel within the Communist underground ranks and ended with a massacre of perhaps scores of Jews, including women. The victims were robbed and buried. The secret came out when, in the spring of 1944, the clandestine Polish National Armed Forces (NSZ) routed the Communist unit and found the looted gold, along with other evidence of the crime. Superb research by Piotr Gontarczyk unearthed additional facts, further corroborating the story and its details.[12]

Banditry, both common and revolutionary, scourged the Polish countryside. It was precisely because of robberies that the Polish independentist guerrillas destroyed the multinational band of "Golden Johnny" (*Złoty Janek*), who terrorized the Białystok area, stealing, among other things, gold both Polish and Jewish, in all its forms. Historian Kazimierz Krajewski documented and described this case in 1993 in one of his monographs, though there were many more instances of murder and robbery during the Nazi occupation of Poland. After the so-called "liberation," for example, Red Army troops excavated for "Jewish gold" at Treblinka. The Soviets did so on an industrial scale, using explosives and Polish peasants as slave laborers.[13]

---

[11] For the Wyszków and Kraśnik cases see Marek Jan Chodakiewicz, *Narodowe Siły Zbrojne: Ząb przeciw dwu wrogom* [National Armed Forces: Against Two Enemies] (Warsaw: WAMA, 1994; second, expanded edition published by Fronda, 1999); and Marek Jan Chodakiewicz, Piotr Gontarczyk, and Leszek Żebrowski, eds., *Tajne Oblicze: Dokumenty GL-AL i PPR, 1942-1945*, 3 Volumes [Secret Face: The Documents of the Communist Underground] (Warsaw: Burchard Edition, 1997-1999).

[12] Piotr Gontarczyk, *Polska Partia Robotnicza. Droga do władzy: 1941 - 1944* [The Polish Workers' Party: The Road to Power] (Warsaw: Fronda, 2003).

[13] Kazimierz Krajewski, *Uderzeniowe Bataliony Kadrowe 1942–1944* [The Cadre Shock Battalions, 1942-1944] (Warsaw: PAX, 1993); Kazimierz Krajewski, "Kto profanował groby ofiar Treblinki [Who Defiled the Graves of the Treblinka Victims]," *Nasz Dziennik*, 16 March 2011, posted at http://www.naszdziennik.pl/bpl_index.php?typ=my&dat=20110316&id=my03.txt.

Reflection 4: The international context

The war and the resultant collapse of law and order created a fertile ground for the spread of banditry and other pathologies. This phenomenon is confined neither to Poland nor to the Second World War. Even in relatively remote and insular cultures, such as pre-Meiji Japan, unspeakable cruelty invariably accompanies armed conflicts and the social upheavals they precipitate. Throughout the centuries, the peasants despoiled and dispatched wounded *samurai* left helpless on the battlefields. The warriors (*bushi*) habitually looted, raped, and killed the peasants during military campaigns and, sometimes, in peacetime – one could test a new sword with virtual impunity on a peasant (*inakape*).[14]

Invoking analogies from far-off lands may help us understand periods and places with which we are more intimately connected, but wielding emotionally charged metaphors imposes serious logical constraints. In *Golden Harvest,* J.T. Gross compares the Poles during the Second World War to the Hutu killers in Rwanda. He harnesses all the emotive power of the African tragedy ignoring the lack of any logical connection that would justify its use in reference to Poland under the Nazi regime. There is no analogy between the Hutus, who dominated their genocidal government in Rwanda, and the Poles, who were governed and terrorized by the occupying Germans. In fact, from the point of view of the Nazi occupation policy, the attitude of the Germans toward the Poles was analogical to that of the Hutus toward the Tutsis.

The African analogy would only make sense if Gross compared the actions of the Hutus to the attitudes of the German neighbors in Poland – the *Reichsdeutsche* and *Volksdeutsche* – to the Polish Jews. After all, the regime of the Third Reich was a government of the Germans, and not of the Poles. The Poles were not the privileged citizens, *après* the

---

[14] See *Nihongi: The Chronicles of Japan from the Earliest Times to A.D. 697* (Rutland, VT, and Tokyo: Charles E. Tuttle and Company, 1998); *Taiheiki: A Chronicle of Medieval Japan* (Rutland, VT, and Tokyo: Charles E. Tuttle and Company, 1985); Miyamoto Musashi, *The Book of Five Rings* (Boston and London: Shambhala, 1994); Yamamoto Tsunetomo, *Hagakure: The Book of the Samurai* (Tokyo, New York, and London: Kodansha International, 1983); R.H.P. Mason and J.G. Caiger, *A History of Japan* (Tokyo: Charles E. Tuttle Company, 1989); George Sansom, *A History of Japan*, 3 vols. (Stanford, CA: Stanford University Press, 1987-1998); Oscar Ratti and Adele Westbrook, *Secrets of the Samurai: A Survey of Martial Arts of Feudal Japan* (Rutland, VT, and Tokyo: The Charles E. Tuttle Company, 1992); Nobuo Ogasawara, *Japanese Swords* (Osaka: Hoikusha, 1984); Helen and William McAlpine, *Japanese Tales and Legends* (Oxford and New York: Oxford University Press, 1989).

slaughter; the NSDAP (German National Socialist Workers' Party), which ran the government of the occupied Polish territories *without any Polish participation*, was not the Polish National Socialist Party. Moreover, the Germans in Poland were not punished by death for shielding Jews; the Poles were, which further renders the Rwandan analogy nonsensical.

If, for some reason, one really must compare Rwanda to occupied Poland at all, the only analogical period would be the colonial times, when the Belgians ruled the African country. Only then can one ponder the differences and similarities between the conquered Tutsis and Hutus, on the one hand, and the Polish Christians and Jews, on the other. Gross has failed to do so. Instead, he tried, once again, to shock the reader with a false analogy. It is not clear whether he chose this approach because of his superficial understanding of the Rwandan tragedy,[15] or because of his habitual over-reliance on emotive arguments and propensity to offer proofs by assertion *in lieu* of logic.

It may well be quite educational to consider comparatively the role of the native troops in maintaining the colonial order in Rwanda and in Poland, but from a perspective on which J.T. Gross' discussion does not touch. In her work on Russia as a colonial power, Ewa Thompson offers brilliant insights into the complex problem of Poland's colonial dependence, from the Partitions (1772-1918) to the Nazis (1939-1945), and the Soviets (1939-1941, and 1944-1993, when the last Red Army soldier left Polish soil).[16]

The colonial framework may be a productive comparative paradigm, and it may be useful not only in examining collaborationist non-

---

[15] See Marek Jan Chodakiewicz, „Rwandyjska tragedia, polska odpowiedzialność," [A Rwandan Tragedy, and Polish Responsibility] *Tygodnik Solidarność*, 18 February 2011. See also Martin Meredith, *The Fate of Africa: From the Hopes of Freedom to the Heart of Despair: A History of Fifty Years of Independence* (New York: PublicAffairs, 2005); Philip Gourevitch, *We Wish to Inform You that Tomorrow We Will be Killed With Our Families: Stories From Rwanda* (New York: Picador, Farrar, Straus and Giroux, 1998); Michael Barnett, *Eyewitness to a Genocide: The United Nations and Rwanda* (Ithaca, NY, and London: Cornell University Press, 2002); Linda Melvern, *Conspiracy to Murder: The Rwandan Genocide* (London and New York: Verso, 2004); Gerard Prunier, *Darfur: The Ambiguous Genocide* (Ithaca, NY: Cornell University Press, 2005); Rene Lemarchand, *The Dynamics of Violence in Central Africa* (Philadelphia: University of Pennsylvania Press, 2009); Gerard Prunier, *Africa's World War: Congo, The Rwandan Genocide, and the Making of a Continental Catastrophe* (New York, NY: Oxford University Press, 2009).
[16] Ewa M. Thompson, "Nationalist Propaganda in the Soviet Russian Press, 1939–1941," *Slavic Review*, vol. 50, no. 2 (Summer 1991): 385–99; Ewa M. Thompson, *Imperial Knowledge: Russian Literature and Colonialism* (Westport, CT: Greenwood Press, 2000).

German units under the Nazi occupation in Eastern Europe, but also as a scholarly approach to Stalin's "Polish People's Army" (LWP), which, under the command of the NKVD, the Red Army, and the Polish Communist secret police, destroyed the anti-Communist underground in Poland between 1944-1956 with little-publicized brutality which claimed at least 50,000 lives.

But instead of invoking spurious analogies with Rwanda, a Holocaust scholar could consider existing serious research about the question of carrying out orders and coercing one's underlings to perpetrate criminal deeds. The much respected scholar, Christopher Browning, has argued that practically any human being can be coerced, directly or indirectly, to do anything, and that no physical compulsion is required – an appropriate psychological atmosphere, peer pressure, and proper institutional framework will suffice. Browning has arrived at this controversial conclusion during his in-depth research on a rather typical German reserve police battalion active in occupied Poland.[17]

But Gross shows no interest in Browning's work, methodology, or the conclusions he reached. Instead, he chooses to emulate Daniel Jonah Goldhagen, who responded to the thought-provoking hypothesis put forth by Browning with an intellectually simplistic argument published in book form as *Hitler's Willing Executioners*.[18] Ignoring the human factor behind the crimes, Goldhagen, argued that the Germans Browning aptly refers to as "ordinary men" were responsible for the Holocaust because of their in-born, pathological prejudice against the Jews, because their ideology was "exterminationist anti-Semitism."

Factual inaccuracies, contradictions and wildly selective and manipulative use of the archival material earned Goldhagen a scathing and embarrassing critique, *A Nation on Trial: The Goldhagen Thesis and Historical Truth*,[19] written by a team of two prominent scholars – an American political scientist, born to Warsaw Ghetto and concentration camp survivors, specializing in exposing the excesses and opportunism in Holocaust literature as opposed to rigorous Holocaust research; and a German-born chief historian of war crimes and crimes against humanity in the Canadian Justice Department who is also the foremost international authority on the German archives which served as Goldhagen's main source.

---

[17] Christopher R. Browning, *Ordinary Men: Reserve Police Battalion 101 and the Final Solution in Poland* (New York: HarperCollins, 1992).
[18] Daniel Jonah Goldhagen, *Hitler's Willing Executioners: Ordinary Germans and The Holocaust* (New York: Alfred A. Knopf, 1996).
[19] Norman G. Finkelstein and Ruth Bettina Birn, *A Nation on Trial: The Goldhagen Thesis and Historical Truth* (New York: Henry Holt & Co., 1998).

Despite an army of influential supporters, the egregious methodological, factual, and conceptual flaws of Goldhagen's work, including his follow-up "revelations" about the responsibility for the Holocaust of the Catholic Church and Pope Pius XII, discredited the erstwhile Harvard professor as a serious scholar, and his effusions elicited thunders from Raul Hilberg, the founder of Holocaust studies himself. Unlike the members of what Finkelstein referred to as the "Holocaust Industry,"[20] Hilberg believed that "when it comes to the truth, it has to be said openly, without regard to any consequences that would be undesirable, embarrassing."[21]

In putting the Polish nation on trial, Gross has visibly adopted Goldhagen's methodology and rhetoric. Like Goldhagen, he rejects multifarious and multifaceted individual human experiences as a window into understanding human action; he eschews any good-faith efforts to reconstruct history through painstaking micro-level research from which a general pattern may be discerned and the past may emerge in all its true complexity. Following Goldhagen's example, instead of rigorous scholarship, Gross favors emotive arguments, manipulation and selective use of evidence, and generalizations, in effect limiting his contribution to creating and propagating stereotypes and spreading propaganda.

Reflection 5: Human nature

Both *Golden Harvest* and Gross's earlier works unfortunately fail to consider human nature as a factor. To appreciate the character and scale of any phenomenon, including crime and atrocity, one must know how – and be willing – to compare. Comparison is a basic methodological tool across disciplines, at least as far as the logocentric, empirical school is concerned. Comparing a variety of atrocities across the ages demonstrates plainly that unbelievable ruthlessness is a feature inherent in the whole of the human race, and not just Polish peasants. To invoke a *bon mot*, "if it walks on two feet, it is capable of any atrocity."

To acknowledge as much does not justify any persons, of any nationality, who robbed and killed Jews, but it helps explain the mechanism of their actions. Killing innocents is an atrocity with no justification, but cruel crimes perpetrated on the Jews by a few cannot

---

[20] Coined by Norman Finkelstein, the phrase is the title of his book, *The Holocaust Industry: Reflections on the Exploitation of Jewish Suffering* (Brooklyn: Verso, 2001).
[21] Raul Hilberg interviewed by Roberto Antonini, *Swiss National Radio (SBC-SSR)*, 31 August 2000.

be used to justify condemning collectively all Polish peasants, even all Christian Poles. The cultural and moral consequences of such collective blaming are plainly visible in the mainstream imagery and phraseology to anyone who cares to notice.

Some journalists casually refer to "the Polish concentration camps,"[22] rather than "Nazi concentration camps in occupied Poland," simply mimicking the pronouncements and unproven accusations flowing from academia, where stereotyping increasingly masquerades as research, and the dialectic of identity politics supplants the intellectual rigors of logocentrism.

Even without any research, the religious among us believe that we strive to overcome our nature and make wise choices, that individual action matters, and that each person shall answer individually before the Lord for his or her faults, sins, and crimes.

Secular Western law, including the American legal system, reflects the same understanding of crime and punishment and of individual, not collective responsibility for any human action.

Reflection 6: The Polish context

While it is only too human to be weak, cowardly, and cruel, it is no less human to overcome weakness and fear and draw on one's capacity to do good. Weakness and cruelty are hardly an aspiration, while goodness is the standard against which we measure ourselves and others. Gross' latest work acknowledges as much, at least implicitly if inadvertently, by being unforgiving of all acts of human smallness behind the perpetration of crimes against Polish Jews.

Gross concentrates on the village of Wólka-Okrąglik, the alleged nest of Nazi-time pathologies involving "Jewish gold."[23] Such pathologies must indeed be exposed. But they must be exposed precisely as pathologies, rather than serving as a tool for collective national character assassination. Gross, defying both logic and scholarly decency, chooses to wield a tool: extrapolating from his fallacious

---

[22] The skewed image of a Pole in the popular mind is fused so much with the Nazis that it leads to absurd statements, such as a local paper referring to Nazi concentration camps in central Germany – not even in occupied Poland – as "Polish," recalling with respect "the liberation of four Polish concentration camps, most notably Buchenwald and Mittelbau Dora" by the British. See Bill Hall, "Veteran faced off against Germans in Luxembourg," *The Carrol County Times*, 1 May 2010, http://www.carrollcountytimes.com/news/veteran_profile/veteran-faced-off-against-germans-in-luxembourg/article_9332627c-54d0-11df-9b2d-001cc4c03286.html.

[23] A case study of Wólka-Okrąglik by Paweł Styrna follows below.

"because a few, therefore all," he accuses and condemns an entire people with dictatorial efficiency and without any regard for the burden of proof or the rudimentary demands of logic.

Without verifying his examples, the author of *Golden Harvest* assumes that criminal behavior was the all-Polish norm. That norm is indeed obtainable, but through painstaking comparative microstudies of a large number of localities – a far more demanding, honest, and time-consuming process than listing a few pathological aberrations that fit Gross' foregone conclusion *cum* hypothesis. The checking and cross-checking of the examples given are entirely absent.

Let us stress that Gross's opinions about Wólka-Okrąglik are based on a few unverified passing remarks in a couple of memoirs and propped up by an unrelated photograph whose provenance has since been discredited. His judgments have been formed without any comprehensive micrographic research. It is a cut-and-paste narrative, and it fails as scholarship.[24] Cherry picking off the ash heap of history whatever fits our theories may make the life of a scholar easier, but it may not substitute for research any more than plagiarism would. And yet, such a methodology informs the Grossian *oeuvre* throughout. Conclusions have to come from honest research, not the other way around.[25]

To realize how deeply flawed the stereotypes purveyed by the author are, and to see how poorly substantiated his latest book is, one needs only to familiarize oneself with the monumental output by the Canadian independent scholar Mark Paul. Paul has documented several thousand instances that completely contradict the aberrations listed as norms by Gross. Paul conducted in-depth research into available Jewish memoirs and testimonies, publishing his findings in the historical-social quarterly *Glaukopis* and on the Polish-Canadian

---

[24] Marek Jan Chodakiewicz, "O Polakach i Żydach bez retuszu: rozmowa z prof. Markiem Janem Chodakiewiczem [About Poles and Jews Without Censorship: An Interview with Prof. Marek Jan Chodakiewicz]," *Glaukopis*, no. 7-8 (2007): 289-312; and a shorter version in: "Skąd się wziął *Strach* [The Origins of *Fear*]," *Niezależna Gazeta Polska*, no. 6 (4 August 2006): 32-36; "Oni mają Żydów w nosie [They Couldn't Care Less About the Jews]," *Goniec*, 11-17 August 2006, 14-15; "Historia jak wycinanka [History as a Cut-and-Paste Exercise]," *Nowy Dziennik: Przegląd Polski*, 25 August 2006, 5, 11; "Gross kontra prawda: Rozmowa z prof. Markiem Janem Chodakiewiczem [Gross Vs. the Truth: An Interview with Prof. Marek Jan Chodakiewicz]," *Najwyższy Czas!*, 9 September 2006, XLVII-LII.

[25] Marek Jan Chodakiewicz, "Research Before Conclusion: The Problems of Shock Therapy in Jedwabne," *Glaukopis*, February 2001, http://glaukopis.pl/pdf/czytelnia/ResearchBeforeConclusion.pdf.

Congress website.[26] Whether Gross is unaware of Paul's research or deliberately ignores it, he raises questions about the integrity and depth of his own scholarship.

Because of the paucity of Gross' research, whether primary or secondary, we are faced with a serious dilemma. Why should we follow him in considering the village of Wólka-Okrąglik as the wartime symbol of the Podlasie or Białystok region? Based upon very few unverified sources, Gross claims that the local population was degenerate. The men robbed Jewish property, and the women prostituted themselves with the SS men for "Jewish gold." One wonders why Gross chose that particular settlement to illustrate what he implies and suggests was the Polish moral norm. But if it was the norm – and if Wólka-Okrąglik was indeed a fitting symbol to represent the Polish countryside - then what about the nearby settlements? A look around the area proves most valuable – and informative. But it hardly confirms Gross's imputations about the region or the representative value of the village of his choice.

In nearby Paulinów in February 1943, the Germans shot fifteen Polish farmers, including women, for sheltering Jews. The entire village knew about the Jewish neighbors in hiding, and a few actively helped the sheltering family and the sheltered in a variety of ways. Paulinów would constitute a beautiful symbol of good, even if we disregard for the time being that the Polish Christian rescuers of Paulinów and their Jewish cares were denounced to the Nazis by a Jewish *agent provocateur*. That Paulinów did not even merit a mention in Gross' book again raises some questions about the author's motives and his attitude towards historical evidence.

Brzostowica Mała, another settlement absent from *Golden Harvest*, may also serve as emblematic of the area and the nature of its wartime violence. According to Mark Paul, in September 1939, nearly two years before the infamous events in Jedwabne, a Communist band of Jewish and Belarusian neighbors from the nearby Brzostowica Wielka descended upon the village and the manor armed with axes and scythes to exterminate the entire Polish Christian population of Brzostowica Mała. By the thugs' measure, the raid was successful – the victims, including the handicapped Countess Ludwika Wołkowicka, were tortured horribly before they were sadistically killed. Research by historian Krzysztof Jasiewicz confirms Paul's gruesome account. Though tempting, despite visible social and racial aspects of the crime,

---

[26] See: www.glaukopis.pl and www.kpk-toronto.org/fundusz_obrony.html. For Mark Paul's essay on Treblinka and its environs see below.

forming sweeping generalizations based on this attrocity about the character of national minorities in the occupied territories during the Second World War would be unjustifiable, though that is precisely the sort of "logic" to which Gross routinely resorts.

Reflection 7: Regional studies

Only in-depth regional research and a series of case studies can assist us in forming any general opinions whatsoever about the Holocaust in Poland's countryside. Though there are many strong opinions on the subject, so far there have been precious few of such studies, and many more are warranted if we ever want to have a fuller understanding and factual knowledge of the times. The Institute of National Remembrance (IPN) in Poland, largely thanks to the vision, leadership, and perseverance of the late director Janusz Kurtyka, supported regional research and case studies, but much more work is necessary before one could offer a solid synthesis of Poland's modern history. However, even the IPN microstudies of single localities have so far focused on select issues rather than researching individual regions, towns, and villages comprehensively. Appropriate methodological training and paradigms are lacking, and the condition of post-Communist Polish scholarship leaves much room for improvement. It is unfortunate that the trend-setting newspaper of record, *Gazeta Wyborcza*, primitively mocks the scholarly achievements of the IPN, reserving its vitriolic disdain for microstudies in particular.[27]

On the other hand, the *Gazeta Wyborcza* applies a different measure to similar phenomena. Was not the Holocaust revisionist *Neighbors* by Gross also a case study, albeit a seriously flawed one, of Jedwabne?

The same *Gazeta Wyborcza* praises Gross' *Neighbors,* arguably the author's attempt at a Holocaust case study, if a revisionist and flawed one, pointing to the newspaper's bias not against case studies as such, but against some conclusions the editorial board may find all the more exasperating because of the strength of the research from which they are derived. After all, works by Jan Grabowski and, to some extent, by Barbara Engelking-Boni met with the newspaper's enthusiastic approval, even though they can be considered case studies[28] – as can all

---

[27] Adam Leszczyński, "Czy IPN może być zbawiony [Can the IPN be Redeemed?]," *Gazeta Wyborcza*, 10 January 2010, http://wyborcza.pl/1,75515,8922040,Czy_IPN_moze_byc_zbawiony_.html?as=1&start sz=x.

[28] Barbara Engelking, *Jest taki piękny słoneczny dzień: Losy Żydów szukających ratunku na wsi polskiej, 1942-1945* [It is Such a Beautiful, Sunny Day: The Fate of

the precious historical details, mined at the lowest "micro" level in villages and in the recollections of ordinary people, the forgotten, the overlooked, and the ignored, now frequently mentioned in the debate over *Golden Harvest* by the same scholars, pundits, and moralizers who would not stoop to gather them themselves.

Those down-to-earth details and sources are precisely what microhistory is all about: the vaunted "lower depths" theoretically so cherished by scholars on the left, but not, it seems, when studying the Holocaust or any subject on which they already formed an opinion and for which they need an intellectualized alibi, or an excuse, rather than evidence.

Naturally, one must crosscheck all data, whatever the source. The first step for a serious professional scholar or amateur researcher alike is to verify the sources independently. The second stage of verification is to disseminate the information gathered, unadulterated and unredacted, no matter how inconvenient the evidence gathered. Therefore, one should promptly share newly discovered revelations with one's peers and, next, with the public at large. To share and disseminate means not only to publish once, but consistently beam the available information to the world, including the details about its author. The internet allows for almost instantaneous sharing and verifying. Thanks to this process, other researchers will be able to find quickly the source of any new information, and they may be able to point to verifying or discrediting facts about the sources and actors in any historical drama.

Unfortunately, this mechanism for data and idea exchange and review often fails, especially among scholars, pundits, and journalists on the political left, because of their penchant for excluding the inconvenient and unwanted. The process of peer review cannot perform its function when the purportedly "tolerant" intellectuals believe that certain names must not be named and certain facts should remain unmentioned, no matter what the merits of the scholarship reviewed – and rejected. Political correctness, a tactic of silencing the opposition by keeping quiet about the dissidents, and a desire to show off one's

---

Jews Seeking Rescue in the Polish Countryside] (Warsaw: Stowarzyszenie Centrum Badań nad Zagładą Żydów, 2011); Jan Grabowski, *Judenjagd: Polowanie na Żydów, 1942-1945: Studium dziejów pewnego powiatu* [Judenjagd: Hunting for the Jews, 1942-1945 – A Study of the History of One County] (Warsaw: Stowarzyszenie Centrum Badań nad Zagładą Żydów, 2011). For a scathing critique of these deeply flawed works see Wojciech Jerzy Muszyński, "Holokaust stereotypami i wrażeniami opisany [The Holocaust Described Through Stereotypes and Sensationalism]," *Glaukopis*, no. 21-22 (2011): 320-327.

allegedly original contributions to the field, which had already been discovered and plowed over by the unmentionables, all conspire to handicap research sharing, principled scholarly exchange, and the search for the truth.

Does the name of the discoverer really change the objective merits of the discovery? The great Raul Hilberg himself freely admitted that he read the revisionist David Irving's analysis of various documents as well as his historical writings. Doing so allowed him to keep up even with the most obscure sources and to learn about the arguments used by his intellectual opponent. The "tolerant" scholarly *milieu* in Poland is not nearly as open-minded. The most recent monograph published on the fate of the Jewish population in the Warsaw Rising of 1944 virtually ignores important original research by Leszek Żebrowski, likely because of his vocal refusal to conform to the provocative *a priori* thesis that during the insurrection "the AK and the NSZ [Polish underground] slaughtered a plethora of Jews."[29]

Żebrowski's research is symptomatic of a larger tendency to gloss over in silence any inconvenient truth or intellectual dissent, trying to create an illusion of scientific consensus by intimidation and without proof. There are many examples of such anti-intellectual practice. To reinforce Gross's thesis about the pathological being the norm in Poland, his echo chamber of experts invoked the cases of Rechta and Stanin in the Lublin area, where Jews were killed by the Polish peasants and navy blue policemen.[30] The findings were published in the leftist Catholic *Tygodnik Powszechny*, but the experts forgot to acknowledge and cite the original source, a behavior that in some circles meets the definition of plagiarism.

Not only did they fail to mention the name of an intellectual opponent of theirs, whose original research unearthed these facts and introduced them into the scholarly discourse over a decade earlier,[31] but they also neglected to admit the existence of a more complex, alternative interpretation of the tragic events.

---

[29] See Leszek Żebrowski, *Paszkwil Wyborczej: Michnik i Cichy o Powstaniu Warszawskim* [Slander by the Electoral Gazette: Michnik and Cichy on the Warsaw Uprising] (Warsaw: Burchardt Edition, 1994); and Barbara Engelking i Dariusz Libionka, *Żydzi w powstańczej Warszawie* [The Jews in Insurrectionary Warsaw] (Warsaw: Stowarzyszenie Centrum Badań nad Zagładą, 2009).
[30] Dariusz Libionka and Jacek Leociak, "Sny o Bezgrzesznej [Dreams of a Poland Without Sins]," *Tygodnik Powszechny*, 16 January 2011, http://tygodnik.onet.pl/30,0,57862,sny_obezgrzesznej,artykul.html.
[31] Marek Jan Chodkiewicz, *Polacy i Żydzi 1918–1955: Współistnienie – Zagłada – Komunizm* [Poles and Jews, 1918-1955: Coexistence, the Holocaust, and Communism] (Warsaw: Fronda, [1999] 2000), 2nd. ed. 2005, third in print (2011).

Incidentally, the same work was responsible for the first mention in scholarly literature of the 1941 events in Jedwabne, including the Polish factor in the massacre of the Jews, but without the now-famous, if forensically and logically unsubstantiated, interpretation offered later by Gross in his shocking – and best-selling – *Neighbors*.

Using existing research, Stalinist interrogation documents and "confessions," remembrances by unverified witnesses, including Communist secret police officers to support his thesis, Gross applied his shock therapy to readers with characteristic methodological crudeness aided by fantasticaly violent imagery. The Polish intelligentsia, deprived of any solid knowledge about Poland's contemporary past by fifty years of Communist dictatorship, uncritically accepted *Neighbors* as a scholarly, not literary work. In the United States, the spirit of *Neighbors* was simply consistent with the popular perception of Poland during the Second World War. Meanwhile, the only empirical and logocentric microstudy of Jedwabne and the crimes committed there has been published – and glossed over in silence.[32]

Scholarship is the opposite of censorship, whether the censor functions through suppression or through silence. Scholarship is about the open-minded gathering and presenting facts as well as about the free exchange of opinions. Scholarship also means spreading knowledge and referring to all relevant works and authors contributing to the field, including those we disagree with. Naturally, one can exclude inconvenient voices. One can also try to monopolize the discourse, but it is to the detriment of scholarship and at the price of the truth. The threat of exclusion alone, instead of encouraging the greatest possible number of historians to engage in multifaceted research, imposes upon the profession a straight jacket of political correctness sadly modeled after Communist censorship.

Because Polish local historians from the provinces feel intimidated by the politically correct Coryphaeuses from Warsaw, Kraków, and, in particular, the newly accessible – and aspired to – West, they reflexively adjust to the expectations of the reigning orthodoxies. In no area of research is it more visible than in the history of Polish-Jewish relations during the Second World War and in its immediate aftermath. Neglect and, even more regrettably, warping of microstudies is this widespread phenomenon's direct consequence, as the "provincial"

---

[32] Marek Jan Chodakiewicz, *The Massacre in Jedwabne, July 10, 1941: Before, During, After* (New York and Boulder, CO: Columbia University Press and East European Monographs, 2005).

scholars seek approval by striving to tailor their research and conclusions to the expected *a priori* thesis about the role of all Polish Christians in the Holocaust. Naturally, not everyone can be intimidated into distorting documents and compromising scholarship, as evident, for example, from the work on the Podlasie region by Dariusz Magier and his team, who publish the Eastern Humanist Yearly (*Wschodni Rocznik Humanistyczny*, formerly the *Radzyński Rocznik Humanistyczny*).

Reflection 8: Our own case study

Surprisingly, there are virtually no case studies to turn to if one wants to understand the basis for the currently prevalent generalizations about life, events, trends, and norms of behavior in the Polish countryside under the Nazi and Soviet occupations. That these generalizations came to be in the first place, without rigorous research to back them up, is in itself a comment on methodology and the quality of evidence, which created them, even on their veracity. For stories, no matter how compelling, cannot become history merely on the strength of their literary qualities. Such stories are mere literature, but not scholarship. To have historical value, a historian's narrative needs to be based on evidence, documents, and facts – and that requires research. If the scholar's ambition is to discern patterns and be able to generalize about certain phenomena, case studies, or examining the particulars, are a necessary, if time-consuming, first step before any conclusions can be reached about the whole.

The present author's monograph on the county of Kraśnik-Janów near Lublin is the only comprehensive case study to date in any language concerning the demography, economy, politics, underground, institutions, elites, majority population, minorities, and the occupiers between 1939 and 1947.[33] The Lublin region on which the study focuses is particularly interesting, not only as the first official seat of the Soviet-installed Communist government in Poland and home to the notorious German concentration camp of Majdanek, but also the area abutting the Podlasie region in which Gross anchors his gold-digging narrative and the misattributed photograph meant to symbolize that gruesome loot in *Golden Harvest*.

Published in 2004, the case study is an expanded version of the doctoral dissertation defended at Columbia University, a fruit of nearly

---

[33] Marek Jan Chodakiewicz, *Between Nazis and Soviets: Occupation Politics in Poland, 1939-1947* (Lanham, MD: Lexington Books, 2004).

a decade of original, on-the-ground research into primary and secondary sources in Polish, German, Russian, and English, including sixteen archival collections and document depositories, both private and public, interviews with survivors, memoirs, forensic expert opinions, and others. No serious scholar may aspire to generalizing any aspect of that time without first analyzing it in detail.

Meticulous research and analysis contained in the study led to the conclusion that first, the Nazi and, later, Communist terror caused the occupied population to function within a triad: collaboration, accommodation, and resistance. Accommodation – simply attempting to survive – was the most prevalent attitude during the occupation. Not surprisingly, the human moral average turned out to be statistically neither heroic nor despicable, but just average. Only over time, under the impact of the brutal policy of the occupiers, accommodation shifted toward universal passive resistance. The research revealed a tightly controlled community, paralyzed with fear, and completely pauperized, yet sometimes resisting, a phenomenon that applies in a nuanced manner to the Polish countryside at large.

The occupiers forcefully collected enormous food quotas from the villages in the case study, increasing in volume and quantity after 1940 in particular, and leaving the population on the brink of starvation. After 1944, the Communists required the same and sometimes even greater food collections than the Nazis, but they were less efficient, at least until 1947, in coercing the population to give up the rations. Further, the occupiers demanded the fulfillment of various other obligations *in situ*, in particular the *corvée*. The Christian locals were also first encouraged, and then coerced and kidnapped, to work as slave laborers in the Reich. About 10,000 Poles – 10 percent of the total local population – were shipped off from the county of Kraśnik.

The peasants were punished for any and all infractions, both perceived and real, with fines, confiscations, beatings, jail, forced labor camps, concentration camps, and, increasingly, death. The occupiers forcibly resettled deportees and refugees, first from western and then eastern Poland. At least 12,000 Christians and about 8,000 Jews were forcibly brought into the county. Individual families and even entire villages were deported or resettled within or without the county as various social engineering projects multiplied and war requirements affected the population.

The occupiers in general, and the Germans in particular, periodically conducted "pacification" – anti-partisan, and economic actions of various intensity and scope. Those considered to be resisting were ruthlessly beaten, seized, or killed and their farmsteads burned.

Between 1939 and 1944, out of some 350 hamlets, thirty-three villages were destroyed partly and fifteen completely. For example, on 2 and 3 February 1944, the Nazis slaughtered about 900 Polish Christian civilians in Borów and its environs as punishment for supporting the far-right National Armed Forces (NSZ) guerrillas. This was the largest pacification action in central Poland.

Reflection 9: Chaos

The countryside was subject to the relentless terror of the occupiers. To make things worse, from September 1939, various criminal bands had been robbing the country people with increasing intensity. Moreover, different guerrilla units supplied themselves in the villages with and without the blessing of the farmers. As a result, gnawing poverty, hunger, and fear gripped the countryside. Basic products were lacking. Diseases were rampant. Mortality was high, both for "natural" reasons, and because of the random "ordinary" terror of the occupiers against the Poles. Terror intensified over time, in particular because of the onset of the Holocaust in the county of Kraśnik in the spring of 1942. Because of the Nazi policy of exterminating the Jews and Soviet POWs, and because of the activities of the robber bands, refugees, and guerrillas, the Polish countryside experienced an almost complete breakdown of law and order from mid-1942 onward.

Chaos reigned. Gradually, local farmer self-defense units, based upon the cadre of pre-war community and political activists of the lowest level, formed spontaneously to oppose it. In the countryside, the self-defense organizers usually harkened from the peasant populist movement. Yet, they also maintained links with a variety of underground orientations of the independentist camp. Further research shows that this phenomenon was present not only in the county of Kraśnik, but also in the Wilno and Nowogródek region as well as elsewhere.[34] A number of historians have confirmed that this pattern was replicated in most other areas of occupied central-eastern Poland's countryside.

Although spared the indiscriminate fury and horror of the Holocaust, the Christian deportees and refugees, the landless and smallholding peasants, who constituted the majority of the population, struggled to

---

[34] Marek Jan Chodakiewicz, ed., *Ejszyszki: Kulisy zajść, epilog stosunków polsko żydowskich na kresach, 1944-45* [Ejszyszki: the background of events, and epilog of Polish-Jewish relations in the Eastern Borderlands, 1944-45], 2 vols. (Warsaw: Fronda, 2002), and 2nd ed. as one vol. (Warsaw: Fronda, 2010).

survive. Up to 20,000 people, or a fifth of the county, needed permanent social assistance to make ends meet. It is estimated that more than half of the county's inhabitants took advantage of the county welfare services periodically in a variety of forms.

Medium-sized holders and wealthy farmers fared better, if they succeeded in hiding food, smuggling it out of the county, and selling it on the black market in starving cities. However, if they fell victim to banditry, they would helplessly and immediately fall to the poorest category; if caught smuggling, they could be executed. The documents of the Main Welfare Council and its county and parish branches, along with the underground reports, as well as even the records of the occupation authorities, reflect best the sheer misery of the predicament of the Christian population in the county.

Reflection 10: Pathologies

Poverty, hunger, fear, and terror inherent in both the German and Soviet occupation systems, manifested themselves in a particularly horrific form during the war and gave rise to a plethora of pathologies.

First, totalitarianism encouraged the settling of personal scores through "political" denunciations. Informing was a plague. For example, in a village between Zakrzówek and Wilkołaz, a farmer had a stallion, which brought him an income, by illegally inseminating the mares of his neighbors and, thus, denying the Nazis their taxes on animal reproduction. In one instance, after the coupling, a neighbor refused to pay. Because the owner of the stallion was also a deputy hamlet head and a member of the local forced food quota committee, he increased the volume of food products to be delivered by the mare's owner hoping to collect his due in that convoluted manner. The peasant felt persecuted and therefore denounced his creditor to the authorities at the local government (*gmina*) level, accusing him of illicit profiteering with a stallion. Conflicts of this kind and their resolution through blackmail or denunciation were quite common.

In the best-case scenario in Kraśnik County, the culprits were fined or their forced food quota was punitively increased. Usually, however, they were beaten, held in jail, or sent to the local forced labor camp. Less frequently, they were dispatched to the Lublin Zamek (Castle) prison, the camp at Majdanek, or even Auschwitz. *In extremis* they were shot. Other transgressions were punished in a similar manner. Punishments for anything and everything became a daily occurrence. After all, prostitution, drunkenness, looting, and violence were common. The lack of respect for private and public property was universal. Illegal felling of trees, poaching, and other forms of illicit exploitation of natural resources were constant.

Naturally enough, crime and social problems existed before the war, but during the occupation they multiplied to hitherto unimaginable proportions. Theft and robbery were common, much more frequent than in the pre-war period. They commenced already in September 1939.

Following the retreat of the Polish army from Kraśnik, local Christians and Jews despoiled the base of the 24th Lancer Regiment, including the apartments of the families of its officers and NCOs. Bombed out trains were looted. Individual refugees were set upon. Houses were broken into, in particular when the men were at the front and no one could protect the property. After the collapse of military resistance, some peasants stole from the retreating and fleeing Polish troops. If the exhausted soldiers fell asleep, they lost their horses, boots, and jackets – and these were almost exclusively ethnic Polish territories, except for Otrocz and a few other Ukrainian villages beyond the San. In some places, the self-appointed "red militia," encouraged by the Red Army units penetrating as far as Urzędów, engaged in robbery in late September 1939.

Things calmed down, albeit not immediately, when the Nazis took control of the area by early October 1939. In some localities, Janów for example, the occupiers initially encouraged looting of the local stores, mostly Jewish-owned. The mob would ravage the establishment and fight for the merchandise, with the choicest items falling to the soldiers of the *Wehrmacht,* who also photographed the action. Next, the Germans restored order with an iron hand; they imposed the death penalty for looting and for failing to return stolen property, state-owned items in particular.

Some local perpetrators, however, continued their criminal activity. They concentrated on the manor houses, ecclesiastical residences, wealthy farms, and Jewish businesses. Jewish merchants were accosted on the highway; the bandits took everything, including, for example, eggs. At first, the German gendarmerie and the Polish police counteracted the wave of banditry vigorously. The police defended initially both Jews and Christians.

For example, in 1940 the gendarmerie punished a Pole who blackmailed a Jew. In Modliborzyce, the police arrested perpetrators who had targeted a Jewish trader. However, the occupier gradually limited his regular police functions. Consequently, from mid-1941 the plague of banditry intensified and the thieves operated with virtual impunity until the village self-defense units and the independentist underground made an effort to protect the population and deal with the bandits in the fall of 1942.

Not only did the Germans curtail routine police activities but, ever more frequently, the Nazis also used the random violence as an instrument of fear and control. They resorted to approximated terror, which targeted mostly the bystanders, hardly ever connected to the bandit groups. The real perpetrators rarely suffered at the hands of the Nazi police. In the subsequent years, banditry continued with varied intensity, until after the war, when the Communist government, no longer in need of organized "spontaneous" violence against the pre-war elites or minorities, put a stop to it in the late 1940s – with no productive experience to offer, some erstwhile bandits often volunteered their professional services to the infamous Stalinist terror apparatus.

The bandits were known for their ruthlessness. They were indiscriminate killers, who would stop at nothing to extract goods or information from their victims. According to an underground report, to force a farmer to surrender his hidden property, bandits stripped and tortured his wife in front of him. Far from being an isolated incident, this was a regular occurrence, one of many acts of violence perpetrated on the people of the countryside during the six years of the war and in its immediate aftermath.

This universe, subject every day to acts of terror directed against the entire local population – by the Nazis and by the criminals let loose on ordinary people by the occupiers' deliberate neglect of law and order – is entirely missing from *Golden Harvest* or, for that matter, from any of Gross' writings about the Holocaust and its aftermath.

For all its deeply judgmental aspect and a tendency to accuse the local population of anything and everything from callousness to criminal involvement in the extermination of Poland's Jewish minority, *Golden Harvest* is surprisingly devoid of any serious discussion of the context or background information.

In Gross' rendering, the world in which that extermination was taking place lacks any governing details, whether sociological, political, or legal. There is much naturalist, almost pornographic violence - intellectualized, theorized, and psychologized in turn - but the prose of life, which, after all, is not just an insignificant backdrop against which all the horrific events of the war took place, is not to be found. The events reported are charged with value judgments, but they almost seem to take place in a reality vacuum. Indeed, to take Gross at his narrative's word, occupied Poland has all the complexity of a morality play – Jewish victims, German perpetrators, and their Polish Christian henchmen.

A complex and serious subject deserves more than a simplistic triad of the good, the bad, and the ugly. There is naturally no comparison between living as a target of a focused racial cleansing campaign, and living in fear of random terror which promises to kill one and one's family if one aided that target in any way, but which may – or may not – spare one if one does not. But whoever one was, one was never safe, one did not have enough food, and one did not experience comfort. The terror was everywhere, and everyone in occupied Poland lived in its shadow. It is surprising that Gross would repeatedly ignore its impact.

Reflection 11: Jewish-Jewish relations

The reign of terror to which Poland's entire population was subject during the German occupation is not the only aspect of wartime reality missing from Gross's narrative. In his writings, Gross almost entirely overlooks the vexing issue of Jewish-Jewish relations. In contrast, Hannah Arendt wrote with characteristic frankness about the negative role a portion of the Jewish elite played during the Nazi occupation.[35] Apart from being an integral part of Holocaust history, Jewish-Jewish relations also shed a light on the ethical and sociological question at the heart of the Browning-Goldhagen debate.

The debate comes down to the following question: Can one coerce human beings to perpetrate despicable deeds, deeds they would never even consider under normal circumstances? Goldhagen believes that anti-Semitism underpins all acts of violence against the Jews, explaining that the difference between prejudice and murder is merely one of degree –moving from one to the other is only a matter of time. Browning, on the other hand, suggests that while anybody is free to say "no" and suffer the consequences, most, especially under extreme circumstances, have the tendency to conform. Despite free will, resistance, lonely resistance in particular, appears to be an exception rather than a rule in any ethnic or religious group.

The microstudy of Kraśnik, including the county's Jewish community, under occupation, confirms what Browning saw as a pan-human phenomenon, and what Hannah Arendt asserted about the behavior of some Jewish elites under the Nazi regime. The traditional Jewish leadership in Kraśnik served its people well.

---

[35] Hannah Arendt, *Eichmann in Jerusalem: A Report on the Banality of Evil* (New York: Penguin Books, 1992).

However, the Germans quickly eliminated prominent local Jews and community leaders, such as Rabbi Friedling of Zakrzówek or Pinkwas Wagman of Urzędów, and put in their place pliable individuals, who could be trusted to serve the Nazis at the expense of their own community. The newly appointed leaders' obedience towards the Germans bestowed upon the collaborating prominent Jews a degree of security, but it failed to protect their people. The chairmen and other employees of the Jewish Councils, as well as ghetto policemen, or Jewish Order Service, directly oversaw and implemented German orders concerning property confiscation, slave labor, and other forms of economic exploitation of the Jews.

At the end, it was the leaders, Jewish policemen in particular, who carried out the Nazi command to round up and deport their fellow Jews to the death camps. Without their participation, it would have been much harder for the Nazis, first, to manage the Jewish community and then, with infamous efficiency, to perpetrate mass murder on it.

Historian Isaiah Trunk claims that collaboration benefitted the Jewish leaders because, percentage-wise, the leadership was more likely to survive than common members of the community.[36] This concerns the ghetto policemen in particular, whose survival rate was approximately 25 percent. However, the generalization does not apply to the county of Kraśnik – the local Jewish policemen and their commander Pesach Kawa indeed outlived most members of their community, but in the spring of 1944 they were all shot for attempting to escape from the concentration camp at Budzyń.

Thus, while the Holocaust was designed and perpetrated by the Germans, the Germans had various collaborators. Some of those collaborators were Jewish. This fact, largely considered a taboo, deserves more scholarly attention – both for its value in explaining the infernal mechanism of the Holocaust, and for the complex insight into human agency it offers. The Nazis, whose policies imposed the framework of collaboration on the Jewish community and its elites with apocalyptic consequences, were all too keenly aware of the persuasive power of terror and the human desire simply to survive – at any cost. Similarly, their occupation policies in effect shaped the character of accommodation and resistance, not only among the Jews, but also among the Polish Christian population and its leadership.

---

[36] Isaiah Trunk, *Judenrat: The Jewish Councils in Eastern Europe under Nazi Occupation* (Lincoln: University of Nebraska Press, 1972).

Reflection 12: The occupiers and their victims

Let us start with the victims. The Jewish community was the main victim of the German terror in Poland, including the county of Kraśnik. Most of the Jews were gassed by the Germans at the death camp in Bełżec. Demographic data analyzed in the course of the microstudy of Kraśnik demonstrates that during the Holocaust the Nazis murdered between 15,000 and 17,000 Jews in the county, which represents 13 to 15 percent of the total wartime local population and puts the death rate among the Jewish population of the county under German rule at a staggering rate of 90-95 percent. Most of the dead were local, but there were also other victims, deported from elsewhere. The likelihood of death for the Christian Poles in the same period was similar to the Jewish minority's chances of survival: between 8,000 and 10,000, that is 8 to 10 percent of the county's total pre-war population, or 5 to 7.5 percent of the local Christian population, perished at the hands of the Nazis.

The county's small parish of Chrzanów may help illustrate the difference in the scale and dynamics of violent death during the Second World War. Throughout the entire period of the German occupation, one hundred and four Poles, mostly peasants, were killed in that area. In contrast, the entire Chrzanów Jewish community of about 200 people was exterminated – shot – in one day in the fall of 1942. But this ethnic "key" to the slaughter of civilians, so clearly visible from the historical perspective, was not at all apparent in the early years of the war.

In the beginning of the occupation, the proportions of Jews and Christians killed by the Germans statistically reflected the demographic make-up of the county of Kraśnik as a whole. For example, in October and November 1939 the Jews constituted 10 percent of all executed hostages countywide (5 out of 50 people). However, from the start of the war, they were more discriminated against legally. At the same time, research shows that, in practice, they were subject to fewer police repressions than the Poles. For example, between March and July 1940, the German gendarmerie arrested 82 Poles and only 4 Jews for a variety of infractions against the occupation law. An average Christian was thus twice as likely to be repressed as an average Jew at that point. Possibly the occupiers saw terrorizing and instilling fear of persecution in the majority as an effective tool of controlling the local population as a whole.

Nonetheless, from the beginning of the German occupation the mortality rate for "natural" reasons among the Jewish population was much greater than among the Christians. In August 1940, about forty Jews died of starvation in the small town of Ulanów. To compare, in April 1940, twelve Christians were reported deceased of similar "natural" causes in Kraśnik, the county's largest town. In all of 1940, 125 Christians died there, including 109 of "natural" and 16 of "violent" causes, while in the month of April 1941 alone, 51 Jews died throughout the county of various diseases. Throughout 1941, there were approximately 600 such Jewish deaths. Jews were six times more likely to perish of "natural" causes at the time than Christians. Available data from the Kraśnik area suggests that altogether around 1,000 Jews perished of hunger and disease between the fall of 1939 and the spring of 1942, i.e. before the Holocaust commenced.

Afterwards, the mortality among the persons of Jewish origin who managed to avoid gas chambers or shooting remained very high. In June 1943, in the camp at Budzyń, where the surviving remnant of the local Jewish population was permitted to live "legally," the mortality indicator for the 2,000 prisoners averaged 20 persons, or 1 percent, per week – a direct result of horrid conditions and ruthless treatment by the SS guards and prisoner trustees.

High "natural" mortality rates reflected, of course, the Nazi occupation policy: isolation, segregation in the ghettoes, overcrowding, denial of basic food and commercial products, including soap and medicine. Before mass murder commenced, the Germans put into place a system of total occupation. They exacted absolute obedience from their Jewish and Christian slaves. They severely punished anything they considered resistance, including, from time to time, even passive submission. From the beginning of the war, they ruthlessly implemented all the decrees of the occupation law. In the county of Kraśnik, "according to the decree of the [Nazi] county supervisor of 23 October 1942, [...] all inhabitants and *their neighbors* who shelter Jews, supply them with food, or assist them in escaping, in particular by supplying horse-drawn carts to Jews, will be punished with death" (emphasis in the original).

It is estimated that at least fifty Christian Poles were punished with death for saving Jews and therefore violating this Nazi decree.

Reflection 13: Solidarity and profit

Christian-Jewish relations were multifaceted. In some aspects, they may be considered positive, in particular when individual predilections or self-interest dictated kindness and solidarity. One of the most important fields of constructive engagement between Polish Jews and

Christians was trade. Until the fall of 1942, despite regulations and laws to the contrary, and harsh punishment, the Jewish population endeavored to continue its pre-war patterns of existence, including plying trade. Several factors facilitated the endeavor. There were only open ghettos in the county of Kraśnik. The Germans failed to erect walls, and the perimeters were guarded by the Jewish and Polish policemen, either friendly, corruptible, or both, making it easy to sneak in and out. The clients were waiting eagerly for the Jewish middlemen because the peasants preferred to obtain a good price from a familiar Jewish merchant than to surrender their agricultural products to the Nazis for the imposed food quota.

By the end of 1940, the Nazis had perfected the control of population movements, and the local Jews found it nigh impossible to reach larger towns with their wares for sale. The profit evaporated and, in its absence, so did the capital for further trade. The Jewish savings vanished. Moreover, the Jewish merchants had been running out of industrial merchandise to barter with the peasants. Despite all this, in 1941 and 1942, the denizens of the ghettoes continued their peregrinations in the familiar countryside swapping various leftover items for food. They begged for sustenance with some success, in particular among some friendly Gentile families.

Begging continued, though in a much more surreptitious form, as the Jewish fugitives from the Nazi extermination machine criss-crossed the county of Kraśnik, hiding, circling about, or proceeding elsewhere, between March 1942 and July 1944.

The Christian population was rather sympathetic to the Jews, although the level of their generosity fell gradually as a direct result of the Nazi terror and the extreme pauperization of the county population. Aside from trading with the Jews and supplying them, the Christian Poles also served as liaisons and guides between separated Jewish families and friends in various parts of occupied Poland. They also escorted Jews, traveling illegally for a variety of reasons and to different localities, in and out of the county. After the Holocaust commenced in the spring of 1942, at least some of the liaisons and guides continued their activities to some extent.

Gunnar S. Paulsson, in his *Secret City*, has described the intricate mechanism of rescuing Jews in Poland as essentially a chain of people of good will reacting to Jewish pleas for help.[37] Although Paulsson

---

[37] Gunnar S. Paulsson, *Secret City: The Hidden Jews of Warsaw, 1940-1945* (New Haven, CT: Yale University Press, 2002).

developed his model to fit the urban setting, particularly Warsaw, the pattern applies to the Polish countryside as well.

First, to obtain help, a Polish Jew had to show initiative – i.e. escape and turn to a Christian for assistance. The majority of the ghetto prisoners did not take those risks. They remained passive for a variety of reasons – family obligations, lack of contacts outside, poor or no knowledge of the Polish language, or false hopes of survival fostered by the Germans.

Meanwhile, the majority of the Poles, including the peasants, extremely poor and aware of the death penalty for the entire family and neighbors for any such efforts, failed to initiate offers of assistance. Some Christians helped nonetheless. Many accepted money or goods for their services, usually to cover the black market costs of the upkeep of the fugitives but sometimes also simply taking advantage of the unfortunates. Many Christians helped sporadically. Very few of them resolved to host and shelter Jews permanently. Many more Poles were capable of sporadic acts of assistance and cordiality, such as offering temporary shelter, feeding someone a few times, sharing some clothes, organizing fake "Aryan" documents, or transporting a fugitive to another safe spot.

At least 5,000 people of good will in the area of Kraśnik, mostly peasants, are estimated to have participated in aiding Jews. They engaged sporadically in assisting about 1,000 Jewish fugitives. An additional one thousand Christians sheltered approximately 400 Jews for extended periods at various times during the Nazi occupation. Some of the helpers as a rule operated for profit; others accepted money or goods sometimes; and still others simply offered their charity for nothing. The local chapter of the national underground Council to Aid Jews (*Żegota*) was also active in the county, mostly helping assimilated Jews and Poles of Jewish origin.

Some assimilated Jews, converts to Christianity in particular, continued to live as they had before the war, knowing that unlike their Polish neighbors, the Germans were not aware of their Jewish origin. Ewa Sowiakowska, the Jewish wife of the Ukrainian physician Dr. Jeremiasz Sowiakowski in Janów, was one of those hidden from the Nazis in plain view. About 100 assimilated persons living in the county survived thanks to false "Aryan" documents furnished by the Polish underground.

Based on the available evidence, between March 1942 and July 1944 an estimated one thousand unassimilated Jews risked the escape from certain death and hid in the county. While in hiding, all of them, though to a varying degree, had to rely on the assistance, good will – and courage – of the Christian Poles who would shelter and feed them. Only about 300 of those fugitives survived until the arrival of the Soviets in mid-1944.

It is important to consider the circumstances under which the Jewish fugitives died. According to Gross, the principal agents of their deaths were the Polish peasants. Although the case study of the Kraśnik area confirms the impact of social pathologies on the deteriorating situation of Poland's Jewish population, Gross's assertion that the impetus to kill Jews came from "anti-Semitism" and "greed" is simplistic at best, and a false, twisted caricature of reality at worst.

Reflection 14: Death in details

The detailed analysis performed in the course of the case study of Kraśnik has yielded incontrovertible data that the Germans killed an estimated 17,000 Jews in the county. Around 16,000 Jewish victims were gassed at Bełżec. Approximately 700 Jews died while in hiding. At least 400 of the Jewish fugitives were killed by the hunter units of the SS, gendarmerie, and the German police. An estimated 300-400 died under various circumstances and for different reasons as a result of Polish actions, direct and indirect. Among the victims there were some transient Jews from other areas, approximately 150 to 300 people, who found themselves in the county as partisans, fugitives, or prisoners.

To understand what took place over the six years of the war in the county of Kraśnik – indeed, in every county of occupied Poland – it is important to examine carefully the various categories of people responsible for Jewish deaths, the reasons behind their actions, and the circumstances of the killing.

Carefully scrutinizing the actions and motives of the perpetrators sanctioned by the Germans and operating within the institutions approved by the occupier, of the criminal element, and of the underground active in the county, allows for a more nuanced and focused historical analysis of the past and a better understanding of what actually happened, how it happened, and why, based on available evidence, rather than theories or sheer conjecture.

In the absence of any Polish government institutions at any level, local Polish officials, such as county mayors, hamlet heads, policemen, or watchmen, served under the German occupiers and reported to the German administrators. The Polish police essentially did not participate directly in the Holocaust. Its activities were limited to guarding prisoners or handing over Jews captured by the unarmed peasant catchers used by the Germans. Handing the fugitives to the occupiers meant near certain death for the captives – by carrying out Nazi orders, some Polish officials became directly implicated in Jewish deaths.

It was extremely unusual for Polish officials to initiate anti-Jewish actions. Some officials did so, however, usually for personal reasons, such as avarice, anti-Semitism, and, in some cases, self-defense. Based on the analysis of all the available materials and documents from the county, Polish policemen may have been responsible for ten Jewish deaths. A policeman in Wilkołaz, who killed two Jews to ingratiate himself with the Nazis, was an exception. Another policeman, in Polichna, shot a captured Jewish fugitive to prevent him from revealing to the occupation authorities the names of the Poles who had sheltered him. Several Polish policemen were used as guides and interpreters in combined hunter units of the SS and gendarmerie who searched for Jews, but there is no evidence that they took part in executions. Nonetheless, they were there – indirect accessories to murder.

To pursue Jewish fugitives, the German authorities employed the night watch, the field watch, and the volunteer fire guards. They were composed of peasants and lacked firearms. The "work" was far from voluntary, though the peasants' enthusiasm in executing the objectives of the pursuit depended on the individuals' predilections, and most commonly on the seriousness of their Christian faith, the award offered by the occupier, and the attitude of the local leaders who headed such outfits. Generally, the peasants abhorred fulfilling any task ordered by the Germans. They considered it a form of *corvée*. Thus, they treated participating in the round-up, running around the forests with sticks, and looking for Jews, exactly as they would any other forced obligations: a punishment akin to road construction, snow removal, transport duty, and other onerous services exacted by and for the Nazis.

Though rare, there were also voluntary "Jew chases." The members of the very same official guard outfits participated in them for a variety of reasons. First, they pursued the Jewish fugitives who robbed food to survive, in particular if the robbery was violent, especially if a peasant was murdered in its course.

Some volunteer "Jew catchers" were motivated by money – they robbed the unfortunates or turned them over to the Germans for a reward. In the county of Kraśnik, each seized Jewish fugitive was worth between two and five kilograms of sugar, a highly prized commodity. Captured Jews were generally turned over to the authorities, which equaled death.

The scope of this phenomenon is difficult to establish. About one hundred persons in the county of Kraśnik fell victim to the catchers, and perhaps half of the apprehended were killed on the spot, chiefly as revenge for real and suspected banditry. For example, a gang of volunteer catchers operated out of the village of Pasieka, managing to catch at least one fugitive in Antolin. In Godziszów, the supervisor of the volunteer fire department and his deputy voluntarily caught Jews for money. Clearly on the moral fringes of the village, they maintained intimate links with common bandits, who also engaged in catching Jewish fugitives.

There are cases of individual fugitives killed for loot or for sadistic pleasure by certain degenerate single peasants. After all, the killers operated with virtual impunity, and pathologies remained deliberately unchecked by the occupiers.

"Ordinary" peasants, hitherto rescuers, would also rescind earlier offers to shelter Jews and either expel, denounce, or even kill their cares – out of fear or greed. Approximately 50 persons died as a result of such actions in the county of Kraśnik, though it is hard to gauge the scale of this phenomenon. It does seem, however, that these were rare occurrences. Deemed repulsive by all decent people, the stories were much discussed by many with revulsion; the perpetrators would be known, pointed out, and quietly condemned. The local Christians themselves feared the perpetrators.

Jews died sometimes because of quarrels between Polish neighbors, misunderstandings, which in the times of terror and extreme deprivation, had the power to metastasize into existential duels. Things would turn bloody when, to settle scores, the parties involved called on the Nazis, the underground, or the bandits. Such neighborly misunderstandings claimed approximately 50 Jewish and 200 Christian lives in the county.

These horrific events usually originated in personal or political disagreements. For example, the Gajdur family of four and a five-year-old Jewish girl they sheltered died because Jan Kowalik, a hamlet head and a Communist sympathizer, perceived them as "uppity" and disapproved of their independentist ties – the Gajdurs' son had earlier died in Auschwitz when the camp was still reserved for Polish political prisoners. Kowalik denounced the Gajdurs to the Nazis, and on 1 June 1943, in Majdan-Obleszcze near Brzozówka the Nazi gendarmes burned alive the Christian family of four – two toddlers and an elderly couple – and the five-year-old Jewish girl whom they were hiding.

For this denunciation, the hamlet head was sentenced to death by a Polish pro-Western underground court. The sentence was carried out two weeks after the killing – Jan Kowalik was executed for his crime by a Polish "blue" collaborationist police sergeant Wiśniewski, a clandestine soldier of the underground National Armed Forces (NSZ), who used a false pretense to mete out justice.

The fate of the Gajdurs was precisely what all Poles knew to expect for interfering with the Final Solution, not only in the county of Kraśnik, but throughout all counties – Poland, home to Europe's biggest Jewish population, had the dubious distinction of having the most draconian Nazi laws for helping its Jews, which succeeded in making the fear of German reprisals the single greatest deterrant from helping the hunted Jewish minority. And Jews were simply not able to survive without Christian help – without food, shelter, and money.

Not only the Gajdurs, but numerous families which took the risk and hid their Jewish neighbors paid the ultimate price – many trees around Yad Vashem tell their stories. In Słonim near Grodno, in the eastern Borderlands, several hundred Polish Christians were massacred for the community's effort to shelter local Jews. In Huta Stara near Buczacz, in historic Galicia, the Nazis herded the settlement's entire Polish Christian population, and the Jewish countrymen they were hiding, and burned them all alive in the local church. The stories can be multiplied.[38]

So much for what Gross cynically – and perversely – dismisses in his writings about Poland, not as a moral gesture and an act of courage, but a supposedly lucrative enterprise. The estimated 50,000 to 100,000 Jews who survived the war in hiding and who were saved could not have survived on their own. It is therefore not surprising that fully 25

---

[38] Walerian M. Moroz and Andrzej Datko, eds., *Męczennicy za wiarę 1939–1945: Duchowni i świeccy z ziem polskich, którzy prześladowani przez nazizm hitlerowski dali Chrystusowi ofiarę życia świadectwo miłości* [Martyrs for Faith: The Religious and Lay of the Polish lands who, while persecuted by Hitlerite Nazis gave Christ, through the sacrifice of their lives, a proof of their love] (Marki-Struga: Michalineum, 1996), 385–86 and 390–91; Stanisław Łukomski, "Wspomnienia," [Memoirs] in *Rozporządzenia urzędowe Łomżyńskiej Kurii Diecezjalnej* [Administrative Decrees of the Łomża Diocese Curia], no. 5–7 (May–July 1974): p.62; Witold Jemielita, "Martyrologium księży diecezji łomżyńskiej 1939–1945," [Priest Martyrs of the Łomża Diocese] in *Rozporządzenia urzędowe Łomżyńskiej Kurii Diecezjalnej (Administrative Decrees of the Łomża Diocese Curia)*, no. 8–9 (August-September 1974): 55; Jan Żaryn, "Przez pomyłkę: Ziemia łomżyńska w latach 1939–1945." [By mistake: The Łomża region 1939-1945: Conversation with Rev. Kazimierz Łupiński from Szumowo parish], *Biuletyn Instytutu Pamięci Narodowej (Bulletin of the Institute of National Remembrance)*, no. 8–9 (September–October 2002): 112–17, cited in Mark Paul, ed., *Wartime Rescue of Jews by the Polish Catholic Clergy: The Testiomny of Survivors* (Toronto: Polish Educational Society of North America, 2007), 252, posted at http://www.internationalresearchcenter.org/research_center/media/WartimeRescueOfJewsByThePolishCatholicClergy_MarkPaul.pdf.

percent of Righteous Among Nations were Poles, surely an underestimation because of the rigidity of Yad Vashem standards.

While Poland had its share of the righteous ones, each province, county, and village also had regular criminals. The greatest number of Jews who died at the hands of the Poles in the county of Kraśnik – over 100 people – were killed by the bandits, in particular the robber band of Stanisław Kiełbasa ("Dziadek"). Originally of the independentist underground, the boss of the group and a few of his partisans went rogue and formed a thieves' alliance in the beginning of 1941. In the fall of 1942, Kiełbasa's underlings lured Jews to join them with promises of paid protection. The bandits robbed and killed all of them. Later, some of them joined the Communists and continued their banditry.

Some Jews perished at the hands of the Communists. Some of them were victims of violent robberies. Others died as a result of struggles within the ranks of the Communist Party or the fight against the Nazi *agentura*. Some were victims of anti-Semitism. The People's Guard (GL), the People's Army (AL), and other groups connected to the Communist Polish Workers Party (PPR) were responsible for up to 150 Jewish deaths.

The independentist underground, known for executing "*szmalcownicy*," individuals who denounced Jews in hiding and their caretakers for reward money, was nevertheless responsible for some killings of the Jewish fugitives as well. An estimated 50 people may have been killed as real or imagined Communists, bandits, or Nazi agents.

Anti-Semitism was not the reason for such actions. Counteracting agents, provocateurs, and robberies were. Village self-defense units, incorporated into the Popular Security Guard of the Peasant Party (LSB SL) and the Self-government Watch of the Government Plenipotentiary (DR), fought the bandits and any persons considered as such.

Desperate Jews roaming the countryside and robbing to survive would be seen as a threat to a village. In addition, any fugitive may have been perceived to be a Communist agent or a Nazi provocateur – some in fact were, which made the possibility and the risk of executions which followed such encounters very real. Therefore, fugitives could have been considered a threat not only to a village, but to the survival of the local underground units as well. Both the National Armed Forces (NSZ) and the Home Army (AK) participated in anti-Communist and anti-Nazi agent operations to a comparable degree.

Overall, between 300 and 400 Jews of the Kraśnik county, or about 1 percent of the group's pre-war population, perished at the hands of

Poles. To put these deaths in perspective, between 1939 and 1944 in the county of Kraśnik, the soldiers of the underground killed between 102 and 450 Germans (*Reichsdeutsche* and *Volksdeutsche*, civilian, police, and military), and about 500 Nazi collaborators, mainly ethnic Poles, but also Ukrainians. German losses include 102 local Germans, either residing in or billeted in the county, whose deaths are fully substantiated in Nazi documents (but the available statistics concern only the period between May 1943 and July 1944), and at least 200-350 visitors, either passing through or staying longer, such as soldiers killed during underground sabotage actions against transports or policemen from other counties, districts, or units participating in major pacification operations in the county of Kraśnik.

On the other hand, the Germans killed on the spot at least 787 underground fighters and other armed persons, and captured 224 clandestine operatives, most of whom were subsequently killed (again, the statistics are available for the period between May 1943 and July 1944 only).

Further, the Nazis liquidated 126 and captured 84 supporters of the underground; most of the captured did not survive the encounter. Out of approximately 7,000 soldiers of the underground (at its peak in the summer of 1944), an estimated 1,000 perished at the hands of the Germans.

This does not include the victims of various Nazi pacification actions, which killed at least 1,200 Poles, mostly civilians, peasants in particular, only a few of whom were members of the underground. At the same time, once again for comparison's sake, between 1939 and 1947 the independentists killed about 400 Communists (240 of them by July 1944, including 120 by the National Armed Forces), and the Communists killed 875 independentists (375 of them before the second entry of the Soviets). In addition, the Soviets shipped off between 300 and 550 inhabitants of the county of Kraśnik to the Gulag.

The lack of documentation renders practically all wartime and postwar statistics unreliable. This fact alone makes it necessary to delve into existing primary sources and examine the down-to-earth, often mundane details only a case study can offer. A past unreliably documented cannot be reconstructed with an image or a metaphor.

The mechanism of the Final Solution turned the Jews, especially the unassimilated Jews, those *without* familiar Polish neighbors, into the most vulnerable and isolated group in wartime Poland. Anti-Semitism may well have been a factor influencing almost every instance of anti-Jewish violence, but, among the local population, it was certainly not its cause. Similarly, peasant greed was neither the cardinal nor the only motif for killing Jews.

Fear, however, did play a serious role in many anti-Jewish actions. But contrary to what Gross would have his readers believe, it was not the fear of the Jews, but of the Nazis and their killing machine. Seeing a Christian family burned alive for harboring a little girl or an entire village massacred for hiding its Jewish neighbors did much to give all Poles pause, the brave and the cowardly alike.

Reflection 15: Propaganda

The main perpetrators of the Holocaust, the Nazi Germans, disappear in Gross's narrative. Instead, an all-consuming wave of peasant violence engulfs the Polish countryside. In his musings, Gross neglects to give any serious thought about the chief beneficiary of the extermination of the Jews. And yet the answer is right before his eyes – before our eyes – all along. It is the property-confiscating totalitarian state. The first beneficiary of the killings was the Third Reich and next, the Soviet colony known as the Polish People's Republic.

In his books, Gross asserts that the chief beneficiaries of the Jewish tragedy were the Poles, peasants mainly, but also other representatives of the lower social strata. The supposed ill-gotten gains advanced them to the ranks of craftsmen and merchants. But the Grossian narrative only repeats, inexplicably, the basest facets of Nazi propaganda. In the context of wartime terror, poverty, and near-starvation, not to mention the Communist take-over of post-war Poland, his assertion is positively bizarre if not outright Orwellian.

One may only read the so-called reptile press (*prasa gadzinowa*), such as the *New Lublin Daily* (*Nowy Dziennik Lubelski*), published by the Germans in the Polish language, to appreciate fully the intellectual pedigree of Gross's argument. Already in July 1941 the paper averred that "during the Polish era the participation of Jews in trade was between 80 to 90 percent, and on the territory of the General Gouvernment [Nazi-occupied central Poland] the number of Jews plying trade could be estimated at 100,000 enterprise owners. Nowadays, in step with the progress of the de-Jewing of trade, the liquidation of many small and large Jewish-managed enterprises is carried out."

In June 1943 the editors wrote about "the transformation of crafts in the Government General" thanks to the Holocaust. In July the paper rejoiced that "the Lublin [Polish] painters have taken over from the Jewish craftsmen." Thus, the Holocaust was depicted as benefitting the

Poles precisely in the way Gross seems to see it. But neither the Nazi propaganda nor its embrace by Gross can change the fact that there were but two beneficiaries of the Shoah: the Nazis and the Communists.

Reflection 16: Property and institutions

The Nazis benefitted from the Holocaust first. During the war they expropriated and exploited Jewish property, as well as destroyed to a large extent private trade, crafts, and enterprises. Then, after the war, the Communists took over Jewish possessions and, in addition, eradicated almost everything that remained of private trade, crafts, and enterprises. Thus, one totalitarianism assisted and laid the groundwork for the succeeding one. *Golden Harvest* fails to emphasize that fact, while Gross's earlier *Neighbors* positively obfuscates it, going as far as to refer to the Communist security apparatus-exacted confessions as scholarly "evidence," and its officers as "witnesses," and constructing the "truth" of his interpretive narrative around those "documents."

For a book that concerns itself with expropriation of astounding proportions – down to valuable prosthetic parts and remains of a charred human body – *Golden Harvest* is remarkable in its avoidance of the robbery of Jewish property and the property of others by the state.[39] The mechanism of expropriation is known, and it is illuminating in its details.

First, the Germans introduced appropriate legislation, confiscating literally everything from the Jews. The definition of "Jewish property" was of course extremely elastic and based upon the Nuremberg Laws. Not only did Christian converts lose everything, but it was sufficient for a single member of the board of an enterprise to be of Jewish origin

---

[39] On the expropriation of Jewish property in Europe see Martin Dean, *Robbing the Jews: The Confiscation of Jewish Property in the Holocaust, 1933-1945* (New York: Cambridge University Press, 2010). On the confiscation of property in Poland by the Nazis see Bernhard Rosenkötter, *Treuhandpolitik: Die "Haupttreuhandstelle Ost" und der Raub polnischer Vermögen, 1939-1945* [Trusteeship Policy: The "Central Trust Agency for the East" and the Robbery of Polish Property] (Essen: Klartext Verlag, 2003). To compare with Lithuania see Valentinas Brandišauskas, "Lietuvos žydų turto likimas Antrojo pasaulinio karo metai [The history of the property of Lithuanian Jews during the Second World War]," *Genocidas ir reistencija*, no. 1 (15) (2004): http://www.genocid.lt/Leidyba/15/valentin.htm; Valentinas Brandišauskas, "Žydų nuosavybės bei turto konfiskavimas ir naikinimas Lietuvoje [Expropriation and destruction of Jewish property in Lithuania]," *Genocidas ir reistencija*, no. 2 (12) (2002): http://www.genocid.lt/Leidyba/12/valentin.htm.

for the business to be branded as "Jewish" and, on that basis, confiscated – so much for the upward mobility of the lucky remaining board members, owners, managers, and workers. Further, the Jewish community was burdened with outrageous taxes and contributions. The Jews lost literally everything, except for what they could successfully hide.

An entire perverse machine of exploitation was set up to harness the occupied population to it. The Christians and Jews were forced to carry out a number of obligations. The peasants were burdened in particular with the forced food quota. At the lowest level it was collected by their fellow-villagers in the forced food quota commissions, which consisted of the local elite: teachers, priests, hamlet heads, and their deputies.

Similarly, the institutions exploiting the Jewish population were staffed, at the lowest level, with the Jewish elite of the Jewish councils (*Judenrat*). In the countryside, the Jews were subordinated to the officials in town and parish administrations, appointed mayors and village heads. The heads were usually Christian Poles, but sometimes also Ukrainians, Belarusians, or *Volksdeutsche*. They were subordinated to German officials, usually *Reichsdeutsche*: the county supervisor (*Kreishauptmann*) or town commissar (*Stadtkommisar*) and their underlings in various county bureaus, all of which demanded services and contributions in cash, jewels, nature, or labor from the Jewish community.

Despite the fact that the robbery of private property through the national-socialist state took place through the medium of multiple bureaucratic structures, it was the plenipotentiary office that had the most direct dealings with the Jewish property.

For instance, a Polish leaseholder on a Jewish-owned mill had to pay the monthly lease on it to the Nazi state plenipotentiary official. The lease collector in such instances was usually a Polish Christian. Further, following expropriation, the agent of the plenipotentiary of the Jewish properties and land (*Treuhänder für den jüdischen Haus-und Grudbesitz*) collected a monthly rent from the "former" Jewish owner of a house and a garden. In other words, the expropriated Jewish owner had to pay for the "privilege" of using his (formerly) own property. The collection agents were either Jewish or Polish Christians.

As in a typical colonial system, it was convenient for the occupier to have some natives despoil other locals for the benefit of the colonial state. This partly explains the great resentment felt toward Polish officials in many recollections by Jewish witnesses. After all, they hardly ever met a German commissar. They usually dealt much too frequently with a Polish rent collector, tax collector, or a plenipotentiary agent for Jewish properties.

After the entry of the Soviets in 1944, the property conquered by them from the Third Reich was not returned to the rightful owners, but taken over by the puppet Communist Polish state. This concerned both Jewish and Polish possessions. In practice, at the lowest level, it meant that the town administration continued to collect rent from the tenants of Jewish apartment houses, and the parish administration continued to demand lease money for a grain mill or a sawmill. And it really did not matter that the names of the real owners were still listed in property registers. The Communists seized everything. They confiscated big industry, enterprises, and banks right away. Next, the Polish plenipotentiaries of the Kremlin gradually took over everything, including even the tiniest enterprises and real estate: all the Jewish ones, but also the ones owned by the Christians.[40]

In this light, Gross's assertion that "the Poles" somehow benefitted from the expropriation of Jewish property is peculiar, or, possibly, given the scholarly standard of his works, simply uninformed. Poland did not win the Second World War, and any talk about Christian economic "gains" amounts to imagining a different outcome of history.

Or perhaps Gross confuses Poles with Communists. After 1944 Communism destroyed the private merchants, artisans, craftsmen, and all other persons who during the war had started fulfilling economic

---

[40] Communist expropriations progressed in stages but they were usually completed by 1949 or so. Initially, for propaganda reasons, the Communists pretended to favor Jewish owners and returned some properties to them briefly, as described by Barbara Gorczycka-Muszyńska below. On Jewish property during the war and the attempts to reclaim it in its aftermath in central and western Poland see Marek Jan Chodakiewicz, *After the Holocaust: Jewish-Polish Conflict in the Wake of World War II* (New York and Boulder, CO.: Columbia University Press and East European Monographs, 2003); and in the eastern Borderlands (Soviet-occupied Belarus in particular) see Leonid Smilovitsky, "The Struggle of Belorussian Jews for the Restitution of Possessions and Housing in the First Postwar Decade," *East European Jewish Affairs,* vol. 30, no. 2 (2000): 53-70. For Europe in general see: Martin Dean, Constantin Goschler, and Philipp There, eds., *Robbery and Restitution: The Conflict over Jewish Property in Europe* (New York and Oxford: Berghahn Books, Published in Association with the United States Holocaust Memorial Museum, 2007), including a rather superficial treatment of the topic by Dariusz Stola, "The Polish Debate on the Holocaust and the Restitution of Property," s. 240-255. Further see Marek Jan Chodakiewicz, "*Restytucja*: The Problems of Property Restitution in Poland, 1939-2001," in *Poland's Transformation: A Work in Progress*, ed. by Marek Jan Chodakiewicz, John Radzilowski, and Dariusz Tolczyk (Charlottesville, VA: Leopolis Press, 2003), 159-93. See also Adam Hlebowicz, "Straty materialne kultury polskiej na Wschodzie [The Material Losses Suffered by Polish Culture in the East]," *Biuletyn Instytutu Pamięci Narodowej,* no. 3 (March 2007): 23-28.

functions traditionally held by Jews until their extermination by the Germans. In addition, had Poland won the war, Jewish survivors and other private owners would have claimed their properties and jobs back, as was the case in Western Europe.

The claim about the alleged Polish benefits from the Holocaust is a colossal misunderstanding of history. Interestingly, a Communist historian, Czesław Madajczyk, appreciated the disappearance of free market infrastructure because it was easier ("more rational") to build Communism.[41] This raises another question: was Communism in the Polish interest? Did the Poles benefit? Or perhaps it was Soviet Russia that benefited from the conquest of Poland and the confiscations that followed.

The claim that the Polish peasants enriched themselves at Jewish expense is spuriously false. The peasant looting of the leftover Jewish possessions, so-called "abandoned" property, often junk, did take place. Indeed, a few dilapidated houses in the ghetto were demolished for building material and fuel in Zakrzówek and Radomyśl.[42] The "abandoned" Jewish property belonged to the Third Reich. The grand theft, the robbing of a people had already taken place before the looting. The phenomenon is analogous to the theft of the possessions belonging to the Poles and others in the eastern Borderlands who were deported to the Gulag by the Soviets between 1939 and 1941 and after 1944. That robbery had also already taken place when the former Ukrainian, Belarusian, and Jewish neighbors picked up the scraps left by the deported Poles. The main beneficiary of that mass expropriation was the Soviet Union.[43]

---

[41] Czesław Madajczyk, *Polityka III Rzeszy w okupowanej Polsce* [The Policies of the Third Reich in Occupied Poland] (Warsaw: Państwowe Wydawnictwo Naukowe, 1970), vol. 1: 574.

[42] More comprehensive research at the microscale is needed to ascertain the scale and character of the phenomenon.

[43] The Soviet expropriations and the history of the property left behind by the Poles and other victims of the Communists remain grossly under-researched. See two case studies, about Lithuanian motor vehicles and Poland's state forestry employees in a single region, respectively: Vidas Grigoraitis, "Lengvųjų automobilių nacionalizavimas Lietuvoje," [The nationalization of cars in Lithuania under the Soviet occupation] *Genocidas ir reistencija*, no. 1 (5) (1999):
http://www.genocid.lt/Leidyba/5/vidas.htm#Nationalisation%20of%20motorcars%20in%20Lithuania%20After%20Soviet%20Occupation; and Michał Gnatowski, "Deportacja osadników i służby leśnej oraz ich rodzin z regionu łomżyńskiego na wschodnie obszary ZSRR w lutym 1940 roku [The Deportation of Settlers, Foresters, and Their Families From the Łomża Region to the Eastern Areas of the USSR in February 1940]," *Studia Łomżyńskie*, vol. 7 (1996): 49-66.

Reflection 17: National consciousness

Gross and his adherents, expounding upon *Golden Harvest*, often employ the first person plural nominative, asserting that "we are guilty," or "that is the [horrible] way we are." The use of an implicitly accusatory "we," instead of "you," is disingenuous. Apart from the fact that one's guilt can only be assessed individually – it is *mea culpa,* not *nostra culpa* – Gross always stresses his liberal and secular separateness from the conservative and Christian Polish mainstream.

To whom, then, is the "we" referring? Is the use of that pronoun a sign of self-confessed guilt or a crafty rhetorical ploy that allows Gross to put a nation on trial in a seemingly more palatable manner? Or is Gross confessing the alleged sins for another person, putting his own words into the mouths of others – of an entire nation? And is that nation, accused collectively, identified with the pathological underclass that kills the most vulnerable for money or sadistic pleasure?

If that is in fact Gross's moral and rhetorical thrust, his approach raises another question: to what extent did the village primitives, crude bandits, and marginal people who perpetrated crimes against Jews and others, consciously think of themselves as Poles? True, they certainly spoke Polish, and they were likely baptized in the Catholic Church. But did they consciously think of themselves as Polish? Did they have a thought-out sense of identity? Their Jewish neighbors probably saw them as Gentiles or "the peasants" rather than "Polish," or perhaps all of the above interchangeably. Foreigners, Germans for instance, who deliberately thought in terms of ethnicity and nationality, considered them Poles. This form of perception is certainly important.

National consciousness is a complex phenomenon. The Nazi terror expedited the development of national consciousness among the people it ruled. But to what degree? There are no studies or scholarly monographs which can help examine to what extent the murderers of Jews considered themselves to be Polish.

Gross seems to take fringe, pathological behavior and utilize it to comment about the consciousness of mainstream Poles, ascribing criminal intent and base instinct to all. An exception may confirm a rule, but Gross uses exceptions to manufacture a rule of what it means – and what it meant during the Second World War – to be Polish. In the caricature of a nation he constructs, being Polish meant to kill your neighbors, to fear them murderously, and to desecrate their remains lest a valuable golden shred be left in the ashes.

In this sense, *Golden Harvest* reads like another prejudiced assault on Polishness, patriotism, Christianity, tradition, and the sense of national identity. Gross resorts to logical fallacies, for Socratic logic will be of no help as he tries to discredit a people whose values he resents by equating them with the pathologies and fringe behaviors which any civilized nation – indeed, any individual – would abhor.

Reflection: The last one

In the spring of 2010, a young intern and historian from Poland, Paweł Zyzak, visited the famous Hoover Institution at Stanford University, California. His visit coincided with Jan Tomasz Gross's guest lecture for Stanford faculty and students. Paweł Zyzak decided to attend. Professor Gross retreaded his standard joke about Swiss bankers and Polish peasants, who allegedly have one thing in common: Jewish gold. The intern stood up and deadpanned: "I am a Pole of peasant origin, but we never had any Jewish gold." Gross was duly embarrassed. And we wish the same to his uncritical admirers in Poland and elsewhere.

INSULTS INSTEAD OF FACTS: NOTES ON THE RECENT DEBATE ON POLES AND JEWS

Peter Stachura

Jan Tomasz Gross, the historian of Polish-Jewish background presently based in the United States, boasts an extraordinary and seemingly inexhaustible capacity for depicting Poles in general, and the Second Polish Republic in particular, in the most unflattering, denunciatory terms. In a number of previous publications, beginning with his book on Jedwabne,[1] wild generalization, based on the flimsiest or most partial and limited of evidence; distortion or wanton manipulation of material; and the ignoring of important facts which would disprove or, at the very least, impugn his line of argument and interpretation; constitute his trademark.[2]

A substantial volume of sophistry is another frequent ingredient. Moreover, these extremely dubious characteristics are expressed in a prose style that is not only invariably acerbic, but also susceptible to low-level sensationalism. In a word, Gross and traditional notions of sound, empirically supported, objective scholarship – which aims to ascertain the true facts of historical circumstances, and to weigh these calmly in the interests of balance and clarity – are irreconcilable.

---

[1] Jan T. Gross, *The Destruction of the Jewish Community in Jedwabne, Poland* (Princeton and Oxford: Princeton University Press, 2001). The most comprehensive and convincing refutation of this work is provided by Marek Jan Chodakiewicz, *The Massacre in Jedwabne July 10, 1941: Before, During and After* (New York and Boulder, CO: Columbia University Press and East European Monographs, 2005). Interestingly, some of Gross's earliest studies, such as *Revolution from Abroad: The Soviet Conquest of Poland's Western Ukraine and Western Belorussia* (Princeton and Oxford: Princeton University Press, 1988), were generally proportionate, informative, and useful.

[2] Notoriously, his *Fear: Anti-Semitism in Poland after Auschwitz: An Essay in Historical Interpretation* (Princeton and Oxford: Princeton University Press, 2006).

In many knowledgeable academic quarters, both in Poland and throughout the world, Gross's reputation as an anti-Polish propagandist with a craving for attention and publicity – as opposed to that of a serious, credible historian – is so well-established now, that one can only wonder at the sheer audacity of someone blissfully forging ahead in the same vein in a further work. If nothing else, Gross confirms the sad fact that some individuals simply never learn, or want to learn. They suffer from an entrenched aversion to anything that might challenge, contradict, or disprove what they are *determined* to state. Those pursuing such a premeditated agenda – whose provenance and ongoing inspiration is often a profound, irrational personal animosity towards something or someone – invite not only ridicule, but also unqualified contempt.

Gross's latest, somewhat provocatively titled publication, which is complemented by correspondingly provocative content, may be assessed from at least three principal perspectives.

In the first instance, Gross's account of an obviously contentious subject incorporates all, if not more, of the fundamentally serious, even perverse, flaws and shortcomings of his offerings in the recent past. Behind a *façade* of conventional scholarship, including the customary footnoting apparatus, lies another blatant example of a disjointed, tendentious narrative. It is an interpretation and appraisal resulting in a veritable piece of propaganda rather than a genuine study of historical merit.

Through the presentation of selective, unrepresentative, and invariably trivial or localized incidents and data, much of which derives from the work of Jewish and minor leftist Polish-based scholars,[3] Gross aims to paint an unedifying and damning picture of Poles during the German occupation of Poland (1939-1944). In his opinion, the Poles were avaricious, malevolent, and cunning neighbors who quickly seized the opportunity to exploit the German repression and maltreatment of Jews for their own material enrichment. Jewish misfortune, we are told, became the Poles' opportunity (see pp. 109-

---

[3] Such as Saul Friedlander, *The Years of Extermination: Nazi Germany and the Jews 1939-1945* (New York: HarperCollins, 2007); Jan Grabowski, *Rescue for Money: Helpers in Poland, 1939-1945* (Jerusalem: Yad Vashem, 2008); Alina Cała, *The Image of the Jew in Polish Folk Culture* (Jerusalem: Magna Press, 1995), as well as studies by Alina Skibińska, Dariusz Libionka, Andrzej Żbikowski, and the famous Emanuel Ringelblum.

120, in particular). Or, in other words, as far as Gross is concerned, the Poles were criminals.[4]

The foremost problem with Gross's account is that none of it rings true. Indeed, much skepticism, if not outright disbelief, must be the ineluctable reaction to the nature of the evidence he presents. While a small number of rogue Poles may have dotted the country, they cannot be reasonably declared in any way representative of the nation as a whole, as Gross argues implicitly that they were. He downplays the well-known fact that the vast majority of Poles were, on a daily basis, engaged in a bitter struggle for survival, not only against the Germans, but also against something as prosaic as hunger and starvation.

In any case, it is now certain that for every random Pole who might have stolen something from a Jew, there were also Jews who stole from their fellow Jews. A disconcerting conclusion is unavoidable. Once again, Gross is intent on perpetuating, in his usual sensationalist and disproportionate manner, his unremittingly negative view of the Second Polish Republic. In essence, his work is not merely a case of much ado about nothing. It also constitutes a case of indulging in unjustifiable mischief-making about a country in a particular epoch that he unmistakably loathes.

Secondly, Gross's present work reveals a total ignorance of the dynamics of German occupation policy and, specifically, those regarding property and other material assets in the hands of both Poles and Jews in occupied Poland.

In addition to the well-known racial imperatives of National Socialism, which designated Poles and Jews alike as subhuman *Untermenschen*, there was no possibility within German occupation policy, *especially where the ownership of goods and property was concerned*, for one of these groups to benefit materially at the expense of the other. German policy in Poznania (*Gau Wartheland* for most of the occupation period), and in the Generalgouvernement under Hans Frank, provide irrefutable proof of the latter point.

For example, in the *Warthegau*, whose *Gauleiter* (Nazi Party leader) and *Reichsstatthalter* (Governor) was the notorious Arthur Greiser, a

---

[4] In light of Gross's interest in "criminality," one might suggest that he direct his attention to the prominence of Jewish influence and control in Warsaw's pre-war and wartime criminal underworld, involving not only material assets, of course, but also human beings.

ferociously-pursued policy of Germanization[5] resulted in the stripping of Poles and Jews of their homes, businesses, real estate, cars, bicycles, savings, and other household valuables without compensation. All the proceeds were channeled into the coffers of the Reich.

As early as October 1939, the Central Trust Agency for the East (*Haupttreuhandstelle-Ost*: HTO) was set up to coordinate and supervise, in conjunction with the SS-controlled Reich Commissariat for the Strengthening of Germandom (*Reichskommissariat für die Festigung deutschen Volkstums*: RKFDV), the registration and sale of the entirety of the large quantity of property confiscated from both Poles and Jews. At the same time, and for good measure, the Germans introduced, through the newly established Land Office (*Bodenamt*), new rules governing the holding of property. These were designed to facilitate the program of registration and confiscation.

Later on during the following year, the Polish Assets Decree (*Polenvermögensordnung*) closed any loopholes which might have appeared, and ensured that virtually all Polish and Jewish property and associated assets in the *Warthegau* were liable to outright confiscation. The official justifications ranged from the ubiquitous "needs of the Reich" to "the public good."[6] All major German civil, Nazi Party, police and military organizations subscribed without deviation to this all-engulfing *modus operandi*. Of course, this did not mean that they desisted from haggling over the proceeds with one another.

---

[5] See Arthur Greiser, *Der Aufbau im Osten* [Building the East] (Jena: Fischer-Verlag, 1942); his personal role is examined in Czesław Łuczak, *Arthur Greiser* (Poznań: POS, 1997), and Catherine Epstein, *Model Nazi: Arthur Greiser and the Occupation of Western Poland* (Oxford: Oxford University Press, 2010). See also, Michael Alberti, *Die Verfolgung und Vernichtung der Juden im Reichsgau Wartheland 1939-1945* [The Persecution and Extermination of Jews in Reichsgau Wartheland 1939-1945] (Wiesbaden: Harrassowitz, 2006).
[6] Further details in Bernhard Rosenkötter, *Treuhandpolitik: Die 'Haupttreuhandstelle Ost' und der Raub polnischer Vermögens 1939-1945* [Trusteeship Policy: The "Central Trust Agency for the East" and the Robbery of Polish Property 1939-1945] (Essen: Klartext, 2003), and Ingo Loose, *Kredite für NS-Verbrechen: Die deutschen Kreditinstitute in Polen und die Ausraubing der polnischen und jüdischen Bevölkerung 1939-1945* [Credit for National Socialist Crime: The German Credit Institute in Poland and the Robbery of the Polish and Jewish Population 1939-1945] (Munich: Oldenbourg, 2007). For the wider context, see Richard C. Lukas, *The Forgotten Holocaust: The Poles under German Occupation, 1939-1944* (Lexington, KY: University Press of Kentucky, 1986), and Diemut Majer, *Non-Germans under the Third Reich: The Nazi Judicial and Administrative System in Germany and Occupied Eastern Europe, with Special Regard to Occupied Poland, 1939-1945* (Baltimore, MD: Johns Hopkins University Press, 2003).

Another relevant factor in the takeover of Polish and Jewish property was the presence of some 500,000 ethnic Germans who, by the spring of 1943, had moved into the *Warthegau* and other German-administered areas in Poland, thus filling the void created by the mass killings (of Poles and Jews) and deportations (of Poles) to the Reich. In other words, the machinery of confiscation was rendered watertight, even if there may have been occasionally and in unusual circumstances, perhaps in the ethnic chaos prevailing after 1941/1942 in the Eastern Provinces (*Kresy*), a degree of flexibility and improvisation on the ground, which may have permitted an exiguous amount of illegal, transient theft.

However, it is significant that by early 1941, there remained hardly any Polish or Jewish property/assets still to be confiscated in the *Warthegau*. Consequently, it is not at all surprising that there are no credibly recorded examples of any of the confiscated loot passing to one oppressed group, the Poles, from another, the Jews, in this region. Such solid and verifiable evidence indicates that Gross has manipulated contemporary rumor and hearsay, in addition to embittered post-war Jewish memories, as a foundation for his baseless allegations of Poles, in effect, robbing the Jews in the Wartheland.

That the same pattern of the non-seizure of Jewish assets by Poles prevailed in the Generalgouvernment, for example, is corroborated, ironically, by Gross himself, in an earlier monograph.[7] Similarly, in other parts of occupied Poland no concrete evidence exists to support Gross's claims. Gross merely exaggerates scattered and unconvincing reports, such as the Germans "encouraging" the locals to "plunder" Jewish property.[8] It is also telling that recent, generally well-received studies, which encompass the wartime situation in Poland, make little or no mention whatsoever of the theme of Gross's latest attack book.[9]

Thirdly, it strikes one as outrageous that a country like Poland, pulverized by wartime Nazi and Soviet barbarism, followed by almost

---

[7] Jan T Gross, *Polish Society under German Occupation: The Generalgouvernement, 1939-1944* (Princeton: Princeton University Press, 1979).
[8] As cited, e.g. in Mark Mazower, *Hitler's Empire: Nazi Rule in Occupied Europe* (London: Allen Lane, 2008), 453.
[9] To name but a few: Norman Davies, *God's Playground: A History of Poland. Volume II, 1795 to the Present*, Revised Edition (Oxford: Oxford University Press, 2005); Ian Kershaw, *Hitler, 1936-1945: Nemesis* (London: Allen Lane - The Penguin Press, 2000); and Michael Burleigh, *The Third Reich: A New History* (London: Macmillan, 2000), despite its tendentiousness when discussing Polish-Jewish relations both prior to and following 1939.

half-a-century of Soviet Communist military and political domination, should in the 21st century be denigrated as a race of people. Gross's blanket assault calls for a full reassessment of the Princeton scholar's own academic integrity as a Holocaust revisionist of a new stripe.

IF THE FACTS ARE AGAINST US, TOO BAD FOR THE FACTS: ON JAN TOMASZ GROSS'S SCHOLARLY METHOD IN *GOLDEN HARVEST*

Piotr Gontarczyk

Analysis of a single photograph

In 2008, two Polish-based journalists, Piotr Głuchowski and Marcin Kowalski, published a photograph of a group of people in the left-liberal daily *Gazeta Wyborcza*. The individuals in question supposedly plundered the burial grounds of human remains in the area of the former Treblinka death camp.

The picture's caption read as follows: "Diggers from Wólka-Okrąglik and the surrounding villages pose for a common photograph with militiamen, who caught them red-handed. The peasants' pockets were filled with gold rings and Jewish teeth. By the feet of the sitting individuals: arranged skulls and tibias of the gassed."[1]

The controversy surrounding the photograph became a point of departure towards broader discussions on the general stance of Christian Poles towards the Holocaust, which Princeton University Professor Jan Tomasz Gross – along with his ex-wife, Irena Grudzińska-Gross – introduced in his *Golden Harvest*: "A seemingly calm image pertains to two central themes of the Holocaust – the mass murder of Jews, and the plundering of Jewish property that accompanied it."[2]

Step-by-step, Gross subsequently introduces dramatic events and incidents occurring within the dynamic of Polish-Jewish wartime relations in order to arrive at generalized conclusions:

---

[1] *Gazeta Wyborcza*, 7 January 2008.
[2] Citations from the pre-publication, Polish-language version of *Golden Harvest* by Jan Tomasz Gross come from the material made accessible to the author in December 2010 by the hosts of the TV show "Tomasz Lis na żywo" [Tomasz Lis Live].

The behavioral norm in Polish society – remembering, of course, that the majority of people were not interested in anything that did not directly affect them, and that the same majority remained neutral about the fate of the Jews – was tracking and hunting down hidden Jews, and not, assisting the persecuted Jews. Jewish property had suddenly become an easily achievable desire and only a 'chump' [*niedołęga*] would not seize the given opportunity.[3]

I am far from embracing the opinion that Poles, in their relations with Jews, behaved solely positively. Along with advances in Holocaust research, I verify my previous, rather optimistic viewpoints. I do this, however, only in a situation when the texts at hand are solidly documented and written in accordance with the canon of honest scientific inquiry. This last element calls into question the reliability of the assertions presented by Gross.

The starting point for *Golden Harvest* became the aforementioned photograph: taken just after the end of Second World War, and thus in the middle of the twentieth century, the image depicts a group scene somewhere in Central Europe. In the picture, beside the cluster of farmers, a hill of ashes of 800,000 Jews gassed and burned in Treblinka from July 1942 to October 1943 became immortalized. The Europeans seen in the picture most likely occupied themselves with the unearthing of charred human remains in search of gold and jewelry overlooked by the Nazi murderers.[4]

Indeed, the regrettable act of digging-up mass graves by the local populace in pursuit of gold, jewelry and other valuables did take place in the wake of the war. We cannot be sure, however, that the individuals in the photograph were actually engaged in such heinous treasure hunting. According to postwar documents, both Communist Party and state authorities, as well as the underground anti-Communist resistance, found this practice to be absolutely reprehensible and actively combated it by, e.g., dispersing the "diggers," fencing the area off, and cleaning up the excavated cemetery.

It is also unknown who took that photograph, where, or even in what circumstances. There is no definite proof that it was taken near Treblinka, although it most likely was. Finally, there is no evidence about the identities of the photographed individuals and why they were present at the location. Were they "diggers"?

---

[3] *Ibid.*
[4] Jan Tomasz Gross and Irena Grudzińska-Gross, *Złote żniwa. Rzecz o tym, co się działo na obrzeżach zagłady Żydów* [Golden Harvest: Concerning the Events on the Peripheries of the Holocaust], (Kraków: Znak, 2011), 18 (further as *Golden Harvest*).

Or were they restoring order to the graves? Let us explore the question by asking about the circumstances of the photo. The people photographed form a mixed group of both uniformed men and civilian men and women. Is it logical that uniformed officials would pose with grave robbers? Is it logical that grave robbers would conduct their ghoulish work in broad daylight? Would grave robbers truly want to document their crimes with photographs? And why would such a photograph be required by the militia, which was supposed to apprehend them? Did the Citizens' Militia (*Milicja Obywatelska*, MO) document these types of crimes? If so, then how did this photo fall into private hands?

Or, perhaps, it had been in private hands all along and was kept precisely by someone who did not see anything blameworthy in the image. Perhaps because the keeper of the photograph was memorializing the returning of a cemetery to its normal state, witness to the performance of what devout Catholics call "corporal acts of mercy" – to bury the remains of the dead.[5] Perhaps, then it had never occurred to the individual who preserved the photo that someone, someday, would accuse the people of "digging."

The problem does not appear to be trivial, since a lack of critical analysis of images may sometimes lead to serious consequences. A couple of years ago, a group of German scholars who – like Gross – had embarked upon the path of least resistance, began to analyze a series of photographs of Germans next to piles of corpses. These pictures were later presented at a famous exposé entitled "Wehrmacht War Crimes."

A Polish-born historian, Bogdan Musiał, upon viewing the gallery of photographs, proved that the Germans did not intentionally photograph their own crimes, but, rather, documented those perpetrated by the Soviet NKVD. Musiał found that in the case at hand, the Germans in June 1941 had discovered and unearthed the remains of NKVD victims in Lwów, Złoczów, and Borysław, and other Eastern Borderland towns.

---

[5] The Catholic Church and some other Christian denominations teach seven corporal acts of mercy. The first six, based on Matthew 25:31-46, are: feed the hungry, provide drink to the thirsty, shelter the homeless, clothe the naked, visit and if possible free the captive, and visit the sick. The ultimate penalty for failure to perform such acts of mercy, as Christ Himself said (Matt. 25:41), is eternal damnation. The seventh corporal act of mercy, based on the ancient Hebrew Book of Tobit (or Tobias) and considered sacred scripture in the Catholic and Orthodox churches, is to bury the dead.

The "Wehrmacht War Crimes" exhibition ended in an atmosphere of scandal, and the authors were completely discredited.[6]

For Gross, issues such as factual analysis are of little importance. He therefore has no doubt that the symbolic photograph to sensationalize his book depicts a group of Polish grave robbers, seemingly the participants in the Holocaust:

> A signal that this photograph belongs to the category of *trophy pictures* is the neat assembly of skulls and tibias in the foreground. Similarly to hunters following a successful wild game expedition, the murderers of Jews photographed themselves on the sites of executions; or, as persecutors, [photographed themselves] around a tortured victim, who was publicly forced to perform humiliating acts or, to the amusement of the public, had his beard chopped off.[7]

Later, Gross equates the individuals in the picture to a Jew-murdering Nazi, writing that those in the photograph, by digging up graves, were committing "an action directly tied to the Holocaust, namely, the despoiling of Jewish property."

Soon after the publication of *Golden Harvest*, two investigative journalists from the Polish newspaper *Rzeczpospolita*, Michał Majewski and Paweł Reszka, arrived in the Treblinka area. Their account clarified that Gross's anchor photograph depicts not "diggers" caught by the militia, but a team of men and women cleaning up the gravesite. The version presented by *Gazeta Wyborcza*'s writers was most likely a deliberate fabrication, they concluded.[8] The newspaper removed the false caption under the archived photo, and *Gazeta Wyborcza* reporters Głuchowski and Kowalski admitted, "We do not know the circumstances under which that photo was taken."[9]

It is worth remembering that both reporters co-authored a book titled *Odwet* [Retaliation], which was to tell the history of the fate of the Bielski brothers, Jewish wartime partisans from the Nowogródek

---

[6] See.: Piotr Gontarczyk, "Fałszywe obrazki z wystawy" [False images in the exhibition], *Życie*, 8–9 May 1999.
[7] Manuscript in author's collection.
[8] Michał Majewski and Paweł Reszka, „Zagadka starego zdjęcia" [The Mystery of the Old Photograph], *Rzeczpospolita*, 21 January 2011.
[9] For the whole report, see „Wyborcza (rakiem) wycofuje się z opisu zdjęcia z Treblinki i (półgębkiem) odcina się od Grossa. Co zrobi wydawnictwo 'Znak'?" [*Wyborcza* is quickly backtracking and quietly distancing itself from Gross. What will Znak Publishers do?], information found on wpolityce.pl, 27 January 2011, wpolityce.pl/view/6556/Wyborcza__rakiem__wycofuje_sie_z_opisu_zdjecia_z_Trebli nki_i__polgebkiem__odcina_sie_od_Grossa__Co_zrobi_wydawnictwo__Znak__.html.

region. The book not only turned out to be an intellectual *curiosum*, but also a plagiarized version of a monograph that had appeared earlier in the United States. All printed copies were soon redirected to recycling plants.[10]

The controversy put Gross in a difficult position. Nevertheless, he did not reconsider publishing his *Golden Harvest*. Instead, he inserted an annotation that decidedly rejected any attempts to question his interpretation of the contentious photo. Gross initially stated, "Another possible interpretation of the photo at hand describes people from local villages herded to clean up the previously dug-up gravesite."[11] But why is this version, according to Gross, false? Because – as he says himself – "It is difficult to ignore the information provided by the photo's owner to the journalists at *Gazeta Wyborcza*, who clearly said that the people in the picture were 'caught red-handed.'"[12]

Thus, even after the unmasking of a story possessing all the indications of a hoax, and his own sources' dual admission that the story was probably a deliberate fabrication, Gross continued to rely on the recanted word of those same sources. He continued to repeat all the accusations and insinuations directed towards the photographed peasants. He even added a new paragraph:

> Familiarity with the commercial economy around the camps and transports sheds new light on our photograph. The villagers from the Treblinka region were not only diggers occupied with searching for valuables on the premises of the former camp. They were also experienced traders, the parents of the camp guards' girlfriends, and hostesses cooking nutritious meals for them. They were farmstead owners, reselling formerly Jewish watches and rings.[13]

Thus, the photographed men were not solely "diggers." They now became parents, who – as Gross claims bluntly earlier in the book[14] – greedily pimped out their daughters as prostitutes to Nazi death camp

---

[10] Piotr Skwieciński, "Karygodny grzech obiektywizmu" [The Condemnable Sin of Objectivity], *Rzeczpospolita*, 18 February 2009; M. Wójcik, „Książka reporterów *Gazety Wyborczej* plagiatem?" [The Book by *Gazeta Wyborcza's* reporters is plagiarized?], *Dziennik*, 4 February 2009; T. Zdunek, "Kolejny błąd autorów *GW*" [Another mistake by the *GW's* authors], *Gazeta Polska*, 23 January 2011; *Plagiarism disappears from the shelves,* a note from tvn24.pl, 10 February 2009, www.tvn24.pl/12690,1585575,0,1,plagiat-znika-z-polek,wiadomosc.html.
[11] *Golden Harvest*, 13.
[12] *Ibid.*
[13] *Ibid.*, 71.
[14] *Ibid.*, 64.

guards. It appears that the whole issue is less and less concerned with history, and instead becomes a truly interesting assessment of Gross's credibility.

Source analysis methodology

After the 2011 publication in Poland of *Golden Harvest,* similar Grossian "scholarly theses" met with a crushing critique. Unsurprisingly, the cross-examination appears to have had little to no effect on Gross. A genuine scholar would scrap his flawed work and start over. Instead, Gross chose a much different approach by conducting minor stylistic corrections and inserting small tidbits that would suggest the author's objectivity, but fail to alter the book's message. Yet, such cosmetic touch-ups caused significant inconsistencies and contradictions in *Golden Harvest*.

For example, Gross added a piece of information received from the historian Bożena Szaynok regarding cases wherein priests, during confession, instructed the faithful to behave respectfully towards the Jews.[15] The subsequent sentence, however, was retained from the original version of the work: "The question of why there was so little interest in the Jewish fate during the Holocaust can [. . .] also be posed to village priests in every [sic!] location inhabited by Jews."[16] Apparently, this did not apply to "every" locality, since even by Gross's revised standard at least certain priests behaved decently, as mentioned in the previous sentence by Szaynok. Similar inconsistencies populate the book.

The greatest recent change occurred, however, in relation to the number of Jews allegedly murdered by Poles during the Holocaust. Initially, Gross claimed the figure to approximate "100-200,000." He later scaled the number down to "tens of thousands." Gross cited as his source various numerous recent interviews and articles.[17] And what about the previous figure? What is the credibility of an author who, under the influence of newspaper publications, significantly alters previously mentioned data? Has the author verified these new media claims? Are they supported by serious scholarship? I argue that neither of these numbers has any solid basis in historical sources.

Other fragments of Gross' book are also devoid of the most elementary credibility. An instance in which Gross attempted to

---

[15] *Ibid.*, 184
[16] *Ibid.*
[17] *Ibid.*, 83.

critique a source resulted in a rather amusing example. While analyzing Rachel Auerbach's book on Treblinka "diggers," titled *The Polish Colorado,* Gross commented "the author most likely meant El Dorado."[18] The problem is that Auerbach was correct, because the Gold Rush did not take place in the mythical South American city (whose Spanish name coincidentally means "The Golden One" or "The Golden Place"), but during the middle of the nineteenth century and in the territories of the modern-day American states of California (officially nicknamed "The Golden State"), and to a larger but less famous degree, Colorado.

Yet, these errors do not constitute the greatest problem plaguing Gross's writings. Of much greater importance is the manner in which the author utilizes other scholarly texts or sources cited by others. The examples are abundant. In his typical manner, Gross used the internet-based fragment of the chronicle of the 6th Wilno Brigade of the Polish Home Army, and cited it extensively in a footnote:

> 2 February 1946. We are approaching the infamous Treblinka. According to the accounts of the locals, constant digging-up and theft of corpses has achieved the highest level of animalistic behavior. Teeth are ripped out, jaws taken whole, arms are cut, [as well as] legs, [or] heads, just for a piece of gold. This is defilement, but the local authorities do nothing to protect this one-of-a-kind gravesite, the resting place of 3 million Jews, Poles, Gypsies, Russians, and other nationalities.
>
> 3–4 February 1946. Chmielnik. We are three kilometers 'from the death camp.' Reconnaissance conducted in the 'camp' has confirmed information of gravesite desecration. On the evening of 4 February 1946, we are headed to the village of Wólka-Okrąglik to punish the gold diggers of Treblinka.[19]

The historian who edited this chronicle commented later that Brigade patrols subsequently apprehended random "diggers and their sinful actions were punished with many lashes."[20]

The picture presented by the chronicle is thus unequivocal. The underground resistance unit in question held an extremely negative opinion of grave robbing and general looting in the death camp area, seeing it as an ultimate act of human bestialization. The Polish insurgents condemned the Soviet occupation authorities for failing to secure the gravesite properly, and soon undertook a punitive expedition

---

[18] *Ibid.,* 46.
[19] *Ibid.,* 52.
[20] *Ibid.*

to enforce justice by themselves. How did Gross treat the whole matter? He merely inserted the story into a footnote, while preserving the main text with his previous conclusions: "In this way, the remainder of the 'Jewish gold' which had not filled the treasury of the Reich, fueled the budget of the postwar anti-Communist underground through the efforts of the 'diggers.'"[21]

Therefore, according to Gross, the chronicle of the 6th Wilno Home Army Brigade is proof of Polish greed. And yet, the aforementioned fragment does not even hint at the confiscation of any valuables from the "diggers." And even if the dug-up items had indeed been confiscated by the underground, there is no reason to treat is as anything other than additional, painful punishment of the demoralized cemetery hyenas.[22] This time, however, as a result of Gross's specific scholarly methodology, those who in the name of obvious humanitarian and ethical reasons defended the eternal peace of the victims of Treblinka, became accessories of the Holocaust and robbers of Jewish property.

In his *Golden Harvest*, Gross continues further in the direction of such risky interpretations. Based on his own understanding of the 6th Brigade, Gross arrives at a general conclusion about postwar Polish behavior at large: "The plundering of Jewish property was an important element of the circulation of goods, a factor of the socio-economic structure of life, and not an aberrant behavior of a group of demoralized individuals."[23]

This generality constitutes a classic example of the fact that the book's narrative remains at odds with its quoted sources, and has turned out to be *de facto* confabulation by Jan Tomasz Gross.

Certain additional doubts surface upon analyzing the veracity of the sources cited in *Golden Harvest*. The author writes: "Wojciech Lizak assessed the number of legal successors of the Jewish at half a million."[24] An investigation reveals that the sentence appears to reference an article published in the liberal Catholic weekly *Tygodnik Powszechny* in 2004. I was unable to locate any scholarly research by

---

[21] *Ibid.*
[22] The fact that the NSZ's action against the "diggers" was guided by such a motivation is confirmed by a fragment of another work referenced by Gross. See Mariusz Bechta and Leszek Żebrowski, eds., *NSZ na Podlasiu w walce z systemem komunistycznym w latach 1944–1952* [The NSZ in the Podlasie Region While Fighting the Communist System in 1944-1952] (Siedlce. Związek Żołnierzy NSZ, 1998), 201.
[23] *Golden Harvest,* 52.
[24] Wojciech Lizak, "Z perspektywy ludu" [From the people's perspective], *Tygodnik Powszechny*, 7 November 2004.

that author on the topic. The list of contributors within the weekly provided only the most rudimentary biographical data: "Wojciech Lizak (born in 1951) is a lawyer and an art historian. He owns an auction house, and lives in Szczecin. [He] Contributes to *Tygodnik Powszechny* and other publications."[25]

Everything indicates that Lizak's data pertaining to the number of legal successors to Jewish property is unsupported by any scholarly basis whatsoever, thereby relegating it to the realm of pure conjecture. Reliance on such sources constitutes a complete antithesis of solid research standards.

Various Grossian statements on Polish actions and the circumstances of Jewish deaths are often historically unfounded. For example, the author writes: "One ought to presume that torture of Jews and the rape of Jewish women was a common occurrence at the time."[26] My observations point to the very opposite. In such an important case a scholar would be advised to rely on more than mere *presumptions*.

Many other pieces of information in Gross's book are similar presuppositions, speculations, and bits passed on to the author by word of mouth that are impossible to verify. Some of them have been removed during earlier editorial corrections. New pieces of evidence have replaced them, some of them just as dubious as the initial ones. One of the most significant fragments pertains to Poles seeking Jewish gold around the Auschwitz-Birkenau camp area. Gross relates the matter:

> The exploitation [...] of ashes of millions of Jews murdered in Auschwitz by the local populace is explained by a former worker of the State Museum of Oświęcim-Brzezinka, who wrote on an internet forum: this procedure was conducted under the cover of night; bags were filled with ashes and placed on some mode of transport, and subsequently rinsed in the Vistula. Yes! Exactly the same way as during the Gold Rush in the Wild West [...]. It's no secret that all of Pławy, Harmęże, and half of Brzezinka are built on Jewish gold. Many caravans passed through on a daily basis long after the war – even from faraway villages – laden with 'spoils' and headed for the 'rinse.'[27]

In a footnote, Gross indicated the source of his information: "An entry on the blog of Krzysiafish-przemyślenia.blog on the website onet.pl." However, the blog is not authoritative and nothing is really

---

[25] *Ibid.*, 76; Lizak, "Z perspektywy ludu" [From the People's Perspective], *Tygodnik Powszechny*, 7 November 2004.
[26] *Golden Harvest*, 104.
[27] *Ibid.*, 51.

known about the author. The readers are left to wonder where he received this information and whether he really worked at the mentioned museum. Nothing concrete can be established in this matter. It appears that by citing similarly dubious historical sources, Jan Tomasz Gross only emphasizes the unscholarly nature of his work.[28]

Between truth and falsehood

One of the more interesting topics addressed in *Golden Harvest* concerns individuals who helped Jews for financial compensation. As a result of last-minute critique-induced corrections, Gross conflates two groups of people: those who helped Jews and received money on the side (for food, clothing, shelter, or as bribes), and those who helped Jews specifically for profit.

Nechama Tec and Marcin Urynowicz tackled a similar problem earlier. Both of them, having worked individually with testimonies of those saved from the Holocaust, estimate that the group seeking profit amounted to 10 to 15 percent of all the rescuers.[29] Jan Grabowski attempted to debunk these statistics but failed to offer concrete numbers, and his methodology appears less convincing than the one employed by Tec and Urynowicz.[30]

It appears that the main claim to fame of Grabowski's article will boil down to the translation of the English neologism "paid helpers" into Polish. Grabowski concluded that the Polish equivalent would be the term "biorcy" ("takers"). In this simple manner, those who admittedly "gave" something on account of the risks involved under Nazi occupation, were transformed into ones who only "took."[31]

When considering questions of content, it is important to remember that one of the chief sources used by Grabowski are the so-called August Cases (*sierpniówki*), i.e. postwar Communist proceedings against individuals accused of collaboration with the Germans. The murderers of Jews were included in this definition. On the other hand, it seems problematic to construct an accurate picture of the Polish countryside based on cases so extreme that they made it into postwar courts. In short, it is an attempt to extrapolate a norm from a pathology.

---

[28] The blog also happens to contain numerous dubious references to Polish history and a sarcastic poem dedicated to the late President Lech Kaczyński in the wake of the April 2010 plane crash.
[29] Jan Grabowski, „Ratowanie Żydów za pieniądze – przemysł pomocy" [Saving Jews for Profit – The Aid Industry], *Zagłada Żydów. Studia i Materiały* 4 (2008): 84.
[30] *Ibid.*, 84, 106–108.
[31] *Ibid.*, 82.

It is nonetheless worth mentioning that Gross rejected not only Tec and Urynowicz's figures, but also Grabowski's suppositions. Apparently, the author of *Golden Harvest* comprehends reality without the necessity of undertaking serious research. In his own words, "The fact that payment for sheltering Jews was regularly demanded is proven emphatically through the *consensus* of opinion in Polish society, according to which people aiding Jews must have enriched themselves in the process."[32] This logical fallacy ("I know that something happened, because it was spoken of") appears to be a grave methodological abuse, and not only due to the fact that concurring opinions resounded throughout the centuries about Jews using the blood of Christian children to make their Passover Matzo.

It is also worth remembering that Gross consciously and consequentially relies on information he himself knows is untrue. Some pieces of information, which had been exposed as blatant abuses, are intentionally repeated in further publications, guided solely by the principle of utility. These examples can be multiplied.

The author of *Golden Harvest* relies heavily on a book by historian Emanuel Ringelblum on Polish-Jewish wartime relations. Yet, even the title of Ringelblum's book does not indicate that we are dealing with an in-depth scholarly study, which has been repeatedly pointed out to Gross.[33] The book was written in a bunker in which the author was hiding until his death in 1944. He was at that time not in a position to undertake rigorous research, and his work does not possess much scholarly value.

Yet it is Ringelblum whom the author of *Golden Harvest* consistently cites, claiming that navy-blue police functionaries murdered "tens of thousands of Jews" during the war.[34] I wrote in *Rzeczpospolita*,[35] a major Warsaw newspaper that is considered the peer rival to *Gazeta Wyborcza*, that Ringelblum's figure lacks a scholarly basis. The critique would have come to the attention to any serious Polish-speaking scholar of the matter, as well as to Gross himself, because of *Rzeczpospolita*'s high profile in Poland and its publication of my critiques of his own work. Yet Gross did not excise the data because – although false – it provided the highest quantity he could cite.

---

[32] *Golden Harvest*, 158.
[33] Emanuel Ringelblum, *Stosunki polsko-żydowskie w czasie drugiej wojny światowej. Uwagi i spostrzeżenia* [Polish-Jewish Relations During WWII: Comments and Perspectives] (Warsaw: Czytelnik, 1988).
[34] *Golden Harvest*, 81.
[35] Piotr Gontarczyk, „Wszyscy jesteście złodziejami" [You're All Thieves], *Rzeczpospolita*, 8–9 January 2011.

In another part of the book, Gross mentions situations in which Jews entrusted their material wealth to Christian Poles, and were consequently deceived or even denounced to the Germans. Certainly such cases occurred, although it appears that the problem lies beyond the limits of statistical description. Yet Gross appears certain that the figure was an overwhelming 95 percent. This data was extracted directly from Ringelblum's volume.[36] While referencing this information, the author writes: "Of course, this cannot be taken literally – since occupation-time phenomena cannot be grasped numerically – but it does possess a great persuasive power." However, the decisive scholarly criterion is the credibility of a piece of information, not its "persuasive power." For that matter, the controversial photo of the "diggers" possesses great persuasive power to help Gross state his case, but that power does not equate to truth.

In other cases, Gross disregards impermissible errors and manipulations pointed out by others. An example may be found in the case of the interrogation protocol of Helena Klimaszewska in the study *Wokół Jedwabnego* [Surrounding Jedwabne]. She described a dramatic scene, which took place in Radziłów after the murder of its Jewish inhabitants in 1941:

> I went from Goniądz to Radziłów in August of 1941, I think, with the intent of finding a place to live for my husband's parents because I knew that after the liquidation of the Jews there would be many available ones. Godlewski, whose first name I can't recall, informed me that the apartments are all taken. He said: 'When it was time to liquidate the Jews, you were nowhere to be found, and now you're all coming here for their homes.' The now-deceased mother of my husband then announced: 'Now they don't want to give me a home, even though they already sent my grandson to spray the barn with gasoline.'[37]

Having discussed this incident in his previous book, Gross stated: "And here we are witnessing a conversation, whose message – implicitly accepted by one older lady, one middle-aged lady, and one man – is the recognition that the title to Jewish valuables is premised on participation in the murder of their former owners"[38]

---

[36] *Golden Harvest*, 64.
[37] Krzysztof Persak and Paweł Machcewicz, eds., *Wokół Jedwabnego. Dokumenty* [Surrounding Jedwabne: Documents], (Warsaw: IPN, 2002), 2: 932.
[38] Jan Tomasz Gross, *Strach. Antysemityzm w Polsce tuż po wojnie. Historia moralnej zapaści* [Fear: Anti-Semitism in Poland after Auschwitz] (Kraków: Znak, 2006), 86.

The context in which the "older lady" uttered these words is unclear. One can lean towards the interpretation formulated by Gross. But, in the case of the other two, the matter becomes much more complicated. Zofia Klimaszewska did not take a position towards the described affair, but merely related her account of it. Gross's thesis, that she accepted such methods of redistributing formerly Jewish homes, is debatable.

Problems arise, of course, in the case of Wacław Godlewski, whose name recurs on a constant basis in the documents pertaining to the crimes in Radziłów. He was not a "typical Pole," but a renegade, and, what was obviously omitted by Gross, a German gendarme as well.[39] And the German gendarmerie was hardly conterminous with Polish society. Meanwhile, in *Fear* the whole matter becomes a vehicle to illustrate and prove the narrative of "norms and mechanisms of Jewish property redistribution" in Polish society.

This particular distortion of reality to suit an *a priori* thesis has been critically analyzed in an extensive article on *Fear* authored by myself and published in *Rzeczpospolita*.[40] The entire section about "norms and mechanisms of Jewish property redistribution" has been copied and reinserted into *Golden Harvest*.

It is as a direct result of such research methods that the vision of Polish-Jewish relations is slowly becoming less complicated, ambiguous, and riddled with contradictions. The necessity of understanding German occupation policies completely disappears, for the author knows little on this subject.[41] There is no need to systematically analyze human behavior or to investigate the essence of social and economic processes. As Gross recycles in *Golden Harvest*,

> Suddenly we begin to notice shocking statements and events – each initially surprising or even impossible – which complement one another and create a complete picture. And it is precisely this aligning, [and] this complementarity of mentioned perceptions and situations, that we judged at a first glance to be a pathology, a violation of normalcy, [and] an aberration, which forces us to consider them, in the end, as manifestations of *social practices*; [i.e.] concrete embodiments of dealing with the Jews. And thus

---

[39] See the interview protocol of Feliks Godlewski from 29 December 1950, or the Supreme Court Decision with regards to Feliks Godlewski from 28 September 1954, *Wokół Jedwabnego...*, 2: 952, 961–962.
[40] P. Gontarczyk, "Daleko od prawdy" [Far from Truth], *Rzeczpospolita*, 12 January 2008.
[41] The above was marvelously explained by Bogdan Musiał in "Prowokacja, podwójne standardy i zakłamanie" [Provocation, Double Standards, and Lies], *Uważam Rze*, no. 2, 14–21 February 2011.

we begin to understand[42] that Jewish property suddenly became an easily achievable desire and only a 'chump' would not seize the given opportunity.[43]

Informing the author that he consistently relies on doubtful, and even false information produces no results. In response to a fact-based critique one will be met with odd reflections, *ad hominem* arguments, and sometimes even cynicism. Regarding his book on the Jedwabne tragedy, I accused Gross of, among other things, creating a false scenario of the tragic events without consulting any of the more significant documents, but based primarily on three, rather untrustworthy witnesses. One witness was lying about his presence in Jedwabne in 1941, since he had been deported to Siberia a year earlier for stealing a gramophone. In response, the author of *Neighbors* concluded that he had not defined that person in his book as an "eyewitness."[44] The problem is that prior to Gross's work, the "non-eye witness" who observed events over thousands of kilometers away never existed in honest scholarship. This illustrates one of the effects of attempts to engage in a factual discussion with Gross, i.e. absurd semantic games and circular logic.

Dubious accusations

Not a single document, behavior, underground leadership decision, or social mechanism escapes Jan Tomasz Gross's ability to persuasively interpret phenomena as fragments of the universal Polish plan to plunder Jewish gold.

An earlier interpretation of the 6th Wilno Brigade's chronicle proves this expressively. Even such common market occurrences as demand, supply, fluctuation, and speculation can assume an entirely new meaning. They can, for example, become manifestations of robbery, murder, and anti-Semitism.

---

[42] These words were placed in the initial Polish language edition of this book, which we translate as follows: "The behavioral norm in Polish society – remembering, of course, that the majority of people were not interested in anything that did not directly affect them, and that same majority remained neutral about the fate of the Jews – was tracking and hunting down hidden Jews, and not, assisting the persecuted Jews." Evidently, Gross retracted even this opinion, although it constitutes the spirit of his book.
[43] *Golden Harvest*, 193.
[44] Jan Tomasz Gross, "A jednak sąsiedzi" [Neighbors Nonetheless], *Rzeczpospolita*, 11 April, 2001. The mentioned text contained many invectives directed toward Prof. Tomasz Strzembosz, while the present author was labeled an "adolescent (*młodociany*) historian."

Yet, war changed the value of goods and, consequently, prices and social relations. Shortages of certain goods, and the banning or strict rationing of certain other products, immediately gives life to the "black market." Value is, after all, a subjective term in economics.

After the outbreak of war, many members of the Polish intelligentsia – as a result of the closing of schools, offices, and research centers – eagerly accepted any employment open to them. Attempting to survive, they sold their possessions, including heirlooms that had been in their families for generations. Hence, one's loss was another's gain. For instance, some peasant farmers benefited from highly inflated food prices.

Obviously the war and German policies also affected the Jews. But this occurrence is assigned a much different meaning by Gross:

> The poor Jews that sold their bed sheets, furniture, household items, and even winter clothing to Aryans for pennies […] were robbed […], because the ensuing pauperization pushed them to the edge of destitution. Everyone that used the opportunity to acquire Jewish property for a marginal price of its real value[45] – regardless of how valuable the items were [or weren't] – took part in the looting of European Jewry.[46]

Therefore, whoever conducted business with a Jew during the war could easily become a "looter of European Jewry" or even a "participant in the Holocaust." It is not surprising that the author of the essay includes, among the real participants of the Holocaust, "millions of ordinary people, who in this way helped rob their Jewish neighbors."[47] The problem lies in the flawed and self-contradictory argument, which pertains to the appropriation of Jewish property in forced wartime transactions, and is therefore difficult to accept.

This matter is important, however, even if only on account of the armies of smugglers supplying food to the Warsaw Ghetto, perhaps at market or black market prices where they could incur huge expenses to get the food through, thus usually profiting, but engaging in this risky endeavor nonetheless. Will they too acquire the label of thieves and – like the guards from Treblinka – be counted by Gross among the accomplices of the Holocaust?

---

[45] It is worth noting that Gross replaced those words with: "They took every opportunity to acquire Jewish property for a price lower than its value." The significance of this paragraph was changed after sharp critique from the author of the article in *Rzeczpospolita* („Wszyscy jesteście złodziejami").
[46] *Golden Harvest*, 73.
[47] *Ibid.*, 74.

I am omitting of course the obvious examples of shocking abuses, such as the selling of water to Jews being shipped to Treblinka. The wartime situation was incredibly complex; the exchange of goods often took place in circumstances imposed by the policies of the German occupier, for which neither the Poles nor the Jews bore responsibility.

But if one was to apply Gross's logic to concrete events during the occupation, problems begin to arise. If a Polish peasant was to profit from a Polish city dweller and charge exorbitant prices during the entire duration of the war, well then – as Gross would likely argue – such were the unfortunate effects of war. If a Jewish trader bought a family heirloom from a subsistent Polish university professor during the winter of 1939, then that would not constitute anything extraordinary either. But if a Pole bought something from a Jew, and if one is not familiar with Gross's price register, then the whole matter begins to reek of the Holocaust.

One begins to wonder, how could it be possible that Poles avoided exposure to accusations of "robbing their Jewish neighbors" in such a grossly defined world? Apparently only by adhering to German orders, which prohibited any commercial contacts with the Jews whatsoever.

Similarly to greatly overestimating the number of robbers of Jewish property, Gross multiplies the number of active participants in the Holocaust. It is important to recall that the Princeton University professor had previously categorized the Catholic Church as "collaborators through omission."[48] In reality, churchmen provided enormous help to the persecuted Jews by hiding thousands of them and, in many cases – which are documented in publications and elsewhere in this volume – paid for it through martyrdom.

Yet, Gross considers this irrelevant. He writes in *Golden Harvest*, "Grabowski, after having read a couple hundred August Cases, concluded in surprise that the word priest does not appear even once."[49] I would consider such a conclusion a source of optimism. After all, the August Cases make crystal-clear that priests – contrary to some claims – neither participated in, instigated, nor looked on in indifference on the killing of Jews. Grabowski and Gross interpret this phenomenon much differently, however. For them, the absence of priests in the August Cases is proof of a "lack of reaction on the part of Catholic priests towards the crime of genocide occurring exactly in their

---

[48] Jan Tomasz Gross, "O kolaboracji" [On Collaboration] in *Zagłada Żydów* 2: 416.
[49] *Golden Harvest*, 183.

parishes, a crime in which, as we know, the local populace was involved."⁵⁰

Parishes are not merely church communities. They are geographically defined areas that often comprised well over tens of square kilometers of jurisdiction, including ones containing over ten villages. Many murders of Jews took place on the fringes of villages: in barns, bunkers, fields, or forests. There are grounds to doubt that the potential criminals, upon conceiving their murderous intentions, first rushed to inform the priest. Even if the priest had learned of such a crime *post facto* from his parishioners, then his reaction would not have been included in the postwar August Cases. The cases were not created to chronicle the life of the Polish countryside, but rather constituted an attempt to target the crimes of quite concrete individuals.

Accusing the Catholic clergy in general of passivity in the face of the Holocaust is a gross exaggeration based on Jan Grabowski's dubious observations. It is obvious that the priests could not monitor every crevice of their parishes, just as they cannot monitor the actions of their parishioners. Grabowski asserted that there are "no priests" in the records of the August Cases. If so, then is every priest responsible, even without the necessity of proving his guilt?

Polish "elites"

It is worthwhile recalling that the results of Jan Grabowski's research constitute one of the more important sources of Gross's knowledge about the realities of the German occupation. The author of *Golden Harvest* also utilizes other works, chiefly by authors affiliated with the Polish Center for Holocaust Research of the Institute of Philosophy and Sociology of the Polish Academy of Sciences, directed by Barbara Engelking-Boni, who publish chiefly in the journal *Zagłada Żydów* [Shoah].

The problem lies in the fact that the quality of these works varies considerably. The Center and its journal contain good texts, whose fact base is difficult to question, and which force deeper reflection. But the venue also prints articles of low quality.⁵¹ Some of them could even be suspected of intentionally promoting an agenda. For example, the

---

⁵⁰ *Ibid.*, 184.
⁵¹ I find the following authors' articles to be the most interesting and educational (alphabetically): Grzegorz Berendt, Dariusz Libionka, and Sebastian Piątkowski. However, there are also poor texts. In some cases, the main reason for an article being published appears to be not its insight, but the complicated relations of the author with the Catholic Church.

Center's researchers appear intent on proving that Polish elites committed crimes against Jews as well.

Grabowski, as cited in *Golden Harvest,* concluded – based on certain German criminal court cases – that blackmailing Jews (*szmalcownictwo*) was a widespread phenomenon among the general Polish population: "We find [here] all social groups: skilled workers, bureaucrats, artists, peasants, merchants, confectioners […], and even a French language tutor. The extortionist with the best pedigree was undoubtedly a young count."[52] These findings would be significant if Grabowski's sample was not limited to a group of only 73 people.

In another section, Gross cites the fruit of a study conducted by Alina Skibińska and Jakub Petelewicz and published in *Zagłada Żydów*. Based on these, the author of *Golden Harvest* wrote that "Jews were murdered during the war by members of the local elite in the Kielce-region countryside. The direct perpetrators, the most active participants in the crime, were often eminent members of local society. Some of them, as we have read about earlier, belonged to the Communist Party after the war, and we find them in the Citizens' Militia (*Milicja Obywatelska*)."[53]

Yet, the treatment of PPR and MO officers as a "local elite" is one of the substantive problems of Skibińska and Petelewicz's text. A serious study of the epoch in question will demonstrate that MO and PPR structures constituted one of the most significant hotbeds of crime in the Polish countryside directly after the war. In light of the powerful animosity on the part of authentic elites and many ordinary Poles towards Communist rule and their "class-based" recruitment methods, the MO, UB, and PPR became a magnet for Communist partisans, ordinary criminals, and *lumpenproletarians*.

Even during the years of the Nazi occupation, the leadership of the Communist underground realized exactly what segments of society they were dealing with, but this failed to deter them. After the war, one of the close collaborators of the high-ranking officer of the People's Army (AL), Marian Spychalski *nom de guerre* "Marek," related his superior's visit to a unit commanded by Stanisław Gać "Kuba":

> He became familiar with their mindset and operating procedures, which were quite different from the way city people imagined. We could be struck by those watches that the partisans were wearing, [and] those rings they had on their fingers. […] These are the real, not the romanticized Polish soldiers

---

[52] *Golden Harvest,* 155.
[53] *Ibid.,* 93.

of the occupation era – stated Marek – precisely these people are leading us to freedom, and no one else.[54]

During the Communist period, Stanisław Gać eventually became a colonel and a diplomat. So, is this the definition of the Polish elite?

According to their logic, Petelewicz and Skibińska would classify the MO commandant in Siedlce, Stanisław Laskowski, an erstwhile Communist partisan, as a member of the elite as well. A wartime witness wrote:

> His activities were purely criminal, rather than political. [...] They sold horses, while the money fueled drunkenness and partying. They raped women, even mothers and daughters together. They placed grenades under their breast and raped them, stole clothes, furs, money, jewelry and other valuables [...] They stole two horses and a wagon from the monastery. When the nuns tracked them down and came to reclaim their horses in the forest, they [...] intimidated them, and when that did not suffice, they forced them undress and perform various tricks [...]. [Laskowski along with others] also murdered three people in the village Pełczanka, in the Parish of Cegłów in Mińsk Mazowiecki County. Their names are: Czerwiński Jan, and two others named Jacek.[55]

One of the most interesting members of the postwar "Polish elite" was definitely Grzegorz Korczyński, who, as a local commander of the Communist partisans in 1942-1943, murdered over 100 Jews in the Lublin region. He immediately afterwards divided up the spoils with his coconspirators.[56]

Had the war and the ensuing Communist revolution never occurred, Korczyński would have remained a common brawler and gangster, or continued to work as an errand-boy or servant. Yet, he became a general, a parliamentary deputy, a diplomat and one of the most influential Communist activists. But can this product of Communist "upward mobility" be truly considered a member of the Polish elite?

Such examples are legion. Gross was surprised to learn from researchers associated with the above-mentioned Center for Holocaust Research that Władysław Spychaj/Sobczyński, the postwar head of the WUBP (Provincial Public Security Agency, i.e. the secret police) in Kielce, and the Stalinist-era Voivode (provincial governor), Tadeusz

---

[54] Piotr Gontarczyk, *Polska Partia Robotnicza. Droga do władzy 1941–1944*[Polish Workers' Party; The Road to Power 1941–1944] (Warsaw: Fronda, 2006), 248.
[55] *Ibid.*, 416–617.
[56] *Ibid.*, 180–182.

Maj, were involved in killings of Jews during the war.[57] Yet, this fact is already well documented in historical literature.[58] In another section, Gross makes reference to his own book, *Fear,* in which he describes the supposed pogrom in Rzeszów.[59] The difficulty lies in the fact that a book, which convincingly proves that no pogrom occurred in Rzeszów, was already published in 2008.[60] Gross thus not only fails to conduct serious research, but also lays bare his unfamiliarity with the basic literature concerning the subject.

But *why* are Gross and his supporters so determined to "prove" that Polish elites partook in such reprehensible acts as blackmailing or murdering Jews during the Holocaust? The most likely answer is that such proof would facilitate the transfer of responsibility for anti-Semitic crimes from single individuals to society in general. It would provide a basis for the claim that the criminals were not only specific individuals, such as certain peasants or navy-blue policemen, but even nobles and "local elites," i.e. Polish Catholics, and Poles in general.

This appears to be an intentional abuse, based on a rather specific perception of Poles. Prof. Engelking-Boni expressed this view in the TV program "Kropka nad i" (Dotting the "i").[61]

When asked about the difference between the situation of Jewish escapees in the countryside and the city, she answered: "The cities did not see as many murders, [because] it wasn't so simple, [and] one couldn't dispose of the body that easily." Thus, Poles refrained from murdering Jews in cities primarily because they would be hard-pressed to find a place to dump the bodies.

In the introduction to *Golden Harvest*, Jan Grabowski described the Polish stance towards the Holocaust as twofold: "achieving physical annihilation or accepting that annihilation."[62]

It becomes clear that the *milieu* we are describing is propelled by a definite agenda. During Monika Olejnik's TV show, Prof. Engelking-Boni described an event from the Połaniec region. A Jewish escapee

---

[57] *Golden Harvest,* 114.
[58] See Marek Jan Chodakiewicz, Piotr Gontarczyk, and Leszek Żebrowski, eds., *Tajne oblicze GL-AL i PPR. Dokumenty* [The Hidden Face of the GL-AL and the PPR. Documents], (Warsaw: Burchardt Edition, 1997), 3:14; Gontarczyk, *Polska Partia Robotnicza,* 346–347.
[59] *Golden Harvest,* 120.
[60] Krzysztof Kaczmarski, *Pogrom, którego nie było. Rzeszów, 11–12 czerwca 1945 r. Fakty, hipotezy, dokumenty* [The Pogrom That Never Was: Rzeszów, 11-12 June 1945. Facts, Hypotheses, and Documents] (Rzeszów: IPN, 2008).
[61] Author's note from 9 February 2011. Full content of the program can be found on www.tvn24.pl.
[62] *Golden Harvest,* 10.

knocked on the door of a farmhouse on a Sunday and asked for aid. However, the peasants, who had been busy drinking vodka, refused to help him. Instead, they led him to the local police station, despite his pleas that they spare his life.

While recounting this sad story, Prof. Engelking-Boni sarcastically interjected into the middle of the sentence that this event took place on a Sunday: "after the High Mass, as one can surmise." Why such an interjection? Do we have any evidence that these drunkards even attended church?

Such rhetoric allows the Grossians to draw a connection between, on the one hand, the drunken peasants who denounced Jews and, on the other, Christianity in general, and the Catholic Church in particular. In fact, researchers affiliated with Prof. Engelking-Boni's research center resort to this parallel quite frequently.

It appears that, when describing various rural dregs of society, denouncers, and murderers of Jews, it is absolutely imperative to add that the culprits "belonged to the Roman Catholic faith." Yet, the vast majority of Polish peasants was at least nominally Roman Catholic. Why constantly dwell on this fact, if not for its propaganda effect?

Distorted history

In Gross's postulated vision of Polish-Jewish relations, a certain group of Poles has been overlooked: a segment of society compelled to aid Jews out of a sense of civic or Christian obligation. Such opportunities were certainly plentiful, and the best example is the previously mentioned Emanuel Ringelblum. The Jewish historian could only have produced his book on Polish-Jewish relations as a result of Polish assistance.

After being deported from the Warsaw Ghetto in 1942, Ringelblum was sent to the German camp in Trawniki. The Polish underground rescue organization Żegota saved him. For the next two years, he was sheltered, along with a group of other Jews, in a property on Grójecka Street in Warsaw, under the care of the families of Mieczysław Wolski and Władysław Marczak. Germans discovered the safe house on 7 March 1944. Ringelblum was captured and sent to the infamous Pawiak Prison. He was executed soon thereafter, along with the two Poles who sheltered him (the rest had escaped), including Marczak himself.[63]

---

[63] Jerzy Ślaski, *Polska Walcząca* [Fighting Poland] (Warsaw: PAX, 1990), 593–594.

Entirely missing in Gross's essay are examples of Polish rescuers of Jews. Not a single multi-generational family – such as the *entire* Ulma family, from the village of Markowa in the region of Podkarpacie, which was executed by the Nazis for sheltering Jews – is mentioned. Names of villages which jeopardized their own existence are nowhere to be found. Gross also fails to mention, sources such as Ewa Kurek's important book about Jewish children surviving in convents, under the care of Polish nuns.[64]

Scores of other authors' works who addressed this subject are also missing from Gross's register. There is no information about the death penalty awaiting not only those that helped Jews hide, but also over those who helped transport them, or even passed them a slice of bread. We shall not even find traces of information about those who – using Nazi terminology – "instigated" such actions.

Gross has treated all such behaviors as ultimately guided by ulterior motives. Despite certain attempts to nuance his work, and the resulting contradictions and ambiguities in the final edition of the book, it appears that the author considers only one statement as true: "Jews were taken in because harboring them in exchange for payment brought incredible profits."[65]

Even more interestingly, he attempts to convince his audience that sheltering Jews did not always result in the application of an unconditional death penalty, since there were cases of peasants being spared. But does the fact that certain Germans showed mercy negate the existence of a threat?

Rather than answering this question, the author wrote that once Jews were discovered on a premises, villagers would be punished at most with the confiscation of the dishonestly-earned profits: "A farmer caught harboring Jews during the occupation had his farm looted (thus depriving him of the alleged profits)."[66] According to Gross, the sheltering of Jews for money was not really an act of assistance, but a "blackmail process extended over time."[67]

---

[64] Ewa Kurek, *Dzieci żydowskie w klasztorach. Udział żeńskich zgromadzeń w akcji ratowania dzieci żydowskich w Polsce w latach 1939–1945* [Jewish Children in Monasteries: Nuns Saving Jewish Childen in Poland, 1939-1945] (Lublin: Clio, 2001). Kurek has been criticized by scholars associated with *Zagłada Żydów* for allegedly over-exaggerating the number of children saved in the convents. Does this mean that children were not saved and that it is not worthwhile to remember?
[65] *Golden Harvest*, 157.
[66] *Ibid.*, 158–159.
[67] *Ibid.*, 163.

Thus, relations between Jew-hiding Polish peasants and Jew-killing German Nazis became defined as financial transactions between thieves and murderers. But was the occupation-time reality this simple and straightforward?

Furthermore, while commenting on the postwar digging-up of the Treblinka gravesite, the author writes: "The Shoah was the result of a 'horticultural' (*ogrodnicza*) perspective on society, i.e. one whereby certain people are seen as weeds. Only then does their (full) elimination appear to be a rational and purposeful activity. The persistent efforts of decades of unearthing, exhuming, and organizing of the post-camp areas constitute such a 'horticultural' activity."[68]

What is the relationship between the admittedly reprehensible and condemnable acts of grave robbing in Treblinka and the Nazi plan to exterminate the Jews? The issue of the looting of gravesites is as old as human civilization. The stripping and desecration of corpses in search of valuables occurred in ancient times, as well as in the recent past. The villagers from Treblinka almost certainly excavated the camp site for the same reasons that motivated the stripping of corpses during both world wars, the American Civil War, the Napoleonic Wars, and countless other armed conflicts. Can digging in the area of the former death camp of Treblinka, however reprehensible and revolting, be convincingly classified in the same category as the willingness to eliminate Jews from society as "weeds"?

In 1944, an American plane crashed in the south of Poland while returning from a Polish supply mission. When a priest finally arrived at the tragic place, it turned out that the American pilots had to be buried in their undergarments. Their uniforms, boots, warm bomber jackets, and silk parachutes had already been stolen. But based on this event, can one conclude that the Polish peasantry took part in a great plan of robbing and exterminating US citizens?

At one point in his essay, as a result of a certain linguist's advice, Gross volunteered a very assumption-ridden reinterpretation of events that took place in 1941 in Jedwabne:

> By pulling [Jews] from their homes, chasing them through the streets, heaping verbal abuse upon them, throwing of stones at them, as well as giving the Jews the humiliating order to carry the statue [of Lenin], and finally the arrival at the barn, the Poles instinctually organized a Way of the Cross procession. The adult inhabitants of Jedwabne, guided by automatic

---

[68] *Ibid.*, 57.

behavioral processes, but also in pursuit of a model 'final march,' recreated Christ's suffering and passion.

Ironically, Jews, who had once been "justifiably" persecuted for killing Christ, were now appearing in the role of the Redeemer, whilst the Poles filled all the roles that were typically assigned to Jews. On that day, they were the Judases who betrayed, the guards that forced the cross on Christ's back [here: Lenin's statue], and finally the executioners, who brought Christ to the final site of his death. By activating the Way of the Cross scenario, Jedwabne's residents – guided by an anti-Semitic interpretation of Christianity – knew not only how they were supposed to behave, but were also convinced that their actions thoroughly justified.[69]

So far, we have known that Jedwabne's Jews were herded into the market square because it offered a large amount of space. Generally, marketplaces attract large crowds of people, for which they were designed. The Jews were later forced into a barn near the edge of town, because the brick buildings in Jedwabne were too small for the task. Lastly, an attempt to light something on fire in a dense urban environment (in mid-July 1941) probably would have culminated in the entire town being consumed by flames. The Jews were ordered to make their way on foot to the periphery of town since there were no means of mass transportation available. They were saddled with the Lenin statue because they were universally accused of collaboration with the Soviet occupiers. A scholarly investigation always appeared to be the best formula to analyze such events. But Gross has rejected this method.

Outside the realm of scholarly positivism

Gross eagerly emphasizes the philosophical profundity of his observations, resorting even to the Way of the Cross, Golgotha, and Christ's removal from the cross. On the other hand, sometimes the intentions informing his actions appear most mundane. For example, he added a paragraph just before concluding his book concerning the famous political activist Stefan Korboński (a leader of the underground Polish Peasant-Populist Party during the Second World War). As one of the chief Polish Underground State figures engaged in providing aid to the Jews, he was awarded the "Righteous Gentile" medal in 1980.[70]

---

[69] *Ibid.*, 181–182.
[70] For more, see: Małgorzata Ptasińska-Wójcik, ed., *Stefan Korboński 1901–1989* (Warsaw: IPN, 2009).

However, in the cited fragment of *Golden Harvest*, Gross completely omits Korboński's meritorious service. Instead, he cites epithets directed at him by left-liberal writers, Maria Dąbrowska and Jarosław Iwaszkiewicz. Referring to Korboński, the latter claimed in his *Dziennik* (Diary) that: "This guy's short-sightedness and stupidity astounds me. Not one interesting idea. No political conceptions." Maria Dąbrowska expressed her sentiments in a similar manner.[71]

The whole fragment about Korboński was pasted into the book in an artificial manner and without any logical connection to his argument. Most likely, scholarship was not the motivating factor. Rather, Gross was paying close attention to his regular critics during the manuscript editing process. Prof. Jerzy Robert Nowak is certainly such a critic and, in fact, authored an entire book enumerating the Princeton professor's numerous factual errors.[72] Prof. Nowak's discourse may be considered controversial, but, evidently, everyone (including Gross) reads him attentively.

On 24 January 2011, Nowak published an article in the Catholic weekly *Niedziela* [Sunday] entitled simply "Gross is lying once again." Nowak cited several famous Poles who have voiced their negative opinions about him and his work.[73] One of them was Jerzy Giedroyć, a man deeply involved in Polish-Jewish dialogue. In 1981, he wrote the following in a letter to Jan Nowak-Jeziorański: "Gross and his wife are people overcome with psychological issues (*nafaszerowani kompleksami*), and their 'university' lectures have (beyond their social circle) the worst opinion possible in the whole country."[74]

Among the critics of the author of *Golden Harvest*, Prof. Nowak mentioned Korboński as well, who strongly emphasized Gross's numerous lies in the journal *Zeszyty Historyczne* [Historical Notebooks]. Moreover, shortly before his death in 1989, Korboński accused Gross of burdening the Polish conscience in the hope of "personally profiting from it."[75]

Gross could not write anything negative about Giedroyć because of the high esteem in which the thinker is held by *Gazeta Wyborcza*.

---

[71] *Golden Harvest*, 177.
[72] Jerzy Robert Nowak, *100 kłamstw J. T. Grossa o żydowskich sąsiadach i Jedwabnem* [J.T. Gross's 100 Lies About Jewish Neighbors and Jedwabne] (Warsaw: von borowiecky, 2001).
[73] Jerzy Robert Nowak, "Gross znów kłamie" [Gross is lying once again], *Niedziela*, 24 January 2011, http://www.niedziela.pl/artykul_w_niedzieli.php?doc=nd201104&nr=37.
[74] *Ibid.*
[75] *Ibid.*

Nothing prevented him from taking revenge against a Pole who had distinguished himself as a rescuer of Jews. The apparent moral is that Gross approaches his works as an opportunity to settle personal scores.

Dr. Bożena Szaynok once spoke about her experience with Gross's scholarly methods. She caught the author, (by now) a professor at Princeton University, cutting a source up, thereby changing its original meaning. She later told *Gazeta Wyborcza*: "This appeared to be a manipulation, the utilizing of historical materials in a way that transmits the clear message of anti-Semitism being a widespread, normal, accepted, and universal phenomenon in Poland, without truly analyzing its important causes."[76] How did the author reply to such a *dictum*? "Gross disregarded my suggestions," Dr. Szaynok admitted.[77]

Gross's evident manipulations have been pointed out not only by the undersigned, but also by Dr. Bogdan Musiał[78] and, more recently, Dr. Śmietanka-Kruszelnicki.[79] Earlier critiques included those by Prof. Tomasz Strzembosz,[80] Dr. Jacek Walicki,[81] Dr. Paweł Machcewicz,[82] Dr. August Grabski,[83] as well as numerous other scholars.

Prof. Jerzy Eisler described Gross's most famous work *Neighbors* in the following terms: "Any student who turned in such a Master's thesis would be quickly flying out the door."[84] The aforementioned Prof. Jerzy Nowak contributed a perhaps overly emotional, but nevertheless valuable chronicle of various examples of scholarly fraud committed by Gross. The criticized author fails to offer constructive rebuttals to the

---

[76] „Gross – moralista, a nie historyk" [Gross: A Moralist, Not a Historian] (Aleksandra Klich's interview with Bożena Szaynok), *Gazeta Wyborcza*, 25 January 2008.
[77] *Ibid.*
[78] Bogdan Musiał, „Tezy dotyczące pogromu w Jedwabnem, cz. 1: Uwagi krytyczne do książki 'Sąsiedzi' Jana Tomasza Grossa" [Theses Pertaining to the Jedwabne Pogrom, Part 1: Critical Comments on Jan Tomasz Gross's Book *Neighbors*] in *Dzieje Najnowsze* 3 (2001).
[79] Ryszard Śmietanka-Kruszelnicki, „W poszukiwaniu wartości poznawczych książki Jana Tomasza Grossa 'Strach'" [In Search of the Scholarly Value of Jan Tomasz Gross's Book *Fear*], *Zeszyty Historyczne WiN* 32/33 (2010).
[80] Tomasz Strzembosz, „Przemilczana kolaboracja" [Collaboration Passed Over in Silence], *Rzeczpospolita*, 3 February 2001.
[81] Jacek Walicki, „Bezdroża nauki i publicystyki – o nowej książce Jana Tomasza Grossa" [Into the Scholarly Wilderness: Jan Tomasz Gross's New Book] in *Dzieje Najnowsze* 1 (2007).
[82] Paweł Machcewicz, „Odcienie czerni" [Shades of Black], *Tygodnik Powszechny*, 8 January 2008.
[83] August Grabski, „Krew brata twego głośno woła ku mnie z ziemi..." [Your Brother's Blood Calls Me Loudly from Earth], *Kwartalnik Historii Żydów* 3 (2006).
[84] Zbigniew Nikitorowicz, „Pole minowe" [A Minefield], *Kurier Poranny*, 1 December 2000.

accusations. In fact, he has resorted to attributing them to Polish anti-Semitism.[85]

Naturally, Gross's numerous errors and failures would require significantly more space to discuss than he himself dedicated towards the issues described within his works. However, the observations above permit one to draw certain general conclusions, albeit not very optimistic ones. Just like Gross's previous work *Fear*, *Golden Harvest* was not based on the most basic primary sources. This complete lack of archival research prevents Gross from offering any original or novel interpretations. How can he contribute anything at all to scholarship, especially since he has failed to undertake any original research for decades? Does he stand a chance of competing against any serious, hard-working scholars in the field of Holocaust studies?

Of course, the problem of violence towards and aid to Jews in the Polish countryside during the Holocaust merits a factual investigation. It is therefore imperative that one investigate and observe where, when, how, why, and in what circumstances specific Jews were killed. That data must be subsequently balanced and interpreted before it can be utilized to construct general conclusions. Only after the completion of this tedious process may one reflect on its greater meaning.

Unfortunately, it appears that such logocentric methods of reconstructing the past are outside of Jan Tomasz Gross's sphere of interests. His approach seems to be predicated on the view that "if the facts are against us, too bad for the facts." By attempting to achieve personal fame, the author employs any and every method to distort reality whilst utilizing methods generally used in and transplanted from mass culture. These aim to shock, offend, scandalize, and attract attention. Authors employing such a strategy have little reason to be offended when they are treated as, first and foremost, manifestations of popular culture, rather than professional scholars.

---

[85] Discussion between Jacek Karnowski and Janusz Kurtyka, Channel 1 of Polish Radio, program "Nowe wydawnictwo IPN – historia »żołnierzy wyklętych«" [A new IPN publication: The history of the "Cursed Soldiers"] from 17 January 2008, www.polskieradio.pl/7/129/Artykul/217622.

The Attitude of the Polish Population Towards Jewish Escapees from the Treblinka, Sobibór, and Bełżec Death Camps in Light of Jewish and Polish Testimonies[1]

Teresa Preker

(Translated by Paweł Styrna, Klaudiusz Wesołek, and Anna Gwarnicka)

The following essay is based upon the testimonies of fifty-seven people: forty-eight Jews, mainly former death camp inmates, and nine Poles. There are sixty-one testimonies in total, reconstructing, in part or in total, the attitude of Poles toward Jewish escapees. The complete listing of the content is provided at the end of this article. Twenty-seven reports have not yet been published and are deposited at the New Documents Archive of the Jewish Historical Institute (Żydowski Instytut Historyczny: ŻIH) as well as the author's personal collection. Thirty-four were originally published in various books and journals.[2] Twenty-seven testimonies deal with Treblinka, and the same number with Sobibór and Bełżec.

---

[1] Originally published in Polish as "Stosunek ludności polskiej do żydowskich uciekinierów z obozów zagłady w Treblince, Sobiborze i Bełżcu w świetle relacji żydowskich i polskich," in *Biuletyn Głównej Komisji Badania Zbrodni Przeciwko Narodowi Polskiemu Instytutu Pamięci Narodowej* [The Bulletin of the Main Commission to Investigate Crimes Against the Polish Nation of the Institute of National Memory], XXXV (Warsaw: Instytut Historyczny Uniwersytetu Warszawskiego, 1993): 100-114.

[2] The following works have been used: *Dokumenty i materiały z czasów okupacji niemieckiej w Polsce, I. Obozy* [Documents and Materials from the Era of the German Occupation in Poland, Part I. The Camps] (Łódź: CZKH, 1946) [cited as Documents]; Władysław Bartoszewski and Zofia Lewin, *Ten jest z ojczyzny mojej* [He is from My Fatherland], second edition (Kraków: Znak, 1969); *The Death Camp Treblinka: A Documentary*, ed. by Aleksander Donat (New York: Holocaust Library, 1979) [cited as *Treblinka*]; *Sobibór: Martyrdom and Revolt. Documents and Testimonies Presented by Miriam Novitch* (New York: Holocaust Library, 1980) [cited as *Sobibór*]; in addition to the journals *Biuletyn ŻIH* and *Dzieje Najnowsze*.

As far as Treblinka was concerned, seven prisoners (authors of testimonies no. 7, 8, 9, 14, 16, 19, and 22) escaped during the rebellion in August 1943, and eight of them (testimonies no. 1-5, 12, 15, and 19) managed to do so earlier. They employed different ways, usually hiding in heaps of clothing and other objects confiscated from the murdered victims and shipped off to the Reich. Afterwards they leaped out of the railroad cars along the way. This work contains also four testimonies (nos. 10, 11, 17, and 20) written by escapees from the Treblinka I forced labor camp because they experienced identical problems and difficulties in contacts with the Polish population as Treblinka II inmates.

Most of the authors of testimonies from Sobibór won their freedom following the uprising on 14 October 1943, but two of them (nos. 28 and 31) escaped after killing the Ukrainian guard escorting them to work outside of the camp. The escapees included not only Jews from Poland, but also from Holland (report 46), France (40), the Soviet Union (43), and Czechoslovakia (42).

Only one prisoner, Rudolf Reder, survived the camp in Bełżec. He managed to trick a guard while working in Lwów. He had resided in the city prior to his imprisonment in the camp and had many contacts in Lwów. Hence, his case diverges significantly from the experiences of the other escapees. The experiences of the latter category bear a closer resemblance to the testimonies of prisoners who jumped from Bełżec-bound trains, and most of the collected information concerns them.

Most of the escapees were young, sometimes even teenagers; in 1942 or 1943 only five of them were forty years of age or older. Not all of them specified their jobs, but there were a few cobblers, tailors, bakers, a potter, a furrier, and a bookkeeper. Younger people, who were too young to work, also came from families of craftsmen.

Among the ten Polish authors we will find: two peasants, a train dispatcher from Treblinka Station (no. 26), a member of a Communist People's Army unit, a bridge-building engineer (no. 24), an author with a PhD degree, and the son of a Treblinka-area peasant (currently an Associate Professor at the Warsaw Politechnical Institute) (no. 27); the professions of the remaining two are unknown. Five of these authors speak of individual acts of assistance extended to escapees by themselves or someone else. Four (mentioned in parentheses) shed light on the broader context.

The first issue that surfaces upon viewing the testimonies is the disparity between the number of extant Jewish and Polish ones. It is true that the intensity associated with survival attempts on the part of Jewish escapees was far greater than the turmoil the Poles dealt with.

The former were therefore more inclined to share their internal struggles. In addition, those who most interacted with the escapees were peasants, and they constitute a class least capable of expressing themselves in writing. Nevertheless, shortly after the war, the problem of the basic dearth of Polish testimonies was never addressed. Nor were Poles encouraged to write down their experiences.[3] The Jews, on the other hand, tended to collect them. From 1945 on, they had already lobbied different *Voievodships* (Polish provinces) for the creation of the Jewish Historical Commission, followed by the Jewish Historical Institute. Jewish traders and laborers had problems writing about their experiences. Hence, their testimonies were sometimes taken down by Committee or ŻIH clerks (ten such testimonies may be found in the index). Had Polish peasants been provided with similar incentives and support, documentation regarding this period would have certainly been far greater on our part.

Recently, Jewish historians have continued to seek out survivors to persuade them to record their experiences for posterity. Unfortunately, testimonies generated so many decades following the Holocaust possess far less historical value.

May the testimonies discussed here be considered a sufficient basis for characterizing the relations between Poles and Jewish escapees? Is the quantity sufficient for drawing conclusions? It is estimated that 40-60 Treblinka prisoners survived, along with 30-40 from Sobibór prisoners, which adds up to a total of approximately 70-100 people. From among these, 38 have written testimonies cited in this article (excluding the authors of nos. 1-5, who most certainly died after their return to the Warsaw Ghetto). Thus, we have a total of 40-50 Jewish survivor testimonies at our disposal. This appears to be a suitably representative sample. The disadvantage of these testimonies is the brief and laconic nature of passages on subjects of interest to us. Nevertheless, both the brevity and the omission of certain matters are telling, which I shall elaborate upon in another section of the text.

Due to their quantity, Polish testimonies are much less representative.

In general, Jewish authors considered the attitudes of the Polish population towards the escapees as negative. Critical mentions and comments are usually to be found in the middle of a testimony. Some

---

[3] A questionnaire regarding aid provided to the Jews, published by Władysław Bartoszewski in (the liberal Catholic weekly) *Tygodnik Powszechny* in March 1963, failed to penetrate to the peasantry. Even if the peasants became aware of its existence, it constituted an insufficient incentive for them to fill it out.

already describe the moments when the transports reached the death camps; at the train stations on the way to Treblinka peasants sold water for about 100-200 złotys per glass (no. 5); those shipped to Bełżec "begged the Polish railroad worker for some snow. He didn't give any" (no. 58). The escapees related how people refused to help them and took large sums while giving little or nothing in return (nos. 3 and 8).[4] Sometimes they refused to sell anything (nos. 14 and 28); others organized ambushes, mainly in the forests, and stole money, shoes, and anything else they could (nos. 3, 8, and 14). Some escapees became the victims of group robberies, often performed with weapons in hand (nos. 20, 30, and 43).

Some accusations were obviously exaggerated. The author of testimony no. 17, a tailor, was allegedly warned by a peasant against his neighbor, who supposedly had already killed seven Jews and dumped their bodies into his well. But why the well? To make the water unfit for drinking? This information sounds like the repetition of a crudely sensational piece of gossip.

A tale contained in Samuel Rajzman's 1946 testimony (no. 7) may be viewed from a similar perspective. The author claims that, in a small forest in which he successfully hid, the forester, being "a dark character, murdered probably several thousand Jews all by himself" and "the local peasants kidnapped [Jewish] children and led them to their death at Treblinka on a string like calves. Perhaps they received ¼ [of a measure] of sugar for it, or perhaps nothing at all." This piece of information is not corroborated by a single Jewish or Polish testimony. It is also important to note that, while publishing his testimony thirty years late in a collection entitled *The Death Camp Treblinka*, the author omitted both bits.

Most negative assessments do not involve information regarding concrete incidents but general judgments. The authors of a testimony state that in the vicinity of Treblinka, "the peasants helped the Germans in their own way. Even as we escaped, we could see the bodies of murdered Jews from whose feet the shoes had been pulled. The peasants knew that Jews had money, and that was sufficient cause to ambush and murder them [...]" (no. 9).

"It is possible to state that the peasants from all the local villages (adjacent to Treblinka) immediately led anyone they caught to the

---

[4] The testimony of Abraham Krzepicki (item no. 3) indicates that, as a fugitive, he encountered an identical penchant for exploitation and gouging in the ghetto. Thus, when the Jews in Stoczek discovered that he was an escapee from Treblinka, they charged him prices ten times higher than the local market ones.

Germans [...]. If anyone jumped from a train, they undressed, robbed, and turned them over to the Germans. Perhaps there were some exceptions, but they were very few [...] They received nothing from the Germans for this. They did it out of anti-Semitism" (no. 8a).

"It was they [Ukrainian and Polish bandits from the Sobibór area] who are to blame for the fact that so few inmates saw the end of the war" (no. 4).

"Our enemies, apart from the Germans, were the Ukrainians and Polish fascists" (no. 29).

"Near the railroad track [leading to Bełżec] there roamed the local population, mainly Ukrainians, who robbed, stole shoes and coats, and often delivered [Jews] to the Germans" (no. 57).

It is important to add that some of the authors cited here mentioned instances of far-reaching assistance they sometimes received from Polish peasants as individuals. Others limit themselves to purely negative opinions.

Undeniably, the above assessments are based on real observations. But did the young age of the authors, the violent nature of their experiences, and, a probable lack of preparation for generalized reflection (two were cobblers and the third author a carpenter, all of whom came from small towns) not lead them to hasty conclusions?

As we have seen, the authors trace Polish behavior to two main causes. Some claim that the Poles were driven by greed. They wished to appropriate the money, which escapees usually carried large sums of, in addition to clothing and shoes (especially the latter are a reoccurring theme!). Others are convinced that the cause was Polish anti-Semitism (sometimes, in English-language testimonies, the phenomenon was also dubbed "Polish fascism"). But how do Polish authors view this question?

Three longer and more general testimonies (I am omitting the longest testimony, i.e. the railroad worker Franciszek Ząbecki's book) confirm the observations of the Jewish escapees. Their authors also believe that the motive most often propelling individuals toward criminal acts was greed.

Dr. Janusz Peter of Bełżec (no. 59) mentioned the empathy felt by the peasants for the Jews who jumped from the death transports as they approached the camps, often breaking their arms and legs in the process. Yet, according to Peter, this empathy rarely translated into active help. He adds: "We must mention here that plenty of spies and jackals in human form – ready to snitch or kill for profit – traversed the areas adjacent to the tracks."

Similar situations around Treblinka are described more extensively by engineer Jerzy Królikowski, who was at the time constructing a bridge nearby on the Bug River (no. 24a). The local population, Królikowski writes, was demoralized by ethnically Ukrainian guards serving in the camp who flaunted the money and valuables they seized from Jews being sent to the gas chambers. Failing to recognize their value, they squandered them on vodka and drinking bouts or lavished them upon the local girls with whom they cohabited. "The poverty-stricken Podlasian region turned into an Eldorado, which attracted scum from all over the country." Such unsavory individuals no doubt "supplemented" the local peasants' "education." He continues: "In a segment of the local population greed killed off all moral principles."

Associate Professor (*docent*) Ludwik Kołkowski writes in the same spirit: "People were accustomed to the fact that every Jew who escaped from the camp was loaded with money and valuables, which he either owned or acquired at the camp. Thus, a peasant who had already tasted money, upon seeing a Jewish escapee could only think of ways to despoil him [...] Usually, he [the peasant] robbed [the Jew], took everything he could, and let the escapee go [...] The worst types lived in the very neighborhood of the camp: about 200-300 meters away. Those who lived 2,000 meters away were completely different [...] Thus, making one's way through this first perimeter could have been dangerous. Jews knew that after escaping from the camp they had to flee as far away as possible, [and] that they couldn't stop anywhere nearby. That is where the largest number of Germans could be found, but the Polish peasants did not have an entirely clear conscience either."

Neither Peter nor Królikowski mentioned anything about anti-Semitism as the motivation behind the above crimes. When asked about this directly, Kołkowski categorically denied that it played any role. In his view, the peasants of Podlasie were not anti-Semitic before the outbreak of the Second World War because no conflict of interests existed between them and the Jews. If the propaganda of various political groups – usually employing such invectives as the "Jew-Communist" or the "Jew-Anti-Christ" – penetrated into the area, it wasn't sufficiently strong to provoke violent actions.

During the war facts seemed to support misleading opinions regarding apparent manifestations of anti-Semitism. In reality, greed, not anti-Semitism was the driving force in these cases. Yet, it was quite easy to interpret as an expression of anti-Semitism an act such as disclosing to the Germans a secret location in the woods where a group of Jews had been hiding. The claim that the locals disclosed Jewish hiding places for several kilograms of sugar fails to stand up to scrutiny. The Germans did not reward snitches with sugar in the Podlasie region, as Jewish sources confirm, and even had they offered such compensation the peasants would not have denounced the Jews for commodities of such relatively modest value. They sought much greater profits. After all, they had excellent knowledge of which Jews carried money and other valuables. They were also aware of the fact that the Jews did not store these riches in their hiding places, but buried their wealth in nearby locations in the woods. Thus, the local informers launched a systematic excavation operation in the forest after the Germans apprehended the Jews in the wake of their (often anonymous) denunciation.

The fact that anti-Semitism was not the primary motive behind the robberies is also confirmed by other occurrences. For instance, Zilberman, a wealthy Jew from Kosów, entrusted his money to a peasant by the surname of Iwanowski from an adjacent village. The villager soon became the victim of a deadly robbery. It was the Pole, not the Jew, who was killed in this scenario.

According to Kołkowski, another significant factor fueling the denunciation of Jews stemmed from conflicts between peasants, such as vendettas or rivalries. The context of the Nazi occupation provided fertile ground for the settling of squabbles over land, conflicts between families and neighbors (so common in the Polish countryside), and various other scores. Once notified, the Germans shot not only the Jews hidden by the peasant but executed him and his entire family as well. This was exactly the goal. Only those who enjoyed good relations with their neighbors could afford to shelter Jews or circumvent any other German laws.

These observations from the Treblinka area find corroboration in a testimony from the vicinity of a different death camp. A young girl by the name of Irenka Sznycer, whose distinctly Semitic features had hindered efforts to hide her on the "Aryan" side of the Kraków and Warsaw ghettos, found shelter in the home of Maria Leszczyńska, a poor resident of the town of Bełzec. "'I felt good at this lady's place,' Irenka told a clerk recording her testimony at the Jewish Historical Commission after the war, 'and I didn't fear anything. The neighbors knew I was a Jewess but, because this lady didn't have any enemies, nothing could have happened to me'" (no. 56).

Thus, in an area located 200-300 meters away from one of the worst death camps (Irenka often saw it from the outside), among "jackals in human form ready to kill for profit," as Peter described them, a girl with a "bad appearance" was able to survive the occupation because she and her caregiver were poor (which everyone knew) and had no enemies!

Icchak Lichtman (no. 43) – one of the authors – adds vendettas for the Soviet occupation of eastern Poland in 1939-1941 to the list of factors contributing to anti-Semitic acts. In Żółkiewka, where he lived before the war, the relations with the local Poles were friendly, and anti-Semitism was not considered a problem. Following the entry of the Soviet Army in late September 1939, "the young Jewish Communists joined the militia." Afterwards, some of them retreated along with the Soviets, while others preferred to remain in the area. "That is when the atrocities started: crowds murdered wealthy families and looted their wealth. The young people who had happily welcomed the Russians were murdered as well [...]."

Some of the negative comments expressed by the fugitives refer to the partisans as well. Many Jews in hiding could only dream of joining a guerrilla detachment. Five of them (nos. 32, 39, 44, 47, and 48) managed to join the Jewish partisans, two others (nos. 8 and 14) joined some unspecified groups (perhaps also Jewish). Although this allowed them to associate with their fellow Jews, they continued to lack any significant opportunities or prospects.

The role of the Soviet partisans is described in various ways. Peczorski (no. 44), Knopfmacher (no. 38) and Ilona Safran (no. 48) joined well-armed units, which provided former concentration camp inmates with a sense of security. Quite the opposite was bluntly reported by Hersz Cukerman in his 1945 testimony (no. 30): "The escapees were being murdered by Home Army soldiers and Soviet partisans." However, this information was omitted in an altered version published in 1980 (no. 47). Cukerman also excised other details that implicated only the Home Army.

Eliasz Rozenberg, along with several of his friends, experienced an unpleasant encounter with a Soviet partisan unit near Treblinka (no. 14). Following an ostensibly courteous initial exchange, the escapees were coerced to surrender their shoes and whatever nice clothes they possessed. The Soviets also refused to admit them into the detachment.

Testimonies no. 23, 33, and 55 (and perhaps 31) discuss the situation of escapees finding themselves in the branches of the Communist People's Army (*Armia Ludowa*; or AL). Testimony no. 37 demonstrates that even these contacts sometimes resulted in tragic consequences. The author's young friend, who was accepted into the AL as a result of his continuous efforts, was murdered only several days later in unexplained yet quite unequivocal circumstances.

The depiction of the Home Army is quite specific. In her first testimony, stored at the archives of the Jewish Historical Commission (no. 32a), Zelda Metz states: "Those who managed to escape the camp [in Sobibór] died either as partisans, or were murdered by AK." However, while repeating this account a year later for *Dokumenty i materiały*, she changed the name of the underground allegation under accusation from the AK to the NSZ. Later still, she employed the term "Polish fascist" in a book about Sobibór published in the US.

The eventual removal of negative comments regarding the Home Army by Hersz Cukerman was already mentioned. Tomasz Blat (no. 37 a, b) excised such passages as well. According to his testimony, recorded in 1957, Home Army soldiers harassed him (*nachodzili*) several times (albeit unsuccessfully) at his expensive hideout on a peasant's property, which he shared with two additional Jews. Eventually, the partisans colluded with the peasant and, with his active assistance, attacked the escapees, killing one of them, while the other two barely survived. Later on, however, in a book about Sobibór, Blat condensed the entire event to a single intrusion upon the "shelter" by some unknown group of (perhaps) intoxicated individuals, who (perhaps incidentally) killed one of them.

Upon reading and comparing the above two versions of the same testimony, it appears most likely that the initial report was written under the heavy pressure exerted by postwar Communist propaganda, which labeled the AK as the "spittle-besmattered dwarf of reaction." Subsequently, in a less politically intense context, the testimonies were altered appropriately. Unfortunately, some of those testimonies, especially the initial versions, and sometimes even the subsequent ones, often influenced by various negative emotions (e.g. the 1968 "anti-Zionist" campaign in Communist-run Poland), remained in the archives. Some were eventually published and continue to be viewed by some historians as the ultimate proof.

In his initial report (written in 1957), Blat described an encounter with a Home Army platoon commanded by his old schoolmate, Tadek, who explained: "We are the real AK, so we don't kill Jews, unless we find one harassing someone with weapons in hand. Of course, it is possible that certain individuals, masquerading as the AK, kill Jews on their own while committing robberies."

Initially, Blat disbelieved his old classmate. Yet, Tadek was indeed correct; at least in respect to the general situation. A plethora of groups and gangs roamed the country during the occupation, claiming to represent "the Polish Army," "the units of the Government in London," or "peasant organizations" (specific names were either eschewed or unknown).[5] It is possible that the partisan unit that attacked Rozenberg's group near Treblinka was only one such outfit, which simply happened to include a few Soviets.

In this case, of all the charges levied against the Home Army, only one remains tenable, namely: the AK did not accept Jews (nos. 20, 37 et al.). This allegation was never denied by Polish authors.[6]

As this necessarily brief survey indicates, certain harsher judgments made by some Jewish authors regarding the behavior of the local population are, to a significant extent, corroborated by some Polish authors. Yet, discrepancies appear when a quantitative assessment of these phenomena is concerned. In Szymon Goldberg's testimony (no. 8a) we read that nearly all of the denizens of the villages adjacent to Treblinka "robbed and handed [Jews] over to the Germans. Perhaps there were exceptions, but these were few." On the other hand, Michał Knopfmacher from the Lublin region (no. 38) states: "Some peasants help, [and] others want to turn us over. More [peasants] help, although people are afraid." In turn, when asked about these proportions, Kołkowski pointed out that it is insufficient to merely speak of a ratio. Crimes were sporadic, although they generated tragic consequences. Yet, assistance was provided on a daily basis on the premises of many peasants' properties.

To a degree, differing perspectives of Polish and Jewish authors may be responsible for this divergence. The Jewish escapees were primarily concerned with themselves and their fellow former inmates. The Poles generally focused on all the Jews hiding in a certain area. In this context, it is important to remember that all three death camps were organized in regions with large Jewish populations. The Germans ghettoized approximately 20,000 Jews in several towns located within a thirty kilometer distance from Treblinka, such as: Kosów, Sterdynia, Węgrów, Lochów, and Jadów. Ghettoes in Włodawa, Chełm, and Siedliszcze – located within a similar distance from Sobibór – contained almost as many people. The Germans liquidated these ghettoes between the spring and fall of 1942. Yet, many Jews managed

---

[5] Not only ethnic Poles impersonated the Home Army (AK). This was also done by armed groups of Jews, provided that a few of the members could pass themselves off as "Aryans." When writing about food procurement in the villages, the author of testimony no. 19 relates: "Of course we said that we were from the Polish Army, operating in the underground."

[6] In this article I am omitting the murder of a few Jews in Kosów right after the liberation [sic!] (no. 10 and 11) and the activist Feldhendler in Lublin (no. 29 and 30), which had been blamed on the Home Army. If the members of the AK indeed participated in these incidents, the basis behind them was completely different.

to escape them. Finding shelter in the countryside was considerably easier because of the numerous connections of the local peasants. While some testimonies (such as nos. 10, 11, 22, and 27) mention farm owners sheltering over a dozen Jews, perhaps only two or three were actual escapees. The remaining Jews were local. Similar proportions undoubtedly applied to Jews hiding individually as well. Hence the differing quantitative assessments and divergent judgments about the attitudes of the local population.

But how did Poles and Jews view Polish assistance? Practically all authors mentioned individual help. Only one – Franciszek Ząbecki in his book *Wspomnienia dawne i nowe* (item no. 26) – describes organized assistance.

As a railroad traffic supervisor at the Treblinka station, Ząbecki, a Home Army member, prepared reports on the state of the camp and the movement of trains for AK intelligence. Upon the orders of the Home Army's Main Command in Warsaw, he developed a blueprint of the camp based upon the information available to him. The blueprint was to serve as a guide for a planned military operation, which never materialized, however.

Following a revolt, Ząbecki writes, a large group of escapees swam to the eastern bank of the Bug River. The ex-inmates were assisted and provided with covering fire by a Home Army unit. Yet, no other testimony corroborates this version of the river crossing. Moreover, we know that Jews did not congregate in large groups. Instead, they crossed the Bug in teams of four or five individuals, either paying a fisherman to ferry them across, or crossing alone and employing a combination of wading and swimming under the cover of darkness. Ząbecki's claim appears exaggerated to say the least.

Ząbecki also appears to have overestimated the scale of assistance organized by the railroad workers – at both Treblinka and other stations along the route – for Jews locked in the death transports. "The railroad workers gave the Jews water, in spite of the ban. Even the wives of the station employees, such as Pronicka, a stationmaster's wife, Bąkowa [...], Wierzbowska [...], and my own wife [...] cried and rushed buckets of water to the cars [...]. This was very dangerous. A railroad service worker (*robotnik służby drogowej*) was shot at Treblinka station for providing water [...]."

Indeed, the Germans guarded the transports closely. Thus, without even mentioning that the impressions of Jewish authors were quite different, if water was provided on such a massive scale at Treblinka and other stations, in addition to (as Ząbecki states) hammers, pliers, and crowbars, and, finally, if the railroad workers opened the rail car doors at night (and during the day as well) or otherwise enabled the Jews to escape, then such actions would have undoubtedly resulted in the deaths of many railroad employees, not merely one worker.

It is telling that Ząbecki says nothing about the peasantry and the local population. Apart from railroad workers, he mentions only an engineer, Tadeusz Kączkowski, who was arrested for keeping a record of "Jewish transports" (his name is also mentioned by Królikowski in no. 24). Kączkowski later died at Auschwitz.

Undoubtedly – just as in the case of young Jewish authors – the authentic events were the starting point for Ząbecki as well. However, he removed all the darker shades from the story, thereby lending it a somewhat improbable appearance.

Individual assistance was provided in various ways, in part selflessly, and less often in exchange for payment. The most common form of aid consisted of giving food. On their way, the escapees frequently stopped at nearby huts, where they asked for bread and milk. Sometimes they received soup or some other cooked meal. After receiving something for the road, they continued on their journey. At times, the escapees paid for the food they were given (no. 19). In general, however, they did not pay, regardless of the fact that their benefactors were often very poor themselves. Rajzman (no. 21), on a run with his friend, remembered an old woman, very close to Treblinka, gave them some bread and water in front of her hut, asking "please give me back my mug, as I have no other." She refused to accept any money. Other peasants acted similarly (nos. 1 and 34). Obviously, the wealthier ones offered the escapees more generous portions (nos. 4, 14, 20 et al.).

A more common form of assistance consisted of the distribution of food for continuous periods of time by the denizens of one village or a so-called colony. After establishing a "shelter" in a nearby forest, frequently, a group of several Jews dispatched their representative every morning or evening to a different peasant each time, asking for food. The purpose of constantly changing benefactors was to spread the burden to the peasants as widely as possible, and to increase the safety of Jews themselves. After all, if every peasant could be held accountable for helping Jews, none would dare to denounce them.

Such safety precautions were important because – in the rural context – if Jews were not hidden by individual peasants in specially prepared "bunkers," they frequently walked around the village freely. Thus, everybody knew about them. Dr. Kołkowski speaks about this in detail, as do other testimonies. For instance: "we walked around the villages until December" (no. 30), "everybody around knew me well" (no. 15), "Bronisława Lancberg came out (from the woods) to see us, and other neighbors" (no. 25), "the farm hands knew everything about us, and so did their 6-7 year old children, who attended school" (no. 11).

In general, the Jews hiding in the woods changed their hiding places every so often. They preferred be "on the move." However, there are reports stating that some of them remained near a certain village or a particular peasant for extended periods of time. For example: "I lived for ten months or so near Wyszków. Good people lived there, [who] helped me, and gave me food" (no. 8a); Rajzman, along with his friend (no. 21) stayed hidden in a forest near Ceranów for a period of almost identical duration. A son of a local farmer, Gołoś (a member of a right nationalist organization, who became a judge after the war) brought him food, and sheltered him in his own house throughout the winter (Gołoś Sr. knew the Rajzman family).

Dr. Kołkowski's father sheltered several local Jews for free, and later supplied five escapees with food. Mendel Rzepka, along with "an entire cohort [*gromada*]" of other Jews, hid for about a year at the peasant Góral's residence. They were treated as guests (no. 22).

Several reports are so phrased as to render unclear whether the Jews paid their hosts or not. For example, this relates to the report of Lejzor Jakubskind, who wrote: "I survived while hiding at one peasant's hut. I stayed with him for the entire duration, until the entry of the Red Army" (no. 16). In turn, Mosze Hochman (no. 36) was sheltered by a farmer in Papierzyn[a?] for seven months, and Eliasz Rozenberg – along with three Jews from Siemiatycze – stayed with farmer Kosiński for an entire winter (no. 14). Bolesław Pietraszek, a property owner in Sokołów County, sheltered seventeen people from 1942-1943 until the liberation [sic!]. He constructed a special "bunker," and baked 25 kilograms of bread per week for them; "we had plenty of other food as well. All of these Jews survived" (no. 11). It is difficult to ascertain if Pietraszek helped all seventeen Jews for free. We do, however know that the author of the testimony, Szmuel Miodoński, an escapee from Treblinka I, could not afford to make any kind of payment at that time.

In the selection under discussion, there are thirty-three authors (five Polish and twenty-eight Jewish) who mention either certain or probable *pro bono* (i.e. free-of-charge) assistance. They constitute approximately 60 percent of the total.

There are only four testimonies mentioning help in return for money or labor (no. 52). Salomon Podchlebnik (no. 28) hid with three consecutive peasants, paying 50 złotys per day. The hiding place of the previously mentioned Tomasz Blat was probably more expensive yet. Szmuel Grynszpan's situation (no. 19) was even more complicated. He was hiding with ten other Jews in a farmer's underground shelter near

Kosów. When they ran out of money, the peasant refused to continue hiding them. Hence, they carved a "rifle: out of wood, smeared it with ink, and threatened their host with that "rifle" in a dark place, thereby forcing him to care for them for free until the liberation [sic].

However, it was not the sole case of extortion. A group of escapees from Sobibór, who daydreamed about life as partisans, managed to buy a few rifles, which they used to "threaten the peasants to supply them with free food" (no. 43). Testimonies no. 19, 28, 38, 50, and 51 mention the employment of threats or guns to extort food. Two other (nos. 14 and 50) discuss the stealing of foodstuffs: "we became so skilled in our nightly forays into the villages, that ... when we took a few hens or a lamb, nobody even woke up."

It is difficult to condemn hungry escapees unable to procure food in any other way than through theft. Even the nuns from Janów Lubelski acted in a similar manner, when they wandered about with their orphans following the bombardment of their convent: "The older boys roamed around the peasants' fields at night, digging up potatoes, picking cabbage and fruit. There was no other way."[7] There was no other way for the Jews as well. However, the nuns were probably never suspected of theft, whereas the Jewish refugees were suspected of it automatically. Besides, according to peasants, a difference existed between digging up a bucket of potatoes in the field (which was done by all partisans and bands), and the theft of a few animals from a breeder's inventory. In addition, extortion with a gun in hand must have generated even greater indignation. Undoubtedly, such behavior aggravated the peasantry's attitude towards the Jews.

This aspect went unnoticed by the authors, who also never recognized any other motives behind Polish actions. In each refusal, in each lack of help, they saw only aversion and anti-Semitic hostility. They portrayed the peasants' explanations that no food was available on account of Nazi forced food quotas and partisan resupplying operations, as mere excuses (nos. 4, 14, et al.,), regardless of the fact that, in many cases, they must have been true.

The authors discussed the fear among the locals upon their arrival in a similarly contemptuous way. "The Polish peasants were good but too fearful to help us," writes Lea Reisner from Izbica (no. 45). In one hut, the mother was willing to help, but the son was afraid (no. 14), in

---

[7] Ewa Kurek-Lesik, „Udział żeńskich zgromadzeń zakonnych w akcji ratowania dzieci żydowskich w Polsce w latach 1939-1945 (Zarys problematyki)" ["The Participation of Nun Congregations in the Effort to Rescue Jewish Children in Poland during the Years 1939-1945 (An Outline of the Problem)"], *Dzieje Najnowsze* 3-4 (1986): 261.

another hut quite the opposite – the son was benevolent and caring, but the mother experienced a nervous breakdown (no. 20). Certain other testimonies (nos. 17, 37, 44, et al) mention exaggerated and unfounded fears. After all, the Jews have been accused of cowardice so many times, that perhaps – on an unconscious level – they seized any opportunity to charge others with it.

But did the Poles really have nothing to fear?

The authors could not have been unaware of the death penalty facing any and all who dared to help the Jews. Yet, they never mentioned this factor in their testimonies. Szymon Goldberg (no. 8a), as an inmate in Treblinka, witnessed how "a Polish girl, who brought packages for the Jews, was captured by Germans by the fence. Later, the Germans led her into the camp, and Sturmführer Franz himself shot and killed her. She was about 20 years old." That fact (confirmed by other testimonies), however, was relevant to the camp. The only mention of repression for assisting an escapee (who, during the interrogation, provided the last name of the person caring for him) may be found in Blat's testimony (no. 37a): "the gendarmes captured a woman, and it is unclear what they are going to do with her."

Only Aleksander Donat, an editor of a book about Treblinka, wrote in the introduction about two executions for that particular type of "offense." Dr. Kołkowski heard about a significantly greater number of such executions.

"It is very strange," he states, "that this information did not discourage anybody from our village from continuing to help the Jews. We simply believed that it could never happen to us." He also recalls a conversation with Mendel Rzepka, who at that time seemed oblivious to the full implication of those facts as well. Rzepka soon began to take matters for granted – both, his own, now unimaginable, lifestyle from before the war, as well as the help received from peasants, who sheltered him in a hiding place underneath the barn, and brought him food on a daily basis, risking their own lives throughout. Today, however, fully aware of the horror of wartime conditions, he thinks that Poles who helped Jews were outright insane.

I would like to relate my last comment regarding the testimonies in question to Rzepka's observation, that at that time everything appeared normal and ordinary.

As mentioned above, only about 60 percent of the Jewish authors describe, in any broader sense or in passing, their relations with Poles and help received from them. Hence, the remaining 40 percent speaks of interaction with this population in either very general or simply negative terms. Furthermore, both of the books about Sobibór and

Treblinka cited here contain twelve additional testimonies, which do not mention Poles at all. In the archives of the Jewish Historical Institute (ŻIH), a few dozen more testimonies are on deposit. The summaries of these will reveal that only about one-third of the authors/escapees wrote about their dealings with the locals. Yet, the other two-thirds, must have come into contact with the locals, if only to receive or to purchase food – at more or less affordable prices – or to extort it. Such relations must have existed, and must have been sufficiently good, since the escapees survived (continuous extortion was an option only for partisans and gangs). Why then did they fail to mention these contacts?

Mendel Rzepka answered this question. In those days, everything that was recurrent and permanent, just like the events of contemporary everyday life – seemed ordinary and normal – as normal as shopping, working, and other ordinary, everyday activities we do not consider worthy of mentioning. Only rare or unique events – such as escaping, coming into contact with partisans, attacks, and the loss of loved ones – were considered abnormal and extraordinary. The lack of or insufficient information about relations with the local people might signify that these were, at least in some respects, good or decent, i.e. "normal."

Unfortunately, so few Polish testimonies regarding the Treblinka, Sobibór, and Bełżec areas exist. They are necessary not only because their sheer number may be used to cover up certain crimes, which indeed occurred. And not only for the purpose of creating a new basis for the debate on proportions [i.e. the proportion of aid vs. passivity and hostility], which will most likely never be established for certain. That information is considered important precisely because it could assist those, whose task it is to reconstruct the tangled history of the Holocaust in German-occupied Poland, realize that what the Jews saw as "normal" was not always so perceived by the Poles. That is why the predicament of the Polish population, its attitudes, and its view of the current reality in particular – within the context of Polish-Jewish relations – deserves more scrutiny.

Index of Testimonies

The testimonies of the same author containing divergent information regarding Polish-Jewish relations are assigned several numbers (2 and 3; 7 and 21; 30 and 47; 34 and 37). Testimonies characterized by minor discrepancies have been assigned the same number, subdivided, and assigned letters (a, b, and c).

Treblinka: Jewish testimonies

1. Identity unknown (1942), AAN 203/III-115
2. Identity unknown (1942), (probably the first version of no. 3), *Biuletyn ŻIH*, no. 40
3. a. Abraham Krzepicki (1942), fragment, *Biuletyn ŻIH*, no. 43-44
   b. Abraham Krzepicki (1942) *Treblinka* (1979)
4. Dawid Nowodworski (1942), ŻIH Archive 301/689
5. Identity unknown, from Częstochowa (1942), *Biuletyn ŻIH*, no. 40
6. Translation from the Soviet press (1944), ŻIH Archive 301/689
7. Samuel Rajzman (1946), Documents
8. a. Szymon Goldberg (1945), ŻIH Archive, testimony no. 1246
   b. Szymon Goldberg (1946), *Documents* (abridged version)
9. Tanhum Grindberg (1945), *Treblinka* (1979)
10. Szmuel Grynszpan, no data available, ŻIH Archive, testimony no. 1185
11. Szmuel Miodoński, no data available, ŻIH Archive, testimony no. 1186
12. Józef Gutman (1947), ŻIH Archive, testimony no. 2226
13. Szymon Datner (1947), ŻIH Archive, testimony no. 2414
14. Eliasz Rozenberg, no data available, ŻIH Archive VII/151
15. I. Grinberg, no data available, ŻIH Archive, testimony no. 6219
16. Lejzer Jakubskind, no data available, ŻIH Archive 301/83
17. Kałman Krawiec (1949), ŻIH Archive, testimony no. 4086
18. Chaja Markiewicz, no data available, ŻIH Archive 301/162
19. J. Rajgrodzki (1958), *Biuletyn ŻIH*, no. 25
20. a. Mieczysław Chodźko (1958), ŻIH Archive, testimony no. 5712
    b. Mieczysław Chodźko (1958), *Biuletyn ŻIH*, no. 27 (fragments)
    c. Mieczysław Chodźko (1958), *Dzieje Najnowsze*, no. 3-4
21. Szmuel Rajzman (after 1961), *Treblinka* (1979)
22. Mendel Rzepka (1987), documentary film "Ocalałe w pamięci" [*That Which Survived in the Memory*], directed by Z. Raplewski

Treblinka: Polish testimonies

23. Maria Krych, ŻIH Archive, testimony no. 6795
24. a. Jerzy Królikowski (1961), ŻIH Archive, memoir no. 224
    b. Jerzy Królikowski (1964), *Biuletyn ŻIH*, no. 49 (abridged version)
25. Janina Dawidek (1967), ŻIH Archive, testimony no. 6333
26. Franciszek Ząbecki, *Wspomnienia dawne i nowe* [*Memories: Old and New*], (1977)
27. Ludwik Kołkowski (1987), tape-recorded conversation, author's personal collection

Sobibór: Jewish testimonies

28. Salomon Podchlebnik (1944), ŻIH Archive 301/10
29. Yechezkiel Menche (1944), *Sobibór* (1980)
30. Hersz Cukerman (1945), ŻIH Archive, testimony no. 1187
31. Josef Frajtag (1945), ŻIH Archive, testimony no. 5375
32. a. Zelda Metz (1945), ŻIII Archive, 458/z
    b. Zelda Metz (1946), *Documents*
    c. Zelda Metz, *Sobibór* (1980)
33. Mosze Morgenstein (1947), ŻIH Archive, testimony no. 2785
34. Tojwie (Tomasz) Blat (1948), ŻIH Archive, testimony no. 4082
35. Mosze Bahir (1950), *Sobibór* (1980)
36. Mosze Hochman, *Sobibór* (1980)
37. a. Tojwie (Tomasz) Blat (1957), ŻIH Archive, memoir no. 190
    b. Tojwie (Tomasz) Blat, *Sobibór* (1980)
38. Michał Knipfmacher, *Sobibór* (1980)
39. Eda Lichtman, *Sobibór* (1980)
40. Joseph Dunictz, *Sobibór* (1980)
41. Abraham Margulien, *Sobibór* (1980)
42. Thomas Kurt, *Sobibór* (1980)
43. Icchak Lichtman, *Sobibór* (1980)
44. a. Aleksander Peczorski, *Biuletyn ŻIH* (1952)
    b. Aleksander Peczorski, *Sobibór* (1980)
45. Lea Reisner, *Sobibór* (1980)
46. Ajzyk Rottenberg, *Sobibór* (1980)
47. Hersz Cukerman, *Sobibór* (1980)
48. Ilona Safran, *Sobibór* (1980)
49. Jakub Biskupowicz, *Sobibór* (1980)
50. Hela Felenbaum, *Sobibór* (1980)
51. Yehuda Lerner, *Sobibór* (1980)
52. Haim Treger, *Sobibór* (1980)
53. Eliahu Lieberman, *Sobibór* (1980)

Sobibór: Polish testimony

54. Tadeusz Jurjewicz (1945), ŻIH Archive, testimony no. 5300

Bełżec: Jewish testimonies (escapees from trains)

55. Adam Landsberg (1945), ŻIH Archive, 301/199
56. Irena Sznycer (1945), ŻIH Archive, testimony no. 4638
57. Giza Petranker, ŻIH Archive, testimony no. 1213
58. Karol Tenenbaum, ŻIH Archive, testimony no. 1127

Bełżec: Polish testimonies

59. Janusz Peter, ŻIH Archive, memoir no. 221
60. Jan Marzec, *Ten jest z ojczyzny mojej* [This One is from my Fatherland] (1969)
61. Franciszek Mielniczek, *Ten jest z ojczyzny mojej* [This One is from my Fatherland] (1969)

Rescue of Jewish Escapees from the Treblinka Death Camp

Mark Paul

In her article, which is translated and published as the previous chapter of this volume,[1] the late Polish historian Teresa Prekerowa arrived at important findings regarding the attitude of the surrounding Christian population toward escapees from the death camps of Treblinka, Sobibór and Bełżec. In particular, her study underscored that, while the attitude of the local population was not uniform, escapees in fact received a great deal of help from Poles. The extent of that help is underreported because most survivors' testimonies do not elaborate on the assistance they undoubtedly received. Prekerowa's findings are particularly important because she is recognized by Yad Vashem as a "Righteous Gentile."

This addendum chapter, which focuses on Treblinka, takes into account a number of additional testimonies, most of which were not mentioned by Prekerowa, but corroborate her findings.

Approximately two hundred Jews escaped from the Treblinka death camp (Treblinka II) during the uprising on 2 August 1943. At least half the Jews who escaped were caught in the German manhunts that ensued. The local population did not join in these manhunts, on the contrary, the farmers living nearby were terrified by what was happening. As one escapee recalled:

> I manage to run a few dozen meters when I see that the murderers are coming after us with machine guns. An automobile is bearing down on us at the same time. On the roof is a machine gun shooting in all directions. Many fall down dead. There are dead bodies at every step. I change direction and run to the left off the road. The car continues along that Polish road and soon it is ahead of me. We run in various directions. The murderers pursue us from all sides.

---

[1] *Biuletyn Głównej Komisji Badania Zbrodni przeciwko Narodowi Polskiemu–Instytutu Pamięci Narodowej*, vol. 35 (Warsaw 1993), 100–14.

I notice that the peasants working the fields and the shepherds are running away out of fear. Finally, having run about 3 kilometers, we find ourselves in a small woodland area. We decide that there is no point in running further and hide in the dense brush. We number some twenty people. The group is too big, and we divide into two groups of ten men each. The groups are separated by about 150 meters.

We lie there for several minutes and suddenly see that Ukrainians with several SS men have surrounded the wood and are entering it. They encounter the second group and all of them are immediately shot. ...

We lie there for a brief time. Fortunately, they did not notice us and left the wood.[2]

Large forces were employed to conduct a thorough search of the entire area; checkpoints were set up on the roads, villages were combed, and villagers' homes searched. The manhunt lasted for weeks. Scores of Jewish fugitives were killed.

Prior to the revolt, individual Jews managed to escape, usually by hiding in freight trains in which prisoners' belongings were shipped out of the camp. The number of Jews who escaped by stealth from the Treblinka death camp and from Treblinka I, a penal (hard labor) camp for Poles and Jews, is not known. Approximately 80 escapees are believed to have survived the war. Unlike Sobibór and Bełżec, the population in the area surrounding Treblinka was ethnically Polish,[3] so the escapees' interaction was mostly with Poles.

It is worth noting that Prekerowa's findings are diametrically opposed to the views expressed by Yad Vashem historian Yitzhak Arad, who arrived at the following assessment based on his own research: (1) "The local population was of no help. Prominent in the testimonies of the survivors is the assertion that the peasants in the region caught the escapees, took their money and then handed them

---

[2] Chil Rajchman, *The Last Jew of Treblinka: A Survivor's Memory, 1942–1943* (New York: Pegasus Books, 2011), 127–28. Also published as *Treblinka: A Survivor's Memory, 1942–1943* (London: MacLehose/Quercos, 2011), 104–5.

[3] The area immediately adjacent to Sobibór was populated by Ukrainians of the Eastern Orthodox faith, who constituted approximately seventy percent of the population. The territory to the west was ethnically Polish, and that is where most of the Polish Jews made their way after escaping from the camp. The area south of Bełżec was populated primarily by Ukrainians of the Greek Catholic faith, whereas in the territory to the north ethnic Poles predominated.

over to the Germans."⁴ (2) "Indeed, more than a few of the escapees met their death in the forests from … rightist and fascist groups of the Polish Underground, or gangs of common criminals and outlaws who operated in those areas."⁵ (3) "On the whole, with some exceptions, the local population did not aid the escapees."⁶ Teresa Prekerowa's findings refute those sweeping charges.

It is apparent, and to be expected, that the local population would not simply open their doors to fugitives who were being pursued by the Germans in concerted manhunts, especially since every form of assistance to a Jew in occupied Poland was punishable by death, usually by summary execution or being burned alive in one's home. Western Europeans, who were affluent by Polish standards, rarely undertook rescue activities even though they risked considerably less by way of possible punishment—perhaps a fine, occasionally a prison term for repeat offenders, but most often nothing. Fear was the paramount factor for not providing assistance to Jews in Poland.

Put another way, people are not prone to engage in potentially suicidal ventures. The accounts that have been gathered establish that:

- farmers in nearby villages provided a great deal of help, mainly in the forms of food and short-term shelter (see Appendix I). Overwhelmingly, Jewish escapees who turned to Poles received some form of assistance—virtually all of it from complete strangers;
- a number of Jews managed to find long-term shelter with local farmers (see Appendix II);
- there is a lack of compelling evidence that villagers killed Jewish escapees; although a small number of villagers did rob Jews on

---

⁴ Yitzhak Arad, "Jewish Prisoner Uprisings in the Treblinka and Sobibor Extermination camps," Proceedings of the Fourth Yad Vashem International Historical Conference, Jerusalem, January 1980.
⁵ Yitzhak Arad, *Belzec, Sobibor, Treblinka: The Operation Reinhard Death Camps* (Bloomington and Indianapolis: Indiana University Press, 1987), 346. In fact, as Arad later acknowledges, the vast majority of the escapees were caught in German manhunts. *Ibid.*, 298. Arad states there: "*Some* were caught and murdered by local peasants, or handed over by them to the Nazis." However, no accounts of murders by peasants are set out or cited.
⁶ Arad, *Belzec, Sobibor, Treblinka*, 347. Arad adds: "Yet it should be noted that those who did succeed in remaining alive until the liberation were in part saved by the aid extended to them by the local population at critical junctures after their escape from the camps." However, he does not go out of his way to document that aid.

occasion,⁷ there is no evidence that Polish partisans in the area killed and robbed Jewish fugitives;⁸
- there is, however, evidence that at least one Soviet group was responsible for robbing, raping, and killing Poles, as well as Jews who escaped from the camp in Treblinka and jumped from trains. Two members of such a group were killed by peasants defending themselves when they invaded cottages in the village of Orzełek, three kilometers from Treblinka;⁹

---

⁷ Tanhum Grinberg states that, as he fled from Treblinka, while the German manhunt was going on, he saw corpses of slain Jews, with their boots removed from their legs. However, this is clearly inconclusive evidence that they were murdered by peasants, as he alleges. See Alexander Donat, *The Death Camp Treblinka: A Documentary* (New York: Holocaust Library, 1979), 222. Escapee Aron Gelberd was apprehended by Ukrainian farmers and robbed. See Arad, *Belzec, Sobibor, Treblinka*, 260. On robberies by villagers of Jews who were shot by the Germans as they jumped from trains near the village of Sadowne, see Adam Starkopf, *Will to Live: One Family's Story of Surviving the Holocaust* (Albany, New York: SUNY Press, 1995), 160. However, other accounts from Sadowne state that Leon Lubkiewicz, a baker who gave a loaf of bread to two Jewish women, was executed together with his wife Maria and son Stefan when the Jewish women were caught with the bread in their hands and indicated the place where they got it. See Maria Pilarska, ed., *Those Who Helped: Polish Rescuers of Jews During the Holocaust*, Part III (Warsaw: The Main Commission for the Investigation of Crimes Against the Polish Nation–The Institute of National Memory and The Polish Society for the Righteous Among the Nations, 1997), 89. Ruth Altbeker Cyprus, who jumped from a train headed for Treblinka, recalled various instances of assistance from railway guards, villagers, passers-by, passengers, and even a gang of robbers who stole from bodies of Jews who were killed as they jumped from trains. See Ruth Altbeker Cyprys, *A Jump for Life: A Jump For Life: A Survivor's Journal from Nazi-Occupied Poland* (New York: Continuum, 1997), 97, 102–10; translated into Polish as *Skok dla życia: Pamiętnik z czasów okupacji Polski* [A School of Life: A Memoir from the Days of Poland's Occupation] (Warszawa: Philip Wilson, 2001).

⁸ Josef Czarny alleges that he escaped execution by the Home Army while hiding in a forest after fleeing from Treblinka, but the circumstances of that occurrence are not known. See Josef C. Holocaust Testimony (HVT-1065), Fortunoff Video Archive for Holocaust Testimonies, Yale University Library. Kalman Taigman alleges that Home Army men shot at him and his friends in a forest, but there are no details of the circumstances of that encounter. See Arad, *Belzec, Sobibor, Treblinka*, 346. A Holocaust Internet website claims that the group of escapees Samuel Rajzman (Reisman) was part of, were all murdered by Polish partisans. See "Treblinka Roll of Remembrance, <http://www.deathcamps.org/treblinka/roll%20of%20remembrance.html>. However, that claim is not borne out by Rajzman's own testimony. In all likelihood, they were killed in the German manhunt, while Razjman and his colleague went for food. See Donat, *The Death Camp Treblinka*, 245–46.

⁹ Institute of National Remembrance archives, GK 318/416, Akta w sprawie karnej Ufnala Seweryna i Leśnika Jana [case aainst Ufnal, Seweryn, and Leśnik, Jan], and GK 318/418, Akta śledcze przeciwko Ufnalowi Sewerynowi [case against Ufnal, Seweryn].

- apprehending Jews and handing them over to the German authorities by the surrounding population—as the population was enjoined to do and offered rewards for doing[10]—was an infrequent occurrence;[11]
- lack of assistance was generally motivated by fear rather than anti-Semitism: some farmers near the camp refused to provide food even for very large sums of money, yet those who did not take on the risk of helping rarely betrayed Jewish fugitives;[12]
- corruption started inside the camp itself, and included dealings between German overseers, Ukrainian guards, and Jews who worked

---

[10] Rajchman, *The Last Jew of Treblinka*, 134, and *Treblinka*, 107.

[11] Oscar Strawczyński, who escaped from Treblinka during the revolt with his brother Zygmunt, experienced a foiled capture attempt by a group of armed Poles. See Israel Cymlich and Oscar Strawczyński, *Escaping Hell in Treblinka* (New York and Jerusalem: Yad Vashem and The Holocaust Survivors' Memoirs Project, 2007), 187. Szymon Goldberg states that, at one point, he was chased by a Polish gamekeeper with a dog who shot in his direction. See his testimony in Arnon Rubin, *The Rise and Fall of Jewish Communities in Poland and Their Relics Today*, vol. 2: *District Lublin* (Tel-Aviv: A. Rubin, 2006), 381. As a Czech escapee from Treblinka notes, the bandit gangs that roamed around robbing and posing as partisans had "nothing in common with partisans than the name." See Richard Glazer, *Trap With a Green Fence: Survival in Treblinka* (Evanston, Illinois: Northwestern University Press, 1995), 105.

[12] Chil Rajchman, who received help from several Polish farmers, recalled: "It often happens that when we knock at the gates of a peasant house, they refuse to open or to answer questions. ... By day we are afraid to show ourselves since everyone we meet tells us that there are round-ups going on." See Rajchman, *The Last Jew of Treblinka*, 134, and *Treblinka*, 107. Abraham Krzepicki offered large sums of money to peasants who declined to help out of fear, but no one betrayed him. Some peasants did provide assistance for payment, but others refused to accept payment or took very little. One peasant who provided temporary shelter stated that, if he were not afraid of the Germans, he would help free of charge. On one occasion, a peasant took money but did not provide help as promised; on another occasion, Krzepicki's travelling companion, Anshel Mędrzycki, was allegedly robbed. He then conned other Jewish escapees to give him money to make up for his loss, even though he had some money hidden away. Krzepicki described him as "an exploiter, a creature without a moral sense ... from the Warsaw underworld ... he tried to take advantage of me as much as he could." Krzepicki reserved his highest praise for an older peasant women who lived in a village near Ostrówek: "This was the first time since my escape from Treblinka that anyone, Jew or Gentile, helped me get to safety without trying to extort money from me." The woman's relatives in Warsaw were equally helpful when Krzepicki arrived there with his travelling companion. See Donat, *The Death Camp Treblinka*, 134–35, 137–44. According to Eddie (Idl) Weinstein, the fear factor also figured prominently in the amount of money sought by some rescuers, as compensation for the real risk of death for those caught assisting Jews; however, many people were unwilling to take the risk for any sum. See Eddie Weinstein, *17 Days in Treblinka: Daring to Resist, and Refusing to Die* (Jerusalem: Yad Vashem, 2008), 94–95, 98, 100–2, 104–7, 109, 118.

gathering valuables and extracting gold teeth from prisoners,[13] and moved outside the camp where Ukrainian guards disbursed large

---

[13] See, for example, Cymlich and Strawczyński, *Escaping Hell in Treblinka,* 38, 131–32, 152–57. The so-called "Gold Jews" (*Goldjuden*), who received and sorted money, gold, valuables, foreign currency, and bonds taken from Jews upon arrival at the camp and in the undressing area, were considered "extremely privileged, because they could secretly siphon off money and valuables of considerable worth … the SS personnel needed them to secure their share of the wealth that passed through the camp." See Arad, *Belzec, Sobibor, Treblinka,* 108. There are also plentiful accounts of wrongdoings by Jews against fellow prisoners. A group of 60 young Jews were brought from Stoczek to serve as auxiliaries in policing the camp. Armed with sticks, they shoved, jostled, and struck the prisoners. They also seized money and other valuables from new arrivals. See Daniel Blatman, *En direct du ghetto: La presse clandestine juive dans le ghetto de Varsovie (1940–1943)* [Directly from the Ghetto : The Clandestine Jewish Press in the Warsaw Ghetto 1940-1943] (Paris: Cerf; Jerusalem: Yad Vashem, 2007), 477, 479–80. For accounts that detail brutality by Jewish kapos and denunciations of Jewish inmates see: Jankiel Wiernik, *A Year in Treblinka: An Inmate Who Escaped Tells the Day-to-Day Facts of One Year of His Torturous Experience* (New York: American Representation of the General Jewish Workers' Union of Poland, 1944), 17–18; Willenberg, *Surviving Treblinka,* 120–21; Edi Weinstein, *Quenched Steel: The Story of an Escape from Treblinka* (Jerusalem: Yad Vashem, 2002), 59–60; Marta Markowska, ed., *Archiwum Ringelbluma: Dzień po dniu Zagłady* [The Ringelbrum Archive: The Holocaust Day-By-Day] (Warsaw: Ośrodek Karta, Dom Spotkań z Historią, and Żydowski Instytut Historyczny, 2008), 189; testimony of Szymon Goldberg in Rubin, *The Rise and Fall of Jewish Communities in Poland and Their Relics Today,* vol. 2: 380–81; account of Izrael Bramson, Jewish Historical Institute (Warsaw) archive, record group 301, testimony 106; account of Szymon Grynszpan, Jewish Historical Institute (Warsaw) archive, record group 301, testimony 1185. According to one report, Jewish order police from Treblinka were also utilized in manhunts carried out by the Germans to capture Jewish escapees and punish Poles who assisted them. See Mariusz Bechta, *Między Bolszewią a Niemcami: Konspiracja polityczna i wojskowa Polskiego Obozu Narodowego na Podlasiu w latach 1939–1952* [Between the Bolsheviks and the Germans: The Political and Military Underground of the Polish National Camp in Podlasie in 1939-1952] (Warsaw: Instytut Pamięci Narodowej and Rytm, 2008), 414. When wagons of Jewish shoes arrived from Treblinka at the Jewish work camp in Skarżysko-Kamienna, the Jewish commander, Mordechai, would order the shoemakers to take the shoes apart looking for hidden wealth. See David Mittelberg, *Between Two Worlds: The Testimony & the Testament* (Jerusalem and New York: Devora, 2004), 60–61. The postwar Stalinist regime proved to be rather selective in prosecuting collaborators, even those who sent Jews to their deaths in Treblinka. Jerzy Lewiński, a notorious Jewish policeman who rounded up Jews in the Warsaw ghetto and brought them to Umschlagplatz from whence they were dispatched to Treblinka, joined the Communist party and became a prosecutor in Łódź, passing sentences on "collaborators" and enemies of the regime. Despite pressure and threats by co-religionists not to testify against him, Edward Reicher and the renowned pianist Władysław Szpilman refused to succumb. Although he lost his position, Lewiński never faced criminal charges and became the director of the state movie production enterprise, "Film Polski." See

quantities of money and valuables to acquire food and services in nearby villages;
- Jewish escapees often took with them large quantities of valuables and money,[14] and this temptation caused some villagers,[15] as well as Jews in ghettos that the fugitives reached,[16] to steal from or gouge them. Sometimes escapees were met with disbelief and hostility upon returning to their hometowns;[17]

Edward Reicher, *Une vie de Juif* [The Life of a Jew] (Paris and Montréal: L'Harmattan, 1996), 272.

[14] See, for example, Weinstein, *17 Days in Treblinka,* 61 ("several belts filled with gold coins ... taken from corpses"), 69 ("a wad of banknotes, a diamond ring and additional valuables"), 95 ("my share came to 140 gold dollars and 220 gold rubles"), 163; Donat, *The Death Camp Treblinka,* 248 (Samuel Rajzman); A.L. Bombe, "My Escape from Treblinka," in *Czentochov: A New Supplement to the Book "Czenstochover Yidn"* ("a substantial sack with money"), www.jewishgen.org/yizkor/Czestochowa/Czestochowa.html, translation of S.D. Singer, ed., *Tshenstokhover: Naye tsugob-material tsum bukh "Tshenstokhover Yidn"* (New York: United Relief Committee in New York, 1958), 5 ff; Rajchman, *The Last Jew of Treblinka,* 124, and *Treblinka,* 100 ("We, the dentists, have the task of gathering as much gold as possible to take along with us.").

[15] One escapee remarked about a rescuer who turned against the escapee's colleague, after being entrusted with the task of converting their gold coins into Polish currency: "In ordinary times, Zabiniak was an honest man. But when he found that he could gain easy riches, even at the cost of someone else's life, his honesty evaporated. The Germans managed to evoke this kind of anti-social behavior from people who had been perfectly decent in normal circumstances." See Weinstein, *17 Days in Treblinka,* 120–21.

[16] On robbery, gouging and extortion by fellow Jews, see Weinstein, *17 Days in Treblinka,* 72, 75, 92–93. Although Weinstein and his colleagues tried to keep their escape from Treblinka a secret, someone in the Łosice ghetto informed the police they had escaped from Treblinka and were in possession of gold. Abraham Krzepicki reported that, when he arrived in the town of Stoczek (Węgrowski) after his escape from Treblinka, "Life here was normal; there were Jews doing business." Jews in the ghetto demanded "plenty of money" for room and board. "The Jewish population there actually did want to become acquainted with escapees from Treblinka, because they knew that Treblinka people had a lot of money, and so they could charge them prices ten times what they charged normally. ... The population tried to milk Treblinka for all its worth and some brisk trading was done. They bought everything from the Treblinka people: gold and securities." Krzepicki was also robbed in Stoczek, but does not say whether it was by Jews or Poles. See Donat, *The Death Camp Treblinka,* 135–37.

[17] Upon returning to Kielce, Moyshe Mydlo and Yosele Vaser were not only disbelieved, but the head of the Jewish police also had them expelled from the ghetto for spreading panic among the Jews. See Trunk, *Jewish Responses to Nazi Persecution,* 123. No one in Radom believed escapee Nathan Berkowitz's story about the destination of the deportation trains: "I gave a detailed report to the head of the Jewish Council, but he called me a liar and chased me out of his office." See Alfred Lipson, ed., *The Book of Radom: The Story of a Jewish Community in Poland Destroyed by the* Nazis (New York: The United Radomer Relief of the United States and Canada, 1963), 57. Another

- farmers living in nearby villages were profoundly traumatized by their experiences, which included being subjected for long periods to an unbearable stench, audible crying and screaming of prisoners, and being forced to loan their farm carts to transport bones and ashes, and even to disperse human remains themselves;[18]
- the vast majority of farmers lived in extreme poverty, with little or nothing to spare for others, and those in the immediate vicinity of the camp were saddled with the additional burden of requisitions of produce and livestock in order to feed the German overseers, Ukrainian guards and hundreds of Jewish inmates who performed various labor functions without which the camp could not operate;[19]

---

survivor recalled: "Max Rosenblum was in Treblinka. He was deported from my hometown of Kozienice to Treblinka with all the people. He sneaked into Pionki camp where I was, because he had a sister who was there. He told everybody that in Treblinka, everybody was killed, and we didn't believe him. All the people who the Germans took to Treblinka: gassed them. And we called him crazy: 'He's crazy, he must be crazy. Why would they kill everybody, women and children, for nothing?' And he was telling us, 'Believe it! I saw it. They killed everybody—nobody's alive!'" See the interview with David Bayer, First Person, 2009, United States Holocaust Memorial Museum, Washington, D.C.

[18] The people living in the small hamlet of Wólka-Okrąglik, the village closest to Treblinka, related that sometimes the screams of the women being murdered were so horrible that the entire village would be driven out of its mind and run off into the forest, so as not to hear the piercing shrieks. This was repeated three or four times a day. Franciszek Ząbecki, traffic supervisor at the Treblinka railway station, stated: "The population was horrified—not only because of what they saw; they were paralyzed with fear and horror, and then quite soon they became physically ill from the terrible smell that began to emanate from the camp." Some villagers became "pathologically indifferent." It is not surprising therefore that some also succumbed to corruption. The Polish underground punished a farmer who forced his teenage daughter to sleep with a Ukrainian guard, shaved the head of a young woman who came to work as a prostitute, and executed another such woman. About a dozen women who came to do dealings with Ukrainian guards were brought into the camp, whipped and then sent to the nearby hard labor camp. See Gitta Sereny, *Into That Darkness: From Mercy Killing to Mass Murder* (London: Deutsch, 1974), 154–55, 156, 194; Ilya Ehrenburg and Vasily Grossman, *The Complete Black Book of Russian Jewry* (New Brunswick, New Jersey and London: Transaction Publishers, 2002), 474, 479; oral history interview with Isadore Helfing, 9 March 1992, United States Holocaust Memorial Museum, Washington, D.C. There were also Jewish women prisoners in Treblinka who "went to parties, got drunk, and enjoyed themselves to the utmost." Supposedly, they slept around with Jewish kapos as well as Ukrainian guards and German SS, and never suffered physical punishment. See Cymlich and Strawczyński, *Escaping Hell in Treblinka*, 154.

[19] Arad, *Belzec, Sobibor, Treblinka*, 108–13. There was also a Jewish orchestra in the camp that greeted Jews as they arrived, and boxing matches organized for the entertainment of the guards.

- Jewish prisoners who extracted gold teeth and sorted clothing secretly buried large quantities of gold and valuables inside the camp,[20] and it was this buried treasure that was sought by scavengers after the camp was leveled to the ground,[21] rather than the occasional gold tooth that was overlooked by Jewish dentists who worked under very stringent supervision;[22]
- overall, the help provided to Jews is underreported by survivors, many of whom did not leave accounts of how they were able to survive, yet likely did so with at least some Polish assistance. This assistance has not been adequately recognized by Yad Vashem and in Holocaust scholarship;
- conversely, acts of violence are over-reported, as many accounts refer to unverified or untrue events. As noted by Teresa Prekerowa, some of these dubious claims were withdrawn in subsequent testimonies.

---

[20] Oral history interview with Abraham Kolski, 29 March 1990, United States Holocaust Memorial Museum, Washington, D.C.; Mark S. Smith, *Treblinka Survivor: The Life and Death of Hershl Sperling* (Stroud, United Kingdom: The History Press, 2010), 251.

[21] After the war, when some local people started to dig up the site of the camp looking for gold and other valuables, anti-Nazi and anti-Communist units deriving from the disbanded Home Army and National Armed Forces punished those who engaged in such conduct. See Wacław Piekarski, *Obwód Armii Krajowej Sokołów Podlaski "Sęp", "Proso" 1939–1944* [The Home Army District in Sokołów Podlaski: "Sęp" and "Proso"] (Warsaw: n.p., 1991); Mariusz Bechta and Leszek Żebrowski, eds., *Narodowe Siły Zbrojne na Podlasiu* [The National Armed Forces in Podlasie], vol. 2: *W walce z systemem komunistycznym w latach 1944–1952* [Fighting Against the Communist System in 1944-1952] (Siedlce: Związek Żołnierzy Narodowych Sił Zbrojnych, 1998), 201; Kazimierz Krajewski and Tomasz Łabuszewski, *"Łupaszka" "Młot" "Huzar": Działalność 5 i 6 Brygady Wileńskiej AK (1944–1952)* ["Łupaszka," "Młot," and "Huzar": The Actions of the 5th and 6th Brigades of the Wilno AK, 1944-1952] (Warsaw: Volumen, 2002), 255; Kazimierz Krajewski, "Wykreowana historia" [Created History], *Nasz Dziennik*, 5–6 March 2011. Soviet troops stationed in nearby towns played a leading role in these sordid activities and even forced villagers to plant explosives, landmines and bombs that were then detonated to gouge large holes in the surface. Unearthed Jewish corpses were then robbed of any valuables. This was done without interference from the local Communist security officials, who also likely benefitted from the gravedigging. The number of Jews among the security officials in the county seat in Siedlce, as well as among Soviet soldiers, was significant. See Michał Majewski and Paweł Reszka, "Tajemnica zdjęcia z Treblinki" [The Mystery of the Photograph from Treblinka], *Uważam Rze*, 28 February 2011; Kazimierz Krajewski, "Kto profanował groby ofiar Treblinki" [Who Defiled the Graves of Treblinka Victims], *Nasz Dziennik*, 16 March 2011.

[22] Rajchman, *The Last Jew of Treblinka*, 68–69, and *Treblinka*, 60.

Appendix I - Assistance Provided by the Local Population to Jewish Escapees from Treblinka

The following examples do not include many of the cases mentioned by Teresa Prekerowa.

Polish farmers helped Samuel Willenberg on no less than nine separate occasions in the first days after his escape from Treblinka.[23]

Abraham Bomba, Yankel Eyzner (Jacob Eisner), Moshe Rapaport (Rappaport), Yechiel Berkovitsh (Berkowicz), and Yechezkal Kofman (Cooperman) were assisted by several farmers after their escape from Treblinka:

> Laying in the field, we saw a peasant in a wagon go by. We called him over and told him that we had escaped from Treblinka and, perhaps, it would be possible if he could take us into his barn. ... In the end, we convinced him and he showed us his barn in the distance and we went inside. But he doesn't know of anything. And if they would ask, we should say that we sneaked in. That is what we did. We were there the entire day.
>
> At night, the head of the village came and told us that he would lead us out of the village and show us the way to go. He indeed took us to the main road, and we traveled all night until the morning. In the morning, we came to a village. We saw, in front of a house, that a woman opens the door. We went over to the house and the woman told us to come in. We were there for a week. The second week, we were at the friend of the peasant in the same village. I remember this peasant's name: Piotr Supel. ... This was in the village Zagradniki [Zagrodniki] near Ostrovek Vengravski [Ostrówek Węgrowski]. The peasant traveled with us to Warsaw.

The author does not elaborate on the significance of the last point, and the risk involved in escorting a group of Jews to Warsaw: the farmer had to buy train tickets, scout the train station and train, and do most of the talking. Some of the Jews probably had a "poor" appearance and a Jewish accent, making them readily recognizable as Jews.[24]

After their escape from Treblinka, David Lieberman and his friend ran all night until they stopped in a field where they encountered a woman who recognized them as escapees and warned them to go

---

[23] Samuel Willenberg, *Surviving Treblinka* (Oxford: Basil Blackwell in association with the Institute for Polish-Jewish Studies, 1989), 143–48.

[24] See Bombe, "My Escape from Treblinka," *Yidn*, 57ff. See also Arad, *Belzec, Sobibor, Treblinka*, 260.

farther away because the Germans were making their rounds to requisition milk and eggs from the farmers. They walked farther and arrived at a farmhouse:

> the woman was very nice to me. She came out and walked with me and my friend almost for an hour, showed us to go to another road. Closed road where the police is not there. She was very nice. She came with a little baby on her back and walked and then she left us … she took her cross out and made a prayer, God should be with you. And we went on our way.

They walked another mile or two and entered another farmhouse:

> We told the farmer we want to go to a railroad station. He says he's going to take us, but he's not going to walk with us … [but] a distance away. And he opened a barn. He says, 'In case the SS comes, you just walked in yourself. I had nothing to do [with it].' So he walked with us. … And we followed him. Finally, he came to a small little village. The village name was Sadowne.

The fugitives then gave the villager some money with which to purchase train tickets, which he did, and they boarded the train for Warsaw. They also received help from farmers in the vicinity of Częstochowa, their hometown.[25]

Another escapee, Mieczysław Grajewski (Martin Gray), recalled the help he received from farmers:

> I was free. I walked to a village. … I knocked to ask for bread. The peasants looked at me in silence. 'Bread, bread.' They saw my red hands, torn jacket, worn-out slippers, and handed me some hard, gray crusts. A peasant woman, huddled in shawls, gave me a bowl of hot milk and a bag. We didn't talk: my body had turned red and blue from the blows and the cold, and my clothes, everything proclaimed *Jew!* But they gave me bread. Thank you, Polish peasants. I slept in a stable near the animals, taking a little warm milk from the cow in the morning. My bag filled with bread.[26]

After his escape from Treblinka, Chil Rajchman was assisted by several farmers in the vicinity of the camp before making his way back to Warsaw, where he received help from Poles in and near the city. He recalled in an interview:

---

[25] Oral history interview with David Lieberman, 10 July 1990, United States Holocaust Memorial Museum, Washington, D.C.
[26] Martin Gray, with Max Gallo, *For Those I Loved* (Boston and Toronto: Little, Brown, 1972), 178.

The peasant opens the gate but will not let us in. He tells us that the Germans in automobiles and on bicycles have been looking for us all day long. ... The peasant gives us a loaf of bread and some milk, asking for gold in exchange. We give him two watches. ... I decide to leave for Warsaw by myself. ...

After walking several kilometers I come to a village. It is evening. I enter a peasant's house. He is afraid to talk to me. He hands me a piece of bread and tells me that Warsaw is 99 kilometers away. As I stand there, I suddenly hear the sound of shooting in the distance. The peasant runs back into the house and shout[s] to me to run away at once. ... After walking a few kilometers, I see a man [Franek or Franciszek] approaching me. ... I see from his clothes that he is a peasant and ask him the way. He thinks about it for a little while then asks me – Are you one of those who fled Treblinka?

Seeing that he feels compassion for me, I tell him that I am indeed one of those who fled and ask him for help. ... he turns back with me towards his house, some 2 kilometers away. He leads and I follow. When I enter his house I see a woman with a child in her arms. ... She gives me food, and, seeing that I am soaked through, she gives me a shirt of her husband's to put on. She mentions that it is her husband's last shirt. ... After spending half an hour with them, I thank them warmly and want to say goodbye. The peasant points through the window to a [little frequented] barn standing in the middle of the fields not far from us. The barn belongs to a rich peasant and no one ever goes there. He advises me to hide there and come to him in the evenings, when he will give me food.

During Rajchman's two-week stay in the barn, his benefactors provided him with food. They also foiled an attempt by a neighbor who wanted to apprehend Rajchman and turn him in. Despite imploring him to remain, Rajchman decided to leave them and return to Warsaw. Poles he met on the road gave him directions to the train station, and on the train he pretended to accompany a woman he happened to meet.

I am able to get to Warsaw without incident, and thence to Piastów, where my friend Jarosz, a Pole, resides. At first he does not recognize me and tries to give me 5 zlotys [złoty]. Then, when he realizes who I am, he is happy to see me and helps me with necessities. He also provides Aryan papers for me.[27]

---

[27] Rajchman, *The Last Jew of Treblinka*, 133–38, and *Treblinka*, 106–11. In a 1988 interview, Rajchman provided additional details of his interaction with villagers near Treblinka and the assistance he received from many Poles in and near Warsaw: "After a few days with the group, I decided to part. I was with a friend of mine. ... we decided during the night to go to a farm, to a peasant and ask for food. Some decent people

Sixteen-year-old Hershl Sperling was part of a group of three or four Jews who succeeded in getting about twelve kilometers away from the camp. In a statement penned shortly after the war Sperling wrote:

> Being the best Polish speaker, I creep into the nearby village to get something to eat. Slowly, hesitatingly, indecisively, with a pounding heart, I come out of the wood and approach a peasant house standing on its own. ...
>
> Raising my eyes to heaven and praying, I step onto the threshold of the house. One glance at the woman tells me that she realizes what I am. 'You must have escaped from Treblinka,' she exclaims. The state I am in, my clothes, and above all the expression of desperation on my face have all given me away. I am prepared for the worst. But the woman reassures me, saying that I mustn't be afraid, that she will help me as much as she can.
>
> She can't hide me, however. The SS are snooping around and searching all the villages in the area. She is not prepared to expose herself and all her family to mortal danger. She gives me bread and milk and tells me to come back at eleven o'clock. At the appointed hour, all three of us are in her house. This time her husband and daughter are also there. We discuss the situation and decide that the best thing would be to go to a particular place and jump onto the roof of the moving train. At that particular point the train moves with a speed of ten kilometers per hour at most. We have no other way out and we agree to try this. They give us a substantial supper and bread and eggs for our journey. As an expression of our gratitude we leave them twenty gold dollars.

Afraid of a mishap they decide not to jump onto the roof of a moving train and go instead by foot to Rembertów, where they buy tickets and board a train for Warsaw. They manage to get to their destination safely despite their appearances.[28]

Another escapee from Treblinka who managed to return to Warsaw recalled:

---

helped us. Some not ... I parted with my friends. ... I rambled toward a farm house and started talking to peasants. At that moment, we heard shots and shouting. The peasant crossed himself and started to shake. 'Please,' he urged, 'run away! If they will find you with me, I will be killed.' He was afraid that maybe someone noticed me. I hastened back to the potato field, hiding. At dawn, I returned to the peasant, asking him directions to Warsaw to a side road. ... He gave me some food and told me where to go." See the oral history interview with Chiel Rajchman, 7 December 1988, United States Holocaust Memorial Museum, Washington, D.C.

[28] Smith, *Treblinka Survivor*, 251–52.

The peasants near Treblinka didn't want to shelter me even for just one night. They happily gave me food and even money, but they wouldn't hear of my spending the night, because the Ukrainians who were permanently stationed in Treblinka often showed up ... The local peasants told of things that were unbelievable but unfortunately true. ... Everyone I talked to near Treblinka spoke of nothing else. They all told the same thing, in horror. The ones closer to Warsaw let me stay the night, but there was no question of staying there permanently.[29]

After their escape, Samuel (Shmuel) Rajzman (Reisman) and his friend Arie Kudlik approached a peasant's cottage several kilometers from the camp, in the middle of the German manhunt. Understandably, the woman asked them to leave because the Germans were looking everywhere, and if they found the fugitives they would shoot her too. They implored her for some bread and a pitcher of water, which she gave them and said, "Please bring the pitcher back because it's the only one I have." This woman provided them with more food and temporary shelter, before the two fugitives went on their way.

In Brzozów, they received food and temporary shelter from Rajzman's father's friend, Paweł Pieniak and his son. They then went to a village near Węgrów, where Edward Gołoś, another friend of Rajzman's father and member of a "rightist-nationalist organization," agreed to help them live in the forest and, in the winter, hid them in his barn. Their rescuer and his family shared their meager fare with their charges without expecting anything in return, until the arrival of the Red Army in August 1944.[30]

In another account, Razjman (Reisman) states:

After 6 hours of running I found myself with my colleague 12 km from Treblinka. Lying in the forest Celanowo [Ceranów], we heard shots around. We hid ourselves in the potato field. In the night we reached a house in the village of Celanowa [sic], where a woman gave us food. She did not want to take money. She did not let us inside her house, but advised us to hide in the potato field because the Germans and the Ukrainians surrounded the village and the whole forest.[31]

---

[29] Michał Grynberg, ed., *Words To Outlive Us: Voices From the Warsaw Ghetto* (New York: Metropolitan Books/Henry Holt, 2002), 210.
[30] Alexander Donat, *The Death Camp Treblinka: A Documentary* (New York: Holocaust Library, 1979), 245–49; Israel Gutman and Sara Bender, eds., *The Encyclopedia of the Righteous Among the Nations: Rescuers of Jews during the Holocaust* (Jerusalem: Yad Vashem, 2004), vol. 4: *Poland*, Part 1, 245.
[31] Testimony of Samuel Rajzman (Reisman) in Rubin *The Rise and Fall of Jewish Communities in Poland and Their Relics Today,* vol. II, 385.

After a run-in with a gang which wanted to turn him in, easily recognizable as an escaped prisoner, Oscar Strawczyński wandered around for several days seeking directions from Poles he met, yet was not betrayed. He made his way to the village of Jasiorówka near Łochów, where he was taken in by a Polish woman, Stanisława Roguszewska, who was assisting and feeding a group of Jews hiding in the forest. Strawczyński hid with the Roguszewski family for several weeks until he recovered and afterwards joined the Jews in the forest. Yad Vashem has recognized several members of the Roguszewski family for their efforts: Stanisława Roguszewska-Najman, her husband Marian Roguszewski, and her parents-in-law, Bolesław and Stanisława Roguszewski. They also rescued the sisters Ida and Chana Dzierzbowicz.[32]

The following cases are noted by historian Yitzhak Arad:[33] Abraham Goldfarb was informed on and suffered an attempted robbery at the hands of some farmers, but also received assistance from others who fed him and gave him clothes; Jerzy Rajgrodzki and his seven companions received food from farmers; Yechiel Reichman, part of a large group of twenty fugitives, received food from a farmer in exchange for payment. Binyomin Rokh (Rafał Kirszenbojm) escaped from Treblinka by hiding in a railroad car, from which he jumped near Małkinia wearing only his underwear. For about a month he hid out in different Polish villages where he turned to elderly Poles for assistance. He made his way back to his hometown of Siemiatycze where he and five other Jews hid in a bunker under a farmer's barn.[34]

Richard Glazer, a native of Czechoslovakia, passed through quite a few localities after his escape, and when he was finally caught, it was not by a Pole but by a Volksdeutsche.[35] Viliam Fried, a native of Czechoslovakia, and some others broke out of a train as it was pulling into Treblinka. Together with a Polish Jew, he ran and took shelter in a stable where they were discovered by the proprietor's son, who fed them and allowed them to stay for a day.

---

[32] Cymlich and Strawczyński, *Escaping Hell in Treblinka*, 187–88; Gutman and Bender, *The Encyclopedia of the Righteous Among the Nations*, vol. 5 (*Poland*, Part 2), 672.
[33] Arad, *Belzec, Sobibor, Treblinka*, 345–46, 296, 297, respectively.
[34] Isaiah Trunk, *Jewish Responses to Nazi Persecution: Collective and Individual Behavior in Extremis* (New York: Stein and Day, 1979), 100; testimony of Rafał Kirszenbojm, April 1945, Jewish Historical Institute (Warsaw) archive, record group 301, testimony 107.
[35] Richard Glazer, *Trap With a Green Fence: Survival in Treblinka* (Evanston, Illinois: Northwestern University Press, 1995), 149–53.

They were then directed to a person in the next village, a railroad worker who was in the underground and helped escapees. (This is significant because it confirms the claim of Franciszek Ząbecki that railway workers were involved in organized assistance for Jews, which some historians have doubted.) Fried went alone and was allowed to stay in this man's stable and received food. When he left he was given a shovel to allow him to pass as a worker. He went from village to village until he arrived in Międzyrzec Podlaski. Along the way, a village woman, who gave him food, warned him of the presence of German gendarmes who were looking for escapees, and pointed him in a different direction.[36]

After escaping from a train near Treblinka, a wounded David Wolf and his companion hid in forests. At night they knocked on the doors of peasants to ask for food: some helped, others turned them away. Fifteen days later he reached a village near his hometown of Wysokie Litewskie, where he was taken in by a Polish family which sheltered him for 23 months.[37]

Hersh Blutman from Ciechanowiec jumped from a train only three kilometers away from Treblinka. Bruised and limping, he returned to his hometown, asking local farmers from whom his father used to buy produce, for help. Although they all fed him and allowed him to rest, no one was willing to put him up. After many days of wandering, Blutman reached the village of Winna-Chroły where he was taken in by Helena and Aleksander Komiążyk. They invited him into their home and offered to hide him on their farm. The Komiążyks were already hiding Laib Slowczyk and his two brothers, Josef and David. A fortnight later, Komiążyk came to the refugees one evening and told them, with a catch in his throat, that the authorities had been informed that he was hiding Jews on his farm. The four Jewish refugees escaped, just in time. Soon after, the Germans raided their farm, brutally interrogated the Komiążyks, and burned down the barn where the refugees had been hiding.[38]

---

[36] Oral history interview with Viliam Fried, 10 April 1992, United States Holocaust Memorial Museum, Washington, D.C.

[37] David Wolf, "Two Letters from the Other World," in *Entertainment and Ball Given by the United Wisoko-Litowsker and Woltchiner Relief,* Internet: <http://www.jewishgen.org/yizkor/Vysokoye/Vysokoye.html>, translation of Samuel Levine and Morris Gevirtz, eds., *Yisker zhurnal gevidmet diumgekumene fun Visoka un Voltshin* (New York: United Wisoko-Litowsker and Woltchiner Relief, 1948), 22–23.

[38] Gutman and Bender, *The Encyclopedia of the Righteous Among the Nations,* vol. 4 (*Poland,* Part 1), 366–67.

Idl (Eddie) Weinstein escaped from Treblinka together with Michael Fischmann and Gedalia Rosenzweig, secreted in a railway car loaded with bundles of victims' belongings. They received help from several farmers on their way to Mokobody, were robbed once, but were not betrayed.[39] Weinstein mentions a Jew who jumped from a Treblinka-bound train who was helped by some peasants, and turned away by others, yet not betrayed. A woman and her 15-year-old niece, who had escaped from a train en route to Treblinka, were sheltered by a villager until the Soviet entry. (Many more such accounts exist by Jews who escaped from Treblinka-bound trains at some distance from the camp, but are not mentioned here.)

Israel (Srul) Cymlich, who had five gold rubles and some Polish currency when he escaped from the Treblinka hard labor camp, bought some food in two villages, but was told in another village store that there was nothing for sale. A farmer did likewise, explaining that he didn't even have enough food for his own family. Cymlich got rides and directions from farmers a number of times, but is vague on how he managed to feed himself on his way back to Warsaw. He survived the war in Falenica, near Warsaw, with the assistance of Zygmunt and Janina Kobos, who have been recognized as Righteous Gentiles by Yad Vashem.[40]

Henryk Poswolski, who was injured while escaping during the revolt in Treblinka and made his way back to Warsaw, doubtless with the assistance of Poles, was sheltered by Feliks and Marta Widy-Wirski in Podkowa Leśna and nursed back to health. The Widy-Wirskis were recognized by Yad Vashem.[41]

After escaping from Treblinka, Chaim Gradel made his way back to his native town of Bełżyce. He found his brother-in-law and the two of them were sheltered by a farmer, Zygmunt Chlebicki, in the village of Ratoszyn. Afterwards Gradel joined up with a partisan group before returning to the ghetto in Bełżyce, from where he was taken to a series of German camps. He survived the war.[42]

---

[39] Eddie Weinstein, *17 Days in Treblinka: Daring to Resist, and Refusing to Die* (Jerusalem: Yad Vashem, 2008), 69–72, 113, 143.
[40] Cymlich and Strawczyński, *Escaping Hell in Treblinka*, 53–56, 66.
[41] Gutman and Bender, *The Encyclopedia of the Righteous Among the Nations*, vol. 5 (*Poland,* Part 2), 836.
[42] Barbara Engelking, *Jest taki piękny słoneczny dzień...: Losy Żydów szukających ratunku na wsi polskiej 1942–1945* [It is Such a Beautiful Sunny Day ...: The Fate of Jews Seeking Help in the Polish Countryside 1942-1945] (Warsaw: Stowarzyszenie Centrum Badań nad Zagładą Żydów, 2011), 225.

Historian Philip Friedman writes: "A number of priests in the neighborhood of the death camp at Treblinka gave food and shelter to Jews escaping from transports on the way to the camp."[43] A Jew from Warsaw, cut and bruised after jumping from a train in which he had escaped from Treblinka, dragged himself to a church, where a priest gave him clothes and money for a train to Warsaw.[44]

Helping Jews was not without its attendant risks. A warning from a Catholic railway worker about the true nature of Treblinka resulted in his immediate execution when, mistrusting the "anti-Semitic" Pole, the Jew complained to a German guard. A Catholic railroad employee, Jan Maletko, was shot to death by a German guard while bringing water to Jews locked in a boxcar. His companion, Remigiusz Pawłowicz, who also came to the aid of Jews, was saved by falling into a ditch.[45]

Prison guards caught a young Polish woman, around twenty years of age, who was trying to pass some food to the starving inmates through the electric fence surrounding the death camp. Brought inside the camp, she was executed in front of the prisoners.[46]

A farmer, Jan Samsel, who resided in the nearby village of Grądy, was commissioned by the Polish Home Army to deliver arms to the Jewish inmates through a friendly Ukrainian guard. The Germans, however, found out about the plan and arrested the entire Samsel family. All of them perished in the death camp.[47]

On 24 February 1943, two Jews, possibly *agents provocateurs*—one a refugee from Warsaw, the other a local Jew named Szymel (Szmulek) Helman—arrived in Paulinów near Sterdyń, not far from Treblinka, accompanied by a large punitive SS detachment and German gendarmerie to identify Poles who had helped them and other Jews

---

[43] Philip Friedman, *Their Brothers' Keepers* (New York: Holocaust Library, 1978), 126.

[44] Henryk Grynberg, *Drohobycz, Drohobycz and Other Stories: True Tales from the Holocaust and Life After* (New York: Penguin Books, 2002), 151–52.

[45] Franciszek Ząbecki, *Wspomnienia dawne i nowe* [Old and New Reminiscences] (Warsaw: Pax, 1977), 44–46.

[46] Stanisław Wroński and Maria Zwolakowa, *Polacy Żydzi 1939–1945* [Poles and Jews 1939-1945] (Warsaw: Książka i Wiedza, 1971), 439; testimony of Szymon Goldberg, in Rubin, *The Rise and Fall of Jewish Communities in Poland and Their Relics Today*, 2:381.

[47] Stanisława Lewandowska, *Ruch oporu na Podlasiu, 1939–1945* [The Resistance Movement in Podlasie, 1939-1945], Second revised and expanded edition (Warsaw: Wydawnictwo Ministerstwa Obrony Narodowej, 1982), 251.

hiding in the area. A dozen Poles who were identified by these informers perished in the ensuing pacification.[48]

---

[48] Wacław Piekarski, *Obwód Armii Krajowej Sokołów Podlaski "Sęp", "Proso" 1939–1944* [The Home Army District in Sokołów Podlaski: "Sęp" and "Proso" 1939-1944] (Warsaw: n.p., 1991), 25–27; Wojciech Gozdawa-Gołębiowski, "Powiat węgrowski w latach okupacji niemieckiej 1939–1944" [Węgrów County During the German Occupation 1939-1944], in Arkadiusz Kołodziejczyk and Tadeusz Swat, eds., *Węgrów: Dzieje miasta i okolic w latach 1941–1944* [Węgrów: The History of the Town and its Vicinity in 1941-1944] (Węgrów: Towarzystwo Miłośników Ziemi Węgrowskiej, 1991), 357–58; Wojciech Jerzy Muszyński, *W walce o Wielką Polskę: Propaganda zaplecza politycznego Narodowych Sił Zbrojnych (1939–1945)* [Fighting for a Greater Poland: The Propaganda of the Political Base of the National Armed Forces, 1939-1945] (Biała Podlaska: Rekonkwista, and Warsaw: Rachocki i S-ka, 2000), 294–95; Andrzej Krzysztof Kunert, ed., *Polacy–Żydzi, Polen–Juden, Poles–Jews, 1939–1945: Wybór Źródeł, Quellenauswahl, Selection of Documents* (Warsaw: Rada Ochrony Pamięci Walk i Męczeństwa, Instytut Dziedzictwa Narodowego, and Rytm, 2001), 267–68; Joanna Kierylak, "12 sprawiedliwych z Paulinowa" [Twelve Righteous Gentiles from Paulinów], 10 February 2009, Internet: <http://www.muzeum-treblinka.pl/index.php?option=com_content&task=view&id=76&Itemid=69>.

Appendix II – Jewish Escapees from Treblinka Sheltered by the Local Population

The following examples do not include many of the cases mentioned by Teresa Prekerowa.

Isadore (Izak) Helfing and another escapee were taken in by a farmer near Treblinka. They remained with the farmer until shortly before the arrival of the Soviet army. See the oral history interview with Isadore Helfing, 9 March 1992, United States Holocaust Memorial Museum, Washington, D.C. In an earlier interview, Helfing mentioned other assistance received by the larger group with whom he escaped from the camp during the uprising.[49]

Abraham (Abram) Kolski was part of a group of prisoners who escaped during the uprising in Treblinka. All nine fugitives, among them Gustaw Boraks, Heniek Klein, Henoch Brener (Henry Brenner), Stasiek Kohen, Albert Kohen, and Erich (Shaya) Lachman, were hidden for the remainder of the war on a farm in Orzeszówka, a village south of the camp, belonging to Julian Pogorzelski and his elderly father Julian Pogorzelski.

Throughout the entire period the Pogorzelskis provided the fugitives with all their needs, cared for their health, and obtained medicine for them when they fell ill. (Heniek Klein had tuberculosis and passed away in the hiding place.)

When the fugitives emerged from hiding as the Soviet front passed through, their presence became known to the neighbors but no one betrayed them when the Germans returned for a brief period of time. The Pogorzelskis were recognized by Yad Vashem in 1969.[50]

After wandering in forests for about a month, following his escape during the uprising, Josef Czarny was warmly received by Szymon Celka, a farmer near the town of Parysów, who together with his wife, Helena, helped to care for Czarny and a group of Jews hiding in the forest. These Jews were also being cared for by Irena Jankiewicz (later Landau).[51]

---

[49] Isadore H. Holocaust Testimony (HVT-413), Fortunoff Video Archive for Holocaust Testimonies, Yale University Library.

[50] Oral history interview with Abraham Kolski, 29 March 1990, United States Holocaust Memorial Museum, Washington, D.C; testimony of Abram Kolski, USC Shoah Foundation Institute (Interview Code 49970); testimony of Gustaw Boraks, Yad Vashem Archives; Gutman and Bender, *The Encyclopedia of the Righteous Among the Nations*, vol. 5 (*Poland*, Part 2), 625–26.

[51] Mordecai Paldiel, *The Path of the Righteous: Gentile rescuers of Jews During the Holocaust* (Hoboken, New Jersey: KTAV, 1993), 205; "The Funerals of Heroic

Julian and Stanisława Serafinowicz were awarded by Yad Vashem for sheltering Shlomo (Szloma) Helman and Yeshayahu (Szyja) Warszawski, who escaped during the uprising in Treblinka, on their farm in the village of Mostówka, near Wyszków.[52]

Yosef Haezrahi-Bürger, one of the "operatives" of Jewish organizations who, after the war, tracked down Jewish children sheltered by Christian Poles described the fate of two Jewish teenagers who managed to escape from a train on its arrival in Treblinka and were sheltered in a village near the camp:

> in one of the transports, two siblings—a boy and a girl—were among the Jews in the wagons that reached the Treblinka village railroad station before they could be moved to the extermination camp.
>
> While they were waiting, the people in the wagon broke through the wooden floor and several escaped. The guards chased and fired at them but the two children managed to reach a house in the village and hide there, terrifying the owner, whose own children were playing in the yard. When she saw the guards pursuing them, the woman directed the guards to her own house.
>
> The guards shot the woman's children, assuming that they were the fugitive Jewish youngsters who were hiding in the house. The terrified woman regained her composure quickly and decided that if this was her fate, she had no choice but to raise the Jewish youngsters.
>
> The operative did not find the source of the information about these children after the war but was told that emissaries had been sent to remove them several times, failing each time. In 1947, when he was asked to deal with their removal, the children were sixteen and seventeen years old. They knew they were Jewish but refused to leave their 'mother,' as they called their rescuer, since she had lost her own children and had saved them. The mother left the decision up to them: both persisted in their refusal and remained in the village.[53]

Rescuers," 14 April 2010, Atzum–Justice Works, Internet: <http://atzum.org/category/news/>.

[52] Gutman and Bender, *The Encyclopedia of the Righteous Among the Nations*, vol. 5 (*Poland*, Part 2), 703.

[53] Emunah Nachmany Gafny, *Dividing Hearts: The Removal of Jewish Children from Gentile Families in Poland in the Immediate Post-Holocaust Years* (Jerusalem: Yad Vashem, 2009), 202–3, 281.

The Tale of Two Hamlets:
The Cases of Wólka-Okrąglik and Gniewczyna in Nazi-Occupied Poland

Paweł Styrna

A predictable continuity characterizes the works of Jan Tomasz Gross, through his recent *Golden Harvest*, co-authored with Irena Grudzińska-Gross.[1] That continuity is a collective accusation levied against the Poles, in general, and Polish peasants in particular, who, it is alleged, willingly, enthusiastically, and unscrupulously colluded with the Germans in robbing, persecuting, and exterminating the Jews.

Poles, as described by the Grosses, appear as particularly ruthless, merciless, and sadistic brutes utilizing any and every opportunity to appropriate Jewish wealth. Moreover, the expropriated Jews were humiliated and tortured while their (Polish) oppressors took pleasure in not only on depriving their victims of their property but also their very lives.

In fact, the Grosses compare the Poles as a race of people with the Hutu *genocidaires* murdering the Tutsi in Rwanda, and racist lynch mobs in the American South. In addition, they portray practically the entire nation as grave robbers (so-called cemetery hyenas) shamelessly digging up remains of *Shoah* victims – in search for valuables omitted by the Nazis – in the vicinities of death camps. Thus, the Poles not only assisted the Germans in robbing, rounding up, and murdering the Jews. They were also incapable of demonstrating even a modicum of respect for their remains.

---

[1] Jan Tomasz Gross and Irena Grudzińska-Gross, *Golden Harvest*, advance author's copy, electronic version in Polish, January 2011 [henceforward cited as *Golden Harvest*]. To quote the authors: "a social practice, rather than the criminal excesses of the dregs of society." In this chapter, we translate the book's direct quotes from Polish into English; they may be at variance with the English version published in 2012 by Oxford.

According to the Grosses, such outrageous acts were not pathologies typical of the dregs of society. Rather, they were socially condoned practices. The perpetrators included not only so-called rabble, but also representatives of the middle classes and even the elites. In turn, according to the Gross view, the Catholic Church in Poland not only remained indifferent *vis-à-vis* the Holocaust, but churchmen also expressed joy at its effect – as did the entire Polish nation. The main factors fueling such attitudes and actions were hatred of the Jews combined with greed for Jewish wealth. The spoliation of the exterminated Jews amounted to a veritable "golden harvest" for the Polish masses. The Holocaust, according to the Gross logic, thus produced a grand redistribution of Jewish wealth, of which the Polish middle class was a significant beneficiary. In *Golden Harvest* Poland and the Poles are, therefore, presented in the most negative and damaging light possible. The Gross portrayal almost makes one wonder why the Nazis found the need to import Germans and their Baltic, Ukrainian and Belarusian auxiliaries to Poland to carry out the extermination of the Jews.

Yet, the conclusions at which the Grosses have arrived are quite problematic. The events depicted in *Golden Harvest* have been extracted entirely from a very complex historical context. Historian Andrzej Żbikowski, a scholar quite sympathetic to the authors and associated with the Warsaw-based Jewish Historical Institute (Żydowski Instytut Historyczny), agrees with such an assessment:

> Perhaps I wouldn't label it an accusation on my part, but rather an initial reservation against situating the story in our modern-day, contemporary moral context. Of course, he has a right to do so. In fact, it is a way to move the readers and force them to reflect on certain issues. However, a historian is not allowed to do this. A historian must reconstruct the past within its historical context.[2]

Much like Gross's previous works – *Neighbors* and *Fear* – his newest publication is stripped bare of nuances. The authors' approach

---

[2] Wiesław Władyka, "Złote żniwa – ile faktów, ile interpretacji. To jest polska luka. Rozmowa z prof. Andrzejem Żbikowskim o książce Jana T. Grossa 'Złote żniwa', o białych plamach w okupacyjnej historii Polaków i Żydów, o bohaterstwie i zbrodniach czasu Holocaustu," ["The Golden Harvest: How Many Facts, How Much Interpretation? It is a Polish Gap. An Interview with Prof. Andrzej Żbikowski on Jan T. Gross's 'Golden Harvest,' on Gaps in the Occupation-Time History of the Poles and Jews, and Heroism and Atrocities during the Holocaust"] *Polityka*, 29 January 2011, http://www.polityka.pl/historia/1512268,1,zlote-zniwa---ile-faktow-ile-interpretacji.read [henceforward cited as "Interview with A. Żbikowski"].

is reductionist. The methodology employed is inductive, i.e. grounded upon "thick description," and maximizing conclusions based on a tiny handful of examples. After all, the Grosses argue, there is a dearth of research on the Holocaust in Poland. The evidence base is thus necessarily limited. In response, it may be worthwhile to ask whether a comprehensive microstudy of a village in occupied Poland would not contribute to our knowledge of the Holocaust to a much greater degree than a book based mainly on the interpretation of a smattering of tendentiously selected secondary sources?[3]

In addition, the authors display a lack of criticism toward the small amount of sources they chose to utilize. This is especially true in relation to the testimonies of Holocaust survivors. The Grosses cite only sources that appear to corroborate their argument. Simultaneously, they ignore completely any evidence that may question or debunk their conclusions. This is a very serious accusation, since a professional historian is obligated to cite and address the arguments of scholars expressing alternative points of view as well. Quoting only those with whom one agrees is not a tool from the workshop of a professional historian, but a weapon from the arsenal of a professional propagandist.

Furthermore, the Grosses' portrayal of events in war-torn Poland is rigidly static. The authors fail to take into account the dynamic and rapidly changing context of the Second World War. As a result, they ignore the plague of ordinary and revolutionary banditry effecting both Jews and Christians;[4] the cruel and bloody reality of the Nazi and Communist occupations; mass murder perpetrated by Germans, Soviets, and Ukrainian fascists (associated with the OUN-UPA, the Organization of Ukrainian Nationalists – Ukrainian Insurgent Army); intensive economic exploitation; and numerous other factors.[5] A reader unfamiliar with Poland's Second World War history will not find mentions of the deaths of 2-3,000,000 Polish Christians during the war,

---

[3] For a useful model see the groundbreaking microstudy of the Janów Lubelski county by Marek Jan Chodakiewicz, *Between Nazis and Soviets: Occupation Politics in Poland, 1939-1947* (Lanham, MD: Lexington Books, 2004).

[4] For a succinct sociological explanation of the phenomenon of wartime looting see Bethany Paluk, "Looting as a Case Against Racial Determinism," below.

[5] See Richard C. Lukas, *The Forgotten Holocaust: The Poles Under the German Occupation, 1939-1944* (Lexington, KY: University of Kentucky Press, 1986). Lucas explains: "Thus the conclusion is inescapable that had the war continued, Poles would have been ultimately obliterated either by outright slaughter in gas chambers, as most Jews had perished, or by a continuation of the policies the Nazis had inaugurated in occupied Poland during the war – genocide by execution, forced labor, starvation, reduction of biological propagation, and Germanization." *Ibid.*, 5.

or the circumstances in which Poles lived and died, in *Golden Harvest*. This constitutes a major shortcoming.

Holocaust historian Żbikowski assessed the driving thesis of the Grosses' work with caution and reservation: "Gross puts forward – and this includes public appearances – several unpleasant and even accusatory theses, and offers a few generalizations, which arouse vehement objections. For me, someone who has, after all, dealt with the subject for many years, they [Gross's theories] are excessively categorical. The conclusion that hunting down and robbing Jews was a socially-accepted practice in rural Poland appears to me, at this juncture, as cognitively unsupportable."[6] Thus, it would be much more appropriate to label *Golden Harvest* as a work of historically based punditry, rather than historical scholarship.

Many other charges have been levied against the Grosses' recent publication.[7] However, rather than repeating the comments of other reviewers, we will focus on the events in two villages mentioned in the book – Wólka-Okrąglik and Gniewczyna – thereby situating them in the proper historical context.

Wólka-Okrąglik was a small village of approximately 200 inhabitants situated closest to the death camp in Treblinka, to the northeast of Warsaw.[8] The hamlet lacked both a church and a school. The local children were thus compelled to undertake a six-kilometer journey to Kosów, where the closest educational institution was located.[9]

The Grosses portray the denizens of Wólka as particularly depraved individuals. The local women, they allege, collectively engaged in prostitution with Ukrainian SS men, while their relatives collaborated with the camp's personnel. The authors rely on the testimony of an Endek landowner, Józef Górski, according to whom:

> The peasants from this village sent their wives and daughters to the Ukrainian guards employed at the camp and could not control their rage when these women failed to bring back a sufficient amount of rings and

---

[6] Interview with A. Żbikowski
[7] For criticism in Polish see Piotr Gontarczyk, „Jak złapią za rękę ..." ["If They Catch You by the Hand ..."], *Rzeczpospolita*, 19-20 February 2011; in English see Marek Jan Chodakiewicz, "Reflections: A New Work, but the Same Old Method," available above and at www.heartsofgoldpl.com.
[8] Vasilii Grossman, Ilia Ehrenburg, *The Complete Black Book of Russian Jewry* (New Brunswick, London: Transaction Publishers, 2002), 474 [henceforward cited as Grossman].
[9] Gitta Sereny, *Into That Darkness: From Mercy Killing to Mass Murder* (London: Deutsch, 1974), 150 [henceforward cited as Sereny].

other formerly Jewish valuables gained as payment for personal services. These dealings brought tremendous material benefits, of course.[10]

The Treblinka area c. 1936

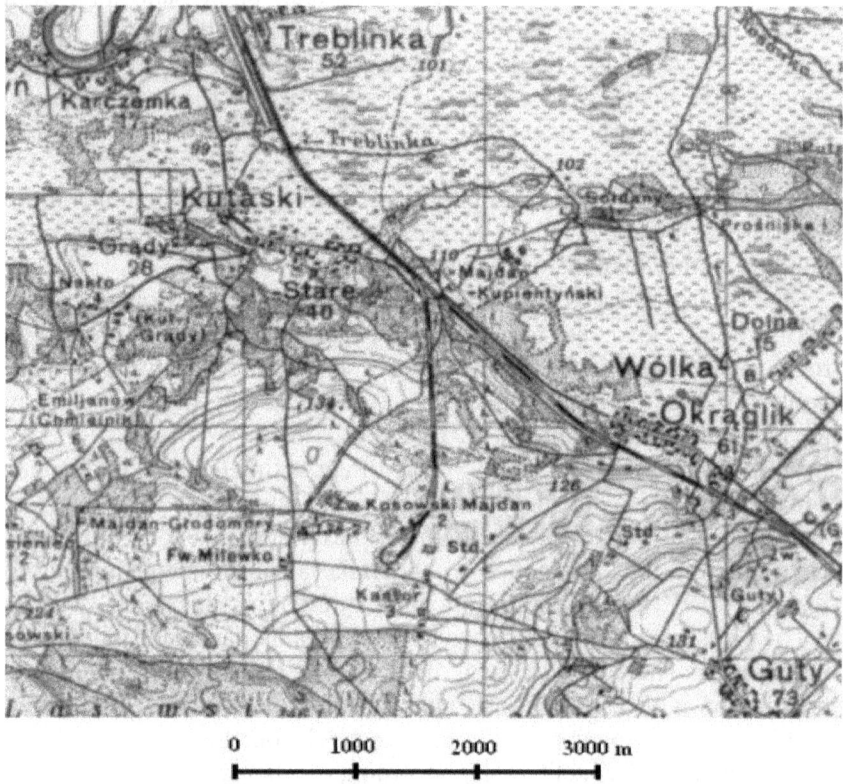

The Grosses also utilize the testimony of engineer Józef Królikowski, who described peasant traders – both male and female – earning windfall profits while gouging exhausted, hungry, and thirsty Jews stuffed into freight cars on Treblinka-bound death transports. Ethnic auxiliaries and/or Polish "navy blue" policemen were bribed with bootlegged vodka or sensuous kisses (and, one may surmise, also with sexual favors). After having thus gained access to the trains, water was sold to the Jews, who were practically dying of thirst, for the mind-boggling sum of 100 złotys. Instances also occurred when no water was given in return for payment received.[11] Thanks to the Holocaust the

---

[10] Józef Górski, op. cit. in *Golden Harvest*, 26.
[11] *Golden Harvest*, 26-28.

local villages therefore became the beneficiaries of a major financial injection. According to the Grosses:

> The peasant men and women in the Treblinka area are not only diggers, busy combing the grounds upon which the camp had been located for gold. They are experienced female traders, the parents of the [camp] guards' girlfriends, housewives cooking wholesome dinners for them [the guards], [and] farmers selling Jewish watches and rings. Most likely, they have already built or remodeled their homes, but the cemetery grounds continue to tempt them. At that point, during the time of the transports [of Jews to the death camp], they transformed themselves from farmers to merchants of death, and they are no longer capable of freeing themselves from this practice.[12]

Is the portrait painted by the authors even remotely complete? Moreover, may it be considered as a norm representative of the occupied Polish lands during the Holocaust? The available evidence calls for a much more nuanced assessment of events, both in Wólka-Okrąglik, in particular, and in Poland, in general.

To begin with, let us ask ourselves how ordinary people would react to the presence of a death factory in their very neighborhood. It is true that war demoralizes, depraves, and numbs the human spirit. At the same time, terrifying atrocities also produce other reflexes and reactions. For example, a Soviet writer of Jewish descent noted that the peasants of Wólka were traumatized victims of the war, who "relate that sometimes the screams of the women being murdered were so horrible that the entire village would be driven out of its mind and run off into the forest, so as not to hear the piercing shrieks that penetrated through the trees, through heaven and earth."[13] In addition, the local peasantry was forced to render free services on behalf of the death camp erected and operated by the German occupiers.[14]

Yet heroism, gentleness and generosity can also emerge from horror. Pity often translated into assistance – usually passive, often active. The testimony of Franciszek Ząbecki, rated highly by historian Gitta Sereny, provides a large amount of valuable information on this

---

[12] *Ibid.*, 29.
[13] Grossman, 474.
[14] See the testimony of Isadore Helfing, United States Holocaust Memorial Museum, RG-50.042*0014, 9 March 1992. Helfing, a Jewish inmate at Treblinka, related that the Germans ordered the local peasants to deliver a horse and cart to the camp's gate on a daily basis. The Jews were then forced to load corpses on the buggy, or simply dragged them on the ground to the burial sites.

subject. He was the stationmaster and railroad traffic supervisor in Treblinka.

In fact, Ząbecki was inserted into this important position as a "mole" by the independentist, anti-Nazi, anti-Communist underground. His objective was to procure and pass on intelligence regarding the movement of German troops and equipment.[15] Ząbecki corroborates that the Germans issued a declaration to the locals, passing a death sentence on anyone assisting Jews, a local reiteration of a general law in force throughout the entirety of occupied Poland. In spite of the lethal danger, quite a few inhabitants of the adjacent countryside helped to hide Jews, transport them under the cover of darkness, or to point escapees in a safer direction. According to Ząbecki, this occurred in the nearby hamlets of Grady, Maliszewa, and Kielczew.[16] Are there grounds to assume that Wólka-Okrąglik was a negative exception? The Grosses certainly do not provide any convincing evidence to prove this.

Moreover, Ząbecki also paints an entirely different image of the peasants approaching the death trains:

'When people realized that not only adults but babies were being killed,' Pan Zabecki said, 'they felt pity. It manifested itself first by their bringing water to the trains. ... At first the train supervisors allowed this. But after a few days it was stopped. But even then, people continued to bring water, until the Germans began to shoot to keep them away from the trains.'

The population was horrified – not only because of what they saw; they were paralyzed with fear and horror, and then quite soon they became physically ill from the horrible smell that began to emanate from the camp. But then too, you see, everybody became terrified for themselves; they were *seeing* all this and one became more and more convinced that anyone who witnessed these unspeakable horrors would have to be eliminated too.[17]

The proximity of the death camp also exerted a negative impact on the health and psyche of Ząbecki's wife:

There was a period – in the beginning – when my wife could no longer function at all; she could no longer do anything around the house; she couldn't cook, she couldn't play with the boy, she couldn't eat and hardly sleep. She had a sort of complete nervous breakdown. When I was a POW

---

[15] Sereny, 149.
[16] Franciszek Ząbecki, *Wspomnienia dawne i nowe* [Old and New Reminiscences] (Warsaw: PAX, 1977); see also
http://www.holocaustresearchproject.org/revolt/zabecki.html.
[17] Sereny, 154.

she had managed, but now she broke down completely. This extreme condition she was in lasted for about three weeks, then she became pathologically indifferent; she did her work, moved, ate, slept, talked – but all of it like an automaton.[18]

The above is a credible depiction of the development of a coping mechanism by a witness of horror. On the subject of prostitution, in turn, Ząbecki also helps fill in the gaps:

[T]he Ukrainians began to have a great deal of money. And they wanted more and more women. One farmer forced his twelve-year-old daughter to sleep with Ukrainians. The Conspiracy [Resistance] learned of this and a group went one night and beat him up. Then there was the case of two Polish girls who came from somewhere, got a room and 'received' Ukrainians; the Conspiracy shaved the head of one of them and executed the other.[19]

Moreover, a "dozen" women approached the camp to presumably offer their "services" to the Ukrainian guards. However, they were brought into the camp, whipped, and dispatched to the nearby forced labor camp.[20] Unfortunately, we are not told if these women arrived separately, or as a group. Nor are we informed whence they came. Nevertheless, the episode indicates that the Nazis frowned upon such "relationships" between the local women and their ethnic auxiliaries. Omitting such a detail created the impression of German approval of these practices.[21]

The train station supervisor's testimony indicates that a phenomenon of mass prostitution among the allegedly depraved local women was

---

[18] *Ibid.*, 155.
[19] *Ibid.*, 156.
[20] *Ibid.*, 154-155, 156, 194; Ilya Ehrenburg and Vasilii Grossman, *The Complete Black Book of Russian Jewry* (New Brunswick, New Jersey and London: Transaction Publishers, 2002), 474, 479; oral history interview with Isadore Helfing, 9 March 1992, United States Holocaust Memorial Museum, Washington, D.C.
[21] In this context, we might also recall the phenomenon of prostitution among Jewish female prisoners in the camps. Some Jewish female inmates in Treblinka "went to parties, got drunk, and enjoyed themselves to the utmost." Allegedly, they serviced Jewish kapos, Ukrainian guards, and even German SS men. In this case, no physical punishment was forthcoming. From an ethical viewpoint, it is admittedly difficult to equate prostitution among rural women who were relatively free, and the doomed and imprisoned women in the concentration camps. The options for survival available to the latter were certainly more limited. Yet, this example further demonstrates that wartime demoralization was by no means limited to ethnic Poles. See Israel Cymlich and Oskar Strawczyński, *Escaping Hell in Treblinka* (Jerusalem: Yad Vashem, Holocaust Martyrs' and Heroes' Authority, 2007), 154.

hardly a common practice. Undoubtedly, pathological cases occurred and stories about them circulated widely.

Individuals such as Józef Górski subsequently proceeded to record these second-hand tales. Thus, Ząbecki's testimony appears to confirm the fact that such pathologies took place in Wólka-Okrąglik. Simultaneously, it calls for a major revision of the simplistic and unidimensional description of the events in Wólka (and other neighboring villages) offered in *Golden Harvest*. The data compiled diligently by the Canadian historian Mark Paul, and based mainly on Jewish testimonies, also further supplement the facts omitted by the authors.[22] For instance, Paul mentions the nearby locality of Paulinów, where the Germans murdered a family of fifteen peasants – including women and children – for sheltering Jews in February 1943. These Righteous Gentiles were not denounced by other villagers, who not only knew about the Jews, but also assisted in various ways. Instead, a Jewish escapee serving as a German agent turned in the Polish family. One may search in vain for similar information, which alters completely the depiction of Wólka-Okrąglik and adjacent hamlets, in the *Golden Harvest*.

The authors also treat very superficially the phenomenon of the so-called diggers (*kopacze*), in whose case it remains unclear whether they resided in Wólka, or any other local village. Individuals engaged in this practice had succumbed to the beastialization accompanying any major war, and particularly one as brutal, total, and bloody as the Second World War.

As Vasilii Grossman's and Franciszek Ząbecki's testimonies confirm, occupation-era terror, omnipresent death, and an unfathomable stench inevitably impacted the collective psyche of the local population. Of course, from the point of view of ethics nothing is capable of justifying such actions. Nevertheless, from the perspective of psychology, it allows us to comprehend the pathology that so shocks the authors. Accordingly, it is important to remember that searching for "treasure" – even in graves (only to mention the pyramids) – is a very human trait indeed, crossing nearly all of human existence and culture.

The Grosses appear convinced that the Polish-speaking "cemetery hyenas" digging up the remains of *Shoah* victims were propelled not only by greed, but also (if not primarily) anti-Semitism. In other words,

---

[22] Some of these are available in English on www.heartsofgoldpl.com, in addition to the website of the journal *Glaukopis* (www.glaukopis.pl) or the site of the Canadian Polish Congress at www.kpk-toronto.org/fundusz_obrony.html. Polish translations are accessible via *Glaukopis*.

the Polish anti-Semitic diggers desecrated the remains of Treblinka victims precisely because they were Jewish remains. Yet, this is a very odd claim. The "hyenas" would have undoubtedly excavated the burial grounds regardless of the ethnicity of the corpses they contained.

In passing, the authors happen to mention that, following the area's "liberation" by the Soviets, Red Army soldiers also joined the ranks of the diggers.[23] As we know, Stalin's army was a multi-ethnic force consisting of all the nationalities inhabiting one giant concentration camp. Unfortunately, the Grosses fail to derive any conclusions from this fact. Their implicit thesis that "treasure"-hunting constituted a unique specialty of greedy and anti-Semitic Polish-speaking peasants is further refuted by the phenomenon of Jewish "hyenas," including the so-called Pinkert group (*Pinkertowcy*). These Warsaw ghetto grave diggers were known to exhume freshly-buried corpses in search of gold teeth and other valuables. They cooperated with the Jewish ghetto police and some even collaborated with the Nazis.[24]

Their fate was described by the Jewish resistance fighter and left-wing Zionist, Yitzhak Zuckerman (Icchak Cukierman) *nom de guerre* "Antek." It is important to reconstruct it precisely on account of the abominable practices in which they engaged. After the crushing of the Warsaw Ghetto Uprising by the Germans, the *Pinkertowcy* escaped into the forests near the small Mazovian town of Wyszków to the northeast of the Polish capital. They were well armed. As a result of grave robbery, they also possessed the necessary means to survive in the countryside. Yet, they chose to terrorize and rob the local population. This aroused the anger of not only the Polish peasants, but also the opprobrium of Zuckerman's outfit, the Jewish Combat Organization (*Żydowska Organizacja Bojowa*).

The *Pinkertowcy* were needlessly antagonizing the locals, whose nerves were already strained by the German occupation. Thus, it was decided to liquidate this group. Soon thereafter, the Pinkert gang was exterminated in a joint action by the Jewish Combat Organization and the Communist People's Guard (*Gwardia Ludowa*, the underground resistance tentacle of the Soviet *agentura* in occupied Poland).[25] Thus, their punishment at the hands of the Jewish and Communist

---

[23] *Golden Harvest*, 17.
[24] Charles G. Roland, *Courage Under Siege: Starvation, Disease, and Death in the Warsaw Ghetto* (New York and Oxford: Oxford University Press, 1992), 17.
[25] Yitzhak Zuckerman, *A Surplus of Memory: Chronicle of the Warsaw Ghetto Uprising* (Berkeley, California: University of California Press, 1993), 397-402, 477-478.

underground did not differ from penalties meted out by the Polish independentist resistance to the local village dregs in Wólka-Okrąglik.

The above information is also missing from the Grosses' new book. Interestingly, Gross cited Zuckerman's memoirs to support his own arguments in his previous book, *Fear*.[26] Why is the data on cemetery "hyenas" significant? It allows us to not only reconstruct the historical and social context, but also to prove, beyond any doubt, that the atrocious phenomenon possessed a universal dimension; it was not limited to ethnic Poles, as the Grosses imply.

In an equally selective manner the Grosses approached the sources describing the events in Gniewczyna. This small village, located between the towns of Jarosław and Przeworsk (the western fringes of former Lwów Province), was selected by the authors to serve as another symbolic example of bestial Polish anti-Semitism. According to the testimony of Tadeusz Markiel (published in 2008 by the liberal Catholic monthly *Znak*), in May of 1942 a gang of local peasants tortured and raped a group of eighteen Jews, including women and children. The following day the perpetrators invited the German gendarmes who executed the victims. Hitherto, the sole source of information on the atrocity in Gniewczyna was the testimony provided by Markiel, then a twelve-year-old.[27] He describes the criminals in the following terms:

---

[26] Jan Tomasz Gross, *Fear: Anti-Semitism in Poland After Auschwitz, An Essay in Historical Interpretation* (New York: Random House, 2006), 102.

[27] See "W Gniewczynie 68 lat temu Polacy torturowali, gwałcili, a w końcu wydali Żydów Niemcom," ["Sixty-eight Years Ago in Gniewczyna Poles Tortured, Raped, and Eventually Handed Over Jews to the Germans"] *Gazeta Wyborcza*, 12 January 2010, www.wiadomosci.gazeta.pl/Wiadomosci/1,80708,8750352,W_Gniewczynie_68_lat_te mu_Polacy_torturowali__gwalcili_.html. The Warsaw-based liberal left daily *Gazeta Wyborcza* portrays Markiel as a "graduate of the Military Technical Academy, engineer, and retired lieutenant colonel of the Polish Army." In addition to Markiel's military career in the service of the Communist regime in Poland, it is also worthwhile to note Markiel's hostility to the Church (he blames Catholicism for the crime and anti-Semitism), as well as to pre-war Poland and the broadly conceived elites prior to Communist rule. The newspaper fails to provide any further details regarding his service in the Polish "People's" Army. Nor are we told of any other potential functions Markiel may have discharged within the structures of the Communist state's military-security complex. A sociologist might also note his hatred towards the community from which he was extracted as a result of Communist "upward mobility." In this case, the effect produced a radical break with the officer's peasant roots, including religion and tradition. Are Markiel's stories about his former neighbors, admittedly grim and horrific – albeit unverified by any research – guided by any personal motives? On the ideological plane (given the author's anti-clericalism and negative attitude toward the pre-war elite), his testimony resembles a propaganda lecture generated by the Communist Main Political Board of the Polish People's Army.

The local – let us call them a collection of the village 'elite' – namely: the head of the Volunteer Fire Brigade (on the basis of a pre-war social mandate), the brigade's activists and simultaneously the Trinczers' closest neighbors, the village administrators and their helpers, known as lackeys [*pachołki*] (on the basis of the occupation mandate) from both parts of the village – Łańcucka and Tryniecka – along with the nonideological [*bezideowe*] wing of the resistance movement […].

The locals, a collection of the village 'elite,' which we would today call the mafia, was recruited from the rural middle class of the time. They represented the administrative power and exercised physical power, including illegal firearms. Their functions overlapped. They had great opportunities to benefit from corruption (including the setting of food quotas for individual farms as well as the drafting of lists for forced labor in Germany) and an insatiable desire for revelry [*niepohamowana ochota na pohulanie*].

The most active, demoralized, and cruel of them all was the head of the local Volunteer Fire Brigade composed of about a dozen or so. He also participated in the pogrom of ten Jewish families in the nearby village of Jagiełła.[28]

As in the case of Wólka-Okrąglik, the Grosses fail to emphasize the context of the events. Instead, they merely satisfy themselves with the demonstration that Polish neighbors (once again) killed their Jewish neighbors. Yet, Markiel's testimony contains additional information enabling us to question not only the details of his interpretation of the above-mentioned events but also his opinions regarding the "Polishness" of the peasantry. After all, in the case of Gniewczyna, this "Polishness" was to constitute a reflection of the national norm. The "statistical" Pole in the Grosses' work is a primitive, greedy, Catholic conservative ultra-nationalist burning with a genocidal hatred for the Jews. In other words, he is a Catholic Endek who considers the spoliation and murder of his Jewish fellow man as a religious and patriotic duty! Can this stereotype be reconciled with the situation in Gniewczyna?

According to Markiel, the village's pre-war denizens suffered intense poverty and failed to identify with Poland:

The shortage of land, and the accompanying poverty, heavy toil, cramped space, and the lack of hope for a better tomorrow caused most people to feel wronged and disinherited by destiny, and thus [to feel] angry and search for

---

[28] Markiel, *ibid.*

scapegoats for their hard lives. Lacking in opportunities to develop themselves, they did not have a sense of patriotism [*nie mieli poczucia patriotyzmu*] because they did not have a reason to feel proud of belonging to free Poland. Their Fatherland was, like during the partition era, the Polish language [*polszczyzna*] and their patrimony, if they were lucky enough to inherit it.[29]

The above passage indicates that quite a few ethnically Polish peasants from the Gniewczyna area did not identify as "Poles." The missing "sense of patriotism" points to a lack of national consciousness. The identity of the Gniewczyna peasants was therefore a local one. In this context, "patrimony" signified the farm or, at most, the village, while the "Polish language" amounted to the continued opportunity to communicate in the local *patois* [*"po swojsku,"* i.e. in "our own speech"], as opposed to a foreign tongue like German or Russian. Moreover, the perception of "the Other" was not strictly reserved for the Jews. "The townspeople, officials, policemen, railroad workers, teachers [the broadly-conceived elites, i.e. the "Poles"] were gazed upon with hatred and resentment."[30] To what degree then were the Polish-speaking peasants, who robbed and sometimes killed Jews, Poles?

Marek Jan Chodakiewicz reached the conclusion that only the Second World War, and the concomitant struggle against both occupying powers, accelerated rapidly the process of "nationalizing" the hitherto mainly indifferent and passive popular masses.[31] Detailed statistics requiring tedious research are, as of yet, unavailable.

On the basis of Tadeusz Markiel's testimony, we do however know that not all of Gniewczyna's residents – regardless of their ethnicity – behaved savagely during the war. After all "there were at most ten perpetrators from both parts of Gniewczyna."[32]

The majority of the hamlet's population probably chose neither the path of collaboration or resistance, but meekly accommodated the occupiers in the hope of surviving the war. "The good people in the village were not well organized, did not invest any energy into

---

[29] *Ibid.* During the Second Polish Republic the illiteracy level in Gniewczyna was slashed significantly. As the negatively predisposed towards pre-war Poland author admits in passing: "Only twenty years before (i.e. following the regaining of Polish independence) were children and youths obligated to attend school. Among their grandparents' generation only very few could read or write, [and] among their parents' generation – half [were literate]."
[30] *Ibid.*
[31] See Chodakiewicz, *Between Nazis and Soviets*, p. 137 n. 3.
[32] Testimony of Tadeusz Markiel. See footnote no. 27.

communal matters, [and] only voiced their opinions behind closed doors. They were fed up with their own problems with feeding the children, diseases, the lack of clothing, fuel, and light."[33] Furthermore: "No one in the village dared to 'take on' these gangsters out of the fear of having their [forced food] quota raised, deportation, or death."[34]

Thus, the vast majority was terrorized by the dregs of the local society in the service of the German occupiers. We may surmise that Markiel's family found itself among this silent majority. Otherwise, the author would have certainly boasted of his family's accomplishments in the ranks of the organized resistance movement.

The depiction of rural life under the occupation also differs completely from the Gross portrayal. To begin with, the picture emerging from Markiel's testimony is far more complex and multi-layered. Gniewczyna could also boast of courageous villagers who sheltered Jews: "[Jews] Hid among trusted people [*zaufani ludzie*] in sub-hamlets on the peripheries of the village, such as Poręby and Zawisłocze. Those without children slept in the cowsheds of the trusted people in the village itself."[35] Thus, Gniewczyna was not solely a nest of anti-Jewish tormentors. In addition to the frightened majority, preoccupied with its own daily problems, there also existed "trusted people" attempting to aid the Jews in their hour of need.

Furthermore, as Markiel's reminiscences confirm, the perpetrators of the anti-Jewish atrocity in Gniewczyna represented the fringes of the local community. After all, they constituted a "mafia." They were "gangsters" beholden to an "insatiable desire for revelry" and alcohol who "collected a ransom for alcohol and disappeared." Hence, they formed merely one of the many common criminal outfits exploiting the peasantry throughout Poland. Allegedly, some of these men also belonged to the "non-ideological wing of the Home Army."[36] If true, materials confirming the demoralization of this local cell of the underground are probably extant. Why did the Grosses fail to locate and consult them?

In any case, the above information contained in Markiel's testimony remains an insufficient source base to support the Grosses' claim that, in the case of Gniewczyna, members of the local patriotic elite perpetrated a crime against defenseless Jews.[37] So far, we have only the

---

[33] *Ibid.*
[34] *Ibid.*
[35] *Ibid.*
[36] *Ibid.*
[37] It is worthwhile to note that Gross perceives "elitism" (i.e. the fact of belonging to an elite) as a function of socioeconomic status. His assumption may be paraphrased as

claims of a retired Communist-era army officer at our disposal. These have recently been challenged by solid research.[38]

The authors encourage us to treat the situation in Gniewczyna, as described in *Golden Harvest*, as a general representation of social interaction in rural Poland. On the basis of above-mentioned examples, however, it is impossible to conclude unequivocally that the mafia in charge of Gniewczyna was representative of the village.

Determining whether the pathologies occurring in Gniewczyna (and Wólka-Okrąglik) may be considered a Polish norm, or exceptions to this rule, poses an even greater problem. The current state of our knowledge favors the latter conclusion. Microstudies of Gniewczyna, Wólka-Okrąglik, and dozens of other villages, towns, and regions will allow scholars to verify multiple stereotypes currently functioning as axioms, both among the post-modernists, and the pop-culture-consuming public starving for the sensational.

---

follows: X, who robbed and killed a Jew, cannot be dismissed as a mere deviant and lowlife because he or she was educated, fluent in foreign languages, a landowner, or was wealthy. Yet, according to the ethical standards developed by Western culture, an individual's worth is defined not by his pedigree, wealth, or education, but by his character, virtue, and actions.

[38] Recent research has cast further doubt on Gross's version. Historian Piotr Chmielowiec has discovered that postwar Communist courts not only established that the Jews were murdered by auxiliary Ukrainian policemen and exonerated fully Józef Lasek, but they found that the latter and other Gniewczyna Poles actually assisted Jews during the Nazi occupation. See Piotr Chmielowiec, "Sprawa Józefa Laska. Z dziejów ludności żydowskiej w Gniewczynie Łańcuckiej w okresie okupacji niemieckiej" [The Case of Józef Lasek: From the History of the Jewish Community in Gniewczyna Łańcucka During the German Occupation] in *Glaukopis* 23-24 (2011/2012): 10-45.

Collective Rescue Efforts by Poles on Behalf of Jews in the German-Occupied Polish Countryside

Ryszard Tyndorf

The state of research on Polish rescue efforts is surprisingly still in its infancy. Only recently has Yad Vashem published two volumes dedicated to 5,333 Polish rescuers recognized as Righteous Gentiles by the end of the year 2000.[1] As of 1 January 2011, the distinction of "Righteous Among the Nations" has been granted to 6,266 Poles, who form the single largest national group honored by that institution.[2]

---

[1] Israel Gutman and Sara Bender, eds., *The Encyclopedia of the Righteous Among the Nations: Rescuers of Jews during the Holocaust,* volumes 4 and 5: *Poland,* Parts One and Two (Jerusalem: Yad Vashem, 2004). The largest compilation of rescue testimonies remains the classic book by Władysław Bartoszewski and Zofia Lewin, eds., *Righteous Among Nations: How Poles Helped the Jews, 1939–1945* (London: Earlscourt Publications, 1969), which is an abridgement of the Polish edition: Władysław Bartoszewski and Zofia Lewinówna, *Ten jest z ojczyzny mojej* [He is From my Fatherland], Second revised and expanded edition (Kraków: Znak, 1969). There are many other smaller compilations and countless memoirs and published accounts, as well thousands of unpublished testimonies.

[2] For a complete list of Poles awarded by Yad Vashem as of 1 January 2011, see www1.yadvashem.org/yv/en/righteous/pdf/virtial_wall/poland.pdf. This list includes only ethnic Poles, as rescuers ethnic or national groups who assisted Jews on the territory of interwar Poland are listed under Ukraine, Belarus, Lithuania, Czechoslovakia (e.g., Czech rescuers from Volhynia), and Germany, as the case may be. For online information about the rescue activity of individual Poles see www.savingjews.org/. On the rescue of Jews by the Catholic clergy see Mark Paul, *Wartime Rescue of Jews by the Polish Catholic Clergy: The Testimony of Survivors,* Internet: www.kpk-toronto.org/fundusz_obrony.html. Additionally, a number of Poles from Lithuania, Latvia, Belarus, Ukraine, Germany, Austria and France have also received recognition. For information about Polish rescuers from those countries see Israel Gutman, ed., *The Encyclopedia of the Righteous Among the Nations: Rescuers of Jews during the Holocaust,* vol. 8: *Europe (Part I) and Other Countries* (Jerusalem: Yad Vashem, 2007), pp.31–32, 70–71, 86–87, 115–16, and vol. 8: *Europe (Part II),* forthcoming.

The vast majority of Poles who extended assistance to Jews have not received any recognition, and in many cases their Jewish benefactors have since died or lost contact with them.³ It is difficult to estimate the number of Poles who sheltered or—much more often—assisted Jews in other ways. Polish historian Teresa Prekerowa, herself a Righteous Gentile, estimated their number could run as high as 300,000. However, this may be a conservative estimate.

It is also apparent that it took the silent support of many additional hundreds of thousands of Poles, in defiance of German decrees that made all forms of assistance to Jews punishable by death, for the rescue efforts to succeed. The toll in human sacrifice that Poles paid for this rescue effort is staggering. Research conducted by Poland's Institute of National Remembrance, which is still ongoing, has confirmed more than one thousand documented cases in which Poles—women, children, and men, often entire families—were executed, burned alive or perished in prisons and concentration camps for helping Jews. Most of these acts of repression occurred in the countryside where the majority of Jews survived.

While there has been no authoritative global assessment of rescue efforts in the countryside, historian Gunnar S. Paulsson, the author of the authoritative study *Secret City: The Hidden Jews of Warsaw, 1940–1945*,⁴ has summarized his findings regarding Warsaw, the site of the single largest rescue effort, as follows:

> In the league of people who are known to have risked their lives to rescue Jews, Poland stands at the very top, accounting for more than a third of all the 'Righteous Gentiles'. ...
>
> Of the 27,000 Jewish fugitives in Warsaw, 17,000 were still alive 15 months after the destruction of the ghetto, on the eve of the Polish uprising in 1944. Of the 23,500 who were not drawn in by the Hotel Polski scheme, 17,000 survived until then. Of these 17,000, 5,000 died in the 1944 Warsaw Uprising, and about 10,500 were still alive at liberation. ...

---

³ See, for example, Bill Tammeus and Jacques Cukierkorn, *They Were Just People: Stories of Rescue in Poland During the Holocaust* (Columbia, Missouri and London: University of Missouri Press, 2009), 21, 69–70.

⁴ Gunnar S. Paulsson, *Secret City: The Hidden Jews of Warsaw, 1940–1945* (New Haven and London: Yale University Press, 2002); translated into Polish as *Utajone miasto: Żydzi po aryjskiej stronie Warszawy (1940-1945)* (Kraków: Znak and Centrum Badań nad Zagładą Żydów, Instytut Filozofii i Socjologii PAN, 2007).

As it happens, there is an excellent standard of comparison, because it is estimated that in the Netherlands, 20-25,000 Jews went into hiding—about the same number as in Warsaw, of whom 10-15,000 survived—again, about the same number. ... The conclusion, then, is quite startling: leaving aside acts of war and Nazi perfidy, a Jew's chances of survival in hiding were no worse in Warsaw, at any rate, than in the Netherlands. ...

The small number of survivors, therefore, is not a direct result of Polish hostility to the Jews ... The Jews were deported from the ghettos to the death camps, not by Poles, but by German gendarmes, reinforced by Ukrainian and Baltic auxiliaries, and with the enforced co-operation of the ghetto police. Neither the Polish police nor any group of Polish civilians was involved in the deportations to any significant degree, nor did they staff the death camps. Nor did the fate of the Jews who were taken to their deaths depend to any significant degree on the attitudes and actions of a people from whom they were isolated by brick walls and barbed wire. ...

The 27,000 Jews in hiding in Warsaw relied on about 50-60,000 people who provided hiding-places and another 20-30,000 who provided other forms of help; on the other hand, blackmailers, police agents, and other actively anti-Jewish elements numbered perhaps 2-3,000, each striking at two or three victims a month. In other words, helpers outnumbered hunters by about 20 or 30 to one. The active helpers of Jews thus made up seven to nine per cent of the population of Warsaw; the Jews themselves, 2.7 per cent; the hunters, perhaps 0.3 per cent; and the whole network—Jews, helpers and hunters—constituted a secret city of at least 100,000: one tenth of the people of Warsaw; more than twice as many as the 40,000 members of the vaunted Polish military underground, the AK [Armia Krajowa or Home Army]. ...

How many people in Poland rescued Jews? Of those that meet Yad Vashem's criteria—perhaps 100,000. Of those that offered minor forms of help—perhaps two or three times as many. Of those who were passively protective—undoubtedly the majority of the population. All these acts, great and small, were necessary to rescue Jews in Poland.[5]

To what extent does Paulsson's thesis apply to the Polish countryside? Despite the publication of a number of books about rescue activities in Poland, there has been no comprehensive count of how many Jews were sheltered and assisted in other ways and how many Poles participated in these rescue efforts. Nor is it likely—or even

---

[5] Gunnar S. Paulsson, "The Rescue of Jews by Non-Jews in Nazi-Occupied Poland," *The Journal of Holocaust Education,* vol. 7, nos. 1 & 2 (Summer/Autumn 1998): 19–44.

possible—that such a count will ever be made, especially now that more than sixty-five years have passed since the end of the Second World War. Therefore, one has to look at other evidence that is indicative of a pattern in order to gauge the true extent of such assistance and the attitude of the population.

It is clearly not enough to focus only, or primarily, on evidence of lack of assistance, as that can be explained by many factors such as fear and not necessarily indifference, or even on evidence of actions perpetrated by individual Poles that harmed Jews, as those may not be representative of the population as a whole. Rescue in the countryside is in some ways different from rescue in Warsaw. It was much more difficult to remain anonymous in a rural setting and therefore rescue activities were much more likely to be known or suspected by neighbors or even the entire village.

The picture of the Polish countryside that emerges from the hundreds of cases that have been collected for this study is clear. Without the active or passive support of the rescuers' neighbors—who engaged in a conspiracy of silence, as it were—it would have been impossible to have carried out the majority of the rescue activities.

Regarding passive assistance, it is important to bear in mind that in occupied Poland *not* reporting a Jew's presence in a village constituted a crime punishable by death. One cannot therefore underestimate the fear factor that loomed large over the lives of the population. It must also be stressed that the accounts relied on in this study are, with few exceptions, the testimonies of *Jewish* survivors, culled from a large number of sources.

Before turning to the testimonies that speak of collaborative or communal rescue efforts in the countryside, it is also important to remember that most Jews who survived the war hiding in Poland received assistance of various sorts from at least several people, often a great number of Poles. Most of that help was casual or short term, and very often from complete strangers. That type of assistance is the least likely to be acknowledged since the benefactors are rarely known by name and no effort has been made by Holocaust commemoration and research institutions to identify them. The following survivors attest to their experiences in this regard:

- In an open letter to B'nai B'rith, dated 7 February 1996, Joseph S. Kutrzeba (born Arie Fajwiszys) wrote: "It was impossible for anyone to singly save a Jew during World War II in Poland; rather, it had taken the cooperation of a number of persons to achieve this—Poland being the only country in Nazi-occupied Europe where a death penalty was mandated for assisting a Jew in any way. In my own case, it had taken the cooperation of nine persons to save my life, not including some 20 who'd aided me along the way. Only one has been recognized by Yad Vashem."

- Hanna Krall, a well-known journalist and author, counted 45 Poles who risked their lives to shelter her.[6] Franciszka Tusk-Scheinwechsler reported a similar number of Polish benefactors.[7]
- After her escape from the ghetto in Łosice, Stella Zylbersztajn took shelter in several villages in the vicinity of Łosice. In total, 25 Polish families helped her survive the war.[8]
- One Jewish woman had to change hiding places 25 times, whereas another woman 17 times.[9] The renowned scientist Ludwik Hirszfeld moved eleven times.[10]
- Anna Forkasiewicz identified as her rescuers three Polish families (consisting of 11 people), three individual Poles, four priests, and a boarding school run by nuns.[11]
- Rose Gelbart (née Grosman), who had at least a dozen different hiding places, recalled: "There were so many places and so many people who did know I was Jewish but who didn't give me away. It had to be at least fifty, even more than fifty."[12]
- When asked, "What help did the residents of Warsaw provide to people of Jewish origin who hid?" Władysław Szpilman replied: "A great deal. Poland is not an anti-Semitic country. Those who state the

---

[6] Bartoszewski and Lewinówna, *Ten jest z ojczyzny mojej* [He is From My Fatherland], 2nd ed., 410–13.

[7] Bartoszewski and Lewinówna, *Ten jest z ojczyzny mojej* [He is From My Fatherland], 2nd ed., 537–42.

[8] Bartoszewski and Lewin, *Righteous Among Nations*, 287–96; Bartoszewski and Lewinówna, *Ten jest z ojczyzny mojej*, 2nd ed., 685–92; Stella Zylbersztajn, *A gdyby to było Wasze dziecko? Wspomnienia antysemitki w getcie, komunistki w klasztorze i uniwersalistki wśród Ludu Wybranego, Umiłowanego* [And If It Were Your Child? Recollections of an Anti-Semite in the Ghetto, a Communist in the Convent, and a Universalist Among the Chosen People] (Łódź: Oficyna Bibliofilów, 1994; Łosice: Łosickie Stowarzyszenie Rozwoju Equus, 2005).

[9] Nathan Gross, "Unlucky Clara," *Yad Vashem Bulletin*, no. 10–11 (1956): 34; Małgorzata Melchior, *Zagłada a tożsamość: Polscy Żydzi ocaleni "na aryjskich papierach": Analiza doświadczenia biograficznego* [Extermination and Identity: Polish Jews Saved Through "Aryan Papers": An Analysis of Biographical Experience] (Warsaw: IFiS PAN, 2004), 129.

[10] Ludwik Hirszfeld, *Historia jednego życia* [The History of One Life] (Warsaw: Czytelnik 1946; Pax, 1957).

[11] Andrzej Chciuk, ed., *Saving Jews in War-Torn Poland, 1939–1945* (Clayton, Victoria: Wilke and Company, 1969), 26–27.

[12] Tammeus and Cukierkorn, *They Were Just People*, 79.

opposite don't speak the truth and perform a bad service that is hostile to Poland. Let us remember that for taking part in rescue activities on behalf of Jews one was threatened with death. Not everyone could muster up the strength to run this risk. Not everyone is born a hero. At least thirty Poles were engaged in rescuing me. At least thirty, at the risk of their lives."[13]

Of the several hundred Poles who came to the assistance of these ten Jews alone, only a few were ever awarded by Yad Vashem for risking their lives, and those of their families.

As for the make-up and profile of Polish rescuers, Lawrence N. Powell offers the following astute observations that discredit the view that rescuers were from the margins of Polish society and not representative of it:

> There is a burgeoning literature on the sociology and psychology of 'righteous gentiles,' but the sociological literature is frankly inconclusive. Rescuers do not cluster on one or two rungs of the social ladder. They derive in almost equal proportions from the working class and the middle class, the peasantry and the intelligentsia, the educated and the unlettered. Nor are they conspicuously religious or unusually politically active. There have been attempts to identify them as social marginals, people who marched to a different drummer and were impervious to the good opinion of friends and neighbors. But, apart from a psychological ability to act independently of social norms, *there is little evidence showing that rescuers were anything but organically embodied in the communities in which they lived* (emphasis added).[14]

---

[13] Tadeusz Knade, "Władysław Szpilman ostatni wywiad" [Władysław Szpilman: The Last Interview], *Rzeczpospolita,* 12 October 2002.

[14] Lawrence N. Powell, *Troubled Memory: Anne Levy, the Holocaust, and David Duke's Louisiana* (Chapel Hill and London: The University Press of North Carolina, 2000), 281–82. Moreover, based on the memoirs from the Warsaw area, Powell noted: "Almost without exception Jewish rescue occurred within networks. Minimally, it required ten rescuers to save one Jew. ... Several of these rescue operations were complex organizations, such as Żegota ... But most underground railroads were informal and ad hoc, carefully woven webs of associates whose involvement started out gradually and then, before they realized what was happening, metamorphosed into major commitments. ... The challenge of starting a rescue network, however, was knowing whom to trust. Which friends and relatives were reliable, who was discreet? Routine intimacies had to be reevaluated, well-worn social conventions sifted through for clues as to who combined the right mixture of empathy and discretion." *Ibid.,* 279–80.

Let us now turn to the focus of our study: collective rescue efforts in the countryside, including small town and villages. Since Jews were removed early in the war from western Polish territories incorporated into the Reich (except for the large enclosed ghettos of Łódź and Sosnowiec), it was in the General Government and the northern and eastern parts of Poland that Jews escaped from the ghettos, mostly into the countryside. Hundreds of thousands of Poles living in the General Government had themselves been deported by the Germans from Western Poland. Poles constituted a minority, sometimes a small one, in many parts of Eastern Poland and were themselves often endangered. In Volhynia and Eastern Galicia, Ukrainian nationalists launched a campaign of ethnic cleansing that resulted in the murder of more than 100,000 Poles and the flight of several hundred thousand Poles to central Poland. The rural population was also terrorized by criminal gangs and Communist partisans who robbed the people mercilessly.

The accounts that concern us are those that attest to assistance that was apparent to others, and not simply rescue stories, of which there are many thousands, where such information is lacking. The rescue involved a collaborative effort on the part a number of people in a community or given area, hence they can be referred to as collective or communal rescue. These are accounts that—based on the stereotypical views expressed by many historians and authors about Poles as virulent, greedy, and near universal anti-Semities—simply should not exist at all, and with absolute certainty, not in any significant number.

Emanuel Ringelblum, the chronicler of the Warsaw ghetto, already noted the phenomenon of widespread and open assistance for Jews in his wartime diary which he wrote while being sheltered in Warsaw by Poles, after his escape from the Trawniki labor camp with the assistance of the Polish underground.

> I heard from Jews of Głowno [northeast of Łódź] how peasants helped them during the whole of the winter. A Jew who went out to a village in search of food usually returned with a bag of potatoes … In many villages, the peasants showed open sympathy for the Jews. They threw bread and other food [through the barbed-wire fence] into the camps … located in their neighborhood.[15]

---

[15] Philip Friedman, *Their Brothers' Keepers* (New York: Holocaust Library, 1978), 116.

In an account penned in 1947, three Jews from Ozorków (north of Łódź) – Hercek Cedrowski, Tojwje Drajhorm, and Jankiel Borkowski – wrote:

> The Jews of Ozorków maintained contact with the Poles. The Polish population did not help the Germans in the liquidation of the Jews. They traded with the Jews and brought food to the ghetto. The Jews were afraid of speaking with Poles, and Poles were afraid of helping Jews, but there were no denunciations of Jews.[16]

Rina Eitani (11 years old at the time), and her mother and sister (10 years old), supported themselves by smuggling farm goods from the countryside to Warsaw. They worked separately to lessen the risk of discovery. While the Germans were ruthless toward smugglers, the natives treated them kindly:

> One day I was buying something in a store. A little girl came in, warning me, 'The Gestapo are in the house where you live.' Right away, the owner of the store, a woman, put me in the cellar. She wouldn't let me go until the Gestapo left. ... We stayed a lot in the villages where we bought the produce. The peasants were nice to us. They would feed us and sometimes, in exchange, we worked for them.[17]

Isadore Burstyn, as a boy of eleven, was able to survive through the friendship of people in the village of Głupianka near Otwock (outside of Warsaw): "In my case the entire village sheltered me even though I know there were still about 20 per cent anti-Semites among them."[18]

When Abram Jakub Zand, a tailor from the village of Bolimów near Skierniewice, "stole back to his village; the local peasants welcomed him back, and he was passed from house to house, working a week or two in each. ... 'If I were to thank everyone, whole villages would have to visit me.'"[19] A number of Jews were sheltered in another unnamed

---

[16] Michał Grynberg and Maria Kotowska, comp. and eds., *Życie i zagłada Żydów polskich 1939–1945: Relacje świadków* [The Life and Destruction of the Polish Jews, 1939-1945: Witness Testimonies] (Warsaw: Oficyna Naukowa, 2003), 488.

[17] Nechama Tec, *Resilience and Courage: Women, Men, and the Holocaust* (New Haven and London: Yale University Press, 2003), 231–32.

[18] "Edmonton Survivor Returns to Poland," *The Canadian Jewish News* (Toronto), 2 August 1990, and "Return to Otwock Brings Back Rush of Memories," *The Canadian Jewish News*, 30 August 1990.

[19] Tatiana Berenstein and Adam Rutkowski, *Assistance to the Jews in Poland, 1939–1945* (Warsaw: Polonia Publishing House, 1963), 27; translated from the Polish *Pomoc Żydom w Polsce 1939–1945* (Warsaw: Polonia, 1963).

village outside Warsaw, with the knowledge of the entire village, and no one was betrayed.[20]

In the village of Osiny, "the peasants arranged among themselves that each would hide a Jewish girl for a certain period so that 'everyone would be guilty and no one could inform.'"[21] Henryk Prajs survived the war passing as a Pole in the village of Podwierzbie near Magnuszew where the fact that he was Jewish was widely known, with the protection of the head of the village.[22] Yitzhak Kuniak from Kałuszyn hid among peasants for whom he was sewing secretly. He moved about in a few villages where he was fed and sheltered.[23] In the small village of Bokowo Wielkie near Sierpc four Jews were taken in by various Polish farmers.[24]

After escaping from the Warsaw Ghetto in August 1942, 13-year-old Chana Ajzenfisz, and her ten-year-old sister Chaya, wandered for two weeks from village to village, in the countryside north of Warsaw. Unkempt and dirty, they were readily recognizable as Jews by their appearance and accent, but received food and temporary lodging from farmers on whose doors they knocked. When they arrived in the village of Krzyczki-Pieniążki near Nasielsk, about 50 kilometers from Warsaw, they were taken in by the extended Krzyczkowski family. The girls lived in the village openly, passed off as distant family members, for the rest of the war. Although the villagers were aware of their Jewish origin no one betrayed them.[25]

A Jew from Serock, north of Warsaw, who escaped from a German execution site badly wounded, was cared for by very many villagers where he sought refuge.[26] Izaak Zemelman of Płock was assisted by a large number of Polish families in the nearby village of Sikórz, where

---

[20] Bartoszewski and Lewinówna, *Ten jest z ojczyzny mojej* [He is From My Fatherland], 2nd ed., 572–73.
[21] Berenstein and Rutkowski, *Assistance to the Jews in Poland, 1939–1945*, 27.
[22] Testimony of Henryk Prajs, January 2005, Internet: <http://www.centropa.org>.
[23] Layb Rochman, "With Kuniak in Hiding," in A. Shamri and Sh. Soroka, eds., *Sefer Kałuszyn: Gehoylikt der khorev gevorener kehile* (Tel Aviv: Former Residents of Kaluszyn in Israel, 1961), 437ff., translated as *The Memorial Book of Kałuszyn*, Internet: <http://jewishgen.org/Yizkor/kaluszyn/Kaluszyn.html>.
[24] Leon Gongoła, "O prawach i ludziach" [On Rights and People], *Polska* (Warsaw), no. 7 (1971): 170–72.
[25] Jacek Leociak, *Ratowanie: Opowieści Polaków i Żydów* [Rescuing: The Recollections of Poles and Jews] (Kraków: Wydawnictwo Literackie, 2010), 123–24, 128–29, 131–35.
[26] Michał Grynberg, *Żydzi w rejencji ciechanowskiej 1939–1942* [Jews in the Ciechanów Region] (Warsaw: Państwowe Wydawnictwo Naukowe, 1984), 134.

he and his family took shelter: the Stawiski, Romanowski, Górski, Danielak, Adamski, Kłosiński, and other families.[27]

Rabbi Abraham D. Feffer, a Holocaust survivor from Drobin near Płock, wrote:

> Yet many fortunate survivors from my own shtetl, remember well and with great fondness and admiration the help of the brave Christian farmers who lived in nearby villages where we worked on cold winter days. (In Poland, hiding a Jew, or feeding him was punishable by death, usually hanging). We remember how these men and women, at great peril, opened their poor 'chatkis' [cottages] to share with us warm soup, bread and potatoes.[28]

Irena Bakowska, then a teenager, was part of a group of six Jews smuggled from Warsaw to the countryside:

> We entered into a single train compartment occupied already by the Christian Poles ... We were greeted in a friendly manner, and the man sitting by himself moved over and sat with his four companions. ... The conductor, a Christian Pole, entered the compartment to check the tickets. ... we uncovered our armbands to identify ourselves. I watched the reaction of the Christian Polish passengers with great apprehension. ... But the attitude of the Christian passengers was sympathetic and not at all hostile. They started talking with us, and urged us to throw away our armbands and our Jewish identity. ... Those five people seemed truly to care about my survival, repeating over and over again that I could be saved and survive as a Pole. They persuaded me that all Poles did not hate us, did not wish us to perish.[29]

Jerzy and Irena Krępeć, who were awarded by Yad Vashem, sheltered and assisted a number of Jews on their farm in Gołąbki near Warsaw. Their son, a 14-year-old boy at the time, recalled:

> the fact that they were hiding Jews was an open secret in the village. At times, there were 20 or 30 people living on the farm. Many of the visitors were urban Jews who spoke Polish with an accent. Their children attended underground schools that moved from house to house. 'The neighbors knew. It would have been impossible to manage this without people finding

---

[27] Janusz Szczepański, *Społeczność żydowska Mazowsza w XIX–XX wieku* [The Jewish Community of Mazovia Province in the 19th and 20th Centuries] (Pułtusk: Wyższa Szkoła Humanistyczna imienia Aleksandra Gieysztora w Pułtusku, 2005), 492.

[28] Rabbi Abraham D. Feffer, *My Shtetl Drobin: A Saga of a Survivor* (Toronto: n.p., 1990), 22.

[29] Irena Bąkowska, *Not All Was Lost: A Young Woman's Memoir, 1939–1946* (Kingston, Ontario: Karijan, 1998), 142–44.

out. But everyone knew they had to keep quiet—it was a matter of life or death.' In fact, many of the Krępeć's Polish neighbors helped, 'if only to provide a meal.'[30]

A Polish Red Cross worker entrusted a Polish couple by the name of Kaczmarek, themselves refugees from Western Poland living in the town of Żyrardów near Warsaw, with a young Jewish girl found abandoned in an empty death train. "Many of the neighbors knew that she was Jewish, yet no one informed."[31]

A 31-year-old barber named Zimler, who wandered with his wife in the vicinity of Wiskitki near Żyrardów cutting hair for farmers, wrote that "the attitude of the farmers to us was extremely good." The farmers in various villages such as Oryszew, Wyczółki and Janówka, allowed them to stay in their homes, gave them food, washed their laundry, and even invited them to a wedding.[32]

Chava Grinberg-Brown, who hailed from the village of Wiskitki, roamed the countryside near Żyrardów for the last years of the German occupation:

> ...at the end of each day, I would beg people to let me come in and sleep. I remember that once someone gave me a place to stay and offered me chicken soup ... In another home, one of the women gave me medication for my skin condition. They knew that I was Jewish ... it was obvious. As I wandered from one little place to another, people fed me and let me sleep in their homes or close to them; in barns, pigstys, etc.

When a Pole who recognized her wanted to turn her in, "Some peasants who realized what he was after threatened to give him a beating he would never forget. That stopped him from bothering me." Her story continues:

---

[30] Peggy Curran, "Decent people: Polish couple honored for saving Jews from Nazis," *Gazette* (Montreal), 10 December 1994; Janice Arnold, "Polish widow made Righteous Gentile," *The Canadian Jewish News* (Montreal edition), 26 January 1995; Irene Tomaszewski and Tecia Werbowski, *Żegota: The Council for Aid to Jews in Occupied Poland, 1942–1945* (Montreal: Price-Patterson, 1999), 131–32, and *Code Name: Żegota: Rescuing Jews in Occupied Poland, 1942–1945: The Most Dangerous Conspiracy in Wartime Europe* (Santa Barbara, California: Praeger/ABC-CLIO, LLC, 2010), 140–43.
[31] Zbigniew Pakula, *The Jews of Poznań* (London and Portland, Oregon: Vallentine Mitchell, 2003), 51.
[32] Marta Markowska, ed., *Archiwum Ringelbluma: Dzień po dniu Zagłady* [The Ringelblum Archive: The Holocaust Day by Day] (Warsaw: Ośrodek Karta, Dom Spotkań z Historią, and Żydowski Instytut Historyczny, 2008), 100–1.

I went to the place I had worked before [the war]. I stayed there for a few days. After that, I kept moving from one place to another. Some refused me work. Then a peasant offered me a more stable job. ... I remained with this peasant for most of the summer. Then I left and went to another village. I went from one village to another. Even during the summer I would change places. When the Poles sent me away, I was not angry. I understood that they were afraid or had not enough food and could not share the little they had. I did not particularly feel their anti-Semitism. ... Most people knew right away when I came in that I was Jewish, but they did not harm me. Only a few times did I have to run away. ... When I entered a village I would go first to the head of the village, and he would send me to a peasant. Usually they were not afraid if they had a note from the head of the village. ... I have no bad feelings toward the Christians. I survived the war thanks to them.[33]

Franciszka Aronson, from a hamlet near Mińsk Mazowiecki, wandered about many villages, including localities where she was known, before she was taken in by nuns at a convent in Ignaców, where several Jews and a Gypsy woman were sheltered.[34]

Dr. Zofia Szymańska, who was hidden by the Grey Ursulines in Ożarów (near Warsaw), received material care and an abundance of spiritual comfort from many nuns and priests, without any effort on their part to convert her. News of her stay was widely known to the villagers but no one betrayed her, not even when a German military unit was, at one point, quartered in the convent. Her ten-year-old niece, who had a very Semitic appearance, was sheltered by the Sisters of the Immaculate Virgin Mary in Szymanów, along with more than a dozen Jewish girls.

All of the nuns were aware that their young charges were Jews, as were the lay staff, the parents of non-Jewish children, and many villagers. None of the Christian parents removed their children from the school despite the potential danger, and in fact many of them contributed to the upkeep of the Jewish children. Dr. Szymańska wrote: "The children were under the protection of the entire convent and village. Not one traitor was to be found among them."[35]

---

[33] Tec, *Resilience and Courage*, 225–27.

[34] Ewa Kurek, *Dzieci żydowskie w klasztorach: Udział żeńskich zgromadzeń zakonnych w akcji ratowania dzieci żydowskich w Polsce a latach 1939–1945* [Jewish Children in Convents: The Participation of the Nuns in Rescuing Jewish Children in Poland During the Years 1939-1945] (Lublin: Clio, 2001), 116.

[35] Zofia Szymańska, *Byłam tylko lekarzem...* [I Was Only a Doctor ...] (Warsaw: Pax, 1979), 149–76.

Hanna Mesz, along with her mother, spent the period from September 1944 to February 1945 in the village of Korzeniówka near Grójec, working for various peasants who knew they were Jews.[36] A similar attitude of widespread assistance in several villages near Łowicz is described by Joseph Szmekura.[37]

Zygmunt Srul Warszawer hid for 26 months moving from place to place among numerous villages, such as Wielki Las, in the triangle formed by Łaskarzew, Sobolew, and Wilga, "visiting every farm because he figured that if everyone helped him no one would turn him in—to do so would mean self-destruction." No one turned him away empty-handed during those 26 months:

> 'No one ever refused to help you?' 'No, not food! In twenty-six months, not once. Sometimes they were afraid to let me into the house, or into the barn. It varied, but their food they shared."[38]

In Grodzisk, a small community just outside Warsaw, an elderly Jewish teacher married to a Polish Catholic woman was able to live openly with his wife throughout the war. "Everybody knew my uncle was Jewish but no one reported him to the Gestapo." This family took in other Jews, also without incident.[39] A foundry in Wołomin, outside of Warsaw, engaged a Jew whose appearance and manner of speaking readily gave him away, yet no one betrayed him.[40]

After leaving the ghetto in Jeżów, Nathan Gold received extensive support from Poles in the nearby villages of Przybyszyce and Słupia:

> Some ten families in the villages took turns hiding him, each one not knowing about the other's activities. They were poor people, many of the older ones illiterate, but all opened their hearts and their homes to him.[41]

---

[36] Wiktoria Śliwowska, ed., *The Last Eyewitnesses: Children of the Holocaust Speak* (Evanston, Illinois: Northwestern University Press, 1998), 120–23.
[37] Gedaliah Shaiak, ed., *Lowicz, A Town in Mazovia. Memorial Book* (Tel Aviv: Lowitcher Landsmanshaften in Melbourne and Sydney, Australia, 1966), xvi–xvii.
[38] Małgorzata Niezabitowska, *Remnants: The Last Jews of Poland* (New York: Friendly Press, 1986), 118–24.
[39] Sylvia Rothchild, ed., *Voices from the Holocaust* (New York: Nal Books/New American Library, 1981), 225.
[40] Antoni Marianowicz, *Życie surowo wzbronione* (Warsaw: Czytelnik, 1995), 159–60, translated as Antoni Marianowicz, *Life Strictly Forbidden* (London: Vallentine Mitchell, 2004).
[41] Tomaszewski and Werbowski, *Code Name: Żegota*, 143.

Z. Ben-Moshe wrote with fondness about compassionate villagers in the vicinity of Łask, south of Łódź:

> We must remined [sic – be mindful of] all those people, not Jews, who gave their hand to save many of our town when they escaped from the Nazi murderers. Also in Lask [Łask] there were good Christians who suffered seeing how the Jews of their town suffered. In the hard days of distress and banishment, they endangered themselves by hiding Jews and giving them from their bread. ... The villagers who disperse pieces of bread and turnip on the ways, for the caravans of hungry people, who went under the watching of the SS. The villagers who gave their shoes to barefooted and weak. How can we forget the villagers who refused to give food [to] the watchers of the women-caravans who were transported from work-camp.[42]

The villagers of Czajków near Staszów were known for the support they gave to Jews who were hiding from the Germans. Gabriel Singer recalled:

> it was something exceptional to see the humane way the villagers behaved. These simple people helped us of their own free will, and without receiving any money in return. From them we often heard some kind words, quite apart from the money, loaves of bread and boiled potatoes they gave us from time to time.[43]

In the village of Dziurków near Radom, a local Jew lived openly throughout the war with two Polish families under an assumed identity furnished by the Home Army, and even took seasonal employment with the Germans, without being betrayed.[44] A Jewish boy of seven or eight years named Abraham, who tended geese for a farmer near Sandomierz, was affectionately known to the peasants as "Żydek" (little Jew), and yet survived unharmed.[45]

---

[42] Z. Ben-Moshe, "Respect for Jew Savers," in Z. Tzurnamal, ed., *Lask: sefer zikaron* (Tel Aviv: Association of Former Residents of Lask in Israel, 1968), 124–25.

[43] Gabriel Singer, "As Beasts in the Woods," in Elhanan Ehrlich, ed., *Sefer Staszow* (Tel Aviv: Organization of Staszowites in Israel with the Assistance of the Staszowite Organizations in the Diaspora, 1962), xviii (English section). More than a dozen villagers have been recognized by Yad Vashem as Righteous Gentiles. See Gutman and Bender, *The Encyclopedia of the Righteous Among the Nations,* vols. 4 and 5: *Poland,* Part 1, 197; Part 2, 670.

[44] Tadeusz Kozłowski, "Spotkanie z żydowskim kolegą po 50 latach" [A Meeting With a Jewish Friend Fifty Years Later], *Gazeta* (Toronto), 12–14 May 1995.

[45] Eva Feldenkreiz-Grinbal, ed., *Eth Ezkera—Whenever I Remember: Memorial Book of the Jewish Community in Tzoymir (Sandomierz)* (Tel Aviv: Irgun yots'e Tsoizmir be-Yisra'l: Moreshet, bet iedut 'a. sh. Mordekhai Anilevits', 1993), 544.

Rabbi Icchok Wolgelernter of Działoszyce stated:

> The simple peasant did not feel hatred toward us – on the contrary, he always willingly contacted a Jew and trusted him in every matter. ... The peasants sympathized with us in our suffering and misfortune. They demonstrated this by giving us bread and water. To be sure they were afraid to take us into their homes, because in every village notices were put up warning that anyone who takes in a Jew or gives him a piece of bread will pay for it with his life. Despite this, when things quietened [sic!] down a little, they allowed us to sleep in their barns, and even took women and children into their homes.[46]

Another eyewitness wrote:

> In Kielce Voivodship I know of cases where an entire village knew that a Jew or a Jewess were hiding out, disguised in peasant clothes, and no one betrayed them even though they were poor Jews who not only could not pay for their silence but had to be fed, clothed and housed.[47]

When a Jew passing as a Christian became a driver and had to transport some German officials to his hometown of Wierzbnik, he wondered "How come no one recognized me? There are many gentiles who knew me in the town where I was born and raised and still I was not exposed." After the war he learned that many had indeed recognized him, but "kept their mouths shut."[48]

In the village of Olsztyn near Częstochowa, four Jewish families passed as Polish Christians with the collusion of the villagers.[49] After escaping from the ghetto in Częstochowa, Ignacy Jakobson and his colleagues joined a partisan unit near Koniecpol where they were assisted by a priest and a number of farmers in Kościelna: "the farmers in that village were most favourably disposed to us."[50]

---

[46] Barbara Engelking, *Jest taki piękny słoneczny dzień...: Losy Żydów szukających ratunku na wsi polskiej 1942–1945* [What a Beautiful, Sunny Day: The Fate of Jews Seeking Shelter in the Polish Countryside 1942-1945] (Warsaw: Stowarzyszenie Centrum nad Zagładą Żydów, 2011), 52–53.

[47] Bartoszewski and Lewin, *Righteous Among Nations*, 361.

[48] Menachem Mincberg, "In the Jaws of Destiny," in Mark Schutzman, ed., *Wierzbnik-Starachowitz: A Memorial Book* (Tel Aviv: Wierzbnik-Starachowitz Relief Society in Israel and Abroad, 1973), 201ff, translated as *Wierzbnik-Starachowitz: A Memorial Book*, Internet: <http://www.jewishgen.org/yizkor/Wierzbnik/Wierzbnik.html>.

[49] Frank Morgens, *Years at the Edge of Existence: War Memoirs, 1939–1945* (Lanham, Maryland: University Press of America, 1996), 97, 99; in Polish as *Lata na skraju przepaści* (Warsaw: Alfa-Wero, 1994).

[50] Bartoszewski and Lewin, *Righteous Among Nations*, 588–89.

In the village of Goszcza near Miechów, everyone was aware that Jews, some of them with a marked Semitic appearance, were being sheltered yet no one betrayed them.[51] A teenage boy with a Semitic appearance, the son of a Jewish beggar woman, lived openly in the village of Głowaczowa near Dębica with the Polish farmer who had taken him in, without being betrayed.[52] Similar reports come from the villages of Gałuszowice and Chrząstów near Mielec.[53]

In the village of Czajkowa near Mielec, where the brothers Zygie and Sol Allweiss were sheltered by the family of Maciej and Zofia Dudzik, neighbors who lived around the Dudzik farm were aware that Jewish boys were hiding there but chose not to betray the family. "In the village, if one knows something, everyone knows. They were our neighbors and they were good people."[54]

A Jewish lawyer was able to continue his practice in Mielec, in defiance of a German ban, with the collusion of the town's entire legal profession until he was denounced by a fellow Jew, first to the Gestapo and then to the Justice Department.[55]

The mother of Mary Rolicka, one other Jewish woman and two Jewish men were sheltered by the Sisters of Charity, with the assistance of their chaplain, Rev. Albin Małysiak, in the Helcel Institute in Kraków and later at an old age home in Szczawnica. Rev. Małysiak, who was awarded by Yad Vashem, recalled:

> All of the charges of the institute as well as the personnel (nuns and lay staff) knew that there were Jews hidden among us. It was impossible to conceal that fact, even though it was known what danger faced those who were responsible for sheltering Jews. After the passage of weeks and months many of the residents of Szczawnica learned of the Jewish boarders. No one betrayed this to the Germans, who were stationed in the immediate vicinity.[56]

The case of Doctor Olga Lilien, a Holocaust survivor from Lwów with a very marked Jewish appearance, who lived with a Polish family

---

[51] Bartoszewski and Lewinówna, *Ten jest z ojczyzny mojej* [He is From My Fatherland], 2nd ed., 643–44.
[52] Bartoszewski and Lewinówna, *Ten jest z ojczyzny mojej* [He is From My Fatherland], 2nd ed., 640.
[53] Bartoszewski and Lewinówna, *Ten jest z ojczyzny mojej* [He is From My Fatherland], 2nd ed., 721–22.
[54] Tammeus and Cukierkorn, *They Were Just People,* 22.
[55] Mark Verstandig, *I Rest My Case* (Melbourne: Saga Press, 1995), viii, 109–13, 130–32.
[56] Mary Rolicka, "A Memoir of Survival in Poland," *Midstream*, April 1988, 26–27.

near Tarnobrzeg, is another example of solidarity among Polish villagers. Germans came looking for a fugitive and summoned the villagers to a meeting to question them about his whereabouts.

> Suddenly he looked at me and said, 'Oh, but this is a Jewess.' The head of the village said, 'Oh, no, she cooks at the school. She is a very good cook.' Nobody said, 'Oh, well, she is Jewish. Take her.' He let me go. The population of the village was about two thousand. They all knew there was something 'wrong' with me. Any one of them could have sold me to the Germans for two hundred deutsche marks, but out of two thousand people nobody did it. Everybody in the village protected me. I had very good relations with them.[57]

The author Jerzy Kosiński and his parents lived openly in Dąbrowa Rzeczycka near Stalowa Wola, where their Jewish origin was common knowledge. The Kosiński family attended church in nearby Wola Rzeczycka, obtained food from villagers in Kępa Rzeczycka, and were sheltered temporarily in Rzeczyca Okrągła. Other Jews were also assisted by the local villagers.[58]

Menachem Superman, who survived in the Rzeszów area, wrote: "the entire village knew that I was Jewish, but [my rescuer] always said to me that I shouldn't be afraid, because no one will hand me over to the Germans."[59] Faiga Rosenbluth, a penniless teenage Jewish girl from Kańczuga, roamed the countryside moving from one village to the next for some two years. She was helped by very many peasants and was not betrayed, even though she was readily recognized as a Jew.[60]

Marian Gołębiowski, who was awarded by Yad Vashem, placed Dr. Bernard Ryszard Hellreich (later Ingram) and his future wife Irena Szumska, who went by the names of Zbigniew and Irena Jakobiszyn, in the village of Czermna near Jasło. Their presence was known to all the

---

[57] Ellen Land-Weber, *To Save a Life: Stories of Holocaust Rescue* (Urbana and Chicago: University of Illinois Press, 2000), 204–6, 246.
[58] James Park Sloan, *Jerzy Kosinski: A Biography* (New York: Dutton/Penguin, 1996), 7–54; Joanna Siedlecka, *Czarny ptasior* [Black Bird] (Gdańsk: Marabut; Warsaw: CIS, 1994).
[59] Elżbieta Rączy, *Pomoc Polaków dla ludności żydowskiej na Rzeszowszczyźnie 1939–1945* [Polish Aid to Jewish People in the Rzeszów Region, 1939-1945] (Rzeszów: Instytut Pamięci Narodowej–Komisja Ścigania Zbrodni przeciwko Narodowi Polskiemu, 2008), 28.
[60] Fay Walker and Leo Rosen (with Caren S. Neile), *Hidden: A Sister and Brother in Nazi Poland* (Madison: The University of Wisconsin Press, 2002).

villagers and they enjoyed the protection of the owners and manager of a local estate.[61]

Many villagers in Głuchów near Łańcut were engaged in sheltering Jews, and did so with the support of the entire community.[62] It was universally known that the young daughter of Reb Moshe of Grodzisko near Leżajsk was sheltered in an orphanage run by nuns in that village, yet no one betrayed her.[63] A poor Jewish tailor survived the war by being passed from home to home in the village of Dąbrowica near Ulanów.[64]

An illiterate Jewish woman, who survived in a village near Lublin, acknowledged that "the entire village rescued me. They all wanted me to survive. And when the Germans were routed, I left the village and shall never return there." When asked why she didn't want to see the people who saved her life, she replied: "Because I would be beholden to the entire village. So I left and won't return."[65]

The villagers of Wola Przybysławska near Lublin took turns sheltering and caring for a young Jewish girl who survived a German raid on a forest bunker. She was passed from one home to another, thus ensuring there wouldn't be any informing.[66]

A Jewish man by the name of Duczy lived openly, without any problems, in his native village of Tarzymiechy near Zamość throughout the entire war. He had always been on good terms with the villagers and was so well liked that he lived there safely, without fear of being betrayed to the Germans. He also arranged for several Jews to hide on the farm of a Catholic family in that village.[67]

---

[61] Piotr Zychowicz, "Ratowali Żydów i nie godzą sie na kłamstwa" [They Saved Jews and Won't Stand For Lies], *Rzeczpospolita,* 30 October 2009; Polish Righteous, Internet: <http://www.sprawiedliwi.org.pl>.

[62] Institute of National Remembrance, Wystawa "Sprawiedliwi wśrod Narodów Świata" [The Exposition of Righteous Among Nations] —15 June 2004, Rzeszów, Poland. Internet: <http://www.ipn.gov.pl/portal/pl/359/913/>.

[63] Bertha Ferderber-Salz, *And the Sun Kept Shining...* (New York: Holocaust Library, 1980), 199.

[64] Jolanta Chodorska, ed., *Godni synowie naszej Ojczyzny: Świadectwa nadesłane na apel Radia Maryja* [Worthy Sons of Our Fatherland: Testimonies Sent In Response to Radio Maryja's Appeal] (Warsaw: Wydawnictwo Sióstr Loretanek, 2002), Part Two, 161–62.

[65] Klara Mirska, *W cieniu wiecznego strachu: Wspomnienia* [In the Shadow of Perpetual Fear: A Memoir] (Paris, n.p.: 1980), 455.

[66] Shiye Goldberg (Shie Chehever), *The Undefeated* (Tel Aviv: H. Leivick Publishing House, 1985), 166–67.

[67] Philip "Fiszel" Bialowitz with Joseph Bialowitz, *A Promise at Sobibór: A Jewish Boy's Story of Revolt and Survival in Nazi-Occupied Poland* (Madison, Wisconsin: University of Wisconsin Press, 2010), 141–42.

A Jewish woman named Berkowa (née Zelman) was rescued by Jan Łoś in the village of Żabno near Żółkiewka; although this was widely known, no one betrayed her. The Wajc family, consisting of Mendel and Ryfka and their two young sons, Jankiel and Zygmunt, survived in the village of Różki near Żółkiewka, where they were known to the villagers.[68]

Mirla Frydrich (Szternzys), from Żółkiewka, was shot in the thigh when she jumped from a train headed for the Bełżec death camp. A Pole who happened to be driving by took her in his carriage and nursed her back to health with the help of another Pole. When Mirla returned to Żółkiewka she received assistance from a number of Poles in several nearby villages.[69]

In Majdan Niepryski, several families sheltered a young Jewish girl thrown from a train headed for Bełżec.[70] Irena Sznycer, a Jewish girl with strikingly Semitic features, who was sheltered by a Polish woman in the village of Bełżec, recalled shortly after the war: "I was well cared for by that lady and was not afraid of anything. Although the neighbors knew I was Jewish, this lady had no enemies so nothing [bad] could happen."[71]

Some Jews came to realize that their guise as Christian Poles was not as foolproof as they had believed, but this had not caused them to be betrayed. One Jew who called on farmhouses in the Urzędów area, near Kraśnik, pretending to be a Christian, recalled:

> I would cross myself, bless Jesus Christ, and ask for something to eat. I had made up a story in case questions were asked. Most farmers were not talkative. Viewed suspiciously, sometimes I would be given soup or bread and asked to leave quickly: sometimes I was just told to go. Later it dawned

---

[68] Chaim Zylberklang, *Z Żółkiewki do Erec Israel: Przez Kotłas, Buzułuk, Ural, Polskę, Niemcy i Francję* [From Żółkiewka to Eretz Israel: Through Kotlas, Buzuluk, the Urals, Poland, Germany, and France], Second revised and expanded edition (Lublin: Akko, 2004), 169, 171 72.

[69] Zylberklang, *Z Żółkiewki do Erec Israel* [From Żółkiewka to Eretz Israel], 181–84.

[70] Bartoszewski and Lewinówna, *Ten jest z ojczyzny mojej* [He is From My Fatherland], 2nd ed., 709–10.

[71] Teresa Prekerowa, "Stosunek ludności polskiej do żydowskich uciekinierów z obozów zagłady w Treblince, Sobiborze i Bełżcu w świetle relacji żydowskich i polskich" [The Attitude of the Polish Population Towards Jewish Escapees From the Treblinka, Sobibór, and Bełżec Death Camps in Light of Jewish and Polish Testimonies], *Biuletyn Głównej Komisji Badania Zbrodni przeciwko Narodowi Polskiemu—Instytutu Pamięci Narodowej*, vol. 35 (1993): 104. See above.

on me that I was crossing myself incorrectly, touching my chin rather than the chest.[72]

Ludwika Fiszer was one of three women who escaped naked from an execution pit where Jews from the Poniatowa labor camp were taken by Germans and their Ukrainian henchmen. Wandering from village to village, despite their disheveled appearances, the women received various forms of assistance, even though the peasants were clearly terrified of retaliation. Although most peasants were reluctant to keep them for any length of time, no one betrayed them, and several weeks later they met up with a Polish woman who took them to Warsaw.[73]

In 1942, Jerzy Mirewicz, a Jesuit priest, escorted a Jewish fugitive by train from Biłgoraj to Milanówek near Warsaw, so that he could join members of his family who were being hidden by a Christian family. Even though the priest had permission to travel, officials were constantly checking the papers of passengers. When the train reached Dęblin, a policeman came into the car and demanded to know if his companion was a Jew. Fortunately for the priest and the fugitive, the whole compartment came to their rescue by insisting that priest was escorting a "lunatic" to a hospital asylum.[74]

Dressed as a peasant, Tema Rotman-Weinstock from the Lublin area roamed the familiar countryside moving from employer to employer, most of whom were hungry themselves and found it hard to feed her. She met a cousin who lived with his wife in a bunker in the forest, but he refused to let her join them. Once, when she was on the verge of collapse, kind peasants took her into their home. After a month, afraid to keep her, they directed her to a woman who lived on a farm with her daughter in the village of Kajetanówka. She remained there until the Soviet arrival, even though word had spread that she was Jewish. "Fortunately, no bad consequences followed because she found a powerful protector in the local priest. He baptized Tema and defended her … 'The priest stood up for me, arguing that conversion was a wonderful Christian deed.'"[75]

---

[72] David Makow, *Dangerous Luck: Memories of a Hunted Life* (New York: Shengold Publishers, 2000), 28.
[73] Account of Ludwika Fiszer in the web site *Women and the Holocaust* (Personal Reflections—In Ghettos/Camps), Internet:
<http://www.interlog.com/~mighty/personal/ludwika.html>.
[74] Vincent A. Lapomarda, *The Jesuits and the Third Reich* (Lewiston/Queenston and Lampeter: The Edwin Mellen Press, 1989), 130.
[75] Tec, *Resilience and Courage*, 227–29.

Ryfka Goldiner, a young Jewish child, was rescued by Stanisław and Helena Wiśliński in Bełżyce near Lublin. Although the villagers were aware of her origin no one betrayed them. The local priest did not agree to formally baptize the child in the event her parents survived the war and returned for her, which they did.[76]

Luba Hochlerer, ten years of age, lived openly with Józef and Bronisława Zając in the hamlet of Witoldów near Wojsławice, where she attended village school, yet no one betrayed her.[77] A teenage boy and his mother lived in a damaged, abandoned house in Drzewica, where he openly played with village boys, yet survived the war despite his Semitic appearance.[78] More than a dozen villagers in Mętów near Głusk, outside of Lublin, sheltered Jews.[79]

Eva Safszycka, not yet 20 at the time, left the ghetto in Siedlce, obtained false identity documents with the help of a Pole, a stranger she happened to encounter, and took a position as a domestic on an estate owned by a Pole. She recalled: "I met with so much kindness from the Poles, so many were decent and helpful that it is unbelievable. ... They hid other Jews, one of them a girl of eleven."[80]

Marian Małowist, who survived the war in the village of Jabłoń near Parczew, said:

> The family with whom I lived knew everything about me—in fact, two families knew. After the war it came out that more families knew, and also the chief of the navy-blue police, a Pole, a very decent person. Juliusz Kleiner was hiding in the neighborhood; in the next village there was a Jewess; in that area many were hiding.[81]

Jewish partisan Gustaw Alef-Bolkowiak identifies the following villages in the Parczew-Ostrów Lubelski area as ones where "almost

---

[76] Anna Dąbrowska, ed., *Światła w ciemności: Sprawiedliwi Wśród Narodów Świata. Relacje* [Lights in the Darkness: The Righteous Among Nations: Testimonies] (Lublin: Ośrodek "Brama Grodzka–Teatr NN," 2008), 56–61.
[77] Dąbrowska, *Światła w ciemności* [Lights in the Darkness], 106–7.
[78] Sven Sonnenberg, *A Two Stop Journey to Hell* (Montreal: Polish-Jewish Heritage Foundation of Canada, 2001).
[79] Dariusz Libionka, "Polska ludność chrześcijańska wobec eksterminacji Żydów—dystrykt lubelski" [The Polish Christian Population Toward the Extermination of the Jews: The Lublin District], in Dariusz Libionka, ed., *Akcja Reinhardt: Zagłada Żydów w Generalnym Gubernatorstwie* [Operation Reinhardt: The Extermination of the Jews in the General Gouvernement] (Warsaw: Instytut Pamięci Narodowej–Komisja Ścigania Zbrodni przeciwko Narodowi Polskiemu, 2004), 325.
[80] Tec, *Resilience and Courage*, 224.
[81] "Marian Małowist on History and Historians," in *Polin: Studies in Polish Jewry*, vol. 13 (2000): 338.

the entire population was actively engaged in helping fugitives from the ghettos": Rudka, Jedlanka, Makoszka, Tyśmienica, and Bójki. He also states that in the village of Niedźwiada near Opole Lubleskie, the foresters sheltered several Jewish families with the knowledge of the entire village.[82] About one hundred and fifty Poles were killed in mass executions in the villages of Białka in the Parczew forest and Sterdyń near Sokołów Podlaski for extensive help given to Jews by those villages.[83]

Cypora Frydman, the daughter of a mill owner in Nowy Orzechów near Ostrów Lubelski, hid in a hut near a lake. She recalled: "All the peasants in the village knew me because all of them used to come to our mill, but not one of them denounced me even though everyone knew I was hiding near the lake. Sometimes they gave me bread for free, sometimes a little milk ... I used to return from the village late at night and hid in my hut."[84]

As a teenager, Marian Finkielman wandered the villages in the vicinity of Dubeczno, where he was employed as a farmhand by various farmers:

> In 1941 and 1942 many young Jews wandered from village to village, offering their services in exchange for room and board. The peasant farmers knew who they were, and for some time took advantage of their help, just as the farmer in the village of Kozaki benefited from my situation.
>
> Luckily, during my stay there [in Kozaki] from April through July 1942, ... none of the inhabitants of the village, Ukrainians or Poles, informed of Jurek's [a Jewish boy from Warsaw who also worked as a herdsman] or my existence. It seemed that there were no informants in this village ...[85]

A 9-year-old Jewish boy by the name of Wintluk (Wintel), who had lost his mother and three fingers when shot at by Germans while

---

[82] Bartoszewski and Lewinówna, *Ten jest z ojczyzny mojej* [He is From My Fatherland], 2nd ed., 533–34.

[83] Wacław Zajączkowski, *Martyrs of Charity: Christian and Jewish Response to the Holocaust*, Part One (Washington: St. Maximilian Kolbe Foundation, 1987), 23–24, 228.

[84] Engelking, *Jest taki piękny słoneczny dzień...* [It is Such a Beautiful, Sunny Day ...], 89.

[85] Marian Finkielman, *Out of the Ghetto: A Young Jewish Orphan Boy's Struggle for Survival* (Montreal: The Concordia University Chair in Canadian Jewish Studies and The Montreal Institute for Genocide and Human Rights Studies, 2000), 34–36; Marian (Finkielman) Domanski, *Fleeing from the Hunter* (Toronto: Azrieli Foundation, 2010), 34–35, translated from the Polish *Moje drogi dzieciństwa 1939–1945* (Otwock: Nowa Ziemia, 2005).

escaping, was taken in by a poor Polish family in Mulawicze near Bielsk Podlaski and then cared for and protected by the entire village who took pity on him:

> The entire village, which was more aware of the danger, took responsibility for his survival. The village administrator gave warning of visits by the Germans, who were stationed in the village school. Thanks to this collective effort, the boy survived the war.[86]

Alfreda and Bolesław Pietraszek sheltered several Jewish families consisting of 18 people on their farm in Czekanów near Sokołów Podlaski for a period of two years. Although they had to rely on the assistance of neighbors for food for their charges, no one betrayed them.[87]

The Idasiak family took in a teenaged Jewish boy by the name of Dawid, whom they sheltered for almost two years near Jedwabne. The neighbors were fully aware that he was Jewish and also helped him. He herded cows and played with the village children.[88] The villagers of Kubra near Radziłów did not betray the family of Helena Chilewicz when the Gestapo came looking for them in July 1942. She and her mother survived the war penniless moving from village to village.[89]

Several Jews were hidden in a forest bunker near the village of Leńce near Białystok. The villagers in the area knew about these Jews, but no one denounced them.[90] Rywka Chus and her husband, a grain merchant from Ostrów Mazowiecki, were protected by the villagers of Króle Duże who respected and helped them survive the war.[91]

The most frequent form of assistance was casual assistance for short periods of time offered by many fearful but courageous Poles whose

---

[86] Alina Cała, *The Image of the Jew in Polish Folk Culture* (Jerusalem: The Magnes Press, The Hebrew Univeristy, 1995), 209–10.
[87] "The Righteous Receive Awards," Internet: <http://www.forum-znak.org.pl/index.php?t=wydarzenia&id=6109>.
[88] Account of B. Idasiak, "Jedwabne: Dlaczego kłamstwa?" [Jedwabne: Why All the Lies?], *Nasz Dziennik*, 26 February 2001.
[89] Danuta and Aleksander Wroniszewski, "...aby żyć" [... Only to Keep Living], *Kontakty–Łomżyński Tygodnik Społeczny*, 10 July 1988.
[90] Bartoszewski and Lewinówna, *Ten jest z ojczyzny mojej* [He is From My Fatherland], 2nd ed., 741–42.
[91] Andrzej Żbikowski, *U genezy Jedwabnego: Żydzi na Kresach Północno-Wschodnich II Rzeczypospolitej. Wrzesień 1939–lipiec 1941* [The Genesis of Jedwabne: The Jews in the Northeastern Borderlands of the Second Polish Republic: September 1939 – July 1941] (Warsaw: Żydowski Instytut Historyczny, 2006), 69.

names will never be remembered and whose deeds are largely forgotten. Survivors from Sokoły recall:

> The village Landowa [Lendowo near Brańsk] had a good name among the Jews who were hiding in the area around Sokoly, and they regarded it as a paradise. Many Jews began to stream there. ... there wasn't a house in Landowa where there weren't three or four Jews. (Liba Goldberg-Warobel)

> Finally, we came to the village of Landowa [Lendowo]. ... we knocked on the door of a house, not far from the forest. An old farmwoman brought us into the house. ... I remained alone with the old farmwoman. ... Over time, it became known to all of them that I was not related to her family and that I didn't even know Polish. The farmwoman did not hesitate to admit that she had adopted me, a Jewish girl, as her daughter. ... The farmwoman began to teach me Christian prayers, and on Sundays I went with her to church. ... The *goyim*, residents of the village who knew I was Jewish, did not hand me over to the Germans. (Tzipora Tabak-Burstein)[92]

> This village Lendowo became a refuge for a lot of wandering Jews, they called this village the Garden of Eden. ... here they opened wide the doors without having any fear. Soon there were Jews in every house.[93]

A Jew from Zabłudów has made an effort to recall the numerous Poles who helped him to survive the German occupation in the Białystok District:

> We heard the shooting and immediately went to the path leading to the village we knew very well. Some farmers gave us flour, barley, and butter ... Early in the morning they took us through the path where we could go to Bialystok ... [The Nazis] kept hitting me until I fainted. ... I dragged myself to the road; some Christians that stood there and saw me started crying. ...

> Other [Jewish families] went through back ways to the village to get some food. I managed to get a job from Vintzig Volnetzvick [Wincenty Wolniewicz?], the Christian ... His son-in-law, Chashick [Czesiek], promised me that if I stayed with him I wouldn't have to work for the Germans ...

---

[92] Shmuel Kalisher, ed., *Sokoly: B'maavak l'haim* (Tel Aviv: Organization of Sokoły Emigrés in Israel, 1975), 188–207, translated as *Sokoly: In the Fight for Life,* Internet: <http://www.jewishgen.org/yizkor/sokoly/sokoly.html>.
[93] Luba Wrobel Goldberg, *A Sparkle of Hope: An Autobiography* (Melbourne: n.p., 1998), 63.

One day Vinchick, the Christian that I lived with drove me to Bialystok ... Zabludow's Jewish women went to the Christian's field to get some potatoes for the winter. ... We hid in Vinchik Velosoviches [Wincenty Wesołowicz's] barn deep in the hay ... The helpful Christian's wife came to the barn begging me to leave. 'There were whispers in the city that you were not seen among the people in the wagons, saying that you are probably hiding.' She asked that I pity her, because if I would be caught her family will be held responsible, and they will be punished severely. I was able to convince her to let me stay until Sunday. ...

I came to Novosad [Nowosady] village, I knew a good Christian there. My appearance scared him, and immediately he told me about the order that they have to bring any Jews without delay to the Nazi headquarters. 'I have to be very careful,' he said. He gave me some food and took me to a place behind the barn where I could escape. When evening came I arrived at a new village. I had a friend there ... He too took me in courteously and brought me food, but refused to let me stay. Fearfully he gave me food quickly and begged me to leave, I continued my wandering ... later on I had the opportunity to find shelter in an agriculture farm of Christian people I knew. I left the place when they told me that the Germans were hunting the area and were planning to sleep in their house.

I wandered all night through fields and forests until I got to Baranke [Baranki] village, where my father used to live. A farmer, a good acquaintance that we knew from the past took me in nicely. I shaved and bathed; they even provided me with clean clothes. I hid in the side section of the house where no one lived. ... I stayed in the forest until the evening, and then I came back to the Christians. The Germans were not in the village anymore, but the farmer didn't let me stay and take the risk. I wandered again, and soon I got to another agriculture farm and stayed there a couple of days. The farmer didn't allow for me to stay with him; he was afraid the children might talk and risk giving me away.

From there I moved to a farm near Araje. ... The farm's owners gave me shelter. I knew his son from the old days where we were both captured by the Germans. For a while I was able to rest. When the Christians' holiday came I took part in the ceremonies, and I acted like them. ... In the forests there were a lot of Russian partisans ... When I realized that the Nazis raided around the farm where I was staying I decided to escape. ... I got to a big village by the name of Zavick [Zawyki]. I slipped away secretly to the barn and laid there until the morning. The barn's owner found me, but he was a good man who was ready to help. He took me to his house, fed me, and helped me hide. It was a secret basement under the dining room.

... the Nazis searched the village and came to the farmer's house. ... They were looking for Jews and partisans. ... I stayed in the hiding place for a few days. I was asked to leave by his wife who had started to cry, saying that I was putting her family in danger. 'I'm a mother of six children,' she said. 'If they'll find out that I am hiding you they will kill us. I'll give you food and drink and be on your way. Have pity on us, and save your soul.' I promised that I would leave that night. ... I got to the previous farm from which I had escaped. The frightened Christian told me that the night I escaped the Nazis searched the house and barn. ... It was dangerous to stay in the village, where to go? I decided to go toward Bialystok. On the way I stopped at different villages. ...

The Christian who told me the news was ready to leave the next morning with his wagon to bring food to Bialystok. I asked him to take me with him in his wagon. His wife gave me bread and fat. We left early in the morning so that nobody would see me. ... When we approached Bialystok the farmer got scared and asked me to get off the wagon. I got off, raised my collar and continued by foot ...[94]

According to three separate testimonies of Jewish escapees from the death camps of Sobibór and Treblinka, they "walked about the villages" and were "known to everybody," including the farm-hands and school children, without being betrayed.[95]

Kalmen Wewryk describes the assistance he received from numerous peasants as he wandered from village to village in an area south of Chełm, after his escape from the Sobibór death camp. The area was populated by decent but frightened Catholic Poles and some Ukrainian Baptists. A family of five Jews hid in Teresin near Chełm: "Everybody in the hamlet knew that this family was hiding, but nobody knew where and they didn't want to know. Moishe told me how they were loved in that hamlet—there were decent people there."[96]

In spite of the death penalty for the slightest assistance to Jews, local Polish peasants helped Samuel Willenberg on no less than nine separate occasions in the first days after his escape from Treblinka. Willenberg stresses the risks involved in assisting Jews. When a group of Jews broke out of Treblinka, the Germans mobilized their forces (including

---

[94] Account of Phinia Korovski in Nechama Shmueli-Schmusch, ed., *Zabludow: Dapim mi-tokh yisker-bukh* (Tel Aviv: The Zabludow Community in Israel, 1987), an English translation of which is posted on the Internet at: <www.jewishgen.org/yizkor/zabludow/>.
[95] Teresa Prekerowa, "The Attitude of the Polish Population ...," *Biuletyn Głównej Komisji Badania Zbrodni przeciwko Narodowi Polskiemu—Instytutu Pamięci Narodowej,* vol. 35 (1993): 108. See above.
[96] Kalmen Wawryk, *To Sobibor and Back: An Eyewitness Account* (Montreal: The Concordia University Chair in Canadian Jewish Studies, and The Montreal Institute for Genocide and Human Rights Studies, 1999), 66–68, 71.

the Ukrainian camp guards) and conducted a thorough search of the entire area, setting up checkpoints on the roads and combing nearby villages and searching villagers' homes.[97]

A.L. Bombe, an escapee from Treblinka, was helped by several peasants in the vicinity of the camp:

> Laying in the field, we saw a peasant in a wagon go by. We called him over and told him that we had escaped from Treblinka and, perhaps, it would be possible if he could take us into his barn. ... In the end, we convinced him and he showed us his barn in the distance and we went inside. But he doesn't know of anything. And if they would ask, we should say that we sneaked in. That is what we did. We were there the entire day. At night, the head of the village came and told us that he would lead us out of the village and show us the way to go. He indeed took us to the main road, and we traveled all night until the morning. In the morning, we came to a village. We saw, in front of a house, that a woman opens the door. We went over to the house and the woman told us to come in. We were there for a week. The second week, we were at the friend of the peasant in the same village. I remember this peasant's name: Piotr Supel. ... This was in the village Zagradniki [Ogrodniki] near Ostrovek Vengravski [Ostrówek Węgrowski]. The peasant traveled with us to Warsaw.[98]

After his escape from the Treblinka death camp, Mieczysław Grajewski (Martin Gray) recalled the help he received from peasants:

> I was free. I walked to a village. ... I knocked to ask for bread. The peasants looked at me in silence. 'Bread, bread.' They saw my red hands, torn jacket, worn-out slippers, and handed me some hard, gray crusts. A peasant woman, huddled in shawls, gave me a bowl of hot milk and a bag. We didn't talk: my body had turned red and blue from the blows and the cold, and my clothes, everything proclaimed *Jew!* But they gave me bread. Thank you, Polish peasants. I slept in a stable near the animals, taking a little warm milk from the cow in the morning. My bag filled with bread.[99]

---

[97] Samuel Willenberg, *Surviving Treblinka* (Oxford: Basil Blackwell in association with the Institute for Polish-Jewish Studies, 1989), 25, 143–48.
[98] A.L. Bombe, "My Escape from Treblinka," *Czentochov: A New Supplement to the Book "Czenstochover Yidn",* Internet: <http://www.jewishgen.org/yizkor/Czestochowa/Czestochowa.html>, translation of S.D. Singer, ed., *Tshenstokhover: Naye tsugobmaterial tsum bukh "Tshenstokhover Yidn"* (New York: United Relief Committee in New York, 1958), 57ff.
[99] Martin Gray, with Max Gallo, *For Those I Loved* (Boston and Toronto: Little, Brown, 1972), 178.

The most significant impediment was the fear of German retaliation. A Jew who had escaped from Treblinka and managed to return to Warsaw recalled:

> The peasants near Treblinka didn't want to shelter me even for just one night. They happily gave me food and even money, but they wouldn't hear of my spending the night, because the Ukrainians who were permanently stationed in Treblinka often showed up ... The local peasants told of things that were unbelievable but unfortunately true. ... Everyone I talked to near Treblinka spoke of nothing else. They all told the same thing, in horror. The ones closer to Warsaw let me stay the night, but there was no question of staying there permanently.[100]

Yet despite the massive German hunt for Jews, some escapees did find shelter with farmers nearby. Szymon Goldberg lived near Wyszków: "There were good people, they helped, they gave me food." Mendel Rzepka was hidden on a farm along with a large group of Jews.[101] Abraham (Abram) Kolski, Erich Lachman, Henoch (Henry) Brenner, Gustaw Boraks, and four other Jews who escaped during the uprising on 2 August 1943, were hidden in the cellar of a farmer's home in the village of Orzeszówka for the remainder of the war.[102]

Wacław Iglicki (then Szul Steinhendler) from Żelechów, who jumped out of a train headed for Treblinka near Łuków or Siedlce, stated:

> People used to really help out. I have to say that objectively: when it came to bread or something else, they shared. But finding a place to sleep was a problem. People were afraid. They wouldn't really agree to have us over for a night, or for a longer stay. That was understandable, because if you consider that in every village, in every community, there was a sign saying that for hiding, for any help given to a Jew, there was the death penalty, it's hard to be surprised that people didn't want to have Jews over and so on. They could tell by my clothes that I was a Jew. Because I looked poor, obviously. Ragged, dirty. Wandered around, as they say, aimlessly, didn't

---

[100] Michał Grynberg, ed., *Words To Outlive Us: Voices From the Warsaw Ghetto* (New York: Metropolitan Books/Henry Holt, 2002), 210.

[101] Teresa Prekerowa, "The Attitude of the Polish Population ...," *Biuletyn Głównej Komisji Badania Zbrodni przeciwko Narodowi Polskiemu—Instytutu Pamięci Narodowej*, vol. 35 (1993): 108. See above.

[102] Oral history interview with Abraham Kolski, by Linda Gordon Kuzmack, 29 March 1990, United States Holocaust Memorial Museum, Washington, D.C.; testimony of Abram Kolski, USC Shoah Foundation Institute (Interview Code 49970); testimony of Gustaw Boraks, Yad Vashem Archives.

know where to go. ... Because of that, many knew immediately they were dealing with a person of Jewish origin.[103]

Ruth Altbeker Cyprys from Warsaw, who jumped from a train headed for Treblinka, recalls various instances of assistance from railway guards, villagers, passers-by, passengers, and even a gang of robbers.[104] In his account dated May 1994, Joseph S. Kutrzeba writes:

> During the first days of September 1942, at the age of 14, I jumped out of a moving train destined for Treblinka, through an opening [window] of a cattle car loaded to capacity with Jews from the Warsaw Ghetto. Wandering over fields, forests and villages, at first in the vicinity of Wołomin, and later of Zambrów, I found myself, in late November, in the area of Hodyszewo [near Łomża]. Throughout my wandering, the peasants for the most part were amenable to put me up for the night and to feed me—some either suspecting my origins or pressing me to admit it.[105]

Henryk Schönker recalled that when he was fingered in Wieliczka by a boy who started to chase him, the passers-by ignored the boy's cry to "catch the Jew." No one made an effort to apprehend him. One of the onlookers seized the boy and admonished him.[106]

Joseph Dattner, from Bielsko in Upper Silesia, recalls: "I survived, like my brothers, by pretending to be Christian. I took the name Poluk but I was well-known and most people knew I was Jewish."[107]

Other examples from central Poland where the fact of assistance was widely known in the community are recorded for the following localities: Niedźwiada near Opole Lubleskie,[108] Runów near Grójec,[109] Gorzyce near Dąbrowa Tarnowska,[110] Przydonica, Ubiad, Klimkówka,

---

[103] Testimony of Waclaw Iglicki, September 2005, Internet: <http://www.centropa.org> under "Biographies."
[104] Ruth Altbeker Cyprys, *A Jump for Life: A Jump For Life: A Survivor's Journal from Nazi-Occupied Poland* (New York: Continuum, 1997), 97, 102–10; translated into Polish as *Skok dla życia: Pamiętnik z czasów okupacji Polski* (Warszawa : Philip Wilson, 2001).
[105] Testimony of Joseph S. Kutrzeba, May 1994, Internet: <http://www.glaukopis.pl/pdf/czytelnia/WartImeRescueOfJewsByThePolishCatholicClergy_MarkPaul.pdf>.
[106] Henryk Schönker, *Dotknięcie anioła* [The Touch of an Angel] (Warsaw: Ośrodek Karta, 2005), 135–36.
[107] Al Sokol, "Holocaust theme underscores work of artist," *Toronto Star*, 7 November 1996.
[108] Stanisław Wroński and Maria Zwolakowa, *Polacy i Żydzi 1939–1945* [Poles and Jews 1939-1945] (Warsaw: Książka i Wiedza, 1971), 269.
[109] Wroński and Zwolakowa, *Polacy i Żydzi 1939–1945* [Poles and Jews], 322.
[110] Wroński and Zwolakowa, *Polacy i Żydzi 1939–1945* [Poles and Jews], 343.

Jelna, Słowikowa, and Librantowa near Nowy Sącz,[111] Rakszawa,[112] an entire street in Przemyśl that was aware of a Jewish hideout,[113] Mchy near Krasnystaw,[114] Piszczac near Biała Podlaska,[115] Kolonia Dworska near Piszczac,[116] Różki near Krasnystaw,[117] villages near Lublin,[118] villages near Skierniewice,[119] villages near Zamość,[120] villages near Radzymin,[121] villages near Otwock.[122]

Another episode worthy of mention is the fate of Jews from Warsaw after the Warsaw Uprising of 1944. Almost all of the Jews who survived the uprising, numbering at least several thousand, were evacuated along with the Polish population to a transit camp in Pruszków, some 20 kilometres away. As historian Gunnar Paulsson points out, these included people who had a conspicuously Semitic appearance and had previously lived under the surface. Along the way, there were many opportunities for hostile Poles to spot and denounce them. However, no concrete evidence has come to light of Jews being betrayed during this exodus. Nor is there evidence that any Jews perished in Pruszków as a result of denunciation by Poles.[123]

The Lewinson family, besides having a conspicuously Semitic appearance, were publicly exposed in Pruszków as Jews by a German soldier, who was then distracted. Poles standing nearby urged them: "Run away, ladies, run away. (...) Hide somewhere, try to save your lives."

---

[111] Wroński and Zwolakowa, *Polacy Żydzi 1939–1945* [Poles and Jews], 349.

[112] Wroński and Zwolakowa, *Polacy Żydzi 1939–1945* [Poles and Jews], 353.

[113] Wroński and Zwolakowa, *Polacy Żydzi 1939–1945* [Poles and Jews], 307.

[114] Thomas Toivi Blatt, *From the Ashes of Sobibor: A Story of Survival* (Evanston, Illinois: Northwestern University Press, 1997), 207ff.

[115] Diane Armstrong, *Mosaic: A Chronicle of Five Generations* (Milsons Point, New South Wales: Random House, 1998), 576–81; Roman Soszyński, *Piszczac: Miasto ongiś królewskie* [Piszczac: A Once Royal City] (N.p., n.p., 1993), 97.

[116] Roman Soszyński, *Piszczac: Miasto ongiś królewskie* [Piszczac: A Once Royal City] (N.p., n.p., 1993), 95.

[117] Gutman and Bender, *The Encyclopedia of the Righteous Among the Nations,* vol. 4: *Poland,* Part 1, 452.

[118] Gutman and Bender, *The Encyclopedia of the Righteous Among the Nations,* vol. 4: *Poland,* Part 1, 95, 317, 326.

[119] Gutman and Bender, *The Encyclopedia of the Righteous Among the Nations,* vol. 4: *Poland,* Part 1, 343–44.

[120] Gutman and Bender, *The Encyclopedia of the Righteous Among the Nations,* vol. 5: *Poland,* Part 2, 647.

[121] Gutman and Bender, *The Encyclopedia of the Righteous Among the Nations,* vol. 5: *Poland,* Part 2, 673, 692.

[122] Gutman and Bender, *The Encyclopedia of the Righteous Among the Nations,* vol. 5: *Poland,* Part 2, 927.

[123] Paulsson, *Secret City,* 191–92.

Suddenly, a tall Pole—a complete stranger to them—comes to their rescue and asks the three Lewinsons to run with him. When they reach the far end of the Pruszków camp, they were hidden in a deserted barn. All the onlookers saw the tall man take them away. Any one of the bystanders could have shown the German soldier where they had been taken. Furthermore, people may well have feared reprisals for not doing so. Yet not a single person denounced them. Paulsson makes the following observations:

> [S]ince a single malicious person would have been enough to betray the Lewinsons, whereas their safety depended on the unanimous silence of the whole crowd, even once such occurrence would border on the miraculous if any significant proportion of the population had been sufficiently hostile. For several thousand Jews to pass through Pruszków without a single known instance of betrayal is strong evidence that there was a general attitude of solidarity at that time.[124]

The Lewinsons did encounter some hostility in an overcrowded train carrying Poles from Warsaw whom the Germans dispersed in the countryside. A woman suddenly yelled out, "Let's throw these three Jewesses out! We'd be better off without them." But this proved unpopular with the crowd: "A powerful hushing makes her hold her tongue. 'One more word,' a crippled man says sternly, 'and you'll be thrown out yourself.'" No one supported the woman's solitary urging.[125]

Jews passing as Poles in labor camps in Germany feared Polish inmates who were suspicious of their origins and sometimes threatened to betray them. But, as Paulsson notes, such anti-Semitism was unlikely to lead to betrayal:

> Undoubtedly cases of denunciation did occur in the labor camps, but none have so far come to light. Again, these are situations where a Jew could have died through denunciation by a single malevolent person, but it required the unanimous silence of the whole barrack—in the face of death threats—to ensure the Jew's survival.[126]

Assistance from Polish farmers in Eastern Galicia and Volhynia (Wołyń) was equally plentiful. Historians Tatiana Berenstein and

---

[124] Ibid., 191–92.
[125] Ibid., 193.
[126] Ibid., 193–94.

Adam Rutkowski list several examples of help extended by entire rural communities:[127]

- In Kretówka, in Tarnopol *Voivodship*, "several dozen Jews were able to move about almost freely because the whole village shielded them from the Nazis."
- In Woronówka near Ludwipol, Volhynia, "the collusion of the peasants was cemented by blood ties: every villager was either a Kuriata or a Torgoń."
- "The peasants in Kościejów, in the vicinity of which ran the railway line leading to the extermination camp at Bełżec, tended to Jews who jumped out of the 'death trains.' They not only brought them food and clothing but also sent word to Jews in the nearby village of Kulików to come and fetch the heavily injured immediately; the rest were taken by the peasants themselves to Kulików under cover of darkness."
- "In Bar villagers supplied a group of 18 Jews hiding in the neighboring woods with food; they came into the village at night for their provisions and thanks to this help were able to hold out until the area was liberated by the Soviet Army." One of the Jewish survivors praises the "noble attitude of the entire population, without exception, of the Polish village of Bar," near Gródek Jagielloński, who helped more than twenty people hiding in nearby forests to survive.[128]

Scores of Jews were helped by the Polish villagers of Hanaczów, about 40 kilometres east of Lwów.[129]

About 12 miles outside Lwów, in the middle of winter, Abraham Trasawucki, dressed only in rags, jumped from a death train headed for Bełżec. Although he was easily identifiable as a Jew on the run, the villagers did not betray him, rather he was offered temporary shelter, food, clothing and money at two random Polish farmsteads, and given

---

[127] Berenstein and Rutkowski, *Assistance to the Jews in Poland 1939–1945*, 27, 45–46.
[128] Gerszon Taffet, *Zagłada Żydów żółkiewskich* [The Extermination of the Żółkiew Jews] (Łódź: Centralna Żydowska Komisja Historyczna, 1946), 62; Bartoszewski and Lewin, *Righteous Among Nations,* 444; Bartoszewski and Lewin, *Righteous Among Nations,* 444.
[129] Jerzy Węgierski, *W lwowskiej Armii Krajowej* [In the Lwów Home Army] (Warsaw: Pax, 1989), 77–78; Eliyahu Yones, *Smoke in the Sand: The Jews of Lvov in the War Years 1939–1944* (Jerusalem and New York: Gefen, 2004), 227–28; Chodorska, *Godni synowie naszej Ojczyzny* [Worthy Sons of Our Fatherland], Part Two, 204–7; Gutman and Bender, *The Encyclopedia of the Righteous Among the Nations,* vol. 5: *Poland,* Part 2, 886–87.

rides in the wagons of other Poles. He was sold a train ticket by an official, allowed on the train by a guard who checked his ticket, and not denounced by the passengers, even though everyone recognized him as a Jew.[130]

Regarding conditions in Kosów near Kołomyja, Bronia Beker states:

> My aunt didn't have to hide. She was so well loved and respected by all because she always helped the poorest of the poor, that while she was walking around freely, living among the ruins nobody gave her away. ... The people in the town also made sure she had food at all times.[131]

Samuel Eisen, a teenager who survived in the forest near Tłuste, recalled: "We had no money, but in the village nearby lived a lot of Poles who knew us and were good to us. They were afraid to hide us but they gave us food."[132]

Maria Fischer Zahn, who hid near Zborów, stated: "Everybody in the neighborhood knew we were hiding, but nobody told the Germans. The people in Jezierna were good people. They didn't give us away. They helped us with food. We couldn't have survived without them."[133]

Shlomo Berger, who passed as a Pole in a small town near Czortków, working for Tadeusz Duchowski, the Polish director of a company, recalled:

> I rented a room in Niźniów with one of the Polish workers. I learned from him that the man who was in charge of the office was the son of a judge who was a Jew who had converted to Catholicism. The son was probably raised as a Christian, but by German criteria he was still Jewish. The people at the office knew who he was, but nobody said anything.[134]

A number of Jews were sheltered by Polish villagers in Ułaszkowce near Czortków.[135] Of Ostra Mogiła near Skałat Jewish survivors wrote:

---

[130] Abraham Tracy, *To Speak For the Silenced* (Jerusalem and New York: Devora, 2007), 165–72.
[131] "Women of Valor: Partisans and Resistance Fighters," www.interlog.com/~mighty/personal/bronia.htm, originally published in the *Journal of the Center for Holocaust Studies*, vol. 6, no. 4 (Spring 1990).
[132] Maria Hochberg-Mariańska and Noe Grüss, eds., *The Children Accuse* (London: Vallentine Mitchell, 1996), 206.
[133] Carole Garbuny Vogel, *We Shall Not Forget!: Memories of the Holocaust*, Second edition (Lexington, Massachusetts: Temple Isaiah, 1995), 280, and also 276.
[134] Ronald J. Berger, *Constructing a Collective Memory of the Holocaust: A Life History of Two Brothers' Survival* (Niwot: University Press of Colorado, 1995), 55.
[135] Abraham Morgenstern, *Chortkov Remembered: The Annihilation of a Jewish Community* (Dumont, New Jersey: n.p., 1990), 83–84, 98.

"The people in this village were friendly to the Jews and provided them with whatever they could. ... Twenty-nine Jews survived in Ostra-Mogila."[136]

Markus Lecker, who joined up with a large group of Jews living in a forest bunker in the vicinity of Borszczów, describes their relations with a Polish settlement that provided them with food:

> The colony ... consisted of six houses with six Polish families living there. ... These 6 Polish families were the main support for us Jewish outcasts who lived in the bunker. We used to go to the Polish colony at night and exchange whatever we had left for food ... But I must say these Polish colonists did supply us with some food ... even if we didn't have what to give them in return ...[137]

Irene Gut Opdyke, a Polish rescuer and recipient of a Yad Vashem award who lived in Tarnopol, recalled:

> There was a priest in Janówka [near Tarnopol]. He knew about the Jews' escape—many of the Polish people knew about it. ... Many people brought food and other things—not right to the forest, but to the edge—from the village. The priest could not say directly 'help the Jews,' but he would say in church, 'not one of you should take the blood of your brother.' ... During the next couple of weeks there were posters on every street corner saying, 'This is a Jew-free town, and if any one should help an escaped Jew, the sentence is death.'[138]

Michael Zipper and his cousins, Maria Goldhirsh and her daughter Ruzia (later Rose Slutsky), and Fella Sieler were among the thirteen Jews, including five children, hidden in a forest bunker near the predominantly Polish village of Zabojki near Tarnopol, for a period of eight months. Rose Slutsky would recall, "The whole village kept us a secret, and when they could, they shared some food with us. (...) good

---

[136] Abraham Weissbord, *Death of a Shtetl*, Internet: <http://www.jewishgen.org/Yizkor/Skalat1/Skalat.html>, translation of *Es shtarbt a shtetl: Megiles Skalat* (Munich: Central Historical Commission of the Central Committee of Liberated Jews in the U.S. Zone of Germany, 1948), 65.

[137] Marcus Lecker, *I Remember: Odyssey of a Jewish Teenager in Eastern Europe* (Montreal: The Concordia University Chair in Canadian Jewish Studies, and The Montreal Institute for Genocide and Human Rights Studies, 1999), 56.

[138] Carol Rittner and Sondra Myers, eds., *The Courage to Care: Rescuers of Jews During the Holocaust* (New York: New York University Press, 1986), 47–48.

Polish people who gave us a bit of food, when they themselves were hungry."[139]

"The few Jews of Gliniany who saved their lives were hiding in the woods near Zeniow [Żeniów]. The Polish peasants of that village supplied their food," Chayeh Kanner wrote in a letter.[140] In Hucisko Olejskie near Złoczów, survivor Rose Metzak recounted, "It is a Polish village ... The gentiles were also very kind. We were there. We slept in barns. We slept here a day, here a day, here a night."[141]

In Huta Werchobuska or Werchobudzka (near Złoczów) and Huta Pieniacka (near Brody), the Polish villagers were simply annihilated and their homes and farmsteads burned down in German pacifications (the primary perpetrators were the SS Galizien forces) brought on in part by long-standing assistance provided to Jews.[142] Feiwel Auerbach, a Jew from Sasów, made the following deposition shortly after the war:

There were 30 of us [Jews] in the forest. We hid in Huta Werchobuska and Huta Pieniacka. The Polish inhabitants of those villages helped us. The peasants were very poor and were themselves hungry but they shared with us their last bits of food. We stayed there from July 1943 until March 1944. Thanks to them we are alive. When there were manhunts, the village reeve warned us. Once 500 Germans encircled the forest, but since they were afraid to enter deep into the forest they set their dogs on us. We were saved because our Polish friends warned us of the impending danger. Because of a denunciation [by the Ukrainian police] all of the villagers of Huta Pieniacka and Huta Werchobuska were killed. Some of them were burned alive in a barn. The village was burned to the ground.[143]

---

[139] Testimony of Rose Slutsky in Belle Millo, ed., *Voices of Winnipeg Holocaust Survivors* (Winnipeg: Jewish Heritage Centre of Western Canada, 2010), 364; testimony of Rose Slutsky, USC Shoah Foundation Institute (Interview Code 23960).
[140] "Letter of Chayeh Kanner," *Khurbn* Glinyane (New York: New York: Emergency Relief Committee for Gliniany and Vicinity, 1946), translated as *The Tragic End of Our Gliniany*, Internet: <http://www.jewishgen.org/yizkor/glinyany1/Glinyany1.html>.
[141] Account of Rose (Raisel) Metzak, posted at
<http.//voices.iit.edu/frames.asp?path+Interviews/&page=meltz&ext=_.t.html>.
[142] Zajączkowski, *Martyrs of Charity*, Part One, 154–55; Tsvi Weigler, "Two Polish Villages Razed for Extending Help to Jews," *Yad Washem Bulletin*, no. 1 (April 1957): 19–20; Reuben Ainsztein, *Jewish Resistance in Nazi-Occupied Poland (with a historical survey of the Jew as fighter and soldier in the Diaspora)* (London: Paul Elek, 1974), 450–53; *Na Rubieży* (Wrocław), no. 10 (1994). 10–11 (Huta Werchodudzka); *Na Rubieży*, no. 12 (1995): 7–20 (Huta Pieniacka); *Na Rubieży*, no. 54 (2001): 18–29.
[143] Feiwel Auerbach's account is the Jewish Historical Institute Archives in Warsaw, Record Group 301, Testimony 1200.

Almost every Polish family in the hamlet of Zawołocze near Ludwipol, in Volhynia, sheltered or helped Jews. None of the Jews was betrayed.[144] Jews hiding in the forests in the vicinity of Berezne (Bereźne) near Kostopol, Volhynia, received extensive assistance from Polish villagers and partisans.[145] Polish villages in the vicinity of Korzec, Volhynia, helped Jews hiding in the forests.[146]

A report about the village of Stara Huta near Szumsk, in Volhynia, states:

> The people of a small Polish village named Stara Hota [sic] welcomed a group of Jews to stay and hide in their homes. The Ukrainians found out about the Jewish presence in the village. They informed the Germans right away. The Poles had managed to help the Jews run into the fields, but they were all caught and killed during their escape.[147]

Dawid Sasower recalls: "near Zaturne [near Łuck], there was a Polish village in which about twenty Jews lived. In the daytime they worked in the fields and at night the Poles gave them rifles so that they could protect themselves from the banderovtsy [Ukrainian nationalist partisans]."[148]

According to the Rokitno memorial book, Polish villagers in Blizhov, Borowskie Budki, Netreba, Okopy, and Snodowicze were very helpful:[149]

---

[144] Chodorska, *Godni synowie naszej Ojczyzny* [Worthy Sons of Our Fatherland], Part Two, 77–78.

[145] Account of Seweryn Dobroszklanka, Jewish Historical Institute (Warsaw) archive, record group 301, testimony 1222; Wroński and Zwolakowa, *Polacy Żydzi 1939–1945* [Poles and Jews 1939-1945], 324–25.

[146] Nyuma Anapolsky, "We survived thanks to the kind people—Ukrainians and Poles,' in Boris Zabarko, ed., *Holocaust in the Ukraine* (London and Portland, Oregon: Vallentine Mitchell, 2005), 10–11.

[147] Ruth Sztejnman Halperin, "The Last Days of Shumsk," in H. Rabin, ed., *Szumsk: Memorial Book of the Martyrs of Szumsk,* Internet: <http://www.jewishgen.org/yizkor/szumsk/szumsk.html>, translation of *Shumsk: Sefer zikaron le-kedoshei Shumsk* (Tel Aviv: Former Residents of Szumsk in Israel, 1968), 29ff.

[148] Rima Dulkinienė and Kerry Keys, eds., *Su adata širdyje: Getų ir koncentracijos stovyklų kalinių atsiminimai; With a Needle in the Heart: Memoirs of Former Prisoners of Ghettos and Concentration Camps* (Vilnius: Garnelis and Genocide and Resistance Research Centre of Lithuania, 2003), 319–20.

[149] E. Leoni, ed., *Rokitno (Volin) ve-ha-sevivah: Sefer edut ve-zikaron* (Tel Aviv: Former Residents of Rokitno in Israel, 1967), 293ff., 317ff., 327ff., 334ff., 342ff., 351, translated as *Rokitno-Wolyn and Surroundings: Memorial Book and Testimony,* Internet: <http://www.jewishgen.org/yizkor/rokitnoye/Rokitnoye.html>.

'I must say that these peasants treated us fairly well. In the area of Blizhov there were no attacks or denunciations of Jews.'

'In the village of Netrebe [Netreba], tens of Jews from Rokitno and the area found shelter. They were helped by the villagers who not only did not harm them but also hid them near the village during the day. At night they took them to their homes. Many Jews survived there until the liberation by the Red Army. In the Polish village of Budki some Jews survived ...

'In the same area, in the Polish village of Okopi [Okopy], some tens of Jews were saved thanks to two special individuals... the Catholic priest [Rev. Ludwik Wrodarczyk, who was awarded by Yad Vashem] and the village teacher. The priest used to give sermons to his followers telling them not to be involved in the extermination of Jews. He asked them to help the Jews to survive ... The village teacher also had compassion for the unfortunate Jews. Their suffering touched her heart and she helped in any way possible. She was killed by a Ukrainian gang on the way from the village of Rokitno where she was helping a Jewish family. The priest was burned alive in his church.'

'In a Polish village near Snodovich [Snodowicze], we found a few Jewish families working in the houses and fields of the villagers.'

In Polish villages near the hamlet of Berezołupy near Rożyszcze:

'When I arrived in the Polish village, someone told me that five kilometers from there, here was another Polish village where I might find my brother ... I went there and asked the farmers about him. They told me where to go, and I found him in a forest, with a group of six other Jews. ... They too had spent the winter in the forest, and at night they had brought potatoes and bread from the Polish village. ... I was accepted by an older couple ... My brother also got a job with another Polish farmer, about four kilometers from the village where I was. ... I stayed with that farmer for almost a year, until the Russians freed our area in April 1944.'[150]

Spontaneous assistance was much more frequent than is often assumed, as illustrated by the following examples. In October 1942, after the liquidation of the ghetto in Zdołbunów, the Germans and Ukrainian militiamen combed the town to locate any signs of survivors·

---

[150] Denise Nevo and Mira Berger, eds., *We Remember: Testimonies of Twenty-four Members of Kibbutz Megiddo who Survived the Holocaust* (New York: Shengold, 1994), 257.

[Fritz] Germ would point to a certain house, always one occupied by Polish citizens, and the guards would crash through the door or a window, emerging with a family and the Jews whom they had hidden. The fate was the same for the rescuers as it was for the Jews. This occurred at four or five different homes.[151]

About twenty residents of Berecz, in Volhynia, were killed during a pacification of that Polish settlement by Ukrainian police in November 1942 for assisting Jews who had escaped from the ghetto in Powursk (Powórsk).[152]

Other examples of assistance by Poles, where the fact of assistance was widely known in the community, are recorded for the following localities: Konińsk near Sarny,[153] Huta Sopaczewska near Sarny,[154] Polish villages near the settlement of Berezołupy near Rożyszcze,[155] Pańska Dolina near Dubno,[156] Świnarzyn near Dominopol,[157] in the vicinity of Bereźne near Kostopol,[158] Karaczun near Kostopol (both the Polish underground and Polish villagers were extremely helpful to Jews who hid in the forest),[159] Huta Stepańska,[160] Woronówka near

---

[151] Douglas K. Huneke, *The Moses of Rovno: The Stirring Story of Fritz Graebe, a German Christian Who Risked His Life to Lead Hundreds of Jews to Safety During the Holocaust* (New York: Dodd, Mead & Company, 1985), 84. See also Edward Prus, *Holocaust po banderowsku: Czy Żydzi byli w UPA?* [The Holocaust, Bandera-Style: Were There Jews in the UPA?] (Wrocław: Nortom, 1995), 82.

[152] Władysław Siemaszko and Ewa Siemaszko, *Ludobójstwo dokonane przez nacjonalistów ukraińskich na ludności polskiej Wołynia, 1939–1945* [Genocide Committed by the Ukrainian Nationalists Against the Polish Population of Volhynia, 1939-1945] (Warsaw: von borowiecky, 2000), 1: 363.

[153] Wroński and Zwolakowa, *Polacy Żydzi 1939–1945* [Poles and Jews 1939-1945], 263; Asher Tarmon, ed., *Memorial Book: The Jewish Communities of Manyevitz, Horodok, Lishnivka, Troyanuvka, Povursk, and Kolki (Wolyn Region)* (Tel-Aviv: Organization of Survivors of Manyevitz, Horodok, Lishnivka, Troyanuvka, Povursk, Kolki and Surroundings Living in Israel and Overseas, 2004), 39–40, 67–68, 74, 85.

[154] Denise Nevo and Mira Berger, eds., *We Remember: Testimonies of Twenty-four Members of Kibbutz Megiddo who Survived the Holocaust* (New York: Shengold, 1994), 209.

[155] Nevo and Berger, *We Remember*, 257.

[156] Wroński and Zwolakowa, *Polacy Żydzi 1939–1945* [Poles and Jews], 265.

[157] Wroński and Zwolakowa, *Polacy Żydzi 1939–1945* [Poles and Jews], 266.

[158] Wroński and Zwolakowa, *Polacy Żydzi 1939–1945* [Poles and Jews], 324–25.

[159] J. Peri, "Death and Sorrow," in Yitzhak Ganuz, ed., *Our Town Stepan*, Internet: <http://www.jewishgen.org/yizkor/stepan/Stepan.html>, translation of *Ayaratenu Stepan* (Tel Aviv: Stepan Society, 1977), 213ff.; Stanisław Siekierski, ed., *Żyli wśród nas...: Wspomnienia Polaków i Żydów nadesłane na konkurs pamięci polsko-żydowskiej o nagrodę imienia Dawida Ben Guriona* [They Lived Among Us ...: Polish and Jewish Testimonies Supplied for the Polish-Jewish Memory Contest to Recieve the David Ben Gurion Prize] (Płońsk: Zarząd Miasta Płońsk, Miejskie Centrum Kultury w

Ludwipol,[161] Obórki,[162] Wólka Kotowska near Łuck,[163] Przebraże,[164] Adamy,[165] Huta Brodzka,[166] Okopy, Budki Borowskie, Dołhań, Netreba,[167] a village near Horochów,[168] Huta Olejska near Lwów,[169] Kurdybań Warkowicki, Bortnica, Pańska Dolina, Żeniówka, all in Volhynia,[170] a Polish village in the vicinity of Międzyrzec near Równe,[171] a Polish settlement near Aleksandria in Volhynia (all the villagers knew about and assisted the sisters Cypa and Rywa Szpanberg),[172] Rakowiec and Hołosko Wielkie, near Lwów,[173] Dzwonica, near Złoczów,[174] Horyhlady or Horyglady near Tłumacz,

Płońsku, and Towarzystwo Miłośników Ziemi Płońskiej, 2001), 121; Andrzej Leja, "Urodzona w ZSRS" [Born in the USSR], Polis: Miasto Pans Cogito, Internet: <http://www.polis2008.pl/index.php?option=com_content&view=article&id=601&josc clean=1&comment_id=843>.
[160] Ganuz, ed., *Our Town Stepan*, 287; Daniel Kac, *Koncert grany żywym* [A Concert for the Living] (Warsaw: Tu, 1998), 183.
[161] Wroński and Zwolakowa, *Polacy Żydzi 1939–1945* [Poles and Jews], 327.
[162] Wroński and Zwolakowa, *Polacy Żydzi 1939–1945* [Poles and Jews], 361, 389.
[163] Wroński and Zwolakowa, *Polacy Żydzi 1939–1945* [Poles and Jews], 386.
[164] Wroński and Zwolakowa, *Polacy Żydzi 1939–1945* [Poles and Jews], 392; Kac, *Koncert grany żywym* [A Concert for the Living], 183.
[165] Prus, *Holocaust po banderowsku* [The Holocaust, Bandera-Style], 153; Bronisław Szeremeta, "Zagłada wsi Adamy—rok 1943" [The Destruction of the Village of Adamy: The Year 1943], *Semper Fidelis* (Wrocław), no. 1 (14), 1993: 19.
[166] Prus, *Holocaust po banderowsku* [The Holocaust, Bandera-Style], 167.
[167] Yehuda Bauer, "Sarny and Rokitno in the Holocaust: A Case Study of Two Townships in Wolyn (Volhynia)," in Steven T. Katz, ed., *The Shtetl: New Evaluations* (New York and London: New York University Press, 2007), 273.
[168] Sonya Tesler-Gyraph, "Memories from the Nazi Period," in Yosef Kariv, ed., *Horchiv Memorial Book* (Tel Aviv: Horchiv Committee in Israel, 1966), 63.
[169] Donald L. Niewyk, ed., *Fresh Wounds: Early Narratives of Holocaust Survival* (Chapel Hill: The University of North Carolina Press, 1998), 164.
[170] Isaiah Trunk, *Jewish Responses to Nazi Persecution: Collective and Individual Behavior in Extremis* (New York: Stein and Day, 1979), 250–52.
[171] Account of Mordechai Tennenbaum in Israel Zinman, ed., *Memorial for Greater Mezirich: In Construction and Destruction* (Haifa: Organization of Meziritsh Association, 1999), Internet: <www.jewishgen.org/yizkor/mezhirichi/>.
[172] Andrzej Żbikowski, ed., *Polacy i Żydzi pod okupacją niemiecką 1939–1945: Studia i materiały* [Poles and Jews Under the German Occupation of 1939-1945: Studies and Materials] (Warsaw: Instytut Pamięci Narodowej—Komisja Ścigania Zbrodni przeciwko Narodowi Polskiemu, 2006), 309.
[173] Stepan Makarczuk, "Straty ludności w Galicji Wschodniej w latach II wojny światowej (1939–1945)" [Human Losses in Eastern Galicia During the Second World War], in *Polska–Ukraina: Trudne pytania* [Poland and Ukraine. Difficult Questions], vol. 6 (Warsaw: Światowy Związek Żołnierzy Armii Krajowej, Związek Ukraińców w Polsce, and Karta, 2000), 240.
[174] Ainsztein, *Jewish Resistance in Nazi-Occupied Poland*, 450–53.

and Wojciechówka near Skałat,[175] Wojciechówka near Buczacz,[176] Matuszówka near Buczacz,[177] Dźwinogród near Buczacz,[178] Nowosiółka Koropiecka near Buczacz,[179] the Polish village of Hucisko near Brzeżany, a Home Army base.[180]

In the predominantly Belorussian area of Polesie (Polesia), Kopel Kolpanitzky describes the helpfulness of the residents of Zahorie (Zahorze), a small village of Polish Catholics three kilometers from Łachwa, which the Germans later burned to the ground.[181]

Shulamit Schreyber Żabinska, a teenage girl who was sheltered by Poles in the Wilno countryside, recalled that many Poles brought food to the ghetto, "otherwise everyone would have starved to death. It was dangerous, and people were shot for this." After escaping from the ghetto she was taken in by Weronika ("Wercia") Stankiewicz and her mother, passing as Wercia's niece. Although the villagers knew she was Jewish no one betrayed her.[182]

Similarly, Estera Bielicka was taken in by the Myślicki family in Matejkany where she lived openly. Although the villagers knew about her Jewish origin, no one betrayed her.[183] The neighbors of a Polish family in Białozoryszki near Wilno were aware that that family was sheltering a Jewish boy.[184] Pola Wawer, a doctor from Wilno, recalled

---

[175] Shlomo Blond, et al., eds., *Memorial Book of Tlumacz: The Life and Destruction of a Jewish Community* (Tel Aviv: Tlumacz Societies in Israel and the U.S.A., 1976), column clxxiv; Alicia Appleman-Jurman, *Alicia: My Story* (New York: Bantam, 1988), 149 (Horyhlady or Horyglady near Tłumacz).

[176] Appleman-Jurman, *Alicia*, 157; David Ravid (Shmukler), ed., *The Cieszanow Memorial Book* (Mahwah, New Jersey: Jacob Solomon Berger, 2006), 190–91.

[177] Etunia Bauer Katz, *Our Tomorrows Never Came* (New York: Fordham University Press, 2000), 98–99.

[178] Elżbieta Isakiewicz, *Harmonica: Jews Relate How Poles Saved Them from the Holocaust* (Warsaw: Polska Agencja Informacyjna, 2001), 106–108, translated from the Polish *Ustna harmonijka: Relacje Żydów, których uratowali od Zagłady Polacy* (Warsaw: Niezależne Wydawnictwo Polskie, 2000).

[179] Yehuda Bauer, "Buczacz and Krzemieniec: The Story of Two Towns During the Holocaust," in *Yad Vashem Studies*, vol. 33 (Jerusalem: Yad Vashem, The Holocaust Martyrs' and Heroes' Remembrance Authority, 2005), 298.

[180] Hersch Altman, *One the Fields of Loneliness* (New York and Jerusalem: Yad Vashem and The Holocaust Survivors' Memoirs Project, 2006), 139ff.

[181] Kopel Kolpanitzky, *Sentenced To Life: The Story of a Survivor of the Lahwah Ghetto* (London and Portland, Oregon: Vallentine Mitchell, 2007), 89–96.

[182] Tomaszewski and Werbowski, *Żegota*, 117–18; Tomaszewski and Werbowski, *Code Name*, 117.

[183] Wiktor Noskowski, "Czy Yaffa Eliach przeprosi Polaków?" [Will Yaffa Eliach Apologize to the Poles?], *Myśl Polska* (Warsaw), 20-27 July 1997.

[184] Chodorska, *Godni synowie naszej Ojczyzny* [Worthy Sons of Our Fatherland], Part One, 104–9.

the help she and her parents received from all of the inhabitants in the hamlet of Zameczek who consisted of the families of five cousins.[185]

Another Jew from the Wilno region recalled the assistance he and his father received from the villagers of Powiłańce on a number of occasions:

> The village was composed of some forty houses strung out side by side on a single street. Each house was inhabited by Poles, but my father knew many of them and had done favours for them in the past. At each house, we knocked and explained our plight. Only a few turned us down ... Very soon our wagon was filled with butter and eggs and flour and fresh vegetables, and my father and I wept at their kindness and at the realization that we had been reduced to beggars. The people of Powielancy were so generous ...
>
> Now we sent out a food gathering group each evening to beg in the neighboring villages where most of the people felt kindly toward us. One of the villages in this area was Powielancy whose people had filled our cart with food when father and I had come from the Radun [Raduń] ghetto. They helped us again most willingly for they sympathized with our plight.[186]

Meir Stoler, who escaped the German massacre of Jews in Raduń on 10 May 1942, managed to reach the tiny Polish hamlet of Mizhantz [Mieżańce], where the villagers took him in and gave him food.[187] Murray Berger of Wsielub near Nowogródek attests to receiving extensive help from numerous villagers from December 1941, when he left the ghetto, until he joined up with the Bielski unit the following year.[188] Sarah Fishkin of Rubieżewicze left a diary attesting to repeated acts of kindness by villagers in that area.[189] The Krepski family of Helenów near Stołpce sheltered Shimon Kantorowicz for two years.

---

[185] Pola Wawer, *Poza gettem i obozem* [Outside of the Ghetto and the Camp] (Warsaw: Volumen, 1993), 71.

[186] Leon Kahn (as told to Marjorie Morris), *No Time To Mourn: A True Story of a Jewish Partisan Fighter* (Vancouver: Laurelton Press, 1978), 55, 124.

[187] Martin Gilbert, *The Righteous: The Unsung Heroes of the Holocaust* (Toronto: Key Porter, 2003), 19. The village of Mieżańce is mentioned in other accounts as friendly to the Jews. See the testimony of Beniamin Rogowski, 14 March 1965, Yad Vashem Archives, 03/2820.

[188] His account is in the U.S. Holocaust Memorial Museum Archives, Washington, D.C.

[189] Anna Eilenberg-Eibeshitz, *Remember! A Collection of Testimonies* (Haifa: H. Eibeshitz Institute for Holocaust Studies, 1999), 285–306.

Even though almost the entire village was aware of this, no one betrayed them.[190]

In Poznań, in Western Poland, a stronghold of the National Democratic (Endek) Party, relations with the Jews imprisoned in the Stadion labor camp in 1941–1943 were amicable. Samuel Bronowski, who appeared as a witness in the trial of Arthur Greiser, Gauleiter of the so-called Wartheland, made the following deposition before the Supreme National Tribunal:

> The only help possible was aid in kind by supplying food. In the camp we received 200 grams of bread and one litre of turnip soup per day. Obviously, those who had no help from outside were bound to die within a short time. A committee was formed in Poznań for the collection of food. This was no easy matter since everything was rationed under the food coupon system.
>
> Many a time, we received bigger parcels which reached us secretly at the construction sites where we worked and met the Polish people. Parcels were also thrown into the camp by night. It is not easy to describe the attitude of the civilian population outside the camp—to say that it was friendly, would be too little. There was marked compassion. There has not been a single case in Poznań of a Pole who would betray a Jew escaping the camp. There has not been a single case on the construction site of a foreman striking a Jew without immediate reaction on the part of the Polish co-workers. Those Jews who survived did so only thanks to the help from the Polish population of Poznań.[191]

Maks Moszkowicz, another inmate of the Stadion labor camp, stated in his deposition for Yad Vashem:

> I wish to stress that the behaviour of the Polish population in Poznań towards us, the Jewish prisoners, was very friendly and when our labor battalions were coming out of the camp, people—mostly women—waited for us in the street in order to throw us food in spite of severe interdictions and punishment.[192]

People readily recognizable as Jews who spoke poor Polish were able to survive in the Western Polish countryside, without being betrayed:

---

[190] Information from Yad Vashem, case no. 5844.
[191] Władysław Bartoszewski, *The Blood Shed Unites Us: Pages from the History of Help to the Jews in Occupied Poland* (Warsaw: Interpress Publishers, 1970), 225.
[192] Bartoszewski, *The Blood Shed Unites Us*, 225.

[Alexander] said that he had gone through the war with a false identity. It sounds like a joke with his Yiddish accented Polish, with his looks. 'I presented myself as a Lithuanian, I had no papers, I had no money, but I was young and strong. ... I escaped westward, to the Poznan [Poznań] region where Jews were hardly known. I worked in the village, at the farm of somebody ... He didn't pay me anything. ... What matters is that he fed me, gave me some rags to wear, and I lived like a king.'[193]

Interestingly, even in Lithuania, enclaves inhabited by that country's Polish minority were identified by Jewish survivors as especially helpful. A Jewish woman from Butrimonys (Butrymańce) recalled: "Parankova [Parankowa] became known among us unfortunate Jews as a Polish hamlet where nobody would hand you over to the murderers; 'to me Parankova is truly the Jerusalem of Lithuania.'"[194]

Based on these testimonies alone, it is evident that many thousands of Poles who have never been and never will be recognized as Righteous Gentiles were actively providing assistance to Jews throughout Poland, and many more were passively supporting this assistance. There is no doubt that had helping Jews not been a capital offence, but only carried a monetary fine, as was the case in the Netherlands and other countries (occasionally, imprisonment was imposed for repeat offenders), the amount of help extended to Jews would have been incomparably larger.

As long as conditions more closely resembled those in Western Europe, Jews fared rather well. A Jewish witness who frequently traversed the Polish countryside recalled the conditions he had observed in Lublin province in the early part of the German occupation:

> Traveling through the Polish countryside in the summer of 1940, the uninformed observer could get the impression that life continued relatively peacefully in those small communities. Most men still wore their Eastern Jewish attire; old Jews, looking like patriarchs out of the Bible were standing dignified in front of their houses, the Star of David on their arms. This picture already belonged to the past in the big cities. It was also

---

[193] Ephraim F. Sten, *1111 Days In My Life Plus Four* (Takoma Park, Maryland: Dryad Press, in association with the University of Wisconsin Press, 2006), 66–67.

[194] Rivka Lozansky Bogomolnaya, *Wartime Experiences in Lithuania* (London and Portland, Oregon: Vallentine Mitchell, 2000), 75. See also *If I Forget The...: The Destruction of the Shtetl Butrimantz. Testimony by Riva Lozansky and Other Witnesses* (Washington, D.C.: Remembrance Books, 1998), passim. Regarding Polish villages near Stakliškės (Stokliszki) see the testimony of Sarah Epstein (Sara Epshteyn) in Joshua Rubenstein and Ilya Altman, *The Unkown Black Book: The Holocaust in the German-Occupied Soviet Territories* (Bloomington and Indianapolis: Indiana University Press, in association with the United States Holocaust Memorial Museum, 2008), 297.

pleasing to notice that most Polish peasants treated the Jews in a rather friendly way. They seemed more tolerant than gentiles in the larger centers. Denunciations were exceptional.[195]

The notion that Poles were eager to see the Jews being deported and relished in their misfortune is discredited even by authoritative German sources. General Johannes Blaskowitz, commander of the Eighth German Army during the September 1939 campaign and subsequently Commander-in-Chief of the Eastern Territories, wrote to Field Marshal Walter von Brauchitsch, the Commander-in-Chief of the German Army, in his report of 6 February 1940:

> The acts of violence carried out in public against Jews are arousing in religious Poles [literally, "in the Polish population, which is fundamentally pious (or God-fearing)"] not only the deepest disgust but also a great sense of pity for the Jewish population.[196]

Poles who denounced Jews often found themselves ostracized by the community, as the following examples illustrate:

- In an unspecified village outside Warsaw, "A Jew who had been starving in the woods turned up one day, asking for water. The farmer called the police, who shot the Jew on the spot. This had so outraged the village that the offender had to flee to Warsaw in fear of reprisal."[197]
- Władysława Słotwińska, a rescuer from Bystrzyca Nowa near Lublin awarded by Yad Vashem, recalled that a Pole who turned a Jewish woman and her two children over to the Germans was ostracized by the villagers. After the war he was sentenced to a long term of imprisonment.[198]

---

[195] Gary A. Keins, *A Journey Through the Valley of Perdition* ([United States]: n.p., 1985), 72–73.
[196] Ernst Klee, Willi Dressen, and Volker Reiss, *'Those Were the Days': The Holocaust through the Eyes of the Perpetrators and Bystanders* (London: Hamish Hamilton, 1991), 4; Jeremy Noakes and Geoffrey Pridham eds., *Nazism 1919–1945: A History in Documents and Eyewitness Accounts,* vol. II: *Foreign Policy, War and Racial Extermination* (New York: Schocken Books, 1988), 939.
[197] Natan Gross, *Who Are You, Mr Grymek?* (London and Portland, Oregon: Vallentine Mitchell, 2001), 248–49; translated from the Polish *Kim pan jest, panie Grymek?* (Kraków: Wydawnictwo Literackie, 1991).
[198] Dąbrowska, *Światła w ciemności,* 171.

Moreover, it was the Poles' refusal to heed repeated German warnings to desist contact and trade with the Jews that led to the death penalty being imposed for assisting Jews in any way:

- On 3 July 1941, *Gazeta Częstochowska*, an official German newspaper published in Polish, complained: "The cases multiply, when Polish peasants, impelled by dangerous sympathy for the Jewish rabble, smuggle products into the ghetto and sell them at even cheaper prices than to their own Polish brethren. Such persons are warned of severe measures against them."[199]
- In October 1941, the German county supervisor in Kraśnik remarked with angry incredulity: "according to my observations, the enforcement of this decree [forbidding the Jews to leave the Jewish quarter] is absolutely necessary because in my entire two years of duty in the East I have never experienced a situation where the Jews wander in such a [free] manner from one locality to another as I have observed here." In January 1942, the Nazis again voiced their anger about the fact that there was no negative reaction on the part of Poles toward Jewish beggars.[200]
- A circular issued on 21 September 1942 by the SS and Police Chief in Radom District stated: "The experience of the last few weeks has shown that Jews, in order to evade evacuation, tend to flee from the small Jewish residential districts [i.e., ghettos] in the communities above all. These Jews must have been taken in by Poles. I am requesting you to order all mayors and village heads as soon as possible that every Pole who takes in a Jew makes himself guilty under the Third Ordinance on restrictions on residence in the Government General of 15 October 1941. Those Poles who feed runaway Jews or sell them foodstuffs are also considered accomplices, even if they do not offer them shelter. Whatever the case, these Poles are liable to the death penalty."
- On 11 April 1942, *Gazeta Lwowska*, an official German newspaper published in the Polish language, stated: "It is unfortunate that the rural population continues—nowadays furtively—to assist Jews, thus doing harm to the community, and hence to themselves, by this disloyal attitude. Villagers take advantage of all illegal ways, applying all their cunning and circumventing regulations in order to

---

[199] Cited in S. (Samuel) Mendelsohn, *The Polish Jews Behind the Nazi Ghetto Walls* (New York: The Yiddish Scientific Institute–YIVO, 1942), 14.
[200] Marek Jan Chodakiewicz, *Between Nazis and Soviets: Occupation Politics in Poland, 1939–1947* (Lanham, Maryland: Lexington Books, 2004), 173–74.

supply the local Jewry with all kinds of foodstuffs in every amount. ... The rural population must be cut off and separated from the Jews, once and for all, must be weaned from the extremely anti-social habit of assisting the Jews."[201]

Some Poles asked for payment for the care of their Jewish charges, just as virtually all Danish rescuers did,[202] but this was to be expected given the material hardships faced by almost every Pole under the German occupation. As a recent study shows, unlike Western Europeans, the overwhelming majority of Poles were simply not in a position to offer long-term material assistance to Jews.[203]

---

[201] The two foregoing announcements are cited in Bartoszewski, *The Blood Shed Unites Us*, 40.

[202] During the initial stages of the rescue operation, only well-to-do Danish Jews could afford the short passage to Sweden. Private boatmen set their own price and the costs were prohibitive, ranging from 1,000 to 10,000 kroner per person ($160 to $1600 U.S. in the currency of that period). Afterward, when organized Danish rescue groups stepped in to coordinate the flight and to collect funds, the average price per person fell to 2,000 and then 500 kroner. The total cost of the rescue operation was about 12 million kroner, of which the Jews paid about 7 million kroner, including a 750,000 kroner loan that the Jews had to repay after the war. See Leni Yahil, *The Rescue of Danish Jewry: Test of a Democracy* (Philadelphia: Jewish Publication Society of America, 1969), 261-65, 269.

That the boatmen were gouging the Jews is beyond question, because Jewish organizations were able to bring Bundists fleeing from the Soviet Union in 1940, from Wilno to the United States via Vladivostok and Yokohama, for $518 US per person. See Daniel Blatman, *For Our Freedom and Yours: The Jewish Labour Bund in Poland, 1939-1949* (London and Portland, Oregon: Vallentine Mitchell, 2003), 28.

It is also worth noting that the Danish rescue effort entailed virtually no risk for the Danes. Until the fall of 1943 Danish Jews were unmolested by the Germans. SS General Dr. Werner Best, the German in charge in Denmark, gave a free hand to Georg Ferdinand Duckwitz, the maritime attaché at the German embassy in Copenhagen, to do whatever was necessary to derail the planned deportation of the Jews. Duckwitz flew to Sweden, where he secretly met with President Per Albin Hannson, who assured him that, should the action against the Danish Jews take place, Sweden would in principle be ready to admit them. When the roundup of Jews was about to begin, Duckwitz made his way back to Sweden to alert the Swedish government to be ready to admit the fleeing Jews.

The local German naval command warned the Danish underground of the impending fate of the Jews, disabled the German harbor patrol, and turned a blind eye to the rescue operation. The Jews who were transported to Sweden by Danish boatmen were allowed entry. Since the rescue operation took place with the connivance of the local German naval command, there were no casualties either among the Jews or among the boatmen.

[203] Grzegorz Berendt, "Cena życia—ekonomiczne uwarunkowania egzystencji Żydów po 'aryjskiej stronie'" [The Price of Life: The Economic Aspects of Jewish Existence on the 'Aryan Side'], in *Zagłada Żydów: Studia i materiały* [The Extermination of the

In closing this compilation, it is worth citing the assessment of the late Raul Hilberg, the foremost Holocaust historian whose knowledge of German archival sources is second to none:

> Overall, the general Polish population is not mentioned in German documents in respect of its participation as harassing Jews and helping the Germans. To the contrary; many German reports indicate that Poles felt anxiety for their own safety after the Jews disappeared. There are some German documents that mention some Poles, notably Polish police, railroad-workers and low-level employees in German offices but there was no Polish central authority collaborating with the Germans, as we find in e.g. Norway and its Quisling government or France and its Vichy regime. This was never the case in Poland.
>
> As was the case in many European countries, there were also Polish individuals that played extortion games with Jews, but then there were also Poles that helped Jews under risk of facing death penalty from the German occupants. Both categories were relatively small in comparison to the general population, albeit one must take into consideration that most survivors made it through the war by Polish help and protection.
>
> A friend of mine, Bronia Klebanski, who is Jewish but lived on the 'Aryan' side of society and was an active member of the Jewish underground in the Bialystok [Białystok] area, once told me a story of how she at a time took the train during the war, and was suddenly pointed out by a little girl who yelled 'Jew!' All the Polish passengers sat quietly, and nobody said

---

Jews: Studies and Materials], Vol. 4 (2008):110-43. Yitzhak Zuckerman, a leader of the Jewish underground in Warsaw, went on record to express his appreciation for all assistance give to Jews, including paid and passive help: "Anyone who fosters hatred for the Polish people is committing a sin! We must do the opposite. Against the background of anti-Semitism and general apathy, these people are glorious. There was great danger in helping us, mortal danger, not only for them but also for their families, sometimes for the entire courtyard they lived in. ... I repeat it today: to cause the death of one hundred Jews, all you needed was one Polish denouncer; to save one Jew, it sometimes took the help of ten decent Poles, the help of an entire Polish family; even if they did it for money. Some gave their apartment, and others made identity cards. Even passive help deserves appreciation. The baker who didn't denounce, for instance. It was a problem for a Polish family of four who suddenly had to start buying double quantities of rolls or meat. And what a bother it was to go far away to buy in order to support the family hiding with them. ... And I argue that it doesn't matter if they took money; life wasn't easy for Poles either; and there wasn't any way to make a living. There were widows and officials who earned their few Złotys by helping. And there were all kinds of people who helped." See Yitzhak Zuckerman "Antek", *A Surplus of Memory: Chronicle of the Warsaw Ghetto Uprising* (Berkeley: University of California Press, 1993), 461, translated into Polish as *Nadmiar pamięci (siedem owych lat): Wspomnienia 1939–1946* (Warsaw: Wydawnictwo Naukowe PAN, 2000).

anything to instigate further interest. This account is a small example of the general practice of non-collaboration among the Poles during the war.[204]

Raul Hilberg was of the empiricist school. He had no impact on post-modernists, like J. T. Gross who, alas, dominate the academic discourse on Polish-Jewish relations.

---

[204] Interview with Professor Raul Hilberg, June 20, 2005, available on line at <http://www.maxveritas.com/pb/wp_1add70b0.html?0.611384753320024>.

LOOTING AS A CASE AGAINST RACIAL DETERMINISM

Bethany M. Pałuk

Ignoring the universal dimension of the human condition, Jan Tomasz Gross, in *Złote Żniwa,* published in English as *Golden Harvest*, virtually equates Polish Christians and German Nazis. Through an examination of the subject of looting Gross attempts to demonstrate the supposed moral, qualitative, and quantitative equivalency of Poles and Nazis.

Gross is able to lead his readers to such a conclusion by basing his arguments on a great fallacy, that man's nature differs fundamentally across national borders. His argument utilizes extreme materialist reductionism; it starts by suggesting that the Germans exterminated Jews to acquire their material wealth. Next, Gross purports to show that the Poles were also guilty of attempting to appropriate their Jewish neighbors' property. By implying that their final goal, to enrich themselves off of Jewish property, was the same, Gross would like his readers to conclude that the Poles were guilty of the same crime as the Nazis.

What is so dangerous about this kind of thinking is not only that it is historically unsupported, but, more importantly, that it classifies human nature along racial and ethno-religious lines. According to Gross, Jews are inclined to act one way, and Christians another. Polish Christians, except for some few exceptions, are painted as motivated chiefly by greed, while Polish Jews are motivated chiefly by a desperate desire to survive. It is that simple: the Poles were evil perpetrators; and the Jews were survivors.

This kind of thinking is the same type of logic that led the Nazis to advocate the extermination of whole peoples. The German Nazi inability to transcend their group identity and see themselves as part of a human race – to which, of course, their neighbors, the Jews, Gypsies, Poles, and other races must also be admitted – is what allowed them to kill millions of people. To suggest the inferiority of certain nations or races is, in effect, to deny those groups a fully human status; this is an extremely dangerous worldview, as the history of the twentieth century has proven.

In order to prove the argument that Gross attempts to make, he would have to move beyond mere anecdotal examples, and apply a very rigorous methodology. Considering the chaos of the epoch and the dearth of the reliable data, it is not unreasonable to conclude that a definite study is most likely impossible. Short of such methodological rigor, we must base our arguments on what we know to be true from the vast evidence that the long history of humanity provides us with to conclude that man is endowed with the same essential nature across nations, ethnicities, and races. What is certain is that cherry-picking examples of Polish-on-Jewish atrocities is insufficiently rigorous to prove that there exists a national tendency or nationwide default character. In extraordinary circumstances, Poles act like all other humans in such circumstances; sometimes with great heroism, and sometimes with terrible barbarism, and most often somewhere in between.

To expose the fallacy of Gross's noxious thinking, we shall present its philosophical critique, and consider the poverty of Gross's reductionist methodology in light of sociological theory, as well as a series of comparativist case studies of looting. From the philosophical point of view, it is indispensable that we focus first on the question of human nature.

Human nature is but one. Every person across the entire globe has certain propensities, certain failings, and the capacity for actions both great and terrible. Looting is not a characteristic activity of any one group of people. Man, unsupported by his community or ritual, is weak in the face of his baser instincts, and his lower will. At the end of the day, each man is judged by what he has done and what he has failed to do. His crimes are individual, and not ascribed to all of his countrymen, and thus the condemnation of the Polish people *en bloc*, as attempted by Gross, is an act of deep intellectual dishonesty.

Every decision man makes is a battle. From the mundane to the most important, he is always presented with two ways of living his life: he either gives in to his lower self and seeks fulfillment of his passions, or he denies his passions and rises to the occasion of his higher self. More men would fall prey to the passions of their lower selves if they are left completely to their own devices. Luckily, man is a social being, and he has the additional support of the law and social opprobrium to help him deny his lower will.

Man's moral predicament can be conceived as a battle between two wills: One towards self-indulgence, and the other towards goodness. Through lived experience, man learns that the latter urge creates a sense of deep fulfillment of a meaningful existence, while the former leaves him empty and wretched. This consciousness, *synderesis* or *conscientia*, acts as a guide to a fulfilling life. With each decision man makes, he learns a little more about what his nature requires to feel happiness and peace in his soul.

Despite this internal compass, man, when left to his own devices, tends towards the fulfillment of his lower self. This is due to the fact that gratification for giving in to the lower desires is immediate, while the knowledge of a meaningful existence is the result of a lifetime of denying one's passions. The sense of deep fulfillment is only possible with fortitude.

Fortunately, man has two crutches he may lean on in order to help him. He has the help of habit and of society. Through habit man can strengthen his will to perform the work of his higher self. He can make it an almost automatic position. If he habituates himself always to listening to his higher self when the decisions are mundane, then the decision is already programmed into him when the temptation is greater. It becomes a question of ritual.

The other crutch that man may lean on is his community. Living in society encourages man to act according to his higher will, and society provides man with both the positive and negative impetus of laws and penalties, social mores, and opprobrium. Families, friends, neighbors, and community members serve as examples to follow. They are the worthy recipients of one's higher being, or the many various manifestations of disapproval. As long as man has these two crutches, ritual and community, he can be counted upon to act decently much of the time.

However, when society breaks down and the support for man's higher will, both negative and positive, disappears, then man quickly reverts to his less noble self. When our crutches disappear, when society breaks apart, when our habits are disrupted, we are vulnerable to the temptation of our passions. We humans are always only a few terrifying moments of disorder away from savagery. When our world crumbles, we, everywhere – in Poland, England, America, Egypt, Pakistan, and Israel – turn violently in pursuit of our own preservation. This includes all kinds of barbarity, including: wantonly destroying, stealing, lying, looting, cheating, deceiving, and killing.

The sociological evidence supports our thesis. There are two main veins of thinking about looting in sociology. On the one hand, there is the classical individual model, which holds each looter responsible for deviant behavior. On the other, there is the newer group model, the relativist school, which claims that societal expectations change and therefore the looting behavior conforms to new norms regarding property.

The classical individual model is very akin to the philosophical ideas of human nature explained above. The difference is that the term socialization is used to express the role that society plays in helping man rise above his lower self. Two scholars who espouse this view write: "Under unusual conditions, the socialization process may be more or less reversed, so that individuals are 'disassimilated' from the social system."[1] They then list the potential unusual conditions that might cause a reversal of the socialization process, which includes most extreme societal stresses, including wars and natural disasters.

An important aspect of the classical point of view echoes the philosophical perspective on alienation. This view holds that the less a person is attached to the affected community, the likelier he is to partake in deviant behavior. This is most clearly shown in examples of natural disasters, wherein locals usually do not loot, but strangers brought in to help, or those who come of their own accord, are more likely to loot. This echoes the idea that our communities help us refrain from giving in to our lower selves.

The newer group model of the relativist school is based on a different presupposition. Man is not, in these instances, only a thin cultural veneer away from his baser instincts. Rather, in times of stress what changes is the definition of what is acceptable behavior. Though the proponents of this view see the source of deviance not in the individual man, but in his social condition, the result is the same.

According to the relativist school, in times of societal stress, what emerges is not total chaos and anarchy, but rather a change in accepted norms. With increased stress, what is considered appropriate behavior is widened. This pertains especially to property standards.

Within this relativist school some sociologists argue for a definition of property as "a set of cultural norms that regulate the relations of persons to items with economic value. In effect, property is a shared understanding about who can do what with the valued resources within a community."[2] Based upon this definition there is a situational

---

[1] John McDavid and Herbert Harari, *Social Psychology: Individuals, Groups, Societies* (New York, Harper & Row, 1968) 388.
[2] E.L. Quarantelli and Russel R. Dynes "Property Norms and Looting : Their Patterns in Community Crises" in *Phylon*, Vol. 31, No. 2 (2nd Qtr., 1970): 176.

flexibility that governs norms of behavior. That is not to say that deviance disappears, but it suggests that in certain situations looting is an acceptable response to the conditions.

Whether one sees the world through a lens of philosophical adherence to human nature, or through sociological views of individual deviance or group conformity to changing norms, what remains is that a stressful societal environment causes men to more readily engage in behavior which most of them would avoid in more stable conditions.

What Gross fails to recognize is that, by virtue of man's human nature, or his vulnerability to desocialization, or his changing standards of acceptable behavior, he is susceptible to barbarism. Society does not only keep Christian, Jewish, Muslim, or atheist impulses in check, it keeps *human* impulses in check.

We have countless historical examples to counter those cherry-picked by Gross. Where he shows Christians looting Jews, we see also Jews looting Christians. Where he portrays Christians exploiting Jews, we have also found Jews exploiting Christians. Where Christians have been barbaric, so have Jews. Where Jews have been heroic, so have Christians. Moreover, we have seen Christian-on-Christian and Jew-on-Jew barbarity.

The whole history of humanity is fraught with examples of looting at the first sign of the weakness of societal infrastructure. Nothing nearly as drastic as war is indispensable for deviant behavior to appear. In fact, it can sometimes be the result of positive events. In Chicago, in 1992, looting was caused by exuberant celebrations in the aftermath of the Chicago Bulls' victory in the Basketball Championship. In one night, 347 stores were looted, countless cars were overturned, and general disorder led to great violence.[3]

During the chaos that the Second World War wrought on the Eastern Front, there was bound to be ample lawlessness that the less noble members of society employed to their own advantage. In fact, it was rampant enough that an entire underground militia was organized around an attempt to keep order in Poland.[4] To claim in any way that looting is the work of any single group of people simply contradicts the historical record. Looting is extremely pervasive; it is such a common

---

[3] Michael J. Rosenfeld "Celebration, Politics, Selective Looting and Riots: A Micro Level Study of the Bulls Riot of 1992 in Chicago" in *Social Problems*, Vol. 44, No. 4 (Nov., 1997): 483-502. Published by: University of California Press on behalf of the Society for the Study of Social Problems

[4] See Marek Jan Chodakiewicz, *"Ząb" przeciw dwu wrogom: Narodowe Siły Zbrojne* [The "Tooth" Against Two Enemies: The National Armed Forces] (Warsaw: Fronda, 1999).

human propensity, that it defies limiting to a people, time, or place. In fact, it is perhaps one of those universal manifestations of man's lower nature.

What follows is an array of historical examples. We will begin with examples of the Polish experience, and then proceed to more general European cases.

The examples from Poland have been purposely chosen to refute Gross. Since the author focuses on the cases in which the violence pitted Christian against Jew, in order to clear the record, ours will necessarily focus on the reverse. Most of our examples have been found in Jewish wartime memoirs. Our goal is not to disparage any religious or racial group, but only to illustrate that the trait that Gross would have his readership believe belongs to a particular group is, in fact, a universally human trait. By showing that wartime crimes were also perpetrated by Jews, we aim only to complete the very skewed and partial image that Gross has painted. Our hope is that in showing the commonality of human actions we might overcome group vilification, and perhaps even forge a path toward an understanding of the universality of human frailty that fosters love.

We begin our account with one Jewish eyewitness who tells of Jews who looted the property of foreign firms in Lublin in September 1939. He wrote: "Even the rich came in their carriages and drove away with the hogs inside. I went up to Shlomo Biderman: 'What has come over you?' I demanded. 'You, the richest Jew in Lublin, grabbing hogs and selling them!' ... 'You,' he said in reply, 'are a fool.'"[5]

In Przemyśl, Ukrainian nationalists and Jews, who had joined together to erect a triumphal arch for the German invaders, participated in looting Polish military buildings.[6]

Emanuel Ringelblum recorded that Polish Jews were quick to seize valuables discarded by deported German Jews, who were afraid that possessing them might lead to serious repercussions at the hands of the German Nazis.[7]

---

[5] See Goldberg, *The Undefeated,* 79–80. For conditions in the vicinity of Tarnów see Andrzej Żbikowski, ed., *Archiwum Ringelbluma: Konspiracyjne Archiwum Getta Warszawskiego* [The Ringelblum Archive: The Underground Archive of the Warsaw Ghetto], vol. 3: *Relacje z Kresów* [Testimonies from the Eastern Borderlands] (Warsaw: Żydowski Instytut Historyczny IN-B, 2000), 327.

[6] See Eugeniusz Buczyński, *Smutny wrzesień: Wspomnienia* [A Sad September: Memoirs] (Kraków: Wydawnictwo Literackie, 1985), 132.

[7] See Emanuel Ringelblum, *Kronika getta warszawskiego. Wrzesień 1939 - styczeń 1943* [The Warsaw Ghetto Chronicle: September 1939 - January 1943], ed. Artur Eisenbach, trans. Adam Rutkowski (Warsaw: Czytelnik, 1983), 69

Various Jewish policemen were well known for their ability to extort money and other valuables, especially during deportations from the ghetto. During the great deportation in the summer of 1942, they looted vacated apartments on an enormous scale, amassing considerable fortunes. Afterwards, the remaining Jews copiously looted property left behind by Jews who had been seized for deportation, and began dealing widely in such property.[8]

After the failed Warsaw Uprising of August-October 1944, Jews who remained in the ruins of Warsaw acquired belongings from evacuated Poles for a pittance and formed expeditions to search for valuables buried by Poles (in the hope of digging them out later) and appropriated them.[9]

Chiel Rajchman, who took refuge in bombed-out Warsaw, recalled how he and other Jews went to abandoned warehouses and homes of people who were forced to evacuate the city and "carried off a couple of hundred pounds of food and clothes."[10]

"Jumpers" left the ghetto in Ostrowiec Świętokrzyski to bring back some of the belongings abandoned by Jews when they were forced to move into the ghetto, considering that they were entitled to inherit ownerless Jewish belongings. Some Jews seized goods left behind by Jews who had been deported from the ghettos.[11]

Other Jews looted Jewish graves is search of gold and other property of value. "Undertakers open graves, take out the jewels and gold teeth [...]. Unspeakably base acts are happening at the cemetery. Mass graves [and] defilement of the dead by the lower orders, who throw them into

---

[8] See Itamar Levin, *Walls Around: The Plunder of Warsaw Jewry during World War II and Its Aftermath* (Westport, Connecticut and London: Praeger, 2004), 90–91, 96, 98, 149–544; Barbara Engelking and Jacek Leociak, *The Warsaw Ghetto: A Guide to the Perished City* (New Haven, Connecticut and London: Yale University Press, 2009), 479, 749; Henryk Makower, *Pamiętnik z getta warszawskiego: Październik 1940–styczeń 1943* [A Dairy From the Warsaw Ghetto: October 1940 – January 1943] (Wrocław: Zakład Narodowy im. Ossolińskich, 1987), 62; Calel Perechodnik, *Am I a Murderer?: Testament of a Jewish Ghetto Policeman* (Boulder, Colorado: Westview Press/HarperCollins, 1996), 104.
[9] See Bernard Goldstein, *The Stars Bear Witness* (London: Victor Gollancz, 1950), 251–52, 262, 270–71.
[10] See the Interview with Chiel Rajchman, December 7, 1988, United States Holocaust Memorial Museum, Washington, D.C.
[11] See Isaiah Trunk, *Judenrat: The Jewish Councils in Eastern Europe under Nazi Occupation* (Lincoln: University of Nebraska Press, 1996), 563; Sara Bender, *The Jews of Białystok During World War II and the Holocaust* (Waltham, Massachusetts: Brandeis University Press, 2008), 202, 211.

the graves like dogs [...] they open graves at night, pull out gold teeth and steal the shrouds.'"[12]

A Jew from Chełm recalled how his property was misappropriated by fellow Jews:

> The Jewish police went to each house after the *Aktion* and made new lists of the remaining population—those who had survived. The Germans then ordered the survivors to live closer together, in a more narrowly restricted area. Two families, with 4 children, were sent to live in my home. [...] My new neighbors resented my presence—they would have preferred to have the house all to themselves.
>
> ...I was completely dejected, totally depressed. In my house there were strangers now who dressed in my wife's clothes; their children wore my little one's clothes. [...] When I saw them in those clothes I just couldn't control my tears. They slept in my bed and I no longer had a bed to sleep in. I kept a bit of merchandise in a chest, so I slept on the lid of that chest. I had lost my bed because I was outnumbered by them; they simply took over the bed and that was that. [...]
>
> A big camp, using the military barracks of Chełm as a nucleus, was built. [...] Then a new order was issued: all Jews *had* to report to the barracks. [...]
>
> I didn't report to that camp. Some of my neighbors in my flat also didn't report. Because of them I could no longer use my false-beam hiding place. Anyhow, they wanted to get rid of me. With me gone, there would be one less body in the crowded room. And they could help themselves to my meager possessions. One woman in the flat lost her husband so she wanted all Jewish husbands everywhere to die. Another had lost two brothers who were my age, so she looked at me and her eyes seemed to say: 'Why are you alive and they're not?'
>
> Somebody in my house squealed on me. One day the Gestapo burst into the flat, ran right over to me and told me to tell them where I had hidden my merchandise. ... I showed them where all the merchandise was. They brought a truck and I had to load all the merchandise on it. ... I had to go with the Gestapo men there and unload the merchandise. When I finished they beat me and drove me straight to the big new military barracks camp and shoved me in. I was no longer a free man.[13]

---

[12] See Levin, *Walls Around*, 98.
[13] See Kalmen Wawryk, *To Sobibor and Back: An Eyewitness Account* (Montreal: The Concordia University Chair in Canadian Jewish Studies, and The Montreal Institute for Genocide and Human Rights Studies, 1999), 25–27.

During the Soviet occupation of Eastern Poland in 1939–1941, the property of Poles often fell into the hands of their Jewish neighbors. The estate of the Kiersnowski family in Podweryszki near Bieniakonie was totally stripped of its belongings in September 1939 by a roving gang led by a local Jew.[14]

When the village of Miłków was cleared of its Polish inhabitants (they were deported by cattle car to Bessarabia in the dead of winter in January 1940), Jews descended on the village with their carriages and dismantled and plundered what remained.[15]

When Poles were evicted from their homes in the villages of Jaremecz and Mikulczyn in the Sub-Carpathian Pokucie area, they were taken over by local Jews.[16]

Frequently, the property of Poles deported to the Gulag was simply confiscated by Jewish militiamen, or by Jewish neighbors who had ostensibly taken it for "safekeeping." See, for example, the account of Izabella Dybczyńska from Telechany:

> Before the war these Jews behaved in a very friendly manner, but as soon as the Bolsheviks arrived they joined forces with them. They pretended to be friendly, but in an underhanded way they "informed" us of what might happen and offered their help [...].
>
> Right after the entry of the Bolsheviks, some Jews told my parents that they should hide their clothing because it would, in all likelihood, be taken from us. I remember very well packing suits and fur coats belonging to my parents [...] Two huge suitcases [that folded twice] were taken by these Jews for safekeeping. Soon after another man arrived—sent, it appears, by these Jews—who told us to get ready by evening a desk and two more suits which would be 'borrowed.' By November [1939] we were living in two nearly empty rooms. Our furniture was 'borrowed' and some people had occupied the remainder of the dwelling.
>
> The situation became progressively worse since we had to live from something. My mother approached Szamszel to return the clothing he had

---

[14] See Ryszard Kiersnowski, *Tam i wtedy. W Podweryszkach, w Wilnie i w puszczy 1939-1945* [Then and There: In Podweryszki, Wilno, and the Forest] (Warsaw: Editions Spotkania, 1994), 39.
[15] See Józef Mroczkowski, "Wojna w Oleszycach" [War in Oleszyce], *Karta* (Warsaw), no. 24 (1998): 108.
[16] See Grzegorz Mazur, *Pokucie w latach drugiej wojny światowej: Położenie ludności, polityka okupantów, działalność podziemia* [The Pokucie Region During the Second World War: The Situation of the Population, the Policies of the Occupiers, and the Activities of the Underground] (Kraków: Uniwersytet Jagielloński, 1994), 44.

taken for safekeeping. This exchange probably lasted for a few days and finally he told her that he would not return anything. It was all his and we shouldn't make any claims or things might get worse. What was "worse" actually occurred on December 21, when my father was taken away. Two days later he was shipped out of Telechany; to this day I do not know where he was murdered. In April 1940 my mother and I were deported to Kazakhstan, where we spent six years.[17]

When the Soviets retreated in June 1941 in advance of the Germans, Jews plundered state property in many localities.[18]

Pillaging of German property and black marketeering were widespread. In the wake of the arrival of the Soviets in 1944 and 1945, groups of surviving Jews set off from central Poland on expeditions to plunder property ("*szaber*" or "*shaber*") in former German territories awarded to Poland, as did Jews who settled there. In some cases, Jews gave young German women "protection" in exchange for sexual favors.[19]

---

[17] See Jerzy Robert Nowak, *Przemilczane zbrodnie: Żydzi i Polacy na Kresach w latach 1939–1941* [Crimes Passed Over in Silence: Poles and Jews in the Eastern Borderlands in 1939-1941] (Warsaw: von borowiecky, 1999), 134–35.

[18] See Kazimierz Leszczyński, "Dziennik wojenny Batalionu Policji 322 (Opracowanie i tłumaczenie dokumentu)," [The War Diary of Police Battalion 322 (Editing and Translation of the Document)] *Biuletyn Głównej Komisji Badania Zbrodni Hitlerowskich w Polsce,* no. 17 (1967): 219 (Białystok); Meir Peker, "In the Bielsk Ghetto & the Camps," in Haim Rabin, ed., *Bielsk-Podliask: Book in the Holy Memory of the Bielsk Podliask Jews Whose Lives Were Taken During the Holocaust Between 1939 and 1941* (Tel Aviv: Bielsk Immigrants' Association of Israel and the United States of America, 1975), 29 (Bielsk Podlaski); Michael Maik, *Deliverance: The Diary of Michael Maik: A True Story*, ed. Avigdor Ben-Dov, trans. Laia Ben-Dov (Kedumim, Israel: Keterpress, 2004), 20 (Sokoły near Białystok); G. Beil, "The Holocaust (The Shoah)," in Betzalel Shwartz and Israel Chaim Biltzki, eds., *The Book of Kobrin: The Scroll of Life and Destruction* (San Francisco: Holocaust Center of Northern California, 1992), 382 (Kobryń); Żbikowski, ed., *Archiwum Ringelbluma* [The Ringelblum Archive], 3: 172, 202 (Słonim); Marek Wierzbicki, *Polacy i Żydzi w zaborze sowieckim* [Poles and Jews in the Soviet Occupation Zone] (Warsaw: Fronda, 2001), 218 (Słonim); Samuel Lipa Tennenbaum, *Zloczow Memoir* (New York: Shengold Publishers, 1986), 167–68 (Złoczów).

[19] See Alexandre Blumstein, *A Little House on Mount Carmel* (Portland, OR : Vallentine Mitchell, 2002), 379–80, 382–85; Sylvie Gerche, *Tout se paye dans la vie: Les terribles pérégrinations d'une famille juive polonaise, pendant la guerre. Témoignages* [Everything is Paid For in Life: The Terrible Wanderings of a Polish Jewish Family During the War: Testimonies] (Paris: L'Harmattan, 2003), 232; Jakub Gutenbaum and Agnieszka Latała, eds., *The Last Eyewitnesses: Children of the Holocaust Speak*, vol. 2 (Evanston, Illinois, Northwestern University Press, 2005), 303; Eugene Bergman, *Survival Artist: A Memoir of the Holocaust* (Jefferson, North Carolina and London: McFarland, 2009), 174 (the author describes how young Jews from Łódź returned from looting trips with trucks filled with valuables and furniture).

Another Jewish prisoner liberated from Ebensee recalls:

> Stores belonging to Austrian shopkeepers were fair game. We walked around with guns and any 'deal' we proposed was accepted.... We were entitled to whatever we wanted, much in the way that the Children of Israel were entitled to the booty they took from the Egyptians after their long enslavement.... The looting raged for a few days, and in the ensuing chaos, even American food supplies vanished—from trucks, warehouses, and kitchens...the Austrian women were sex-starved because most of the local able-bodied men were not back from the front.[20]

An inmate of a small camp in Vaihingen an der Enz near Stuttgart described this scene:

> The next day the rumor spread that the Frenchmen gave us permission to go to town and loot. 'Take revenge on those Germans!' A hoard of prisoners poured out of the camp. ... We swarmed like locusts from house to house. Petrified, the inhabitants gave us anything we asked for at once. These were women, old men, a few middle-aged persons. ... At the end of the day we returned to camp. The town was completely looted.[21]

According to another account: "After the German defeat, the young Jews used to travel on trains and take the German people's luggage. The youth took the luggage in the right moment the train was stopped, and then threw it through the train's window. He jumped off the train, took the luggage and escaped."[22]

Poland was not unique in this regard. Banditry and looting occurred in every country in Europe. The universality of this human tendency is visible in the following examples.

Throughout Europe, there was a wide-scale plunder of Jewish property. A case in point is the city of Thessalonika in northern Greece, home to that country's largest Jewish community. Not only did the local authorities facilitate the expropriation of Jewish property including the large Jewish cemetery, which was destroyed by 500

---

[20] See Joseph E. Tenenbaum, *Legacy and Redemption: A Life Renewed* (Washington, D.C.: The United States Holocaust Memorial Museum and The Holocaust Survivors' Memoirs Project, 2005), 165–66.
[21] See Joanna Wiszniewicz, *And Yet I Still Have Dreams: A Story of Certain Loneliness* (Evanston, Illinois: Northwestern University Press, 2004), 102–103.
[22] See Zalman Urievich, "Pruzhany Jews in Ghettos and Camps," in *Pruzhany Yzkor Book,* Internet: <http://www.purs.org/yzkorpruzhany/guettos_camp.htm>; translation of M. W. Bernstein, ed., *Pinkas me-hamesh kehilot harevot...* (Buenos Aires: Former Residents of Pruzana, 1958), Chapter 93.

Greek workers, but the local population engaged in looting on a massive scale.

Despite a police warning against looting, the deported Jews' empty homes and shops were quickly plundered by Greek gangs looking for valuables which had been left behind: "As soon as they were marched away, people rushed into their houses, tore up floorboards and battered down walls and ceilings, hoping to find hidden valuables." There was a "complete breakdown of law and order" wrote an official at the time, and the second-hand shops of the city began to fill up with stolen goods. Squatters invaded residential property after the authorities removed furniture to warehouses. Only a small number of Greeks helped Jews to hide. Few Jews survived, even though the penalty for helping a Jew in Greece was no more than imprisonment. On their return, the survivors found Jewish tombstones in urinals and driveways; they had even been used to make the dance-floor of a taverna built over a corner of the former cemetery. Because graves had been ransacked for the treasure that had been supposedly hidden there, many Jewish skulls and bones were exposed.[23]

Looting was not limited to poorer nations like Greece and Poland. When Germany invaded France in June 1940, both Frenchmen and Germans soldiers took turns looting stores, homes, and other premises.[24]

In wartime Britain, the problem became critical despite the fact that there was no occupation or breakdown of the state apparatus:

> Looting occurred as soon as the bombs of the Blitz began to fall. Bombed houses were raided. Valuables disappeared. Carpets and lead pipes were ripped out. In the first prosecutions in November 1940, it was members of the ARP [Air Raid Precaution] and of the AFS [Auxiliary Fire Service] who faced the charges. The blackout created ideal conditions for burglars, pickpockets and rapists. Offences proliferated as the rate of police successes dropped.

> Fraudulent claims provided another problem. People who had lost their home were entitled to a £500 advance on post-war compensation up to £20,000. People who took in evacuees or service personnel were entitled to payment of 10s. 6d. per week. The National Assistance Office was swamped with claimants, and found it easier to pay than to verify.

---

[23] See Mark Mazower, *Salonica, City of Ghosts: Christians, Muslims and Jews, 1430–1950* (New York: Knopf, 2005), 397–98, 403, 405, 406, 412–13, 418.
[24] See Richard J. Evans, *The Third Reich at War, 1939–1945* (New York: Penguin Press, 2009), 132.

A British MP called black marketeering 'treason of the worst kind.' But, with food, fuel and clothes rationing in force, illegal trade of all sorts flourished. In Glasgow, many people died from drinking home-brewed 'hooch.'

Murders in England and Wales increased by 22 per cent. The increase was partly due to the ready supply of firearms, and partly to opportunism. Bombed-out ruins provided good cover for murderers, who sought to disguise their prey as Blitz victims.[25]

From the summer of 1944, looting grew more widespread in Germany, especially during nighttime air raids; however, it was only foreign workers caught looting who were executed by the German authorities or lynched by German mobs.[26]

At war's end, Allied soldiers—American, French, and British—engaged in widespread plundering in war-ravaged Europe. Looting began even before the German frontier was crossed in 1945: American reports confirmed that pillage of Belgian civilian property by U.S. troops took place on a considerable scale. Once in Germany, looting became a full-blown epidemic, with the military authorities joining in to confiscate works of art, resources, and technical equipment.[27] In Dresden, British and American POWs and German civilians looted the bombed out ruins of the city. A single German was found to have collected at least 150 rings from corpses before being caught.[28]

As is well known in Poland and elsewhere, Germany in particular, but, in essence, anywhere the Red Army entered, pillaging by the Soviets also took on massive proportions.[29]

The looting was also not limited to Europe. There is documentation of U.S. soldiers desecrating the bodies of Japanese soldiers, breaking their jaws with their rifle butts, and using the bayonets to extract gold fillings.[30]

---

[25] See Norman Davies, *Europe at War, 1939–1945: No Simple Victory* (London, Basingstoke and Oxford: Macmillan, 2006), 382.
[26] See Evans, *The Third Reich at War, 1939–1945,* 703–6.
[27] See Antony Beevor, *The Fall of Berlin 1945* (New York: Penguin/Viking, 2002), 192–93; Giles MacDonogh, *After the Reich: From the Liberation of Vienna to the Berlin Airlift* (London: John Murray, 2007), 240, 269–71, 310, 382, 388–90, 404, 419.
[28] See David Irving, *Apocalypse 1945: The Destruction of Dresden* (Focal Point: London, 1995), 204.
[29] See Giles MacDonogh, *After the Reich: The Brutal History of the Allied Occupation* (New York: Basic Books, 2009), 297, 381–88.
[30] See A. Scott Berg, *Lindbergh* (Bel Air, CA: Paw Prints, 2008).

As previously mentioned, the point of this essay is not to pit one group against another, but to show the limitations of attempting to racially (or ethno-culturally) explain what is, in fact, a universal human phenomenon. There is no question that there is much to condemn. Human beings look pitifully weak and demonically evil, both in our examples and those provided by Gross. This is because that is exactly what we are when we are divorced from those institutions that mitigate the temptations of our lower selves. All but the truly noblest of humans require stability and society in order to pursue their better selves. Even this is sometimes insufficient, but without it we are in terrible danger of giving in to our basest instincts on a widespread basis.

The fact that Polish citizens, Jewish and Christian, participated in barbarity does not mean that they were party to or equivalent to the Nazi attempt to exterminate a whole people from the face of the earth. Nor does the fact that the Nazis made use of the belongings of Jews mean that they simply were interested in killing Jews to benefit from their material wealth. To suggest such a thing is to degrade the memory of the dead and to lessen the great atrocity of the war.

Human nature tends in the same way for all mankind. To argue that certain ethno-cultural groups of a community are more or less likely to commit evil simply does not match the historical record. To make the argument that Gross makes would require an enormous amount of empirical study, which he is very far from achieving, and might simply be impossible.

The most viable conclusion we can draw, based on the facts at our disposal, is that looting occurred on all fronts against all groups perpetrated by individuals from every group. There was enormous suffering during the war. To make the ahistorical and vilifying claims we find in *Golden Harvest* tarnishes the memory of all the victims of the war. Man, every man, is capable of both angelic goodness and diabolical evil. The sad truth about the war is that it was witness to much more of the latter and too little of the former.

Part II: Methodology

MORAL DILEMMAS IN TURBULENT TIMES

Father Waldemar Chrostowski

Wars imprint an indelible stigma and leave lasting marks upon the consciousness and memory of the survivors. The relatively long history of humankind abounds in wars and military conflicts. Yet, never before the twentieth century, and particularly the two world wars, has the Moloch of Death guzzled so much blood. The atrocities characterizing the past century truly surpass one's wildest imagination. Yet, these events were very real. Those who survived the Second World War – especially in Central and Eastern Europe, where the conflict generated the greatest harvest of cruelty and violence – were profoundly transformed by this experience.

Religious and ethical systems, including Christianity, are replete with commandments and sets of norms that reflect and define high moral standards. Such efforts are both noble and necessary. They help individuals avoid evil and strive towards excellence while refusing to settle for mediocrity. Handbooks of ethics and moral theology – nourished by wisdom, prudence, and prayer – are written in the seclusion of academic venues, churches, and monastic cells. The norms they propose are vigorously debated, clarified, and updated. This undertaking is based upon a calm and careful analysis of various proposals, arguments, and options.

The Ten Commandments – further elevated by Christ's Eight Beatitudes – form the foundation of Christian ethics and morality. This provides a Christian with a compass to guide his moral choices, even in conditions quite divergent from the norms with which he is familiar. A constant reexamination of one's conscience is a measure of spiritual maturity and endless self-improvement. In this context, accounting for the past helps shape the future.

While making moral choices in peacetime, one may readily expect advice, search for spiritual direction, take advantage of the experiences and prudence of others, and carefully weigh one's options. In the times of turbulence, these options are very limited, thereby hampering or rendering impossible prudence and judgment.

The Second World War in Poland was a time of absolute derision of nearly all honored and accepted norms and values, which were brutally trampled. Since the scope and character of the committed crimes were unprecedented, we should exercise restraint while judging the attitudes of the survivors.

It is true that the commandments and ethical norms are always binding, regardless of context. It is incumbent upon us to perpetually strive to satisfy them. Yet, troubled times and their aftermath often breed the temptation to examine the conscience of others. This happens not only when evil reaps its deadly harvest, but also later, after the passing of the storm. The self-styled judges often pass their verdicts from the comfort of their own living rooms. They prefer to brazenly condemn and stigmatize the actions of others without bothering to even ask themselves how they would behave in similar situations.

Difficult periods generate *both* heroes and cowards. Even under the worst of circumstances there is usually no shortage of heroes providing a shining example to others. In other situations, the cowards dominate, and their conduct exerts a significant impact on others and the course of events. There are many moralists who envision themselves only among the heroes. Quite sporadic are admissions that trying times would culminate in one's moral defeat. Yet, this is the most appropriate perspective from which to assess various aspects of human conduct in times during which human dignity is disregarded and trampled upon.

On Polish soil the Second World War lasted over five and a half years. The war generated unspeakable calamities and suffering on an unprecedented scale. In September 1939, when the Nazis and Soviets attacked Poland jointly, very few pessimists, prophesying even the darkest of scenarios, could predict that both occupiers would resort to such extreme cruelty and criminality.

The bloody harvest was reaped by two totalitarian systems: the brown one, German National Socialism, and the red one, Soviet International Socialism. The Catholic Church was one of the first to sound the alarm bells against both. The voices of Pius XI and Pius XII, as well as other hierarchs, teachers of the faith, and shepherds of the faithful, unmasked the sinister nature and objectives of two regimes. Yet, there were also plenty of individuals and circles that found the Church's teachings inconvenient, treating its constant reiteration of ethical norms and moral principles as intolerable. Not surprisingly, this contributed to the weakening and anaesthetizing of many a conscience. These attitudes bred catastrophic consequences in moments when listening to one's conscience became indispensable and decisive.

The war witnessed an escalation of violence, terror, and evil. These reached their apogee after the Third Reich's attack on the Stalinist Soviet Union, an erstwhile ally. The territories rapidly conquered by the Germans were home to several million Jews, whom Hitler and his henchmen decided to murder. The extermination of the Poles was to be a continuation of the mass murder of the Jews.

While addressing the representatives of the Religious Association of the Mosaic Faith in Warsaw on 14 June 1987, Pope John Paul II said: "Your danger was our danger. Ours did not come to pass to such degree as yours, for the Nazis lacked sufficient time. It was you who absorbed that terrible sacrifice of extermination. It may be said, that you bore it for the others who were also slated for extermination."

Much has been written about "poor Poles calmly staring at the Jewish ghetto" and "gazing indifferently at the trains transporting the Jews to the extermination camps." There are even texts about "poor Poles eying covetously the former property of the exterminated Jews."

Today, various thinkers and researchers – safe and sound in their studies – attempt to not only penetrate the dark mystery of the times, but also to judge those forced to live through them. Sometimes one cannot resist the impression that the main charge against the wartime Poles was that they managed to survive the slaughter that consumed others. It is paradoxical that such judgments become more aggressive, and the judges increasingly impudent, as more time transpires from the events in question. Moreover, the place of the moralists and the ethicists is now being usurped by ideologues and doctrinaires, who revel in their own supposed humility and shed tears over things which cost them little or nothing at all.

Was it a sin to fear helping the Jews, given that such assistance was punished by the execution of not only the "offender" himself, but also one's entire family and even neighbors?

Failing to help the Jews in their hour of need was conditioned by numerous factors. Some of these are inexcusable regardless of the context. Yet, the situation in German-occupied Poland was unique. Conquered Poland was the only country where assisting the Jews was penalized by death; most frequently it also meant the execution of the trespasser's family and neighbors. Collective responsibility was practiced on a large scale, as demonstrated by round-ups and mass executions.

One may easily gain the impression that it is not the perpetrators who are nowadays subject to condemnation and stigmatization, but rather their terrorized, defiled, and exterminated victims. A common characteristic of such "judges" is that they demand much from others, but very little from themselves.

I can answer the question above (was it a sin to fear helping Jews?) prudently only if I first apply the moral dilemma posed by it to myself and to my loved ones. After all, it is much too easy to accuse others of sin. Deliberation over one's own responsibility and its possible consequences calls for a high level of prudence. Nowadays, the challenges are not as great as during the war and its direct aftermath. Even so, there remain many analogous situations that make the above question relevant.

Is it always a sin to appropriate another's possessions? Many people were confronted with such a dilemma during and after the war. Theft is a sin, but is the appropriation of abandoned property always sinful? As a result of the Second World War, Poland's borders were shifted significantly in a western and northern direction. Millions were dispossessed and, in turn, took over properties that had never belonged to them. Many prewar residents, both Poles and Jews, were missing from the postwar landscape of Polish cities, towns, and villages. The war devoured six million Polish citizens.

Although the Germans plundered and murdered Jews on a mass scale, some of their possessions nevertheless survived. In general, bystanders exhibited three approaches towards these. Some would never consider snatching another's property and remained true to their convictions. Others were always ready to grab someone else's possessions, and they too never altered their "moral" code. Finally, there were others yet who, in normal circumstances, would avoid evil, but proved the maxim that "opportunity makes a thief." To which of these three groups would I belong?

Let us consider a contemporary analogy. The recent financial crisis saw billions of dollars "evaporate." But money does not simply "evaporate." It only changes hands. We may legitimately ask whether the contemporary mass theft is stigmatized and condemned with the same zeal and vociferousness as the above deeds committed decades ago.

The tragic events of the Holocaust occurred during the lives of our fathers and grandfathers. Fair moral judgments cannot sever the continuity and solidarity between the generations. After all, we have no idea how we ourselves would have behaved when confronted with the dilemmas faced by our ancestors. Usually, those who demand much from others ask very little of themselves. It is worthwhile to analyze the origins, development, and objectives of the intense criticism of our forefathers. Clearly, ethics and morality sometimes serve political and economic goals, which easily become tools in the hands of ideologues. The latter demand that "others" reevaluate their conscience while they themselves line their own pockets.

In this context a passage from the Hebrew Bible provides us with food for thought. "Ezra's Prayer," an examination of conscience performed by God's People, is recorded in the Old Testament's Book of Nehemiah 9.6-37. The text was written in the middle of the fifth century BC. It reviewed the Israelites' history from the point of view of the contradiction between God's will and "the Fathers'" conduct. The passages examine the causes, course, and effects of a great catastrophe for the Hebrews, the Babylonian Captivity (587-539 BC). In spite of the passage of seventy years, posterity continued to experience the consequences of the bygone disaster. The people saw and acknowledged that it was a link in the long chain of inequities committed against God. The opposition between His munificence and the perversity of the ancestors was expressed grammatically as an antithesis: "Thou (God)" vs. "they (fathers)." It should be noted that the present meaning of the second part of "Ezra's Prayer" differs from the original one, for it was purposely altered.

The text of the Hebrew Bible was recorded using a consonant script. Originally, verses 33 and 34 read as follows:

> Thou art just in all things that are brought upon us, for Thou hast done right.
>
> We too condemn our kings, our princes, our priests, and our fathers.
>
> They did not keep Thy Law and they did not listen to Thy commands and Thy testimonies given to them.

The meaning of this passage is clear: the inequities of the ancestors were enormous. Their offenses were grave. The result of a lasting inclination towards evil and disobedience towards God and His will, these inequities and offences led the ancestors to ruin. Thus, evil should be clearly labeled an evil to prevent it from reoccurring.

But those uttering the prayer soon realized that it weakened the bonds of their national solidarity. They continued to believe that the past should be subject to honest and sincere moral assessments. Simultaneously, they realized the necessity of prudently restraining the criticism and condemnation of one's ancestors. When the vowels were added to the consonant-based text of the Holy Book, the sense of the above verses changed:

Thou art just in all things that are brought upon us, for Thou hast done right, but we have done wickedly.

For neither our kings, our princes, our priests, and our fathers did keep Thy Law, nor hearkened unto Thy commandments and Thy testimonies, which Thou bestowed on them.

The Israelites ceased reciting the venerable prayer containing a severe condemnation of their ancestors. They remained aware of their sins, but a new realization emerged and developed. It was based on the conviction that limits exist when condemning and distancing ourselves from our forefathers.

We cannot be certain how we would have conducted ourselves in their circumstances. Those who attempt to coerce us to reexamine our conscience and accuse our dead compatriots of heinous deeds, do not benefit from such hindsight either. Of course, it is also possible that they failed to consider the complete ethical dimensions of this issue.

Whose Tenements?
A Legal Analysis of the Status of Former Jewish Property in Light of Postwar Polish Law

Judge Barbara Gorczycka-Muszyńska

(Translated by Paweł Styrna)

In post Yalta Poland, care for and protection of the private property of former owners conflicted with the political doctrine of the ruling Communist system. After all, the ideology of Marxism is at its very core hostile to private property. Yet, initially, the Communist law made certain tactical concessions in regard to property restitution. *De facto*, the main privileged beneficiaries in this case were individuals of Jewish heritage.

Following the announcement, in July of 1944, of the Manifesto of the so-called Polish Committee of National Liberation (Polski Komitet Wyzwolenia Narodowego: PKWN) – a Communist front organization completely subservient to Stalin – which was to constitute the legal basis of Communist rule in Poland and to outline the main objectives of the regime, a series of expropriation edicts were issued. In Communist legal parlance, this confiscation of the private property of certain groups and individuals was referred to as "nationalization."[1]

Such was the nature of, *inter alia*, the so-called land reform laws (land reform decree from 6 September 1944, *Journal of Laws* [*Dziennik Ustaw: Dz.U*, henceforward as "Dz.U"], no. 4, item 17, 1944); the state

---

[1] The term "nationalization" implied that the regime was robbing the private property of individual citizens in the name of the "nation" or the "people." An alternative term for such a government takeover, deriving from the French word for state (*etat*), was also employed: "etatization" (*upaństwowienie*). Both terms were euphemisms understating and obscuring the brutal nature of depriving millions of individuals of their property. "Etatization" is perhaps only somewhat more appropriate, given the mass unpopularity of the Communist regime among the Polish nation. However, the term "expropriation" most accurately reflects the injustice of the phenomenon.

takeover of forests (decree on the appropriation of certain forests by the State Treasury from 12 December 1944, Dz.U., no. 15, item 82, 1944); and the expropriation of industry (law concerning the state takeover of the basic branches of the national economy from 3 January 1946, Dz.U., no. 3, item 17, 1946).

In light of the general tendencies embodied in the above government edicts, we may consider exceptional those laws, which pertained to both movable and immovable property, but did not call for their nationalization. On the contrary, some of these legal acts specified the principles and procedures for the restitution of properties forfeited by their owners during the war and not regained in its wake. The goal of these laws was not only to safeguard them against looting and vandalism, but also, and primarily, to favor a certain group of citizens who lost their property as a result of the dramatic consequences of the Second World War.

Polish citizens of Jewish heritage, the most numerous minority in prewar Poland, also constituted a rather significant percentage of these cases.[2] According to statistics from the 1930s, these citizens amounted to 9.8 percent of Poland's population.[3] In regions of Poland formerly under Austrian or Russian rule during the era of partitions, the percentage of Jews was higher than the national average. For example, in Warsaw it constituted 29.9 percent; 31.8 percent in the industrial city of Łódź; and 24.6 percent in Kraków.[4] The sheer number of Jewish residents of Poland's major cities alone, coupled with the fact that they represented a stratum of greater or lesser entrepreneurs and owners of property (such as tenements, businesses, and workshops), posed a problem. The status of the property abandoned by their former owners,

---

[2] The common claim that Ukrainians constituted the largest minority in the Second Polish Republic – approximately 14 percent – appears incorrect. The label "Ukrainian" has been collectively attributed to the Greek Catholic and Eastern Orthodox population of Southeastern Poland who declared their mother tongue as Ruthenian and or Ukrainian. This included both Ukrainians, who exhibited separatist and nationalist tendencies (10.1 percent), and Ruthenes (4.8 percent), who emphasized their national separateness and loyalty to Poland. The political representatives of both of these ethnic groups were locked in a state of conflict, and competed with one another over influence in their local communities.

[3] This percentage included only those declaring the Mosaic faith in the census. However, this number failed to reflect stateless persons (such as Jewish refugees from Nazi Germany) or persons declaring no particular religion, thereby underestimating the actual number of individuals of Jewish descent residing in Poland at the time. See *Mały Rocznik Statystyczny* [The Little Statistical Yearbook] (Warsaw: 1939), 25.

[4] *Ibid.*

who were murdered by the German occupiers, required appropriate legal regulations.

The PKWN Manifesto promised special treatment for citizens of Jewish descent and their properties. In fact, the Jewish minority was the only one mentioned in the manifesto, which declared that "the Jews, subjected to bestial extermination by the occupier, shall be guaranteed the opportunity to rebuild their livelihoods as well as legal and factual equality."

It appears that this objective was to be facilitated through the introduction of special legal norms pertaining to abandoned properties. This was precisely how Polish courts interpreted this provision at the time. A ruling of the Polish Supreme Court from 13 June 1945 (II CRN, i.e. made by the Second Chamber following Extraordinary Revision [Rewizja Nadzwyczajna] 52/45) may serve as an example. The Supreme Court declared as void any court rulings regarding both affirmative and negative decisions regarding the revendication of abandoned properties, in the cases of which the courts failed to publicize that such a court proceeding was pending.

The situation of the Polish Jews served as the justification of this ruling. The author of the ruling pointed out that "given the fact that the German occupier during the Second World War brought about an almost complete extermination or dispersal of the Jewish population residing in Poland[5] – a public announcements regarding the proceedings regarding individuals from this group of property owners amounted to a principal means of enabling this group to defend its rights within the framework of the legal order at the time."

The first act in Communist-occupied Poland to regulate the status of abandoned properties was the decree from 2 March 1945 ("On abandoned properties," Dz.U., no. 9, item 45, 1945). It was soon substituted by another law from 6 May 1945 (same title, Dz.U., no. 17, item 94, 1945).

There were no significant differences between the two regulations. The successor act merely introduced a new stipulation regarding farms and extended the time available for Municipal Courts (Sądy Grodzkie) to examine the claims of former owners attempting to reclaim abandoned properties (Article 24, Paragraph 1, and Article 26, Paragraph 3). Article 1 of both acts contained the legal definition of an abandoned property, i.e. "any movable or immovable property which,

---

[5] The author of the Supreme Court ruling completely ignored the complicity of the Soviet occupier in the extermination and dispersal of Polish Jewry.

as a result of break out of the war on 1 September 1939, is not in the possession of the owner, his legal heirs, or legal representatives."

According to the stipulations of the decree (Article 3), which were repeated in the succeeding act (Article 3), all transactions with the occupying German authorities regarding abandoned properties became null and void. Moreover, individuals who obtained such properties from the Nazis were considered to possess them "in bad faith" and, therefore, subject to appropriate legal repercussions resulting from this.

The Head Agency of the Provisional State Administration (*Główny Urząd Tymczasowego Zarządu Państowego*) was established to register, prepare inventories of, and oversee abandoned properties. The body functioned through Provincial Branches of the Provisional State Administration, which appointed the overseers of each property. These roles were mainly fulfilled by various social and state institutions, but sometimes also by individuals. Residential buildings were assigned to bodies of local self-government (on the municipal and parish levels), which appointed administrators entitled to rent out flats and collect payments on behalf of the local self-government.

According to the logic of Article 10 of both the decree and the successor act, "every body of state or local government, or any private person, upon obtaining information regarding an abandoned property [...] shall forthwith notify the Provincial Branch of the Provisional State Administration." In this case the provision was particularly binding on individuals administering properties on behalf of the German authorities in the capacity of involuntary overseers, stewards, or trustees, in addition to other persons finding themselves in possession of abandoned property. Failure to immediately report this to the new authorities was punishable by a sentence of up to five years imprisonment and a fine as high as 200,000 złotys (Article 11, Paragraphs 1 and 2 of both the decree and act). This rigorous law was in force in Communist Poland for over two decades, until 1 January 1970. Only as of that date was the provision repealed (Article VII, Point 4 of the act from 19 April 1969, provisions introducing the penal code: Dz.U., no. 13, item 95, 1969).

The decree and the successor act granted the owners of abandoned properties a special privilege. They benefited from simplified and expedited legal procedures while pursuing their property restitution claims, as opposed to the regular civil procedures. The latter included burdening the claimants with the financial costs of the legal proceedings, calculated as a percentage of the value of the property in question. Claims pursued via the provisions of the decree/act waived this demand. The municipal courts, which were tasked with handling such cases, were obligated to rule within especially short periods of time. According to the decree, the hearing was to be scheduled on the eight day, and the court was required to rule "within three weeks of the filing of the claim or sooner" (Article 23, Paragraph 1, and Article 26, Paragraph 3 of the decree). According to the successor act, the hearing was to be scheduled no later than the twenty-first day, counting from the date of the filing of the claim, while the ruling was to be announced no later than within six weeks from the date of filing (Article 24, Paragraph 1, and Article 27, Paragraph 3 of the act).

According to the act's definition, as specified in Article 1 of both pieces of legislation, only the proprietor had the right to pursue a restitution claim. In the absence of the prewar owner, his direct relatives and other descendants entitled to inherit his property, as well as his spouse "regardless of whether the marriage was contracted in a manner specified by the law" (Article 19 of the decree and Article 20 of the act), also enjoyed this right. The Municipal Courts exercising jurisdiction over the appropriate locale were to serve as the proper bodies for judging such cases. Their decisions were subject to appeals to the proper District Courts.

Persons whose ownership was restored in accordance with the administrative track were merely entitled to oversee and utilize their property. Such a ruling did not grant the right to ownership, but merely opened the way to regaining the forfeited right to ownership. Hence, only following a period of ten years – calculated from the date of the ruling – could these individuals obtain a legal title to ownership by virtue of caring for, maintaining, and residing in a given property (*zasiedzenie*) (Article 35 of the decree, Article 36 of the act). Admittedly, both legal acts envisaged the possibility of the nationalization of abandoned properties. Nevertheless, in light of the logic of these laws, expropriation should have functioned as a last resort solution applicable in exceptional situations when a former proprietor failed to file a restitution claim.

A series of Supreme Court rulings emphasized that the assumption of abandoned property by the Treasury Ministry was compelled by the necessity of removing the state of uncertainty in relation to the status of abandoned property stemming from a failure of certain former proprietors to demonstrate initiative in regaining their property. The main concern was the economic losses generated by this legal insecurity.[6] In such cases, the state treasury received the ownership title to real estate after a period of twenty years, and to movable property following a period of ten years, counting from the end of the calendar year during which the war came to an end (1945) (Article 36 of the decree, and Article 37 of the act).

The act "on abandoned properties" from 6 May 1945 was substituted by a decree from 8 March 1946 on abandoned and "post-German" properties (Dz.U., no. 13, item 87, 1946).

According to Article 1, Section 1 of the 1946 decree, an abandoned property was defined as "any movable or immovable property of persons who, due to the war which began on 1 September 1939, forfeited their property and failed to regain it." An important difference existed between the decree and act of 1945, on the one hand, and the decree of 1946, on the other. In the case of the former, expedited-track restitution could occur only upon the request of the owner himself (or a legally-qualified party).

According to the 1946 decree, however, any proprietor, hence also an individual not in possession of a title of ownership, qualified to file a restitution claim taking advantage of fast-track proceedings. Thus, not only an owner, but also a lessee could file. The significance of this amendment meant that individuals whose properties were revendicated through expedited proceedings qualified to obtain titles of ownership following a period during which they occupied and maintained the property originally owned by others.

The decree of 1946 specified the deadline for restitution claims filed with municipal courts. After a twofold extension, the deadline finally lapsed on 31 December 1948. Afterwards, persons filing for restitution could do so only via ordinary civil procedures.

The remaining regulations of the decree of 1946 did not differ in any meaningful way from those contained in the legal acts of 1945.

It may also be considered noteworthy that the decree of 1946 shortened by half the time period following which an abandoned property came under the official ownership of the state. According to Article 34, Section 1, this period was 10 years in the case of real estate, and five years in the case of movable property. In both cases, the period was calculated from the end of 1945. By contrast with the legal acts of 1945, the decree of 1946 introduced legal fees for those claiming restitution and appealing unfavorable rulings (Article 28, Section 1 of

---

[6] See the rulings of the Supreme Court of the People's Republic of Poland form 19 December 1960: I CR 412/60; 26 July 2001: IV CKN 280/00; and 19 September 2002: II CK 51/02.

the decree). The amount was to constitute 1/10 of the proportional fee (*wpis stosunkowy*) calculated on the basis of the value of the property in question. The decree introduced a new special provision limiting the possibility of regaining a property previously leased out to another party. Restitution could occur only after the expiration of the lease. In the case of contracts concluded for periods longer than those expiring prior to 31 December 1948, the time period was six months following the notice of lease.

Of little significance were provisions replacing the Provisional Agency of State Administration with regional and district-based liquidation agencies and the outlining of the duties of these new bodies.

Great similarity existed between the assumptions underlying the decree of 1946 and the two legal acts of 1945 mentioned previously. The provisions contained in all three were essentially identical. Thus, the general legal doctrine developed as a result of the decree of 1946 was also applicable to the two acts of 1945.

The decree of 8 March 1946 was repealed by an act from 1 August 1985 on real estate maintenance and expropriation (Dz.U., no. 22, item 99, 1985). Nevertheless, the rights obtained as a result of the decree remained in force and could find confirmation through a civil proceeding.

A comparison of the legal regulations pertaining to abandoned properties with legislation regarding "land reform" and the expropriation of industry reveals unequal treatment and the conferring of a privileged position to the owners of abandoned properties in relation to the owners of landed estates, businesses, and other goods confiscated in the name of the "law" by the Communist state. Individuals in the latter category were required to vacate their properties within a three-day period. Moreover, they were forbidden to live in their previous county of residence. It is difficult to resist the impression that the reason behind the privileged status granted to the former category may be attributed to the fact that many of the abandoned properties belonged formerly to Polish citizens of Jewish descent.[7] The regulations pertaining to these properties enabled such

---

[7] The testimony of a Jewish man from Lublin, who succeeded in regaining several pieces of real estate due to the assistance of helpful Poles, serves as proof of the atmosphere in Poland at the time: "At that time Somershteyn [Emil Sommerstein, a member of the Communist puppet Polish Committee of National Liberation, and the head of the Central Committee of Jews in Poland in 1944-1946] was a minister in the Polish government. Every surviving Jew, whose real estate had been appropriated by others, received a confirmation of ownership from this minister in order to help him regain this property. [...] In those days legislation was passed that a Jew, who owned a

persons, or their legal representatives, to sell them immediately following revendication. Such cases (the selling of reclaimed properties) were not uncommon, and pertained mainly to property regained by Jews, who were leaving Poland *en masse* after 1945.

This favor conferred upon the Jewish minority was a product of extralegal factors. First and foremost, the goal of such an endeavor was to camouflage the real nature of the Soviet occupation in Poland. The red occupation was built upon violence, terror, and deportations, in addition to the violation of democratic norms, including the freedom of speech, free parliamentary elections, and, most importantly, the freedom to own private property. The Communist occupation was thus a case of the robbery of private property on a massive scale. The issue of Jewish property therefore constituted a convenient smoke screen for the Communists.

In the West, the complaints voiced by Polish *émigrés* and the Polish Government-in-Exile in London fell mainly on deaf ears. On the other hand, influential circles in Western countries expressed greater interest in the fate of the Jewish community in Poland, whose concerns were amplified by the Jewish Diaspora in the United States and Western Europe. The principles of Marxist dialectics convinced the occupying regime in Poland to return Jewish properties as a tactical compromise. The Communist objective was to gain support in the West through lofty propaganda gestures of "reinstituting justice" for the main victims of German extermination. Of course, the Communists dropped the restitution farce rather quickly and confiscated all Jewish properties.

---

store before the war, which came under someone else's possession, can take it back." Shiye Goldberg (Shie Chehever), *The Undefeated* (Tel Aviv: H. Leivick Publishing House, 1985), 215, 220. *The American Jewish Year Book*, which carefully monitored the situation in Poland, informed its readers that – as opposed to Poland's Eastern borderlands, now annexed by the Soviet Union – "the restitution of Jewish property, if demanded by the owner of his heir, and provided that it is not subject to state control, proceeds more or less smoothly." *American Jewish Year Book*, 5708 (1947–1948), vol. 49 (Philadelphia: 1947), 390. The great scope of this phenomenon may be gauged by the example of the city of Kielce, where hundreds of buildings and other real estate were returned to their former Jewish owners by mid-1946. See Marta Pawlina-Meducka, ed., *Z kroniki utraconego sąsiedztwa* [From the Chronicle of the Lost Neighborhood] (Kielce: Kieleckie Towarzystwo Naukowe, 2001), 202; Krzysztof Urbański, *Kieleccy Żydzi* [The Jews of Kielce] (Kraków: Małopolska Oficyna Wydawnicza, 1993), 180–190; Krzysztof Urbański, „Żydzi w Kielcach w latach 1939–1945," ["The Jews in Kielce during the Years 1939-1945"] in Leszek Bukowski, Andrzej Jankowski, and Jan Żaryn, eds., *Wokół pogromu kieleckiego* [Surrounding the Kielce Pogrom], vol. 2, (Warsaw: Instytut Pamięci Narodowej - Komisja Ścigania Zbrodni przeciwko Narodowi Polskiemu, 2008), 41–43.

The only Jews who benefited were those who managed to sell their property and leave Communist-occupied Poland.

In this context it becomes clear that the theory that Polish citizens enriched themselves at the cost of Holocaust victims by appropriating their property fails to stand up to scrutiny. During the Nazi occupation these properties (usually referred to as "post-Jewish" properties in the legal parlance of the Nazis and Communists) were confiscated by the Third Reich. Any violations of this newly-Germanized property, by Poles or members of any other non-German ethnicity, were punishable by imprisonment in a concentration camp or death. The common practice of the occupiers in relation to the appropriated valuables and real estate was to utilize and protect them from theft or perceived misappropriation by the undesirables.

After the war, these properties came under the province of the Communist state apparatus in Soviet-occupied Poland. In part, some of the properties were regained by former owners or their legal representatives. The properties of those former proprietors who failed to claim their possessions, or were unable to do so (often, as a result of death) before 1948, were nationalized. Afterwards, as the Communist regime began to further consolidate its control over the country and its economy (e.g. the so-called Battle for Commerce), even briefly restored properties were once again confiscated.

Jan T. Gross's Methodology in *Golden Harvest* from the Perspective of Sociology

Tomasz Sommer

(Translated by Paweł Styrna)

Many historians emphasize that Jan Tomasz Gross's works do not belong to the genre of "historical" scholarship in the strict sense. Rather, they point out that Gross is a sociologist by training, thereby suggesting that his books should be evaluated primarily through the prism of the methodology prevalent in that discipline.

It appears that Gross employs this as an easy escape hatch from the rigors of the historical method. Such a perspective is quite convenient for both Gross himself and his sympathizers, providing a superficially plausible excuse to explain away the multiple factual and interpretational errors in his works. But do Gross's books truly satisfy the demands of sociological methodology? The following essay is an attempt to answer this question based on *Golden Harvest*.

As a text, *Golden Harvest* may be considered a "sociological essay" because it strives to determine the norms guiding certain social groups in a given historical context. These determinations were based on two sociological techniques: the analysis of a photograph, and the analysis of social action. They, in turn, provided the basis of Gross's conclusions. Below I shall endeavor to verify whether the two techniques were employed correctly and if the conclusions were formulated properly.

Analysis of Gross's Usage of the Photograph

Gross chose to utilize a photograph published by the left-liberal, Polish-based daily, *Gazeta Wyborcza* [Electoral Gazette].[1] Such an

---

[1] Piotr Głuchowski and Marcin Kowalski, "Gorączka Złota w Treblince" [Gold Fever at Treblinka], *Gazeta Wyborcza*, "Duży Format," 8 January 2008. A photograph taken

approach may boast of a long tradition in strictly sociological literature.[2] Thus there evolved quite rigid rules for the usage of photographs:

> Currently, photographs are rarely used in sociological research, although the tradition of their utilization – both as documents "proving" certain theses, or as analytical materials – dates back to the turn of the nineteenth and twentieth centuries. Between 1896 and 1916, the *American Journal of Sociology* published thirty-one articles which employed photographs as either illustrations or evidence proving some sociological theses. As of 1914, a new editor altered the journal's policy and, with the goal of promoting more "objective" statistical reports, ceased publishing articles employing photographs [...]. In spite of such a radical policy change by a single but highly influential sociological journal, the presentation of sociological works continued to be associated with the visualization of their hypotheses.
>
> Almost from the very birth of sociology as an academic discipline, photographs were used as empirical and analytical material, although cultural anthropology employed visual methods or presenting, recording, and analyzing data more often. Photographs were utilized as instruments of social analysis, particularly in reform-minded sociology [...]. Our contemporary image-based civilization increasingly demands research methods using "images," and thus also methods of presenting and interpreting data and research conclusions in which certain "visual images" of concepts and hypotheses play an important role.[3]

The logically justified methods of employing photographs developed during the past one hundred years. The four main ones follow:

1. Taking photographs as the researcher's primary function, followed by an analysis of the developed images.
2. Photographs as artifacts representing certain objects possessing some social value.

---

by an anonymous individual served as an illustration of Głuchowski and Kowalski's article.
[2] A substantial body of literature has developed on this subject. The most comprehensive treatment published in Poland is Piotr Sztompka, *Socjologia wizualna – fotografia jako metoda badawcza* [Visual Sociology: Photography as a Research Method] (Warsaw: Wydawnictwo Naukowe PWN, 2005).
[3] Krzysztof T. Konecki, „Wizualne wyobrażenia. Główne strategie badawcze w socjologii wizualnej a metodologia teorii ugruntowanej" [Visual Images: The Main Research Strategies in Visual Sociology and the Methodology of Grounded Theory], *Przegląd Socjologii Jakościowej* Vol. I, No. 1 (December 2005): 42-43.

3. Photographs as artifacts, coupled with narratives and comments provided by individuals to whom they were shown.
4. Employing photographs as evidence supporting a conclusion, or to illustrate conclusions derived from research wherein the empirical data consists mainly of verbal texts or numbers.[4]

It appears that Gross's use of the photograph in question fits into the methodology described by points number two and four. A closer examination of the demands to which these methods are subjected by a theoretician will enable us to determine if they bear any resemblance to those employed in *Golden Harvest*.

The author of the work on visual methodology cited above states the following regarding the second method:

> The researcher gathers photographs from the analyzed subjects to enrich his ethnographic description of the group in question, or to gain materials to broaden his analysis and interpretation of conclusions already formulated on the basis of field research, or, finally, to employ photographs as evidential material to assist in the verification of his hypotheses. In such cases photographing is not by itself a research strategy. Rather, the researcher gathers and analyzes photographs taken by other individuals.
>
> One may, of course, collect photographs from individuals who have taken them before the researcher began his query or prior to his turning to them with a request for visual materials. Photographic materials serving as artifacts can also be found in generally accessible places, such as the press, periodicals, published photo albums, museums, galleries, or websites […]. E. Goffman (1979) located the photographs for his analyses of the "presentation of gender" in periodicals. Photographs in advertisements provided him with the materials for analyzing certain stereotypic scenarios of presenting given situations and social categories. By contrasting and juxtaposing many visual presentations in advertising photographs (the comparative method) he analyzed the typical presentations of gender in the social and cultural context.[5]

The above passage clearly indicates the importance of utilizing a variety of photographs to draw any viable conclusion. Otherwise, one may easily fall into the trap of what we may refer to as "the UFO effect," i.e. utilizing photographic material depicting a nonexistent phenomenon. The repetition of images also has a quantitative significance. Of course, the usage of photographs as such belongs to the

---

[4] *Ibid.*, 44.
[5] *Ibid.*, 44-45.

category of qualitative, not quantitative sociology. Yet, an image presented by the photographs may also be integrated into some statistical framework.

Nevertheless, an attempt to draw far-reaching conclusions from a single photograph has no methodological justification. Let us imagine a situation wherein a researcher sorting through thousands of photographs of the Soviet dictator, Joseph Stalin, choosing to employ only one, depicting Stalin at work while tilling a garden. Would it be correct to conclude on this basis that Stalin was first and foremost a gardener?

Gross's usage of the photograph may also bear a resemblance to method number four. The author of the previously cited methodological text states the following on this method:

> The fourth strategy involves the employment of a photograph as *evidence supporting a conclusion* (emphasis in original) or to illustrate conclusions reached through research wherein the main data consists of verbal texts or numbers.
>
> It would be difficult to label this a research strategy (it is mainly a data presentation strategy), but it may certainly serve as an auxiliary strategy in various types of research. For instance, a researcher-analyst may wish to thus diversify the evidence to support his ethnographic description, or to visualize his conclusions from other types of research, such as quantitative ones [...]. Photographs broaden and contextualize nonvisual empirical data. They also serve as a kind of "portrait" or "image" of the main concepts or ideal types employed by the author. Thus, photographs are employed here to confirm the validity of the researcher's conclusions and his usage of certain concepts. D. Harper employed aerial photographs to confirm and also broaden his conclusions from field research (including quantitative research) regarding the social structure of dairy farms in the United States [...].[6]

To a certain degree, Gross utilizes the reverse of this method. A single photograph serves as a compass of sorts, allowing him to treat other testimonies and interpreted events as facts. The fact that Gross is unsure of the exact context in which the photograph was taken has not in the least hampered his enthusiasm.[7] The image is employed as a

---

[6] *Ibid.*, 49.
[7] As a consequence, he uses the word "probably" while describing the photograph. In addition, as Głuchowski and Kowalski eventually admitted, in contradiction to their claims in the article cited by Gross, they received the image from a scholar, not the "locals" or an individual actually depicted in the photograph.

metaphor or embodiment of a thesis he wishes to promote. This is, to a certain point, justifiable as a literary device, but not as a scholarly method. Gross's approach means that his book may be treated as a more or less successful work of art, but not as a methodologically sound reconstruction of reality. Thus, it is fair to conclude that Gross's employment of the photograph of the "diggers" is unscholarly.

Analysis of social action

Golden Harvest describes two social actions: digging for treasure, and the behavior of a "secure" social group towards an endangered social group. First, we will address the treasure hunting.

Gross presents the phenomenon as absolutely barbaric. He considers the very fact that individuals searched for gold as something extraordinary, something that should not have occurred. Yet, as a sociologist, he should have been aware that treasure hunting is an almost archetypal activity for mankind. He should also be able to distinguish between, on the one hand, the mythological Golden Fleece suspended from a tree in a grove in Colchis, guarded by a one-hundred-headed dragon which never slept, and eventually captured by Jason with the assistance of the sorceress Medea, and, on the other hand, real treasure, which is usually located at the place of burial. The tradition of combing through gravesites in search of valuables is most likely older than ancient Egypt itself. Moreover, modern archeology may indeed be treated as a treasure hunting operation, albeit ritualized by the state.

If Gross desired to adhere to standards demanded of scholarly works, he would have been advised to contextualize his description of treasure hunters in Bełżec or Treblinka by alluding to these traditions, instead of treating the phenomenon of combing through grave sites and battlefields as highly unusual. The anthropological reality is that such unsavory behaviors are not only "normal," but even predictable.[8]

This suggests that Gross's approach amounts to manipulating evidence. He fails to present the reality of a phenomenon that is, first of all, commonplace throughout the world; and secondly, may be understandable or justified in the context of war, hunger, and poverty;

---

[8] See Simon Sebag Montefiore, *Prince of Princes: The Life of Potemkin* (London: Weidenfield & Nicolson, 2000), 26. "The locals continue to search for Alladin's Cave, which they call 'Potemkin's Treasure.' At the cemetery they only managed to dig their way to the bodies of eighteenth-century women, most likely Potemkin's sisters." J.T. Gross is revolted that someone dug in the area of the former death camp of Treblinka for several decades. Yet, a serious treasure hunting operation may last centuries, if not millennia!

and, lastly, boasts of a rich bibliography. Furthermore, Gross's treatment of the facts is as arbitrary as his usage of the photograph, which hinders their assessment.[9]

Now let us turn to the second social action described and subjected to value judgments by Gross, such as the behavior of a "secure" social group vis-à-vis an endangered one. The change in behaviors and relations between two such groups, resulting from a shift in their external circumstances and different legal status, certainly constitutes an interesting sociological phenomenon. Taxologically, it is probably most appropriate to include it in the sociology of war. Its objective is to observe and analyze war as a social phenomenon.

The father of war sociology, which he termed polymology (from the ancient Greek word *polemos*, i.e. war, fight, or combat), was the Frenchman Gaston Bouthoul (1896-1980). Polymology consisted of three elements: the general sociology of war; a search for the rhythm of belligerence (*wojowniczość*); and analyzing the causes of structural, cyclical, and occasional conflicts, as well as the prospects of war breaking out at any given time.[10] Some of the subjects of wartime sociology are the relations between soldiers and civilians on all possible levels, such as between an occupying force and an occupied population, or between allies at home and outside of their native lands.

The phenomenon of declassization (Polish: *deklasacja*) – defined as a social group's loss of status or prestige – accompanies armed conflicts although it does not necessarily occur during a war.[11] When addressing this problem in a sociologically sound text, Gross would have done well to verify whether such a declassization had occurred earlier and if any changes in behavioral patterns transpired in a similar manner. *Golden Harvest* fails to answer this question, although a scholar need not be an expert in East-Central European history to realize that declassization of many social groups occurred on a massive scale in the neighboring Soviet Union. Many social groups – ranging from aristocrats through the middle class and the clergy to the

---

[9] In reality, it is difficult to establish who exactly participated in the treasure-hunting excavations: Polish peasants or Red Army soldiers? The latter, according to testimonies presented by Gross, apparently utilized dynamite in their digging operations.

[10] This is a definition provided by Fr. Andrzej Zwoliński in the introduction to the book *Wojna – wybrane zagadnienia* [War: Selected Issues] (Kraków: Wydawnictwo Wam, 2003).

[11] The decline of the Polish nobility (*szlachta*), which spanned many decades – from the collapse of the January Uprising in 1864 to the end of the Second World War – should be viewed as a creeping, although sometimes accelerating declassization, which, after all, brought about a shift in the attitudes of other social groups towards the nobility.

peasantry – were subjected to liquidation. The Bolsheviks also exterminated, or attempted to liquidate, entire nationalities, including Soviet Poles.

How did other, temporarily secure groups, behave in relation to their liquidated neighbors in the Soviet Union at this time? Gross's reflections raise this question, although he himself failed to pose it. Thus, the fragments of his work dealing with the above phenomenon should be treated as a collection of unjustified invectives, rather than an attempt to establish some kind of material truth justifying the formulation of a conclusion.

The case of Golden Harvest *therefore allows us to determine that Gross neglected to apply his sociological training to his work, which fails to meet the most basic criteria demanded of publications in the discipline.*

We shall conclude this essay with a quote describing the treatment of exhausted soldiers of Napoleon's *Grand Armée*, in the wake of the disastrous defeat in Russia and the deadly crossing of the Berezyna River, upon reaching the city of Wilno on 10 December 1812: "Jews demonstrated a particular penchant for brutality characterizing the most cowardly and vile. They threw the sick into the streets or killed them with much ado, if they expected some loot in the form of money or an expensive uniform from them."[12]

Such a quote, by no means an exclusive one in this vein, might easily constitute the departure point and compass of a work entitled *Golden Harvest of 1812*. Yet, does the behavior of a minority within the context of war justify tarring an entire ethnoreligious group with the same, negative brush? Moreover, would such a work posses any scholarly value whatsoever?

---

[12] Aleksander Count Fredro, *Trzy po trzy – pamiętnik z czasów wojen napoleońskich* [Idle Chit-Chat: A Diary from the Napoleonic Wars] (Warsaw: Towarzystwo Upowszechnienia Czytelnictwa, 1996), 46.

THE NEO-STALINIST DISCOURSE IN POLISH HISTORICAL STUDIES IN THE UNITED STATES

John Radziłowski

Of all tyrannies, a tyranny sincerely exercised for the good of its victims may be the most oppressive. It would be better to live under robber barons than under omnipotent moral busybodies. The robber baron's cruelty may sometimes sleep, his cupidity may at some point be satiated; but those who torment us for our own good will torment us without end for they do so with the approval of their own conscience.

—C. S. Lewis

This essay seeks to describe a school of Polish historical study that has arisen over the past decade, and which is centered primarily in the United States and other English-speaking countries. The work of this school is characterized as neo-Stalinism, though it is a term not accepted by the historians who make up this school of thought. The purpose of this article is to describe, with greater precision, the characteristics of neo-Stalinist Polish historiography in the English-speaking academic world without judging the individual motives or biases of those who make up this school.[1]

The significance of neo-Stalinism cannot be understated since it is profoundly different from other schools of Polish historiography. Unlike other schools of historical inquiry, the goal of neo-Stalinist history is not disinterested research, the search for objective truth, or bringing greater clarity to our understanding of the Polish past. Rather neo-Stalinism has as its goal the wholesale re-writing of Polish history, and from this, a complete re-ordering of Polish culture and identity.[2]

---

[1] I coined this term in 2008. See John Radziłowski, "'Strach' i rewizja polskiej historii" ['Fear' and the Revising of Polish History], *Rzeczpospolita*, 1 March 2008; reprinted in Robert Jankowski, ed., *Cena "Strachu": Gross w Oczach Historyków* [The Price of 'Fear': Gross in the Eyes of Historians] (Warsaw: Fronda, 2008), 345–52.

[2] It may be fairly argued that other schools of Polish historiography were not necessarily purely objective and had their own political or ideological objectives, for example, the nineteenth-century Romantic and Positivist schools of Polish history. While this matter deserves a discussion that is beyond the scope of this article, a few

The purpose of this project is to create a new "secular" Polish identity that the practitioners of neo-Stalinist history view as more enlightened, progressive, and superior to what has gone before—in sum, a new post-modern Polish man.

This goal is perhaps best illustrated in the words of the scholar whose work has most come to define neo-Stalinism, Jan Tomasz Gross. In an interview in 2008, Gross stated that one of his goals was to compel nationalistic and Catholic Poles to confess their sins, most notably anti-Semitism. Of his book *Fear*, Gross stated "I hope that this book will simply help Poles to be themselves and to clear themselves."[3] In a more recent lecture at Yad Vashem, Gross was even more explicit about his purposes. "His [Gross's] research goals, he makes clear, are broad and ambitious: to create a new historiography, and through this to re-write the history of the Holocaust," the *Jerusalem Post* reported. Polish identity, Gross believes, is based on "lies" and must therefore be changed according to the formula he sets forth.[4]

The desire to use scholarship on the past to remake the present and create a "better" future, however noble or ignoble that vision may be, is a fundamental component of a totalitarian mindset, even if its practitioners are themselves not totalitarians. History, evidence, and scholarship itself become merely a means to an end, an instrument to be used in service to some perceived greater good. The myriad methodological temptations that such an approach poses for the researcher are beyond the scope of this article. Yet, the great dangers of allowing the manipulation of the past to serve the present no matter the goal or ideology, are well illustrated by a glance back at the past century of European history. Thus, the neo-Stalinist turn in the writing of Polish history is important to understand and clearly debate for scholars and the public at large.

Characteristics of neo-Stalinist writing on twentieth-century Polish history

What are the main characteristics of neo-Stalinist historiography? Most neo-Stalinist scholars focus their primary interest on Polish-

---

points may be made. First, no previous school (aside from the original Stalinist historians of the period 1945–56) sought to so fundamentally re-order the Polish past and remake the Polish identity. Nor did they deny the existence of objective truth, as post modern neo-Stalinists do, nor did they treat evidence as purely a means of reinforcing their arguments.

[3] "Gross: I hope Poles will clear themselves," *Rzeczpospolita*, 11 January 2008.
[4] Eetta Prince-Gibson, "Myths and Truths," *The Jerusalem Post*, 31 October 2010.

Jewish relations, the Second World War, and the Holocaust in Poland. Thus, the majority of examples deal directly with these topics.

At one level, neo-Stalinist historians often simply use Stalinist era sources, both primary and secondary, with little or no acknowledgement of the ideological and social conditions under which they were generated.

For example, in his book *Neighbors,* Jan Gross uses confessions of accused perpetrators of the Jedwabne massacre that were obtained under torture. Gross does so knowingly and does not have any qualms about using such sources without subjecting them to intense scrutiny and corroboration.[5]

In *Fear,* Gross continues to cite as fact numbers of Jews killed in the immediate post-war years in Poland that were generated during the Communist era for external propaganda purposes and which have been shown to be false by historians David Engel and Marek Jan Chodakiewicz. But Gross is not alone in his uncritical use of Stalinist era sources. German writer Klaus-Peter Friedrich, whose work accusing Poles of mass collaboration with Nazi occupation authorities finds much support among neo-Stalinists in the English-speaking world, also uses Stalinist-era sources to bolster his claims.[6]

While most neo-Stalinists acknowledge the existence of Soviet terror in Poland and elsewhere, they tend to treat it as largely unimportant.[7] At best, neo-Stalinist scholars significantly downplay Soviet terror in Poland, either ignoring it completely, or explaining it away. Communism more generally is viewed in a neutral or slightly positive way. The role of the Soviet authorities in dramatically worsening relations between local ethnic communities in eastern Poland is largely ignored by Gross in *Neighbors,* even though Gross himself acknowledged this reality in his earlier book, *Revolution from Abroad.*

Since the publication of *Neighbors,* most neo-Stalinist scholars have followed Gross's lead and turned a blind eye toward Soviet

---

[5] On this aspect of Gross's work see Marek Jan Chodakiewicz, *The Massacre in Jedwabne, July 10, 1941: Before, During and After* (New York: Columbia University Press/EEM, 2005), esp. 114–25.

[6] Klaus-Peter Friedrich, "Collaboration in a 'Land without a Quisling,'" *Slavic Review* 64, no. 4 (Winter 2006). Significant criticism of this article by a broad range of scholars in North America and Europe was blocked by the editors of *Slavic Review.*

[7] One neo-Stalinist stated to the author in a private conversation that the theory that Poland had two enemies during the Second World War (Nazi Germany and the Soviet Union) must be "eliminated."

involvement.[8] In *Fear*, Gross describes the imposition of the Soviet terror regime in 1939-41 merely as "Sovietization." Post-war Stalinist terror is described employing Stalin's propaganda term as "liberation." In addition, Gross further praises Communism as an honorable political alternative.[9] Other scholars have taken a similar approach *vis-a-vis* Stalinist Poland, largely ignoring the mass terror, executions, torture, and repression. For example, Polish-American historian Małgorzata Fidelis lauds Stalinist labor policy for allowing women to work in heavy industry as a way to overcome gender oppression.[10]

Another critical characteristic of neo-Stalinist literature is its treatment of Poles as perpetrators or co-perpetrators of the Holocaust. This again echoes Stalinist propaganda of the 1940s and 1950s that blamed Jewish deaths on "Polish fascists." Although few neo-Stalinist academics will openly state that Poles were co-responsible for the Holocaust, virtually all of their work points in this direction. In some cases, the accusation is quite crude. Gross, for example, openly invokes the work of Goldhagen in describing the perpetrators of the Jedwabne crimes as "willing executioners."[11] In a newspaper interview he stated: "The Poles similarly to the Ukrainians, the Lithuanians, [and] the Byelorussians participated in the Holocaust."[12]

Sometimes this is done in a more subtle way, such as in one review of *Fear* entitled "Ordinary Poles." By invoking Christopher Browning's work *Ordinary Men*, the reviewer implies at least a comparison, if not an equation, of the Poles with the men of a Nazi police battalion.[13] Although Gross and other neo-Stalinists tacitly acknowledge the presence of the Nazis, the Hitlerites' role in local massacres of Jews is downplayed and the role of Polish collaborators, no matter how large or small, is placed in the foreground. As Gross notes, for neo-Stalinists the Polish experience in Second World War is little different from that of Lithuanians or Ukrainians.

---

[8] A notable exception in recent American literature is the work of Prof. Timothy Snyder, *Bloodlands: Europe between Hitler and Stalin* (New York: Basic Books, 2010).
[9] See John Radziłowski, Review of *Fear: Anti-Semitism in Poland after Auschwitz*, Jan Tomasz Gross, *Biuletyn IPN*, no. 7 (July 2006): 98–102.
[10] Małgorzata Fidelis, "Equality through Protection: The Politics of Women's Employment in the Postwar Poland, 1945–1956," *Slavic Review* 63, no. 2 (Summer 2004): 301–24.
[11] John Connelly, "Poles and Jews in the Second World War: The Revisions of Jan T. Gross," *Contemporary European History*, II, 4 (2002): 641–58.
[12] "Gross: I hope Poles will clear themselves," *Rzeczpospolita,* 11 January 2008.
[13] John Connelly, "Ordinary Poles," *Commonweal*, 23 February 2007, 28–29.

A third characteristic of neo-Stalinism is that it ignores, minimizes, or relativizes the murder of Polish Christians/Gentiles by the Nazis and Soviets. Similarly, it omits to mention most non-Communist resistance and rescue activities under the auspices of the Home Army (*Armia Krajowa*: AK), unless it is to accuse sections of the AK of anti-Semitism or crimes against Jews.[14] There is a corresponding over-emphasis on the minimal and questionable role of pro-Soviet groups like the People's Army (*Armia Ludowa*) and the People's Guard (*Gwardia Ludowa*).

No neo-Stalinist scholars in the past fifteen years appear to exhibit any interest in portraying the extremely wide range of activities and behaviors in German-occupied Poland. They appear at best indifferent to the activities of anti-Nazi resistance and efforts at rescuing Jews, and have never attempted to provide a corrective to the widespread belief outside of Poland that Poles were Nazi collaborators. Hence, Polish resistance and rescue activities continue to remain virtually unknown among both the scholars and the general public in the English-speaking world.

A fourth characteristic of neo-Stalinist historiography is that it views Polish nationalism and/or patriotism as virtually synonymous with anti-Semitism. It appears hostile to the notion of a Polish past possessing any redeeming qualities whatsoever.[15] Poland's thousand-year history is reduced to Jedwabne and Kielce. For example, one scholar sarcastically referred to Polish criminals who killed Jews as "brave" patriots.[16]

Most neo-Stalinist work, like official Soviet propaganda of the 1940s and 1950s, suggests or implies a link between Nazism and Polish nationalism. It is equally hostile to Polish Christianity and equates Catholicism with anti-Semitism. Gross states: "The Jew was a devil in the Christian culture."[17] He further notes, using the present tense: "In the Polish-Catholic imagination, Jews are God-killers, they use Christian children for matzo."[18] In other words, not only were Polish

---

[14] I discuss one such instance in my review of *Secret City: The Hidden Jews of Warsaw, 1940–1945*, Gunnar S. Paulsson, accessed at H-HOLOCAUST@H-NET.MSU.EDU, 11/12/2003 2:15:48 PM. www.h-net.msu.edu/reviews/showrev.cgi?path=252691081495762

[15] See for example, John Connelly, Response to Prof. Anna Cienciała et al., *Slavic Review* 65, no. 4 (Winter 2006): 888–89.

[16] Gunnar S. Paulsson, *Secret City: The Hidden Jews of Warsaw, 1940–1945* (New Haven: Yale University Press, 2002), 173.

[17] "Gross: I hope Poles will clear themselves," *Rzeczpospolita*, 11 January 2008.

[18] Jan T. Gross, *Fear: Anti-Semitism in Poland after Auschwitz. An Essay in Historical Interpretation* (New York: Random House, 2006), xiii.

Catholics anti-Semites in the past according to Gross, but anti-Semitism is a universal characteristic of all Polish Catholics.

Origins and influences

The use of the term neo-Stalinism is preferred because this school of historiography parallels the work of the original group of Polish Communist historians and writers in the years immediately following Poland's subjugation by the Soviet Union at the end of Second World War.[19] This is *not* to suggest that present-day neo-Stalinist historians are devotees of the Soviet dictator Joseph Stalin, or even that they are doctrinaire Marxists in the strict sense of the term. Yet, most are strongly influenced by Marxist historiography, especially the style of "cultural Marxism" emphasizing race and gender grievances that has emerged as the dominant paradigm in North American historiography since the 1960s.

Stalinist writers and historians of the 1940s and 1950s completely rejected the values and beliefs of the Polish cultural tradition. Patriotism, the Catholic faith, and sacrifice for the nation were equated with collaboration with the Nazis, and especially with anti-Semitism. The Soviet Union was not a murderous foreign power but a "fraternal" liberator. Those who opposed Soviet domination were therefore to be discredited, and not merely discredited, but utterly destroyed – intellectually, if not physically. As one Communist jailor told his captives: *"Our task is not only to destroy you physically, but also to smash you morally before the eyes of society."*[20]

The neo-Stalinists of today's North American academia are not torturers or murderers. Nor are they personally responsible for the crimes of Stalinism. And, in any case, we are now far removed from that dark and bloody period in Polish history. Nevertheless, the

---

[19] The first use of the term neo-Stalinism occurred among Trotskyites in the West in 1948 to describe a kind of statist or top-down communism which rejected the consciousness of the proletariat in favor of an intellectual-bureaucratic elite. See Hal Draper, "The Neo-Stalinist Type: Notes on a New Political Ideology," *The New International* 14, no. 1 (January 1948): 24–26. (Available online at http://www.marxists.org/archive/draper/1948/01/neostal.htm). According to Draper, neo-Stalinists reject "economic" communism. This earlier use of the term, though an artifact of arcane intramural left-wing struggles, is helpful in that it suggests a kind of elite contempt for the lived experiences of ordinary men and women and intellectual arrogance.

[20] Major Wiktor Herer quoted in Czesław Leopold and Krzysztof Lechicki, *Więźniowie polityczni w Polsce, 1945–1956* [Political Prisoners in Poland, 1945-1956] (Warsaw: Wydawnictwo Młoda Polska, 1981), 6.

arguments made by today's neo-Stalinist historians often closely parallel those of Stalinist writers of the immediate post-war period, especially in their attitudes toward the Polish nation, Polish nationalism, Polish Catholicism, and the underlying values of the Polish cultural tradition.[21] In taking the positions they do, neo-Stalinists frequently find themselves—consciously or unconsciously—mirroring approaches taken by earlier Stalinist writers and even copying their language and turns of phrase.[22] (Those earlier Stalinist authors, it should be noted, wrote under intense ideological scrutiny from elements of the Communist security services whose bosses placed a high value on monitoring historical research, publication, and teaching.)

The immediate origins of neo-Stalinist historiography deserve further research and discussion, but it should be noted that its emergence after the fall of Communist regimes in East-Central Europe coincides with the increasing volume of documentation on Communist and Soviet crimes.[23] Prior to and immediately after 1989, the dominant paradigm in research on the Holocaust and the Second World War outside of Poland emphasized Polish indifference toward the Jews and some level of collaboration. Mainstream scholars in Holocaust and East European history almost completely ignored Polish resistance to Nazism and treated resistance to the Soviets as collaboration with Hitler.

By contrast, Soviet and Communist actions were viewed in a relatively favorable light or, if the crimes of the Soviet era were noted,

---

[21] A discussion of those values is beyond the scope of this article, but for a fuller treatment see Leon Dyczewski, ed., *Values in the Polish Cultural Tradition*, Polish Philosophical Studies III (Washington, D.C.: Council for Research in Values and Philosophy, 2002), especially contributions by Profs. Tomasz Strzembosz, Ewa Jabłonska-Deptuła, and Piotr Pawel Gach.

[22] For example, one of the earliest writers to use the neo-Stalinist idiom, Yaffa Eliach, repeatedly used the term "White Poles" to describe the Polish Armia Krajowa, a term that comes straight out of the Soviet propaganda lexicon.

[23] Eliach was among the first American scholars to openly turn toward Stalinist modes of historiography, perhaps under the influence of her father who was for a time a Communist functionary whose task was to hunt members of the AK. I have in the past criticized Eliach for her extremely poor methodology. Although those criticisms remain valid, her work *There Once Was a World* stands out as better documented in term of the number and range of sources than either *Neighbors* or *Fear*. See John Radziłowski "Ejszyszki Revisited, 1939–45," *Polin: Studies in Polish Jewry* 15 (2002): 453–68; *Ibid.*, "Ejszyszki i historiografia konfliktów etnicznych w północno-wschodniej Polsce w latach 1939–1945," in *Polski i żydowski ruch oporu pod okupacją niemiecką w latach 1939–1945* [The Polish and Jewish Resistance Movement Under the German Occupation in 1939-1945] (Warsaw: IPN, forthcoming).

they were relativized or downplayed. It may be hypothesized that the emergence of the neo-Stalinist discourse is in part a reaction in defense of that existing paradigm of Polish villainy as it existed for decades in English-speaking scholarship, and which may be challenged by newly opened Communist archives.

Neo-Stalinism can also be seen as a historiographic offensive in response to the turmoil in Polish intellectual, cultural, and social life in the years following 1989. Because of this turmoil, the terms of debate and points of reference in the understanding of modern Polish history were, or appeared to be, up for "grabs." In the political and economic realm, Poland's elite spoke openly of "catching up" with Europe and, in many cases, sought to shed outward signs of a Polish identity in favor of a "European" one.

The time was ripe, then, for a Polish version of the "long march through the institutions" as proposed by Marxist thinkers, such as Antonio Gramsci and later, the members of the so-called Frankfurt School, who translated economic Marxism into cultural terms. Accordingly, a small intellectual elite could remake society and culture to prepare the way for true socialism by gaining and employing influence within the news media, schools, universities, and all cultural institutions. Literature and history were important targets for this "long march." This movement has become dominant within Western academia, especially in North America, which is highly significant given that the overwhelming majority of neo-Stalinist historians, like Gross at Princeton University, live, work, and/or were trained in the United States or other English-speaking countries. Thus, neo-Stalinism exists within a *milieu* in which the "long march" is already a *fait accompli*.

The disastrous effects of cultural Marxism, and of Gramsci's influence in particular, on academic life in the United States have been discussed in great detail elsewhere. However, it is important to note several trends within American academia that appear to have an important influence on neo-Stalinism, in particular hostility toward Christianity and nationalism (and by extension any form of patriotism or service to one's country); post-modernism (and its variants, post-structuralism and post-colonialism); and a paradigm of ethnic-group relations based on a particular reading of the history of race relations in the United States.

Although hostility toward religion, and especially Christianity, was always a part of Marxism, the followers of Gramsci believe that de-Christianization is a necessary element in creating a "progressive" future. Drawing on cultural Marxism, neo-Stalinist historians also mirror the attitudes of Polish authorities who waged a struggle against the Catholic Church throughout the Communist period, in part by portraying the Church during the Nazi occupation as a collaborationist element. Thus, in neo-Stalinist writing, the Church appears as the main incubator of anti-Semitism in Polish life, and thus a major co-conspirator in the Poles' alleged complicity in the Holocaust. As mentioned above, Gross writes: "In the Polish-Catholic imagination, Jews are God-killers, they use Christian children for matzo."[24] Needless to say, Gross presents no evidence for such a statement, no discussion of the history, theology, or philosophy of Polish Catholicism. His view of Catholicism is largely informed by the anti-Catholic polemics of Daniel Jonah Goldhagen.[25]

Decades of doctrinal and moral pronouncements by leading Catholic churchmen, all the way up to the Polish-born Pope John Paul II, are dismissed or ignored – to say nothing of their own extensively documented personal experiences under Nazi and Soviet occupation. Neo-Stalinist writing is rarely subtle and most often cavalier in its use of evidence, substituting personal prejudice for fact. Thus, the contested nature of anti-Jewish strains in Christian theology is largely ignored, as is the actual emergence of racial anti-Semitism in the late nineteenth-century. Instead, for neo-Stalinists, Polish anti-Semitism can only exist as a kind of primordial religious belief, a constant feature whose existence appears to vary little if at all according to time, place, or circumstance.

Hostility toward nationalism is a strong element in contemporary Western academic circles. This is clearly reflected in the work of many neo-Stalinist authors who equate Polish nationalism with anti-Semitic racism. Indeed, neo-Stalinist invective against perceived "nationalist" deviations among Polish historians is often extreme. For example, one American scholar, John Connelly, described Polish nationalism as a form of megalomania.[26] The same author, in response to criticism of his terminology, responded: "I originally wanted to use the word *pride* rather than *hubris* [in the title of an article describing Polish nationalism]. I held back because I imagined that there is something

---

[24] Gross, *Fear*, xiii.
[25] Neo-Stalinist writers are uninterested in the complexity of Catholic theology or philosophy and what it has to say on the question of Judaism, either before or after Vatican II. Within the American context, neo-Stalinist work draws upon a background of crude anti-Catholicism dating back to the nineteenth century and white nativist groups like the Ku Klux Klan.
[26] John Connelly, "Why the Poles Collaborated so Little and Why That is No Reason for Nationalist Hubris," *Slavic Review* 64, no. 4 (Winter 2005): 771–81.

like 'healthy national pride.' Upon further reflection, however, I am convinced that there is no such thing."[27]

Neo-Stalinist scholars adopt modes of argument and uses of evidence drawn from post-modernist writing, especially literary criticism. This methodology is extremely common in North America among historians and others specializing in studies of race, gender, and so-called queer theory (e.g., gay and lesbian studies). In this approach evidence is a means to an end. What matters is not the objective meaning of the evidence (for they deny the existence of objective meaning), but the perception of the individual employing the evidence. This follows a kind of dialectical reasoning according to which the scholarship and the evidence that supports it serve a larger ideological goal.[28]

The leading adherent to the neo-Stalinist school, Jan T. Gross, is by his own admission an avid reader of post-modernist semiotics.[29] Another example appears in a review in which Gross attacked Jewish-American scholar Rosa Lehmann for painting a too-favorable picture of Polish-Jewish relations. In response to Lehmann's finding that few Poles in the community she studied had clear memories of the Nazi deportation and killing of local Jews, Gross quipped "After Freud, some of us are inclined to think that people may not talk about issues precisely because they *are* relevant to their lives."[30] Hence, lack of

---

[27] Idem, Response to Prof. Anna Cienciała et al., *Slavic Review* 65, no. 4 (Winter 2006): 888–89 (emphasis in original). Connelly further advocates a "post-ethnic" approach to history.

[28] Zbigniew Herbert wrote of such thinking thus: "A good Marxist, like a good sophist, successfully argued for Helen's virginity, and then equally successfully demonstrated that she was a whore.... The beginning of the present semantic collapse goes back to the 1950s. Those who remained faithful to the principles of dialectic did so after massive training. They do not pronounce intersubjective judgments but, instead, treat the language as a form of attack or defense: 'Under Bierut I wrote this, under Gomulka something else,' but always following the rhythm of history, or rather, the Politburo guidelines. This amounts to a betrayal of language, a denial of the unequivocal meaning of certain ideas." See *Tygodnik Solidarność*, 46 (321), 11 November 1994. This passage can be read as a description of the career of Prof. Gross, who wrote one thing in works like *Revolution from Abroad*, and quite the opposite in works like *Neighbors* and *Fear* without the slightest discussion of how his view of important subjects such as the Soviet occupation of 1939–41 changed so dramatically, or how evidence he treated as solid and convincing in one book was rejected completely in the next book.

[29] Jan T. Gross, "One Line at a Time," *Poetics Today* 27, no. 2 (Summer 2006): 425–29 (esp. 425n1).

[30] Idem, review of Rosa Lehmann, *Symbiosis and Ambivalence: Poles and Jews in a Small Galician Town*, in *American Historical Review* (February 2003): 288.

evidence of Polish anti-Semitism or involvement in Nazi actions constitutes evidence of these things.

One of the most critical influences on neo-Stalinism in North America is the poor state of scholarship on race. Many neo-Stalinists, and Gross himself in particular, were influenced by periods of serious racial turmoil and agitation in the United States.[31] Since the 1960s, American academics developed a paradigm of history that emphasized the "victims" of the past, particularly African Americans. Although, on the one hand, this was a necessary corrective to the exclusion, discrimination, and violence suffered by American blacks, it quickly became an overtly political exercise. A racialized view of the past emerged as the chief weapon of Gramscian radicals in the United States.

The scholarship of this era turned to a negative form of American exceptionalism, in which America was not merely responsible for its own racial sins, but those of the world at large, and indeed for all unrealized good in the world.[32] A rhetorical centerpiece of this was to value the testimony of the victims over that of their alleged oppressors.

Testimony from groups viewed by scholars and writers of the time as "oppressors" was disregarded while that of "victims" was to go unquestioned.[33] Perhaps the best example was Frantz Fanon's 1961 book *Wretched of the Earth*, which had an important impact on Western intellectuals. Thus, victims and their descendants were granted the right to critique the "oppressors" and their descendants. The former were to speak, the latter to remain silent under the slogan "we talk, you listen."

This approach revolutionized scholarly and public understanding of American history, most notably through the work of Marxist historian Howard Zinn in which America, American religious and social values, and American nationalism were cast as the enemy of human progress.[34] It also revolutionized how racial and ethnic relations were viewed worldwide. Among ethnic groups in the United States, many other

---

[31] Gross left Poland for the U.S. in 1968, a period of most intensive ideological turmoil in the West and in particular of racial turmoil in the United States.
[32] On this subject, see the seminal work of Joseph A. Amato, *Victims and Values: A History and a Theory of Suffering* (Westport, Ct.: Greenwood, 1990), esp. chapters 6–8.
[33] Cf. Jan Gross' "new approach to sources" and Gross, "One Line at a Time."
[34] Howard Zinn, *A People's History of America* (New York: Harper and Row, 1980). Zinn was open about his Gramscian approach to the past. See Catherine Parayre, "The Conscience of the Past: An Interview with historian Howard Zinn," *Flagpole Magazine Online*, 18 February 1998. Accessed at
http://web.archive.org/web/20010525003828/http://www.flagpole.com/Issues/02.18.98/lit.html. Gross can be viewed as the Howard Zinn of Polish history.

groups began to identify themselves as victims similar to American blacks, most notably Jewish Americans and Polish Americans.[35]

Although such identification was, for many reasons, historically problematic, for Jewish Americans, especially on the political left, relations with African Americans became a vital touchstone of progressive identity. In this sense, the paradigm of black victims and white oppressors in the American South served as a kind of facile intellectual shorthand for the complexities of the Jewish past in East-Central Europe, regardless of the severe historical distortion such a comparison implied.

This view became commonplace among many American intellectuals of the 1960s and 1970s, most of whom were not Jewish. For example, Southern writer William Styron set up his 1979 novel, *Sophie's Choice* with an explicit comparison between Poland and the American South, between black slavery and violent discrimination, on the one hand, and the condition of Jews in pre-World War II Poland, on the other. Thoughtful commentators pointed out how Styron's own American racial complexes were imposed on Poland.[36]

The neo-Stalinist view of Poland and Polish-Jewish relations thus appears to be the importation of this American racial paradigm into a European context for which it is ill-suited. In particular, it makes excessively sharp distinctions between putative "victims" and "oppressors," prizes one group's experiences and testimony over the other's based on the racial or ethnic preferences of the author using them, and is primarily a tool of Grasmcian *desiderata*. Although this general approach to racial relations remains dominant in American academic circles, it is an artifact of a particular moment in intellectual history that provides little value for understanding Polish-Jewish history.

History as a weapon

Neo-Stalinism is impervious to the standard course of scholarly discussion and criticism. This is indeed the case for any group of intellectuals who believe themselves anointed midwives of a better

---

[35] On Jewish American identification with southern blacks, see Hasia Diner, *In the Almost Promised Land: American Jews and Blacks, 1915–1935* (Baltimore: Johns Hopkins University Press, 1977), esp. chpt. 3.
[36] See Thaddeus Radziłowski, "The 'Final Solution' for Southern Guilt," *Polish American Studies* 40, no. 1 (Spring 1983): 59–63; Thomas J. Napierkowski, "Sophie's Choice: The Other Holocaust, Revisited, Revised, and Renewed," *Polish American Studies* 40, no. 1 (Spring 1983): 73–87.

world that will come into being based on their thoughts and writings. Indeed, a final defining characteristic of neo-Stalinism is the extreme level of invective directed against any scholar or individual who criticizes, even mildly, the findings of neo-Stalinist research, especially that of Prof. Gross himself.

One of the biggest targets of neo-Stalinist invective has been the leading critic of Gross' work, Prof. Marek Jan Chodakiewicz, who has been the subject of openly defamatory articles, censorship, and efforts to remove him from university appointments.[37] One leading neo-Stalinist, Prof. Piotr Wróbel, took part in a defamatory article commissioned by the far-left think tank, the Southern Poverty Law Center, in which he stated: "Chodakiewicz, he says, 'has spent almost 30 years in the States—he would never use a phrase or adjective that would clearly identify him as an anti-Semite.' But, he adds, 'There is no doubt whatsoever that he doesn't like the Jews.'"[38] As in the case of Gross' attack on Rosa Lehmann, lack of evidence for a thing is evidence of a thing. The very lack of evidence for Chodakiewicz's anti-Semitism is taken as proof of his anti-Semitism.

Another example occurred in 2008, when the work of Poland's Institute for National Remembrance (IPN), displeased neo-Stalinist authors. Taking to the pages of *Yad Vashem Studies*, historian Jan Grabowski denounced the entire IPN as a nationalist, anti-Semitic plot.[39] In many cases, the defamatory work is so confused that even a cursory glance is enough to disprove the claims made. For example, neo-Stalinist scholar Joanna Michlic took to the pages of *Jewish Social Studies* to attack Chodakiewicz's book *Massacre in Jedwabne*. Michlic cited several pages that had nothing whatsoever to do with the subject she was discussing.[40] The assumption appears to have been that none of

---

[37] See John Radziłowski, "O polskich studiach historycznych w Stanach Zjednoczonych–przypadek prof. Marka Jana Chodakiewicza" [Polish Historical Studies in the United States: The Case of Prof.Marek Jan Chodakiewicz], *Glaukopis* no. 19-20 (2010): 278–85, available in English at www.glaukopis.pl.
[38] Larry Keller, "Night at the Museum: A Controversial Historian at the Holocaust Museum," *SLPC Intelligence Report*, no. 136 (Winter 2009), accessed online at http://www.splcenter.org/get-informed/intelligence-report/browse-all-issues/2009/winter/night-at-the-museum. Rafał Pankowski, a Polish far left-wing activist, also contributed to Keller's article.
[39] Jan Grabowski, "Rewriting the History of Polish-Jewish Relations from a Nationalist Perspective: The Recent Publications of the Institute of National Remembrance," *Yad Vashem Studies* 36, no. 1 (2008): 253–69.
[40] Radziłowski, "O polskich studiach historycznych" [On Polish Historical Studies], Michlic's article appeared in *Jewish Social Studies* n.s. 13, no. 3 (Spring/Summer 2007): 135–76.

the readers of *Jewish Social Studies* would even bother to check her footnotes.

By the same token, reviews of works approved by neo-Stalinists are rarely critical. In fact, there are few examples in the English-speaking world of scholars who have subjected the recent works of Jan Tomasz Gross to rigorous review and analysis free of polemics. Perhaps the fear of being attacked by Gross or his associates and accused of anti-Semitism has something to do with this silence.[41] With the notable exception of John Connelly, who while adopting the neo-Stalinist style, is able to raise some criticisms of Gross's methodology, when neo-Stalinists have reviewed Gross's work themselves the results have often been embarrassingly obsequious. For example, writing on Gross's *Fear* in *Slavic Review* historian Padraic Kenney uses terms like "meticulous" to describe Gross's research on the Kielce massacre, finding none of the deep flaws in Gross' work noted by nearly every Polish expert on the topic. He describes Gross as "brilliant" and claims that "Gross knows more about the war era in Poland than most scholars." *Fear,* Kenney concludes is "scholarship of the highest order."[42]

While, on the one hand, this demonstrates a complete disregard for evidence (if not reality), on the other hand, it illustrates how neo-Stalinists approach history itself: as a form of ideological combat, rather than a search for the truth. Those who disagree with them are not, in their eyes, merely wrong, but enemies who "must be smashed morally in the eyes of the society."

This is truly a contravention of scholarly norms (though admittedly one that is all too common). To quote Zbigniew Herbert: "One of the fundamental things I learned in high school in the Second Polish Republic was how to debate issues fairly. A debate, we were told, was not a fistfight where everything goes, but an attempt to precisely explain one's own position. What counted was proof, not power. Honest debaters are allies who together search for the truth."[43] Such a statement seems very far removed from the approach taken by neo-Stalinists.

---

[41] When *Neighbors* first appeared the author of this article raised several methodological questions about the work on the forum H-Holocaust, an electronic listserv meant to serve scholars, he was subject to a deluge of personal attacks.

[42] Padraic Kenney, review of *Fear*, *Slavic Review* 66, no. 1 (Spring 2007): 108–10. See by contrast the more serious review of Dariusz Stola, *English Historical Review* 122, no. 499 (Dec. 2007): 1460–63.

[43] *Tygodnik Solidarność,* 46 (321), 11 November 1994.

The neo-Stalinist turn in Polish historiography needs to be vigorously, but fairly and respectfully, countered. It does violence to the Polish cultural and historical tradition, and represents an effort at cultural and social engineering by a self-appointed elite, whatever its intentions, that smacks more than a little of a totalitarian mentality. It has worsened honest relations between Poles and Jews, and has greatly complicated writing about difficult subjects in modern Polish history, especially in the North American setting.

Part III: Comparative History

POLES AND JEWS IN POLAND'S EASTERN BORDERLANDS IN SEPTEMBER 1939

Mark Paul

In some respects, what happened to the Poles in the Eastern Borderlands in September 1939 can be viewed as a continuation of Stalin's Great Terror. The group that was targeted for blind retribution, because of its nationality and social status, and not on account of any specific wrongdoings, was the de facto Polish minority. The Terror gave a clear message to the occupied population that those so inclined could act with impunity and benefit from their crimes. These events were thus a prelude to what happened when the Germans invaded the area in June 1941, when they were repeated with the players cast in different roles.

* * *

One of the first reports to reach the West about Polish-Jewish relations in Eastern Poland was authored by the legendary Polish underground courier Jan Karski, who was honored by Israel for his efforts to inform an unresponsive world about the realities of the Holocaust. In his report, transmitted in February 1940, before the massive deportations of the civilian population to the Gulag—as well as the Holocaust—got underway, Karski wrote:

> The Jews have taken over the majority of the political and administrative positions. But what is worse, they are denouncing Poles, especially students and politicians [to the secret police], are directing the work of the [Communist] militia from behind the scenes, are unjustly denigrating conditions in Poland before the war. Unfortunately, one must say that these incidents are very frequent, and more common than incidents which demonstrate loyalty toward Poles or sentiment toward Poland.[1]

---

[1] Jan Karski's full report, in its two versions, can be found in Norman Davies and Antony Polonsky, eds., *Jews in Eastern Poland and the USSR, 1939–46* (New York: St. Martin's Press, 1991), 260–71. The report received prominent notice in an exchange

Karski paints a stark and alarming picture of what he witnessed—one that has generally eluded Western historiography. The portion of the report in which the reproduced passage appears is routinely suppressed by Israeli, American, and British scholars writing on this topic.[2] The English-language literature on inter-ethnic relations in Poland's Eastern Borderlands (*Kresy Wschodnie*) at the time of the Soviet invasion in September 1939 is rather sparse. The events are little known except for some fairly general references and a handful of articles.[3] There is not an

---

("Poles and Jews") between Norman Davies and Abraham Brumberg in *The New York Review of Books*, 9 April 1987.

[2] See, for example, Jan T. Gross, "A Tangled Web: Confronting Stereotypes Concerning Relations between Poles, Germans, Jews, and Communists," in István Deák, Jan T. Gross, and Tony Judt, eds., *The Politics of Retribution in Europe: World War II and Its Aftermath* (Princeton, New Jersey: Princeton University Press, 2000), 74–129, as well as all other writings of that author; Antony Polonsky, "Introduction" and Andrzej Żbikowski, "Jewish Reaction to the Soviet Arrival in the Kresy in September 1939," *Polin: Studies in Polish Jewry*, vol. 13: *Focusing on the Holocaust and its Aftermath* (London and Portland, Oregon: The Littman Library of Jewish Civilization, 2000), 3–33, and 62–72; Martin Dean, *Collaboration in the Holocaust: Crimes of the Local Police in Belorussia and Ukraine, 1941–41* (Houndmills, Basingstoke, Hampshire and London: Macmillan, 2000), 1–16; Paul Zawadzki, "Poles and Jews in World War II" and Antony Polonsky, "Polish Jewry," in Walter Laqueur, ed., *The Holocaust Encyclopedia* (New Haven and London: Yale University Press, 2001), 476–82, 486–93, respectively.

[3] Some recent examples of the cursory treatment of this topic, which do not mention Jews specifically, follow. Richard J. Evans, *The Third Reich at War, 1939–1945* (London: Allen Lane/Penguin Books, 2008), 45: "Their extermination [i.e., Polish officers and officials] was part of a much larger campaign by the Soviets to eradicate Polish national culture. It was accompanied by massive intercommunal violence in which many thousands of Poles were slaughtered by paramilitaries from Ukrainian and Belarusian national minorities in the Polish east, encouraged by the Soviet occupiers." Timothy Snyder, *Bloodlands: Europe Between Hitler and Stalin* (New York: Basic Books, 2010), 125–26: "Soviet occupying forces in eastern Poland placed the lower orders of society in the vacated heights. Prisons were emptied, and political prisoners, usually Communists, were put in charge of local government. Soviet agitators urged peasants to take revenge on landlords. Though most people resisted the call to criminality, chaos reigned as thousands did not. Mass murders with axes were suddenly frequent. One man was tied to a stake, then had some of his skin peeled off and his wound salted before being forced to watch the execution of his family. Usually the Red Army behaved well, though sometimes soldiers joined in the violence, as when a pair killed a local official and then took his gold teeth." An older book that deals specifically with Polish-Jewish relations in Soviet-occupied Eastern Poland is Tadeusz Piotrowski, *Poland's Holocaust: Ethnic Strife, Collaboration with Occupying Forces, and Genocide in the Second Republic, 1918–1947* (Jefferson, North Carolina: McFarland, 1998), 48–58. A more recent example is Alexander V. Prusin, *The Lands Between: Conflict in the East European Borderlands, 1870–1992* (Oxford and New York: Oxford University Press, 2010), 128–48, which is rather selective in its treatment of the Jewish dimension. Prusin says virtually nothing about the conduct of the Jews,

abundance of literature on this topic in Polish either, and what exists, is mostly scattered.[4] Only one major monograph on Polish-Jewish

---

but alleges that the Polish population "overwhelmingly waited for the time of 'bloody reckoning'" with the Jews). (p. 140.) We know with certainty, however, that overwhelmingly the Polish population did no such thing. Relatively few retaliatory acts occurred upon the entry of the Germans in the summer of 1941, and they were the work of a tiny minority of the population. Prusin writes about Polish "reprisals" without providing any background to the events in question: "The reprisals acquired a definite ethnic connotation and were based on the actual behavior of the culprits as much as on anticipation of their disloyalty. In Volkovyska (Wołkowyska) [sic!] in the Hrodna [Grodno] district the troops killed six Jews for their alleged hostile behavior toward Poles." (p. 128.) In actual fact, an armed group of diversionaries, for the most part Jews (and some Belarusians), attacked a Polish army barracks in Wołkowysk, burned part of it down, and looted its contents. Captured rifles were distributed among local pro-Communist elements that formed a militia and took control the town. Understandably, Polish forces retaliated. See Marek Wierzbicki, *Polacy i Białorusini w zaborze sowieckim: Stosunki polsko-białoruskie na ziemiach północno-wschodnich II Rzeczypospolitej pod okupacją sowiecką 1939–1941* [Poles and Belarusians in the Soviet Occupation Zone: Polish-Belarusian Relations in Poland's Northeastern Borderlands Under the Soviet Occupation, 1939-1941] (Warsaw: Volumen, 2000), 148; Marek Wierzbicki, *Polacy i Żydzi w zaborze sowieckim: Stosunki polsko-żydowskie na ziemiach północno-wschodnich II RP pod okupacją sowiecką (1939–1941)* [Poles and Jews in the Soviet Occupation Zone: Polish-Jewish Relations in the Northeastern Borderlands of the Second Polish Republic Under the Soviet Occupation, 1939-1941] (Warsaw: Fronda, 2001), 80. For additional confirmation see Eliyahu Rutchik, "The Russian Occupation at the Beginning of the War," in Katriel Lashowitz, ed., *Volkovysk: The Story of a Jewish-Zionist Community* (Tel-Aviv, 1988), 119–20, Part III of *The Volkovysk Memorial Book* (Mahwah, New Jersey: Jacob Solomon Berger, 2002).

[4] At least several thousand Poles—soldiers, officers, officials, landlords and settlers— were killed in Eastern Poland in September 1939 by members of the ethnic minorities, mostly Ukrainians and Belorussians, representing nationalist, pro-Soviet, or criminal elements. On the murders carried out by Belorussians, see Wierzbicki, *Polacy i Białorusini w zaborze sowieckim* [Poles and Belarusians in the Soviet Occupation Zone], passim. For killings of Poles by Ukrainians see Władysław Siemaszko and Ewa Siemaszko, *Ludobójstwo dokonane przez nacjonalistów ukraińskich na ludności polskiej Wołynia, 1939–1945* [Genocide Committed by the Ukrainian Nationalists on the Polish Population of Volhynia, 1939-1945] (Warsaw: von borowiecky, 2000), two volumes; Henryk Komański and Szczepan Siekierka, *Ludobójstwo dokonane przez nacjonalistów ukraińskich na Polakach w województwie tarnopolskim 1939–1946* [Genocide Committed by the Ukrainian Nationalists on Poles in the Tarnopol Voievodship, 1939-1946] (Wrocław: Nortom, 2004); Szczepan Siekierka, Henryk Komański, and Krzysztof Bulzacki, *Ludobójstwo dokonane przez nacjonalistów ukraińskich na Polakach w województwie lwowskim 1939–1947* [Genocide Committed by the Ukrainian Nationalists on Poles in the Lwów Voievodship, 1939-1947] (Wrocław: Stowarzyszenie Upamiętnienia Ofiar Zbrodni Ukraińskich Nacjonalistów we Wrocławiu, 2006); Szczepan Siekierka, Henryk Komański, and Eugeniusz Różański, *Ludobójstwo dokonane przez nacjonalistów ukraińskich na Polakach w województwie stanisławowskim 1939–1946* [Genocide Committed by the Ukrainian Nationalists on Poles in the Stanisławów Voievodship, 1939-1946] (Wrocław:

relations in the Eastern Borderlands under Soviet occupation has been published in Poland, and it focuses on the interwar Polish territories incorporated into Soviet Belarus.[5] The dominant view in the West is one advanced by Israeli historians and based exclusively on Jewish testimonies; it differs significantly from the conclusions reached by Polish scholars which are based primarily, but not exclusively, on Polish testimonies. This apparent dichotomy raises a number of questions: Is the empirical evidence simply contradictory? Are the interpretations flawed because of reliance on a narrow documentary base? Can they be reconciled?

Stowarzyszenie Upamiętnienia Ofiar Zbrodni Ukraińskich Nacjonalistów, 2008). According to the data of the Organization of Ukrainian Nationalists, from 29 August until 23 September 1939, 7,729 supporters of that organization took part in armed, subversive activities directed at the Polish authorities in 183 localities, capturing 3,610 Poles, killing 796, and wounding 37. (They reported their own losses as 160 killed and 53 wounded.) See Grzegorz Motyka, *Ukraińska partyzantka 1942–1960: Działalność Organizacji Ukraińskich Nacjonalistów i Ukraińskiej Powstańczej Armii* [The Ukrainian Partisans, 1942-1960: The Activities of the Organization of Ukrainian Nationalists – Ukrainian Insurrectionary Army] (Warsaw: Instytut Studiów Politycznych PAN and Rytm, 2006), 72–73. For confirmation of the scale of the killings in Volhynia in Ukrainian and Soviet sources see Andrii Rukkas, "Antypolski zbroini vystupy na Volyni (veresen 1939 r.)" [The Anti-Polish Armed Rebellions in Volhynia, September 1939], in Iaroslav Isaievych, ed., *Volyn i Kholmshchyna 1938–1947 rr.: Polsko-ukrainske protystoiannia ta ioho vidlunnia. Doslidzhennia, dokumenty, spohady* [Volhynia and the Chełm Area, 1938-1947: Polish-Ukrainian Relations] (Lviv: Natsionalna akademiia nauk Ukrainy, Instytut ukrainoznavstva im. I. Krypiakevycha, 2003), 119–38. The massacre of some 60 Polish civilians in the vicinity of Koniuchy, in the Tarnopol area, is confirmed by the testimony of a Ukrainian priest: Pavlo Oliinyk, *Zoshyty* [Notebooks] (Kiev: Natsionalna akademiia nauk Ukrainy, Instytut ukrainskoi arkheohrafii ta dzhereloznavstva im. M.S. Hrushevskoho, 1995), 66.

[5] Marek Wierzbicki, *Polacy i Żydzi w zaborze sowieckim: Stosunki polsko-żydowskie na ziemiach północno-wschodnich II RP pod okupacją sowiecką (1939–1941)* [Poles and Jews in the Soviet Occupation Zone ...] (Warsaw: Fronda, 2001). See also Marek Wierzbcki, "Polish-Jewish Relations in the City of Vilna and the Region of Western Vilna under Soviet Occupation, 1939–1941," *Polin: Studies in Polish Jewry*, vol. 19: *Polish-Jewish Relations in North America* (Oxford and Portland, Oregon: The Littman Library of Jewish Civilization, 2007), 487–516; Marek Wierzbicki, "Western Belarus in September 1939: Revisiting Polish-Jewish Relations," in Elazar Barkan, Elizabeth A. Cole, and Kai Struve, eds., *Shared History, Divided Memory: Jews and Others in Soviet-Occupied Poland, 1939–1941* (Leipzig: Leipziger Universitätsverlag, 2007), 135–46. Marek Wierzbicki's two companion studies dealing with Polish-Belorussian and Polish-Jewish relations contain some overlap. The present article, which draws on these and many other sources, is based on a much larger work, *Neighbors on the Eve of the Holocaust: Polish-Jewish Relations in Soviet-Occupied Eastern Poland, 1939–1941,* posted online at:
http://www.glaukopis.pl/pdf/czytelnia/NeighborsEveOfTheHolocaust.pdf.

In his recent study *The Death of the Shtetl*,[6] Yehuda Bauer reiterates some of the characteristic formulations found in the older Jewish historiography, primarily in the books of Israeli historians Ben-Cion Pinchuk[7] and Dov Levin,[8] while at the same time introducing some new arguments that are gaining acceptance in certain circles. At the outset, Bauer acknowledges, in keeping with Ben-Cion Pinchuk's findings, that Jews were "prominent in the transition to Soviet rule" and that the workers' committees and militias that formed in early stages of the Soviet occupation had, in many places, a largely Jewish make-up. Moreover, they played an active part in the repression of Polish state officials:

> Jewish Communists, though few in number, became prominent in the transition to Soviet rule. The Soviet authorities set up workers' committees, on which there were many Jews, to establish control over towns and villages. ... Jews joined or set up militias [local police] before or immediately following the Soviet occupation. In some Galician and Volhynian localities Jews accounted for up to 70 percent of the militia membership. These militias confiscated major enterprises and arrested many Polish officials.[9]

However, Yehuda Bauer does not allow such facts to color his overall assessment of Jewish behavior toward Poles or the impact it may have had on Polish attitudes toward Jews. What is more, as we shall see, he scrupulously avoids acknowledging evidence of the role played by self-appointed militias and workers' committees in provoking retaliations by the harried remnants of the Polish army.

While acknowledging that "Soviet troops that came to occupy the region were welcomed, in many cases enthusiastically, by the Jews," Bauer then attempts to neutralize this by stating that others did likewise, and he stresses repeatedly that "many Poles" also welcomed the Soviets.[10]

---

[6] Yehuda Bauer, *The Death of the Shtetl* (New Haven, Connecticut and London: Yale University Press, 2009).
[7] Ben-Cion Pinchuk, *Shtetl Jews under Soviet Rule: Eastern Poland on the Eve of the Holocaust* (Cambridge, Massachusetts: Basil Blackwell, 1991).
[8] Dov Levin, *The Lesser of Two Evils: Eastern European Jewry Under Soviet Rule, 1939–1941* (Philadelphia: The Jewish Publication Society, 1995).

[9] Bauer, *The Death of the Shtetl*, 38–39.
[10] Bauer, *The Death of the Shtetl*, 35–37.

Although it is true that many Ukrainians and Belarusians also welcomed the Soviet army, among the Poles, with few exceptions, the welcome was restricted to border towns where the Polish residents initially believed the Soviet claim that they had come to protect Poland from the German onslaught. Not only was the Polish welcome short-lived but, more importantly, it was not accompanied by the pro-Soviet and anti-Polish slogans common among members of the ethnic minorities. A few typical Jewish testimonies from the Białystok district, near the German-Soviet demarcation line, and afterwards from areas closer to the prewar Polish-Soviet border, illustrate these divergent Polish responses. The witnesses are clear as to who came out to greet the Soviets, why they cheered for them, and who did *not* do so.

Michel (Mendel) Mielnicki from Wasilków, a small town outside of Białystok populated by Poles, Jews and Belarusians, has a very vivid memory of those events. Moreover, his recollection is consistent with what is recorded in the town's Jewish memorial book:

> But, as *The Wasilkower Memorial Book* records, everyone in the Jewish community was in such a holiday mood on the evening of 18 September [1939] as they awaited the arrival of the Red Army that they didn't want to go to bed lest they miss any part of this historic occasion. Certainly, this is the way I remember things.
>
> I also can confirm that everyone cheered when our neighbor from across the street, Mordechai Yurowietski, the tinsmith's son, raised a red flag on top of the fire station tower. And cheered again when a Soviet aircraft buzzed the crowd ... to drop leaflets welcoming us as 'Brothers and Sisters of West Byelo-Russia.' And when the Soviet soldiers finally did march in the next morning, ... they did so singing 'Katiusha,' with all the little Jewish and White Russian kids parading along beside them, joining in their song. This was a scene worthy of a Sigmund Romberg operetta. ...
>
> And contrary to Western propaganda, being part of the Soviet Union gave the overwhelming majority of those in our community the security of belonging to a civil society, or at least one that was a hell of a lot more civil than anything we'd experienced before. ... Even my rebbe was a relatively happy man under the atheistic Communists. ... When a plebiscite was held in October and November 1939 on whether we actually wanted to be part of West Byelorussia, the majority of people ... (my mother and father included) voted 'Yes'.[11]

---

[11] John Munro (as told to), *Białystok to Birkenau: The Holocaust Journey of Michel Mielnicki* (Vancouver: Ronsdale Press and Vancouver Holocaust Education Centre,

Michael Maik, a native of the nearby small town of Sokoły, wrote in his wartime diary:

> The next day, soldiers of the Red Army entered the town. The people of Sokoly, from the biggest to the smallest, from the youngest to the oldest, men, women and children, all went out to the streets to greet the liberating soldiers. The Jews received the 'Reds' with shouts of joy and enthusiasm. In comparison, the Poles stood disappointed.[12]

2000), 76–77, 78–79. Later, Mielnicki's father was to play a rather dark role in the service of the NKVD in ferreting out "dangerous" Polish elements in the town (see pp. 82–84):

> I don't know exactly how my father became involved with the NKVD (the forerunner of the KGB), the Soviet intelligence and internal-security agency. ... I do remember, however, the NKVD commissars from Moscow, who would most often arrive at our house after dark, sitting in the living room, smoking one cigarette after another until they could barely see each other through the haze, talking in low voices with Father, as they went over their lists of suspected fifth columnists (so-called *Volksdeutscher* Poles), Polish fascists, ultranationalists, and other local 'traitors' and 'counter-revolutionaries.'
>
> It was my understanding that he served as advisor to the NKVD about who among the local Poles was to be sent to Siberia, or otherwise dealt with. I don't think he had anything to do with the arrest of local Jews, or the expulsion of Jewish refugees who had flooded into the Bialystok area from the German-occupied provinces ... Certainly, it is my firm belief that no one was ever murdered at my father's behest.
>
> Nevertheless, my mother was terribly upset by my father's collaboration with the Russian secret service. ... I remember her begging him not to get involved. He disagreed. 'We have to get rid of the fascists,' he told her. 'They deserve to go to Siberia. They are not good for the Jewish people.' ...
>
> Naturally, word of Father's clandestine activities got out. The black limousine that the commissars parked in our driveway when they came to visit was sufficient in itself to blow any cover he might have desired. Consequently, when the Germans invaded Russia in June 1941, the name of Chaim Mielnicki was on the hit list of both the local anti-Semites (who proved more numerous than anyone imagined) and their new-found allies [sic], the *Gestapo* ... Because I was Chaim Mielnicki's son, I found myself the target of Polish bullets when I returned to Bialystok after the War. That's how much they came to hate him.

[12] Michael Maik, *Deliverance: The Diary of Michael Maik. A True Story* (Kedumim, Israel: Keterpress Enterprises, 2004), 10. Maik is silent about the fate of the town's Polish residents, in particular the prewar authorities. He does acknowledge that the new "municipal functionaries were mostly Jews" and that a number of Jews were denounced for a variety of reasons, but neglects to point out that they were denounced by fellow Jews. Maik even rationalizes their good fortune: "Later, under the evil Nazi regime, all the Jews envied those who had been imprisoned and exiled to the Soviet

As the following accounts from Krynki near Białystok show, jubilation often transformed into active support for the new regime.

Kushnir Eliahu and Friede Zalkin:
The Jewish population of Krinki [Krynki] awaited the arrival of the Red Army, and as soon as our workers heard that the Soviet military had crossed the border, they did not wait long before taking over the government in the shtetl. Before the Polish police managed to leave Krinki, there was already a red flag flying from City Hall.

Jews welcome the Soviets with an outbreak of joy and enthusiasm. Communists jumped up onto the tanks and kissed the soldiers. The people were just plain happy.[13]

Abraham Soyfer:
There was great joy in Krinki. People hugged each other with tears streaming down their cheeks, tears of joy and luck.[14]

Beyl'ke Shuster-Greenstein:
The shtetl was truly dancing in the streets. Everyone was beaming as they met their friends and chatted and talked politics. Everyone was in a holiday mood. People took flowers and called out to welcome the Red Army.[15]

Union." Maik maintains that "the economic situation of the middle-class and small merchants during the Soviet occupation was better than it had been during the Polish regime before the war"; that "unofficial trading flourished and there was plenty of income"; and that "the Jewish merchants felt freer under the Soviet occupation, even though they were legally subject to heavy punishment." *Ibid.*, 14–17.

[13] D. [Dov] Rabin, ed., *Memorial Book of Krynki*, Internet: <http://www.jewishgen.org/yizkor/Krynki/Krynki.html>, translation of *Pinkas Krynki* (Tel Aviv: Former Residents of Krynki in Israel and the Diaspora, 1970), 231. This account goes on to say: "Shortly the enthusiasm on the part of the followers of the Soviet regime began to cool. ... But to them, after the Polish regime, they wanted to try communism. ... Generally, the Jews were happy." *Ibid.*, 231–32. The residents of Krynki had no particular cause to complain about the Polish administration. According to testimonies in that town's memorial book, "the relationship of the Jews and Christians, among them the Poles who were now the ruling and privileged state-forming ethnic group, was usually fair until the Nazi period, and it was not affected by the open and even official anti-Semitic agitation, which intensified during the 1930s." The Polish mayor, Paweł Carewicz, was "a very friendly man, spoke Yiddish well and had a good relationship with the Jews." In 1927 the town council decided that all official announcements would be published in Yiddish as well as in Polish and that Yiddish could be spoken at meetings of the council. *Ibid.*, 147, 177, 223.
[14] *Ibid.*, 233.
[15] *Ibid.*, 233.

In some towns near the Soviet border, Poles and even Polish officials were initially among the crowds that greeted the Soviet army. Indeed, Polish soldiers were often given orders by their commanders not to fire at the Soviet army. Duped by Soviet propaganda, which included leaflets dropped by planes and assurances repeated by many Soviet soldiers in conversations with the local population, these Poles were under the mistaken impression that the Soviets had come to help them fight the Germans, and not to subjugate their country.[16] The Soviet tanks that rolled into Kopyczyńce, in the Tarnopol area, for example, were adorned with Polish flags and slogans of Soviet help in the fight against the common Nazi enemy.[17] The Poles were soon disabused of these illusions. As the confusion gave way to the certainty that Soviets did not come as the defenders of Poland, dejected, the Poles abandoned the cheering multitudes. Many, if not most, Jews, Belorussians, and Ukrainians, on the other hand, openly welcomed the prospect of Soviet rule.

After examining the literature on this topic, Polish historian Teresa Prekerowa reached the following conclusion about the reception

---

[16] In Nieśwież, for example, "the streets ... were overrun with crowds. ... the people stood on the pavement viewing the Red Army in full mass. People began to applaud and throw flowers to the soldiers. Standing in the crowd were *ossadniks* [*osadniks*] ('colonists'), including demobilized officers who had come to settle the lands along the eastern frontier to create a Polish buffer zone. They had always regarded the Russians as 'those damned Muscovites.' But now they, too, threw flowers to the marching columns. Someone cheered: 'They are going to help the Poles beat the bloody *Schwab* [German]." See Shalom Cholawski, *Soldiers from the Ghetto* (San Diego: A.S. Barnes & Company, 1980), 14. In Plebanówka, near Trembowla, the leery Polish inhabitants emerged only after a Soviet officer assured them "Don't be afraid, we're coming to help Poland, so that together we can fight the Germans." See Kazimierz Turzański, *Krwawe noce pod Trembowlą* [Bloody Nights Near Trembowla] (Wrocław: Stowarzyszenie Upamiętnienia Ofiar Zbrodni Ukraińskich Nacjonalistów, 1998), 29–31. In Zdołbunów, even the voivode (provincial governor) and the *starosta* (county supervisor) reportedly came out to greet the Soviet army the morning of 18 September, believing they were coming to fight the Germans. See Piotr Żaroń, *Agresja Związku Radzieckiego na Polskę 17 września 1939; Los jeńców polskich* [The Soviet Aggression Against Poland on 17 September 1939: The Fate of Polish POWs] (Toruń: Adam Marszałek, 1998), 121.

[17] Jerzy Julian Szewczyński, *Nasze Kopyczyńce* [Our Kopyczyńce] (Malbork: Heldruk, 1995), 20. A city official reportedly spoke from the town hall balcony: "Gentlemen, Poles, soldiers, we will beat the Germans now that the Bolsheviks are going to help us," while Red Army commanders embraced the Polish officers whom they soon turned on. See István Deák, Jan T. Gross, and Tony Judt, eds., *The Politics of Retribution in Europe: World War II and Its Aftermath* (Princeton, New Jersey: Princeton University Press, 2000), 122

accorded to the Soviet invaders by a large portion of the Jewish population:

> It appears, then, that it was not fear of the Germans which was the chief reason for the joyous welcome extended to the invading Red Army. The more plausible view, which is now widely accepted, is that an important factor was the level of anti-Polish feelings, the result of the bad relations which had existed during the preceding period, especially the 1930s, which witnessed the negative Jewish policies of the leaders of the Second Republic, antisemitic declarations by the various political parties, and the excesses of the nationalistic thugs. Grudges and resentments produced a situation where among certain sections of the Jewish community the absence of any sense of solidarity with the Polish nation and identification with the Polish state was being demonstratively expressed.[18]

---

[18] Teresa Prekerowa, "The Jewish Underground and the Polish Underground," in *Polin: Studies in Polish Jewry*, vol. 9: *Poles, Jews, Socialists: The Failure of an Ideal* (London: The Littman Library of Jewish Civilization, 1996), 148–57, here at 149. There is more validity to the claim that it was out of fear, and possibly to ingratiate themselves, that Jews built triumphal arches and dispatched delegations to greet the *German* invaders in towns that fell immediately to the German army. For example, in Radom, a Jewish delegation headed by a rabbi and other community leaders marched down the flower-strewn Mikołaj Rej Street on 8 September 1939 to welcome the German army. See Józef Łyżwa, "Pomagałem, a potem siedziałem" [I Helped and Was Later Arrested], *Gazeta Polska* (Warsaw), 10 February 1994. A Jewish delegation led by a rabbi also greeted the Germans in Zaręby Kościelne near Ostrów Mazowiecki. See Tomasz Strzembosz, "Zstąpienie szatana czy przyjazd gestapo" [Satan's Descent or the Arrival of the Gestapo], *Rzeczpospolita* (Warsaw), 12 May 2001. For more examples see Elinor J. Brecher, *Schindler's Legacy: True Stories of the List Survivors* (New York: Penguin, 1994), 56 (Jews greeted the Germans in Kraków); Jake Gelwert, *From Auschwitz to Ithaca: The Transnational Journey of Jake Geldwert* (Bethesda, MD: CDL Press, 2002), 28 (Jews greeted the Germans in Kraków); Eugeniusz Buczyński, *Smutny wrzesień: Wspomnienia* [A Sad September: Memoirs] (Kraków: Wydawnictwo Literackie, 1985), 132 (Ukrainian nationalists and Jews erected a triumphal arch for the Germans in Przemyśl and looted Polish military buildings); Piotrowski, *Poland's Holocaust*, 315 n.167 (Jews greeted the Germans in Janów Lubelski); Tadeusz Bednarczyk, *Życie codzienne warszawskiego getta: Warszawskie getto i ludzie (1939–1945 i dalej)* [The Everyday Life of the Warsaw Ghetto: The Warsaw Ghetto and People, 1939-1945 and Onward] (Warsaw: Ojczyzna, 1995), 242 (Jews built triumphal arches in Łódź, Pabianice, and elsewhere, and Jewish community leaders, headed by rabbis dressed in ceremonial robes, greeted the Germans bearing trays with bread and salt). The last known Jewish delegation to welcome the German army was in Międzyrzec Podlaski on 10 October 1939, after the departure of the Red Army from that town. See Józef Geresz, *Międzyrzec Podlaski: Dzieje miasta i okolic* [Międzyrzec Podlaski: The History of a Town and its Vicinity] (Biała Podlaska and Międzyrzec Podlaski: Ośrodek Wschodni "Civitas Christiana," 1995), 299. Confirmation of these events can also be found in a report of a leftist Italian diplomat who was stationed in Poland: "in the first days of the conflict, numerous Jews greeted the entrance of the

Yehuda Bauer goes further. He *justifies* these displays of disloyalty on the grounds that Jews had been mistreated in Poland, therefore owing no loyalty to their country. In the process he assails Polish "nationalists" who noted the widespread, though not universal, behavior of the country's minorities toward the Soviet invaders:

> Polish politicians and ideologues later accused the Jews of the kresy—and, by association, all Jews—of betraying Poland in its hour of need, of identifying with the Soviet oppressors. This became the main ideological line of Polish nationalists toward the Jews during World War II both in Poland itself and in the Polish government-in-exile in London; it is repeated in Polish historiography, journalism, and literature to this day. The problem with this argument is that from the perspective of most Jews, interwar Poland was an oppressive regime and could hardly demand loyalty from its badly treated Jewish population.[19]

This line of reasoning is spurious for many reasons. The Soviet Union was the most oppressive state in interwar Europe. It had orchestrated an artificial famine that killed millions of its citizens and carried out both class terror and ethnic cleansing on a scale Europe, and indeed the world, had never witnessed.[20] The unprovoked invasion (together with Nazi Germany) of Poland, which had entered into non-aggression pacts with both the Soviet Union and Nazi Germany, was unlawful in light of international law. Poland's citizens had a duty to support their country in such a time or, at a minimum, not to undermine it while Poland continued to fight for its very existence.

Taking the opposite view is descending down a slippery slope which exonerates not only Nazi Fifth Columnists but also disloyalty on the part of disgruntled minorities elsewhere, such as Black Muslims in the United States and Palestinians in Israel. It is also a slap in the face of those many Jews who fought in Poland's defense. It stands in sharp contrast to the actions of those Jews from Eastern Poland who would later secure their release from the Gulag and seek to join General Władysław Anders's Polish army or to repatriate to Poland after the war on the strength of their Polish citizenship. Finally, it should be noted that these vociferous declarations of support for Poland's mortal

---

German armies into Polish cities with cries of joy." See Eugenio Reale, *Raporty: Polska 1945–1946* [Reports: Poland 1945-1946] (Paris: Institut Littéraire, 1968), 204.

[19] Bauer, *The Death of the Shtetl,* 37.

[20] On this see Snyder, *Bloodlands,* chapters 1 through 3. Although the victims also included Jews, they were by far the least likely group to be targeted in the 1930s. See also Yuri Slezkine, *The Jewish Century* (Princeton and Oxford: Princeton University Press, 2004), 273–74.

enemy understandably provided justification for some Poles not to regard Jews as true co-nationals or members of their civic universe.[21]

To his credit, unlike many Jewish historians, Yehuda Bauer acknowledges that Jews also took part in looting, for which there is ample evidence, though none of it is cited by him. Avrahm Trasawucki (Abraham Tracy) penned a detailed account, in 1946, describing conditions in Skała Podolska, a small town on the River Zbrucz in the Tarnopol area, near the Polish-Soviet border:

> Later that night we saw the first Russian patrol on the road, inquiring if we had seen any Polish soldiers. Our joy grew ...
>
> We hurried next door to our neighbor, Eli Yoles, to inform him of the current affairs. Together we celebrated and woke our other neighbors ... We watched the Russian platoons appear on the streets while the Ukrainians walked dejectedly through the village. Many Jewish soldiers accompanied the army and they called out to us in broken Yiddish, 'Peace upon you Jews, you prayed well over the New Year holiday!'
>
> The joy of that night remains in my mind. I doubt that I had ever seen such true joy among my family before that moment. People were jumping about, hugging and kissing each other. Our excitement knew no bounds. ...
>
> We had reached the first houses of the Jewish area near the unfinished synagogue, when we came across a scene that was chaotic at best. It was six in the morning, but the entire shtetl was awake and running through the streets, congratulating each other. Amidst the tumult, we saw a group of unfamiliar Jews running towards us.
>
> 'Have you any butter?' they cried.
>
> 'Yes,' we answered. 'But first we must distribute to our established customers. We will then sell whatever is left to our new buyers.'

---

[21] Once the Germans imposed a death penalty on Poles for providing any form of assistance to Jews, as many righteous Jews who were rescued by Poles stress, Poles had no moral responsibility to endanger their lives to assist Jews (though this in no way condones engaging in activities that harmed Jews). See the statements found in Mark Paul, *Wartime Rescue of Jews by the Polish Catholic Clergy: Testimony of Survivors*, Internet:
<http://www.glaukopis.pl/pdf/czytelnia/WartimeRescueOfJewsByThePolishCatholicClergy_MarkPaul.pdf>.

Suddenly, I heard a voice from behind my shoulder. 'The bourgeois have already devoured enough butter, they can now make ends meet!'

I turned in the direction of the voice and saw Motke Kremitzer's wife. I looked at her, not quite comprehending the implications of her words. Here was the start of a new hatred. Not a hatred between Jews and gentiles but an enmity between the so-called rich and the poor. ...

My father and I did not answer. We proceeded to walk down the street to our usual customers, and stopped on the sidewalk ..., when suddenly, the poor could not wait any longer and began to attack us, tearing away at the butter. My father and I were completely powerless to stop them. We could not even tell who had taken it; all we knew was that when our regular customers came for their orders, we had nothing left. The butter had been taken before my very eyes by people whom I had never seen before. My dear father walked away smiling and called out, 'The money does not matter. Let the Jews eat in good health and enjoy!'

As we walked down the street, we came across a similar incident. The Jews had attacked Moshe Mozner's bakery and were taking away the bread. The scene was dreadful. People in the bakery had shut the doors against the mob and were passing bread through the windows. ...

We continued along the road to my sister, Chaya and her husband, Mendel. Every shop we passed was being looted in the same manner. Every store, be it food or merchandise, was being torn apart.

The Jews who were not looting the streets were rejoicing. Whether old or young, Communist or capitalist, everyone happily greeted the Russian army, our true liberators. We passed by the Polish barracks, now occupied by the Russian military. The windows had been knocked out and there were signs of rifle bullets. ...

Some members of the Jewish community were pro-Communist and immediately cooperated with the Ukrainians. These Jews were rewarded with grand positions and a new militia began to take shape, comprised of both Jews and Ukrainians. These privileged citizens carried weapons on their shoulders and wore red bands on their arms.[22]

---

[22] Abraham Tracy, *To Speak For the Silenced* (Jerusalem and New York: Devora, 2007), 13–19. The author neglects to mention that when the Soviets led captured Polish soldiers through the streets of Skała Podolska in September 1939, Jews and Ukrainians, who converged to observe the spectacle, screamed, "Kill the Polish swine!" and "The Polish swine is dead!" The fate of Polish officials, landowners, and professionals, who suffered the bulk of the repressions, often at the hands of local collaborators, and who

Jews also looted in German-occupied Poland, as did non-Jews. This should not come as a surprise since looting during times of civil strife is pandemic. For example, a Jewish eyewitness recalls the looting of foreign firms in Lublin in September 1939:

> Even the rich came in their carriages and drove away with the hogs inside. I went up to Shlomo Biderman: 'What has come over you?' I demanded. 'You, the richest Jew in Lublin, grabbing hogs and selling them!' ...
>
> 'You,' he said in reply, 'are a fool.'[23]

Jews in Kałuszyn pillaged and then traded in foodstuffs and clothing stolen from a Polish armored train at the Mrozy railway station.[24] Jews participated in looting Polish military buildings in Przemyśl.[25] Emanuel Ringelblum recorded that Polish Jews were quick to seize valuables discarded by deported German Jews, who were afraid that their possession might lead to serious repercussions at the hands of the Germans.[26] Mary Berg confirms that Jews pilfered Polish property. When she was travelling in the countryside with fellow Jews, she came across a bullet-ridden house, containing the body of a dead Polish peasant, which they looted: "The kettle which we 'inherited' from this murdered peasant became our faithful companion on the long road to Warsaw."[27]

Yehuda Bauer tempers somewhat Dov Levin's bald—and totally unsubstantiated—claim that Polish soldiers "savaged any Jews" they

---

were hit the hardest economically, also escapes his notice. See *Na Rubieży* (Wrocław), no. 47 (2000): 52.

[23] Shiye Goldberg (Shie Chehever), *The Undefeated* (Tel Aviv: H. Leivick Publishing House, 1985), 79–80.

[24] Yosef Kermish, "Life of the Jews under the Nazi Regime; the Ghetto of Kaluszyn," in A. Shamri and Sh. Soroka, eds., *Sefer Kaluszyn: Geheylikt der khorev gevorener kehile* (Tel Aviv: Former Residents of Kaluszyn in Israel, 1961), 315ff., translated as *The Memorial Book of Kaluszyn,* http://jewishgen.org/Yizkor/kaluszyn/Kaluszyn.html. For conditions in the vicinity of Tarnów see Andrzej Żbikowski, ed., *Archiwum Ringelbluma: Konspiracyjne Archiwum Getta Warszawskiego* [The Ringelblum Archive: The Underground Archive of the Warsaw Ghetto], vol. 3: *Relacje z Kresów* [Testimonies from the Eastern Borderlands] (Warsaw: Żydowski Instytut Historyczny IN-B, 2000), 327.

[25] Eugeniusz Buczyński, *Smutny wrzesień: Wspomnienia* [A Sad September: Memoirs] (Kraków: Wydawnictwo Literackie, 1985), 132.

[26] Emanuel Ringelblum, *Kronika getta warszawskiego: Wrzesień 1939–styczeń 1943* [A Chronicle of the Warsaw Ghetto: September 1939-January 1943] (Warsaw: Czytelnik, 1983), 69.

[27] Mary Berg and S. L. Shneiderman, ed., *Warsaw Ghetto: A Diary* (New York: L. B. Fischer, 1945), 14.

encountered.[28] Rather, Bauer underscores Jewish victimization by alleging that Polish troops "occasionally" robbed and killed Jews, and that Poles organized unprovoked "pogroms" which, apparently, local authorities did not usually contain and sometimes initiated:

> Polish troops, frustrated and furious at the defeat of their country, also occasionally robbed Jews and killed them. Whether anti-Jewish pogroms were permitted to happen depended on the local leadership. .. In Grodno, … about thirty Jews were killed in a pogrom before the Soviets entered. … In Dereczin [Dereczyn], … Poles—it is unclear whether the Polish army or local police—tried to organize a pogrom, but the local, presumably Catholic priest prevented this from happening.[29]

There is no credible evidence that "frustrated and furious" Polish soldiers simply began to kill Jews; however, there is ample evidence that Jews started shooting at Polish soldiers.[30] In many localities in northeastern Poland, where German forces had never set foot, in

---

[28] Dov Levin states: "As vestigial units of the Polish army fled into Romania, they savaged any Jews who happened to be in the way, especially after they discovered that the Soviet forces were closing in from the east. The pretext for this behavior was their association of Jews with the Bolsheviks and their belief that the Jews had 'stabbed Poland in the back.'" See Levin, *The Lesser of Two Evils*, 32.

[29] Bauer, *The Death of the Shtetl*, 33.

[30] There are numerous recorded cases of Jewish saboteurs shooting at or ambushing Polish troops. See, for example, Jarosław Wołkonowski, *Okręg Wileński Związku Walki Zbrojnej Armii Krajowej w latach 1939–1945* [The Wilno District of the Home Army Union of Armed Struggle in 1939-1945] (Warsaw: Adiutor, 1996), 12 (Wilno); Ryszard Głuski, "Obrona Grodna we wspomnieniach: Żołnierskie relacje" [The Defense of Grodno in Testimonies: Soldiers' Testimonies], *Biuletyn Wojewódzkiego Domu Kultury w Białymstoku*, no. 3/4 (1989): 23 (along the Lida-Grodno highway); Czesław K. Grzelak, ed. and comp., *Wrzesień 1939 na Kresach w relacjach* [September 1939 in the Eastern Borderlands in Testimonies] (Warsaw: Neriton, 1999), 90 (in the Lida-Grodno corridor), 130 (Wilno); Ryszard Szawłowski [Karol Liszewski], *Wojna polsko-sowiecka 1939: Tło polityczne, prawnomiędzynarodowe i psychologiczne; Agresja sowiecka i polska obrona; Sowieckie zbrodnie wojenne i przeciw ludzkości oraz zbrodnie ukraińskie i białoruskie* [The Polish-Soviet War of 1939: The Background in Terms of Politics, International Law, and Psychology; Soviet Aggression and Polish Defense; Soviet War Crimes and Crimes Against Humanity, as well as Ukrainian and Belarusian Crimes], Second and third revised and expanded editions (Warsaw: Neriton, 1995; Warsaw: Antyk–Marcin Dybowski, 1997), vol. 1, 195 (Polesia), 199 (Kołki); Zenobiusz Janicki, *W obronie Przebraża i w drodze do Berlina* [In Defense of Przebraże and on the Road to Berlin] (Lublin: Ardabiju, 1997), 11 (Sarny), 12 (Kołki); Wierzbicki, *Polacy i Żydzi w zaborze sowieckim* [Poles and Jews in the Soviet Occupation Zone], 58–59. As is the common practice in wartime, saboteurs and fifth columnists apprehended with arms in hand, regardless of nationality, were generally executed by the Polish army.

anticipation of the Soviet takeover, organized groups of pro-Soviet Jews and Belarusians took up arms against the Polish authorities—soldiers, police, and other officials: Jeziory, Ostryna, Wiercieliszki, Wielka Brzostowica, Dubno, Wołpa, Indura, Sopoćkinie, Łunna, Zelwa, Wołkowysk, Zdzięcioł, Dereczyn, Byteń, Motol, Janów Poleski, Antopol, Drohiczyn Poleski, Horodec, and Łunin.[31] Polish literature refers to these insurrections as local "rebellions." They were directed against Polish rule and, in all likelihood, would have occurred even if the Soviet Union had invaded Poland alone, and not in concert with Nazi Germany. The reaction of the Polish army was both understandable, and in keeping with accepted practice in times of war.

Bauer's lack of regard for, and *a priori* dismissal of, Polish sources, and indeed any sources other than Jewish ones, which—as we shall see—he uses in a highly selective manner, seriously compromises the objectivity of his scholarship. The events in Grodno were hardly a pogrom. On the eve of the Soviet invasion, after the departure of the Polish military forces, the local authorities oversaw the formation of a poorly organized local self-defense. The atmosphere in the city had already become charged when, on 17 September, sporadic shooting erupted. Armed Jews held clandestine meetings in various places in town. Jadwiga Dąbrowska witnessed how her neighbor's son, a Polish soldier, was ambushed and shot dead by a young Jew who emerged from such a meeting.[32] Young Jews sitting on the roof of a house shot Franciszek Zalewski, who was leading a police unit to dig anti-tank defense trenches.[33]

Preparations for the arrival of the Red Army were also underway in the countryside. One Jewish source notes: "With the publication of the news on the radio that the Russians crossed the Polish border, the Communists of Grodno and its surroundings began to confiscate the weapons from the retreated [sic] Polish soldiers. The Poles looked at this behavior with a lot of anger and hate."[34] On 19 September, the

---

[31] These insurrections are described in Wierzbicki, *Polacy i Białorusini w zaborze sowieckim* [Poles and Belarusians in the Soviet Occupation Zone], passim. Similar rebellions also occurred in Volhynia.

[32] Adam Dobroński, "Obrona Grodna we wspomnieniach: Dyskusja" [The Defense of Grodno in Testimonies: A Discussion], *Biuletyn Wojewódzkiego Domu Kultury w Białymstoku*, no. 3/4 (1989): 17.

[33] Testimony of Helena Platt (Franciszek Zalewski's daughter), cited in Rafał Pasztelański, "Sowieci przywiązywali dzieci do czołgów" [The Soviets Tied Children to Tanks], TVP, September 17, 2009. Helena Platt noted her father was treated by a Jewish doctor when taken to the hospital, so her account cannot be regarded as biased.

[34] Alexander Manor (Menschinsky), ed., *Sopotkin: In Memory of the Jewish Community*, posted on the Internet at www.jewishgen.org/yizkor/spotskin/ ; translation

evening before the Soviets entered Grodno, local Communist supporters, consisting almost entirely of Jews (and only a small number of Belarusians), staged an armed rebellion against the Polish authorities.[35] One eyewitness described the activities of the city's fifth column as follows: "Suddenly some shots rang out on Brygidzka Street. We observe that on the balconies Jews with red armbands are

---

of *Korot ayara ahat: Megilat ha-shigshug ve-ha-hurban shel kehilat Sopotkin* (Tel Aviv: Sopotkin Society, 1960), Chapter 6: "Under the Russian Boot." Perversely, the Poles are then blamed for the ensuing state of events: "No wonder the Jews welcomed the Russians as their redeemers and saviors."

[35] Among the many Polish accounts, see, e.g., Wierzbicki, *Polacy i Żydzi w zaborze sowieckim* [Poles and Jews in the Soviet Occupation Zone], 62–65; Jan Siemiński, *Grodno walczące: Wspomnienia harcerza* [Fighting Grodno: The Recollections of a Boy Scout], Second edition (Białystok: Towarzystwo Literackie im. Adama Mickiewicza, Oddział Białostocki, 1992), 51; Szawłowski, *Wojna polsko-sowiecka 1939* [The Polish-Soviet War of 1939] (1995, 1997), vol. 2, 52–75; Tomasz Strzembosz, *Rzeczpospolita podziemna: Społeczeństwo polskie a państwo podziemne 1939–1945* [The Underground Polish Republic: Polish Society and the Underground State, 1939-1945] (Warsaw: Krupski i S-ka, 2000), 97–98; Ryszard Szawłowski, "Grodno," *Encyklopedia "Białych Plam"* [Encyclopedia of Gaps] (Radom: Polskie Wydawnictwo Encyklopedyczne, 2002), vol. 7, 139–42. According to the Jewish version, "The Poles took advantage of the few days between September 18 and 20, 1939, after the Polish forces had left Grodno but before the entry of the Russians, to perpetrate a large-scale pogrom in the city. However, a few prescient Jews had organized paramilitary units in order to maintain security and order and prevent vandalism and looting. Thus, in the residential suburb at the city's entrance a group of young Jews and Belorussians (co-workers in a glass factory) banded together to disarm a gang of thugs from the Polish army. Another gang, which had organized when Grodno workers had freed political prisoners, decided to 'impose order' in the city. [Since *all* of the prisoners were released by the "workers", including local Communists, and they engaged in looting and other criminal activities, the remnants of the Polish authorities had to respond. *M.P.*] Their leader, a member of the Polish judiciary named Mikulsky [Mikulski], gathered a lawless rabble around him, including policemen and members of the nationalistic organization OZN [*Obóz Zjednoczenia Narodowego*— Camp of National Unity, a pro-government party] armed with rifles and pistols. They wandered through the city, stealing, looting, brutalizing, and killing the defenseless population [i.e., members of armed Communist groups]. Their pogrom claimed twenty-five fatalities. The arrival of the Red Army on September 22, 1939, put an end to the anarchy, uncertainty, and lawless violence. The terrified Jews greeted the Russian forces joyfully, viewing them as their saviors." One Jew from Grodno went so far as to claim: "If the entry of the Red Army into Grodno had been delayed by even one day more, not a Jew would have been left alive. [According to the 1931 census, some 21,159 Jews constituted 42.6 percent of the city's total population. *M.P.*] ... the Soviet regime seemed to its new Jewish subjects to be enlightened and fair ... little was then known about the Nazis' atrocities in Germany and elsewhere." See Shmuel Spector, ed., *Lost Jewish Worlds: The Communities of Grodno, Lida, Olkieniki, Vishay* (Jerusalem: Yad Vashem, 1996), 88–89.

shooting at people in the street."³⁶ Another eyewitness noted that the Jews had mounted a light machine gun on the roof of a house on Dominikańska Street and threw hand grenades out of windows.³⁷ Similar reports came from Orzeszkowa Street.³⁸ Naturally, the Polish civil authorities, police, and remnants of the military had to respond to this unfolding rebellion.

When the Soviet tanks rolled into Grodno early on 20 September, they brought with them as guides Jewish Communists from that town, among them Lew Aleksandrowicz, Margolis, Lifszyc, and Abraszkin, who had fled to the Soviet Union before the war.³⁹ Local Jews flocked to the ranks of the Soviet militia and NKVD and, along with many Jewish civilian supporters, took part in the fighting that broke out once again. Grenades and machinegun fire from Jewish homes were aimed at soldiers who were fighting for Poland's freedom.⁴⁰

Polish children, among them 13-year-old Tadeusz Jasiński, were tied to the front of Soviet tanks who used them as live shields.⁴¹ Jews also took part in the subsequent roundup of Polish soldiers, policemen, activists, and even high school students and scouts, who had rallied to the defense of the city. Bent on revenge, hysterical bands of roving Jews preyed on Poles. Jews fingered Poles to Soviet soldiers, apprehended them, and even attacked them physically.⁴² There were

---

³⁶ Account of Halina Araszkiewicz (Rozmarynowska) in Szawłowski, *Wojna polsko-sowiecka 1939* [Polish-Soviet War of 1939] (1995, 1997), 2: 191.
³⁷ Account of Narcyz Łopianowski in Szawłowski, *Wojna polsko-sowiecka 1939* [Polish-Soviet War of 1939] (1995, 1997), 2: 80.
³⁸ Account of Tadeusz Borkowski in Grzelak, *Wrzesień 1939 na Kresach w relacjach* [September 1939 in the Eastern Borderlands in Testimonies], 175.
³⁹ Szawłowski, *Wojna polsko-sowiecka* [The Polish-Soviet War] (1995, 1997), vol. 1, 110; Siemiński, *Grodno walczące* [Fighting Grodno], 51; Jan Siemiński, *Przyszliśmy, żeby was wyzwolić: Wspomnienia z Grodna i Stanisławowa (1939–1944)* [We Came to Liberate You: Recollections from Grodno and Stanisławów, 1939-1944] (Białystok: Muzeum Wojska, 1992), 9. Another account from Grodno refers to someone, recognized as a Jew, who had fled to the Soviet Union years earlier, shooting at civilians from a Soviet tank. Even though this Jew had just killed three civilians, once himself wounded, the life of this Soviet soldier was spared by the Poles. See the account of Mieczysław Wołódźko in Grzelak, *Wrzesień 1939 na Kresach w relacjach* [September 1939 in the Eastern Borderlands in Testimonies], 183.
⁴⁰ Account of Władysław Adam Ejsmont in Grzelak, *Wrzesień 1939 na Kresach w relacjach* [September 1939 in the Eastern Borderlands in Testimonies], 177; account of Stanisław Góra in *ibid.*, 195.
⁴¹ Testimony of Helena Platt (Franciszek Zalewski's daughter), cited in Rafał Pasztelański, "Sowieci przywiązywali dzieci do czołgów" [The Soviets Tied Children to Tanks], TVP, 17 September 2009.
⁴² Szawłowski, *Wojna polsko-sowiecka 1939* [Polish-Soviet War of 1939] (1995, 1997), vol. 2, 73; Ryszard Szawłowski, "Grodno," in *Encyklopedia "Białych Plam"*

scores of executions throughout Grodno; the bodies of Polish victims, often disfigured, littered the streets.[43] Some 130 Polish students and officer-cadets were executed on Psia Góra (Dog Mountain) and in Sekret forest. Numerous accounts attest to the brutality of the repressions that ensued:

> After the Polish defense had broken down Soviet troops took over all of the important points in the town such as the administration buildings, police stations and jails, etc. Fully armed execution squads descended on the town. In the first days after the town was occupied, those who were arrested were not sent to places of detention, jails, or prisoner of war camps, but were shot on the spot.
>
> One of these Soviet detachments, led to our home by a Jewish co-inhabitant wearing a red armband, arrested my father. My father, Jan Kurczyk, was a 45-year-old schoolteacher. After being taken out of the home he was shot dead. ... My father had not taken part in the defense of Grodno, but it was enough that someone had fingered him because he was a Pole and educated in order to murder him without a trial in the Nazi fashion.[44]
>
> A cruel fate awaited Polish soldiers and hundreds of residents of Grodno, who were taken prisoner after being fingered by Jewish and Belorussian fighting squads. The men were cruelly disfigured: their noses, limbs, and ears were cut off, their eyes were gouged out. Groups of fifteen were then tied together by barbed wire. They were fastened to tanks and dragged for several hundred meters over stony roads. The bodies were then thrown into roadside ditches and bomb craters. The moans and cries of the murdered could be heard over a distance of a few kilometers. The grimness of the situation was intensified by the fires. Polish homes were set ablaze after being ravaged by Jewish youths wearing red armbands and cocards.[45]

[Encyclopedia of Gaps], vol. 7, 142; Strzembosz, *Rzeczpospolita podziemna* [The Underground Polish Republic], 96–97.

[43] Andrzej Guryn, "Zbrodnie sowieckie wobec ludności cywilnej w Grodnie" [Soviet Crimes Against the Civilian Population in Grodno], *Gazeta* (Toronto), 23-25 October 1992. (Guryn's article is based on material deposited in the Hoover Institution in Stanford, California.) See also Tomasz Strzembosz, "Rewolucja na postronku (2)" [Revolution on a String, part two], *Tygodnik Solidarność* (Warsaw), no. 9, 1998; Mariusz Filipowicz and Edyta Sawicka, "Zbrodnie sowieckie na obrońcach Grodna 1939 r." [Soviet Crimes Against the Defenders of Grodno in 1939], *Biuletyn Historii Pogranicza* (Białystok), no. 6 (2005): 11–27.

[44] Account of Mirosław Kurczyk in Szawłowski, *Wojna polsko-sowiecka 1939* [Polish-Soviet War of 1939] (1995, 1997), vol. 1, 364.

[45] Account of Wiktoria Duda, quoted in Jerzy Robert Nowak, *Przemilczane zbrodnie: Żydzi i Polacy na Kresach w latach 1939–1941* [Crimes Passed Over in Silence: Jews

What most sticks in my mind were the terrifying scenes which took place at that time on the streets and outskirts of Grodno. For example, at the corner of Orzeszkowa and Dominikańska Streets, when a vehicle carrying two [Polish] officers and a driver came to a momentary stop, a group of armed Jews ran out of some nearby houses, pulled out the soldiers and assaulted them. They then hacked their bodies up with axes and piled them up on the road.[46]

Once the townspeople were subdued, Jews from Grodno forayed into the countryside as scouts to identify villagers who had taken part in defending the city during the Soviet onslaught. They appeared as militiamen and members of the NKVD and accosted young Polish men they encountered with threats of reprisals: "You went to fight for the *Pans*. I'll give you your Poland, you motherf----r."[47] (*Pan*, in this context, alludes to the pre-Partition Poland of the landed gentry; it was used pejoratively by Communists to refer to the "bourgeois" Poles of the interwar years.) Polish soldiers in the vicinity were also savagely attacked.[48]

Soviet propaganda turned the defense of the city of Grodno into an anti-Jewish "pogrom."[49] However, it is difficult to reconcile the claim of a "pogrom" with the fact that the alleged "pogromists" were not only ethnic Poles, but also included Polish citizens of other nationalities, among them Byelorussians and Jews.[50] Some Jews fought on the side of the Poles and others assisted Poles in other ways. The following year, after the Soviet regime was firmly installed, show trials of "reactionary" Poles were conducted at which Jewish witnesses came forward in large number to level charges against Poles accused of

---

and Poles in the Eastern Borderlands, 1939-1941] (Warsaw: von borowiecky, 1999), 17.

[46] Account of Wiktoria Duda in *ibid.*, 54.

[47] Account of "Grodniak" in Szawłowski, *Wojna polsko-sowiecka 1939* [The Polish-Soviet War of 1939] (1995, 1997), 2: 66.

[48] For an eyewitness report from the Grodno region attesting to atrocities committed against Polish soldiers by local collaborators, see Ryszard Głuski, "Obrona Grodna we wspomnieniach: Żołnierskie relacje" [The Defense of Grodno in Testimonies: Soldiers' Testimonies], *Biuletyn Wojewódzkiego Domu Kultury w Białymstoku*, no. 3/4 (1989): 23.

[49] Szawłowski, *Wojna polsko-sowiecka 1939* [Polish-Soviet War of 1939] (1995, 1997), 1: 148, and 2: 68.

[50] Two of the Jews who sided with the Poles were Chaim Margolis, the teenage son of the director of the State Tobacco Plant, who perished heroically in the struggle, and Oszer Szereszewski, a doctor who cared attentively for wounded Polish soldiers. See Szawłowski, *Wojna polsko-sowiecka 1939* [Polish-Soviet War of 1939] (1995, 1997), 1: 122–23, and 2: 72. Another Jew, Boruch Kierszenbejm, mentioned in the following footnote, was put on trial by the Soviets.

taking part in the fighting. A number of Poles were sentenced and some executed for opposing the pro-Soviet rebellion.[51] Typically, the much more numerous excesses committed against Poles went unpunished.

---

[51] According to one Jewish report, "In June 1940, the thirteen Grodno pogromists [sic]—among them Polish army officers, policemen, and members of anti-revolutionary organizations—were tried in a Soviet court. ... Four of the defendants were sentenced to death; seven received prison terms of six to eight years; and two were released." See Spector, *Lost Jewish Worlds,* 89. According to Evgenii S. Rozenblat, four of the accused were sentenced to death by firing squad, three to 10 years' imprisonment, three to 8 years' imprisonment, and one to 6 years' imprisonment. See Evegenii S. Rozenblat, "'Contact Zones' in Interethnic Relations — The Case of Western Belarus," in Barkan, Cole, and Struve, *Shared History, Divided Memory,* 206. These sources neglect to mention that among those put on trial was a Belarusian (Jemielian Gryko), a German, and a Jew (Boruch Kerszenbejm), thus undermining the notion that this was an anti-Semitic "pogrom." One of the Poles sentenced to death (Franciszek Witul), who had been accused by a Jewish woman, was later acquitted. Virtually all the witnesses called at the trials were Jews. See Tomasz Strzembosz, ed., *Okupacja sowiecka (1939 1941) w świetle tajnych dokumentów: Obywatele polscy na Kresach Północno- Wschodnich II Rzeczypospolitej pod okupacją sowiecką w latach 1939–1941* [The Soviet Occupation of 1939-1941 in Light of Secret Documents: Polish Citizens in the Northeastern Borderlands of the Second Polish Republic Under the Soviet Occupation] (Warsaw: Instytut Studiów Politycznych PAN, 1996), 144 n.7; Wierzbicki, *Polacy i Żydzi w zaborze sowieckim* [Poles and Jews in the Soviet Occupation Zone], 64; Jan Jerzy Milewski, "Okupacja sowiecka w Białostockiem (1939–1941): Próba charakterystyki" [The Soviet Occupation in the Białystok Area (1939-1941): An Attempt at a Description], in Piotr Chmielowiec, ed., *Okupacja sowiecka ziem polskich (1939–1941)* [The Soviet Occupation of Polish Lands (1939-1941)] (Rzeszów and Warsaw: Instytut Pamięci Narodowej—Komisja Ścigania Zbrodni przeciwko Narodowi Polskiemu, 2005), 202; Mariusz Filipowicz and Edyta Sawicka, "Zbrodnie sowieckie na obrońcach Grodna 1939 r." [Soviet Crimes Against the Defenders of Grodno in 1939], *Biuletyn Historii Pogranicza* (Białystok), no. 6 (2005): 19–21. On the other hand, Belorussian peasants charged with murdering a former village administrator and police chief in Małoryta on 26 September 1939, were acquitted because they had committed the murder "out of a desire for class revenge" directed at their "Polish oppressors." See Rozenblat, "'Contact Zones' in Interethnic," 206. Even Rozenblat, who views the events in Grodno as a "pogrom," admits that the outcome was a travesty: "The population of Western Belarus, which closely followed the outcome of judicial proceedings concerning cases of murder stemming from September 1939, received an unambiguous signal from the authorities that a norm of dual standards had been introduced. Assuming from a legal point of view that the murder of Jews and Poles is equally criminal, the court ruling in the case of the Małoryta [Małoryta] peasants was judicial nonsense. Soviet legal proceedings failed to see a criminal offence in the murder of Polish 'oppressors' and acquitted the murderers, but sentenced to death by firing squad those who participated in pogroms against Jews." As Rozenblat points out, there were "clear contradictions between the new regime's propaganda and its actions: on the one hand, the Soviet authorities proclaimed class and national equality of rights, and on the other hand portrayed the enemy of the (Soviet) people as having Polish features." *Ibid.,* 207.

As for Dereczyn, according to Polish sources, armed rebels, consisting of Jews and Belarusians, seized control of the town on 17 September and arrested the deputy commander of a battalion dispatched to that town from Słonim. When his battalion arrived in Dereczyn the following morning, it was fired on by young Jews, whom the Polish forces then drove out of the town. The Polish military conducted a search and found two suspected insurgents, one of whom was killed when he fired at and wounded a Polish soldier.[52]

Several Jewish testimonies found in that town's memorial book essentially confirm the Polish accounts and provide some additional details of what occurred including the attempted lynching, by the revolutionary vanguard, of Rev. Jerzy Poczobutt-Odlanicki, the local Catholic pastor, which was prevented by the arrival of the Soviet forces. While the memorial book contains some vague allegations of an impending "pogrom," in fact the reaction of the Polish forces was measured and did not target the entire Jewish community. Bauer simply ignores the following important Jewish testimonies—found in the same memorial book he cites from—that belie his characterization of the events:

Pesha Feinsilber:
Local Jewish youth, along with [Belorussian] Christians from nearby villages took over the forces in Dereczin on a temporary basis, until the Russians would arrive. They had a little bit of armament.

Immediately on that first night, they came knocking on my door, and ordered me to open the store, and to provide red cloth for banners and tablecloths, in order to receive the Red Army.

On the second night, three vehicles with Polish officers drove through Dereczin, after whom were supposed to come a contingent of the Polish army. The temporary authorities detained the Polish officers, beat them up, confiscated their autos, and arrested them. In town, an uproar and panic ensued: the contingent of Polish army was expected any minute … Many Jews fled the town, and hid out among Christians and in the fields. …

In the early morning, the Rabbi was summoned to the local priest. There it was demanded of him that he should try to influence the young people, and obtain the release of the Polish officers from jail, because of the impending danger attending the arrival of the Polish army contingent who might wreck

---

[52] Wierzbicki, *Polacy i Białorusini w zaborze sowiecki* [Poles and Belarusians in the Soviet Occupation Zone], 162–64.

all of Dereczin. Only after expending considerable energy, did the Rabbi and the priest obtain the keys to the jail, and release the officers.

Meir Bakalchuk:
A group of young people, responsible to no one, but intoxicated with Communist doctrine, attempted to 'seize control' in Dereczin before the arrival of the Soviet army. They detained several Polish officers who were retreating. Following these officers, who were a vanguard for a much larger retreating Polish force, the Polish soldiers arrived ... My father put his life on the line, and went out to the inflamed Polish soldiers, and promised to locate their officers. By exerting great energy, he was able to persuade these young people to release these Polish officers. The retreating Poles were in a hurry to flee as fast as possible from the enemy ...

During those frightful days without a regime in place in Dereczin, another incident occurred: a notification went out all over town that the left wing youth, both Jews and [some Belorussian] Christians alike, were planning to shoot the local Catholic priest, who was known to be a liberal-minded individual, and who also had friendly relations with the Jews. On the prior day, the local priest in Zelva [Zelwa] had indeed been hung [sic-hanged], whom the inflamed young people had accused of being sharply anti-Communist.

When my father learned of the danger that awaited the priest of Dereczin, he resolved to do something to defuse the murder plot, for which the Jews would, ultimately, God forbid, pay dearly. My father went to the priest in the middle of the night, and surreptitiously brought him to our house. The following morning, large groups of young people surrounded our house, demanding that the priest be handed over to them. My father stood himself in the doorway and told them that only over his dead body would they be able to break into our house.

In the middle of this conversation between my father and this gathered crowd, the first vanguard of Soviet officials arrived in town. Seeing a large crowd in front of our house, they asked what was going on. When they found out about the issue with the priest, one of the Soviet officials asked my mother for a small table. He stood on the table and declared to the crowd that 'the Soviet regime does everything according to the rule of law, and nobody has a right to try and sentence anyone out of this process.' The young people were disarmed, and the Soviet military expressed their thanks to my father for his proper and sober position.[53]

---

[53] *Dereczin* (Mahwah, New Jersey: Jacob Solomon Berger, 2000), 206, 324–25. This is a translation of the memorial book *Sefer Derets'in* published in Yiddish and Hebrew in Tel Aviv in 1966. Yehuda Bauer bases himself on just one account—selected from among several in the Dereczyn memorial book—authored by Masha and Abraham-Hirsch Kulakowski, which reads: "The war was already almost two weeks in progress

Did the Polish military or authorities try to organize an unprovoked pogrom, as Yehuda Bauer alleges? There is no evidence of that. Under the circumstances, *any* army would have reacted in like manner. The reception that the Jewish and Belorussian population subsequently extended to the Red Army was ecstatic, though perhaps exaggerated in the following account:

> It is difficult to describe our sense of elation. At the time, I thought I was living the happiest day of my life. The entire Jewish population, and also many of the [Belorussian] Christians from Dereczin and its environs, went forth to greet the Soviet military forces. ... Our joy knew no bounds. It seemed as if the Messiah had come ...
>
> To the celebration gatherings, tens of thousands of people from the entire area came together. Dereczin was literally too small to absorb them all. The masses found many ways to express their enthusiasm and inspiration for the liberating Red military forces, and its shining leader, Stalin.[54]

The platitudes about the rule of law stated so eloquently by the Soviet officer—mentioned in the Jewish account above—were nothing more than a charade. Not only did the Soviets execute thousands of Poles extrajudicially, but they had also encouraged excesses against Poles by the minorities, and took no action to punish the culprits. Meir Bakalchuk was to later run into a member of the local lynch mob in the Soviet interior:

> I must recall Shmuel the youth from Dereczin, a hard-bitten Communist. It was he who demanded of my father in Dereczin that he turn over the priest, who had hidden himself with us. He served the Soviet authorities faithfully in Dereczin, and when the Russians retreated, they took Shmuel with them.[55]

---

before Dereczin received a detachment of several tens of Polish youths, who were sent as a military formation to protect law and order. You are to understand that the 'ordering' started with the Jews. Several Jews fell victim at their hands, and they occupied themselves with instituting their bloody work. With armed weapons in hand, they forced several tens of the Jewish populace into an old abandoned barn, and wanted to torch it. It was only thanks to the energetic intervention of the town priest that these Jews were saved from an awful death." See *Dereczin*, 196. No other witness refers to the alleged attempt by Polish forces to burn scores of Jews in a barn, something that would surely not have escaped their attention, if true.

[54] Masha and Abraham-Hirsch Kulakowski, "This Is How the Jewish Community of Dereczin Was Destroyed," in *Dereczin*, 196.

[55] *Dereczin*, 328.

Although relatively rare, accounts such as those cited above are particularly significant in that they are supportive of Polish reports. Given their paucity in memorial books from Eastern Poland, however, the authors' views do not appear to be representative of their community. The vast majority of accounts simply ignore these shameful episodes, preferring instead to hide behind defensive claims of "unprovoked pogroms." Sadly, the same can be said of Holocaust historiography.

The nearby town of Zelwa, where a revolutionary committee composed mainly of Jews and some Belarusians seized control of the town on 18 September, witnessed much more bloodshed. According to Polish sources, Polish military supply columns were shot at as they passed by the town and some captured Polish soldiers were disarmed. In response, Polish troops stormed the town and arrested some of the armed insurgents, but on the intervention of a priest, who was fearful of Soviet retaliation, they spared the culprits. After the Polish forces retreated, groups of young armed Jews and Belorussians with red armbands continued to terrorize the Polish population, arresting and shooting their victims of choice: settlers, landowners, state officials, officers, policemen, and clergymen.

Among the victims was Rev. Jan Kryński, the 78-year-old local Catholic pastor, and Rev. Dawid Jakubson, the pastor of the Orthodox parish, who were executed together with a dozen Polish captives.[56] No Jew was harmed by the revolutionaries. According to the testimony of a Jewish lawyer named Jacovitzky, which was recorded by Yitzhak Shavlev, exceptionally some Jews were also targeted, but they escaped the fate of the Poles. Unlike the priests, the rabbi of Zelwa, who was also apparently "wanted" by local revolutionaries, received a warning and was therefore spared:

> On one of the nights when there was no government in the town, because the Polish authorities had left the town and the Red Army had not yet arrived, some people knocked on my door, representing themselves as officials of the Soviet regime, and demanded that I [Jacovitzky] open the

---

[56] Wierzbicki, *Polacy i Białorusini w zaborze sowiecki* [Poles and Belarussians in the Soviet Occupation Zone], 86–87, 147–48, 162–63, Mariusz Filipowicz, "Zbrodnia w Zelwie" [A Crime in Zelwa], *Biuletyn Instytutu Pamięci Narodowej*, no. 12 (December 2004): 80–83; Tadeusz Krahel, *Doświadczeni zniewoleniem: Duchowni archidiecezji wileńskiej represjonowani w latach okupacji sowieckiej (1939–1941)* [Experience Through Enslavement: The Clergy of the Wilno Archdiocese Repressed During the Soviet Occupation of 1939-1941] (Białystok: Polskie Towarzystwo Historyczne–Oddział w Białymstoku, 2005), 68.

door. Two men entered the house, both armed, with red armbands on their sleeves. They ordered me to get dressed, and follow after them. When we left the house, they directed me to go to the municipal building, and they followed me with drawn revolvers. In the municipal building, they took me to a room where they told me to sit down and keep quiet. A short while later, the 'American' was brought into the room (this was a descriptor used for a rich gentile who had come from America and had bought himself a small piece of property near Zelva. Everyone knew him as the 'American').

After him, they brought in two other men who owned property in the area (whose names I don't remember) and finally, they brought in the young [sic] Catholic priest from the church on Razboiaishitza Street.

During all this time, we were under the surveillance of three armed men, who did not permit us to talk among ourselves. From the behavior of our guards, and from the fragments of sentences I was able to hear, I gathered that one other individual was still to be brought into the room. After an extended wait, two armed men with red armbands entered the room, and informed the three that they can't find the Rabbi at home. They organized searches in all synagogues, but he was not to be found there either. After a short conference, they decided to send the two original men back to the Rabbi's house and the remaining ones would begin with us. Up to that moment we had no idea of what awaited us.

The first one was the 'American.' He was ordered to get up and go to the exit. Behind him walked two of the guards with drawn revolvers. One was left behind to guard those who were left in the room.

They left the building, went around the structure, and brought the 'American' to the wall of the building that was about three meters from the window of the room in which we were sitting, and with no delay, proceeded to shoot him. When he fell dead, they picked him up and threw his body into a wagon hitched to a horse that was tied up near the window. All this took place in the full view of the rest of the detainees who were sitting in front of the window.

After this they took one of the men who owned property in town, and his fate was the same as the 'American's,' and then the second man who owned land. When it came to the priest's turn, the dawn started to break. I saw him standing against the wall, crossing himself continuously. He was also shot, and his body thrown into the wagon. I was left for last. I heard the steps of the executioners getting closer to the room. I also heard the wagon moving from its place. The door was opened swiftly, and the two entered the room, and ordered me to get up and leave the place as quickly as possible. They warned me, that if I revealed what had happened during the night, my blood would be on my own head. Apparently, after daybreak, when the residents of the area arose to go to work, they didn't have the nerve to continue with their activities.

Thanks to your Rabbi who was not at home, they lost a lot of time, and were unable to finish their work before dawn, and that is how I survived. ... rumors and stories spread about the night of the murders. It was told, that a short time before the Red Underground reached the Rabbi's home, that Ephraim Moskovsky reached the Rabbi and warned the Rabbi about what was about to happen. He advised the Rabbi to flee his house and find a place to hide, until the threat passed. ...

When I [Yitzhak Shalev] reached Israel after the war, my townsfolk told me about what they had heard from the mouth of the *Rebbetzin* Kosovsky. Therefore, it was Ephraim Moskovsky who came to the house of the Rabbi that night and told him what was about to happen, and in this manner, the life of the Rabbi was saved.[57]

The Soviet authorities went through the motions of bringing some of the culprits to trial, but nothing came of it in the end:

The new regime organized an investigation, and the evidence led to five young gentiles from the village of Borodetz that belonged to the Communist underground. They were also regular employees at the factory owned by Borodetzky [a Jew who was later deported to the Soviet interior].

The Soviet regime wanted to demonstrate that there is law and justice in the socialist order, and arranged a public trial for them. I attended several sessions at the courthouse. The defendants sat on the bench for the defense, with broad and insolent smiles on their faces. They didn't lie, and didn't admit anything. All the witnesses that appeared for the defense testified to the appointments the defendants had in the underground, and their heroism there. The spectators at the trial had the impression that the court was on the verge of awarding the defendants laurels of honor and heroism. The trial continued with recesses of weeks, from one session to the next. The defendants, meanwhile, went free, and continued to do their normal jobs. Naturally, the lawyer Jacovitzky kept his secret to himself, and I also kept my word of honor to him. Both of us knew that our testimony would not harm the defendants, but probably would harm us.[58]

Matters were even more complicated elsewhere. The town of Luboml near the River Bug, in Volhynia, changed hands several times. Local

---

[57] Yitzhak Shalev, "The Rescue of Rabbi Kosovsky," in Yerachmiel Moorstein, ed., *Zelva Memorial Book* (Mahwah, New Jersey: Jacob Solomon Berger, 1992), 92–93.
[58] *Ibid.*, 93. According to Soviet sources, a Red Army soldier by the name of Floruk, who oversaw the executions, was arrested but his fate is not known. See Mariusz Filipowicz, "Zbrodnia w Zelwie" [Crime in Zelwa], 80–83.

Jews took turns collaborating first with Germans, who originally occupied the town for two days on 20 September, and then with the Soviets, who took control of the town only on 24 September. Some local Jews and Ukrainians had formed a revolutionary committee that took control of Luboml on 18 September, after the departure of the Polish army. The people's guard (militia), composed of as many as 150 Jews and Ukrainians, arrested the county supervisor (*starosta*), public prosecutor and members of the town administration.

When the Germans arrived, the Jewish-Ukrainian militia apprehended and disarmed Polish soldiers, ripping the Polish insignia off their coats and uniforms, and handed them over to the Germans. As could be expected, when the Germans departed and Polish soldiers in the vicinity learned of what was happening, they struck back at the collaborators during the hiatus before the arrival of the Soviets. Some of the captured insurgents were executed on the spot; others were taken to the Polish garrison in Chełm.[59] Although this sequence of events is confirmed in the town's Jewish memorial book, Yehuda Bauer is apparently unaware of it and states that the Germans "committed atrocities in Luboml during the brief period before they handed the town over to the Soviets,"[60] a claim which the memorial book discredits.

According to the Jewish memorial book, when the Germans entered Luboml for "a few days," "a militia composed of Jews and Ukrainians was formed whose job it was to keep order in the town. (...) Jewish young men were appointed to the town militia by the temporary Jewish-Ukrainian City Council," which worked hand-in-glove with the German military authorities. "During their presence in our town, the Germans behaved like normal occupying authorities. They did no ill to the Jews."

---

[59] The foregoing is based on the following eyewitness accounts: Włodzimierz Wojciechowski, a Polish rescuer awarded by Yad Vashem—see Barbara Stanisławczyk, *Czterdzieści twardych* [Forty Tough Ones] (Warsaw: ABC, 1997), 156–57; Szawłowski, *Wojna polsko-sowiecka 1939* [Polish-Soviet War of 1939] (1995, 1997), vol. 1, 221–22; Piotr Zarzycki, *2 Batalion Mostów Kolejowych* [The Second Railroad Bridge Battalion] (Pruszków: Ajaks, 1994), 37–38; Władysław Jotysz, "Telegram do Stalina" [Telegram to Stalin], *Nasza Polska*, 8 September 1999. The latter account is also cited in Nowak, *Przemilczane zbrodnie* [Crimes Passed Over in Silence], 39 (as Totysz). For additional confirmation based on Soviet sources see Andrii Rukkas, "Antypolski zbroini vystupy na Volyni (veresen 1939 r.)" [Anti-Polish Armed Rebellions in Volhynia (September 1939)], in Isaievych, *Volyn i Kholmshchyna 1938–1947 rr.* [Volhynia and the Chełm Area in 1938-1947], 134–35.

[60] Bauer, *The Death of the Shtetl*, 36.

After the Germans departed, in anticipation of the arrival of the Soviet army, local Bolshevik sympathizers erected a "triumphal arch" at the main entrance to the town "with red flags and other decorations and slogans in honor of the Red army ... which had come to free our citizens from Polish enslavement." "Comrades" armed "with guns, having taken power into their own hands," gathered at the quarters of the "self-defense organization," i.e., the militia, and "walked around arrogantly, with heads held high, and it seemed as if there were none equal to them."

When, unexpectedly, the Polish forces re-entered Luboml, they destroyed the "triumphal arch" and "rounded up the pro-Soviet youths [i.e., members of the self-styled militia] and led them to the station all beaten up and bloodied." And "Comrade" Veyner, who would "ride around with a revolver in his hand on a big thoroughbred horse" and "acted like the former police officer of the shtetl," was the first to be shot.

> There were also *rumors* that before their retreat, the Poles wanted to torch the city, but the Polish priest convinced them not to, saying the victory arch was the work of individuals. (...) The Jews ran to the priest, who, together with the attorney's wife, Mrs. Myalovitska [Miałowicka?], intervened by telling the gentiles that not all Jews were Communists. (...) When the Red Army entered Libivne, the leftists in our town received them with pomp and celebration. There were many Jewish young men among them.

After the long-awaited Soviet arrival,

> [T]he militia reorganized, once again composed of Jews and Ukrainians. (...) Zalman Rubinshteyn [a Communist] made himself the leader of the shtetl. He chose as his aides Moyshe Koltun, Moyshe Bobtses, Rafael Poyntses, as well as a couple of the town's gentile youths. (...) Those Jews who were needed by the Soviets were utilized by the new regime, even though they once had been rich. For instance, Chayim Kroyt, a former owner of a sawmill, was appointed as director of his own confiscated establishment. The same happened to other townspeople. The Soviet authorities did not arrest political opponents, nor the rich of the shtetl.[61]

---

[61] Berl Kagan, ed., *Luboml: The Memorial Book of a Vanished Shtetl* (Hoboken, New Jersey: Ktav Publishing House, 1997), xix, 230–36, 240–43, 261, 290, 343. A careful reading of several Jewish accounts in this book is required to piece together the chronology set out above, as the accounts are fragmentary, contradictory and sometimes incoherent. The introduction speaks of Polish bands of "Andekes" (Endeks) who "overran the town, slaughtering about a dozen Jews in cold blood." One account alleges, most improbably, that "anti-Semitic" Polish soldiers butchered "the peaceful,

Luboml was not the only town in Borderlands where Jews cooperated with the German invaders in striking at the Poles. The Germans armed Jewish Communists in Kobryń, in Polesia, who then carried out diversionary attacks on Polish soldiers. Two flags—a Nazi swastika and a Soviet star—flew over the town simultaneously and in harmony.[62] Tellingly, when German and Soviet armies met at Brześć (Brest) on the River Bug, they celebrated their joint victory over Poland by staging a massive parade. Nazi General Heinz Guderian greeted Soviet General ("kombrig") Semen Krivoshein, a Jew, who saluted the Nazi swastika.[63] The point of the story is not, of course, to stereotype Jews as traitors, but to illustrate—if more illustration is needed—that the Poles were not reacting to (imputed) stereotypes or myth, but to actual facts on the ground. Their response was not directed against all Jews, but only those believed to be responsible for concrete misdeeds, as indeed there were many such people. Moreover, their response was measured and in conformity with accepted wartime practices followed by non-totalitarian states.

To his credit, Yehuda Bauer recognizes that, in the initial stages of the occupation, "the whole weight of the Soviet terror fell primarily on Poles." He writes, "Without doubt, the Soviets saw the Poles as the main enemy and, initially at least, instituted a regime of utmost terror against them, much harsher than their treatment of Jews, Ukrainians, or Belorussians."[64]

But then he performs a volte-face and claims that the "Soviet authorities preferred Poles to Jews, provided they showed real or

---

long-suffering Jewish population, frightened and unarmed. Any Jew encountered on the street was shot and murdered on the spot without any distinction." (There were more than 3,000 Jews living in Luboml at the time, constituting over 90 percent of the town's population.) Allegedly, "Not one gentile [from the self-defense group] received any beating! Those who suffered were Jews and no one else but Jews!" Finally, under Soviet rule, Jews were allegedly relegated to the most menial work: "The pay was not high—otherwise the non-Jews would have gotten the work." Typical of most Jewish memorial books, this one is also rather vague about the fate of the town's Polish population under Soviet rule.

[62] Wierzbicki, *Polacy i Białorusini w zaborze sowieckim* [Poles and Belarusians in the Soviet Occupation Zone], 181.

[63] Vladimir Levin and David Meltser, *Chernaia kniga z krasnymi stranitsami: Tragediia i geroizm evreev Belorussii* [A Black Book with Red Pages: The Tragedy and Heroism of the Jews of Belarus] (Baltimore: Vestnik Information Agency, 1996), 322; Szawłowski, *Wojna polsko-sowiecka 1939* [Polish-Soviet War of 1939] (1995, 1997), 1: 233.

[64] Bauer, *The Death of the Shtetl*, 34, 48.

pretended pro-Soviet sympathies."[65] The evidence he presents to prove his point is rather selective and simply unpersuasive. Bauer also claims that "the number of deported Jews was proportionately much higher than the proportionate number of deported Poles."

However, this is simply not borne out by the documents found in the Soviet archives, which were released in the 1990s.[66] Although Poles constituted about a third of the prewar population of the Eastern Borderlands, their share of the civilian deportations was approximately 70 percent, that is, about 250,000 out of 350,000 deportees. When Polish military personnel and officials that were arrested and executed are added to these figures, the Polish share of the victims of repression is even greater.

The Jewish share of the civilian deportees was 70,000, or approximately 20 percent of the total number of deportees, while their proportion of the overall population was slightly higher than ten percent. Soviet statistics also belie the claim that most of the Jewish refugees from central Poland were deported to the Soviet interior, as Bauer alleges. Refugees from German-occupied Poland accounted for approximately 62 percent of Jewish civilian deportees, and therefore only a small portion of the estimated 200,000–300,000 Jewish refugees from the German zone fell victim to Soviet repressions.

The problem is that Bauer has only a passing acquaintance with Soviet sources, even though they have been available for more than a decade, yet he finds them to be "not convincing" for reasons he does not elaborate on.[67] The lack of in-depth research or any knowledge of sources other than Jewish testimonies, in particular Polish and Russian ones, with only occasional references to the works of German historians, is a significant shortcoming of Bauer's scholarship, and indeed Israeli scholarship.

Unfortunately, some of the unsubstantiated claims and defensive views expressed by Yehuda Bauer are gaining ground among a new generation of historians who show a troubling tendency to endorse

---

[65] Bauer, *The Death of the Shtetl*, 40.
[66] See, for example, O.A. Gorlanov and A.B. Roginskii, "Ob arestakh v zapadnykh oblastiakh Belorussii i Ukrainy v 1939–1941 gg." [On the Arrests in the Western Districts of Belarus and Ukraine in 1939–1941] in Aleksandr E. Gurianov, comp., *Repressii protiv poliakov i polskikh grazhdan* [Repression Against Poles and Polish Citizens] (Moscow: Zvenia, 1997), 77–113; N.S. Lebedeva, "The Deportation of the Polish Population to the USSR, 1939–41," *The Journal of Communist Studies and Transition Politics*, vol. 16, nos. 1/2 (March/June 2000): 28–45; Grzegorz Hryciuk, "Victims 1939–1941: The Soviet Repressions in Eastern Poland," in Barkan, Cole, and Struve, *Shared History, Divided Memory*, 173–200.
[67] Bauer, *The Death of the Shtetl*, 48, 53, 54, 180 (endnotes 77 and 78).

stereotypical generalizations about Poles, often quite strident ones. Some go so far as to dismiss counter-arguments not on their merits, but because of their proponents' alleged "nationalism."[68] Resorting to negative stereotypes, by either side, remains the biggest obstacle facing the historiography of Polish-Jewish relations. Each episode has to be examined individually and conclusions about the behavior of a particular group drawn cautiously, having regard to all of the surrounding circumstances.

There has been a considerable amount of ink spilled over a phenomenon that has been labeled the "Jedwabne state," after the

---

[68] A prime example is Joanna Michlic, a staunch advocate of the Jan T. Gross post-modernist approach to Polish-Jewish relations, who is constantly battling perceived Polish "ethno-nationalist" historians whose views she disagrees with. A typical sample of her writing directed at respected historians reads: "The main representative of the post-1989 historiography characterized by prejudicial views toward Jews ... These historians belong to the school of (ethno)nationalist history writing in which the themes of martyrdom and victimhood of ethnic Poles vis-à-vis other groups play a key role in shaping their arguments and interpretations." The irony of her use of "ethno-nationalist" straw men is, however, lost on Michlic, as her approach to assessing Jewish behavior under the Soviet occupation is consistent with the charges she levels against her "opponents": "they use a range of strategies to rationalize and justify ... violence and to minimize its criminal nature." See Joanna Michlic, "The Soviet Occupation of Poland, 1939–41, and the Stereotype of the Anti-Polish and Pro-Soviet Jew," *Jewish Social Studies: History, Culture, Society*, n.s., vol. 13, no. 3 (Spring/Summer 2007): 135–76, here at 151. Occasionally Michlic has resorted to sheer fabrication to buttress her arguments. In a highly charged letter published in the January 2008 issue of *History*, Joanna Michlic and Antony Polonsky attacked a favourable review of Marek Jan Chodakiewicz's book *The Massacre in Jedwabne, July 10, 1941: Before, During, and After* (Boulder, Colorado: East European Monographs; New York: Columbia University Press, 2005), by blatantly misrepresenting the findings of the prosecutor of the Jedwabne massacre investigation and historians at the Institute of National Remembrance regarding the number of victims, the respective degree of German and Polish involvement in the crime, and the participation of local Jews in the persecution of Poles during the Soviet occupation. See the unpublished responses to *History* posted at: http://glaukopis.pl/pdf/czytelnia/JedwabneReplyToAntonyPolonsky.pdf and http://glaukopis.pl/pdf/czytelnia/RichardTyndorfLetterToTheEditor.pdf. German historian Peter Longerich has pointed out that Jedwabne, where several hundred Jews were killed on 10 July 1941, and other such pogroms were not only inspired but also likely engineered by the Germans, and not by the local population (some of whom were drawn in), as part of a deliberate policy. See Peter Longerich, *Holocaust: The Nazi Persecution and Murder of the Jews* (Oxford and New York: Oxford University Press, 2010), 196. Longerich cites the two-volume study published by the Institute of National Remembrance—Paweł Machcewicz and Krzysztof Persak, eds., *Wokół Jedwabnego: Studia; Dokumenty* [Surrounding Jedwabne; Documents] (Warsaw: Instytut Pamięci Narodowej–Komisja Ścigania Zbrodni przeciwko Narodowi Polskiemu, 2002)—and Marek Jan Chodakiewicz's aforementioned *The Massacre in Jedwabne, July 10, 1941*.

massacre of several hundred Jews in a town in the Białystok district on 10 July 1941. The phenomenon is understood as an outburst of communal violence, culminating in the large-scale murder of members of another ethnic group, carried out with exceptional cruelty and impunity in the knowledge that one has the tacit permission of the occupying authorities to do so. That violence is said to have been integral to a larger pattern of violence carried out by the occupying authorities themselves.

We now know, thanks to efforts of a handful of courageous and dedicated Russian historians, and their champions outside of Russia, that it was the Soviet Union, and not Nazi Germany, that undertook the first shooting campaigns of internal enemies in the 1930s, and it was the Poles who were the first mass victims of the national operations of Stalin's Great Terror. Timothy Snyder has made this point forcefully in his book *Bloodlands*:

> In 1937 and 1938, a quarter of a million Soviet citizens were shot on essentially ethnic grounds. ... the Soviet Union in the late 1930s was a land of unequalled national persecutions. Even as the Popular Front [of the Comintern or Communist International] presented the Soviet Union as the homeland of toleration, Stalin ordered the mass killings of several Soviet nationalities. The most persecuted European national minority in the second half of the 1930s was not the four hundred thousand or so German Jews (the number declining because of emigration) but the six hundred thousand or so Soviet Poles (the number declining because of executions).
>
> Stalin was a pioneer of national mass murder, and the Poles were the preeminent victims among the Soviet nationalities. The Polish national minority, like the kulaks, had to take the blame for the failures of collectivization. The rationale was invented during the famine itself in 1933, and then applied during the Great Terror in 1937 and 1938.
>
> The Polish operation was in some respects the bloodiest chapter of the Great Terror in the Soviet Union. ... Of the 143,810 people arrested under the [false] accusation of espionage for Poland, 111,091 were executed. Not all of these were Poles, but most of them were. Poles were also targeted disproportionately in the kulak action, especially in Soviet Ukraine. Taking into account the number of deaths, the percentage of death sentences to arrests, and the risk of arrest, ethnic Poles suffered more than any other group within the Soviet Union during the Great Terror. By a conservative estimate, some eighty-five thousand Poles were executed in 1937 and 1938, which means that one-eighth of the 681,692 mortal victims of the Great Terror were Polish. This is a staggeringly high percentage, given that Poles were a tiny minority in the Soviet Union, constituting fewer than 0.4

percent of the general population. Soviet Poles were about forty times more likely to die during the Great Terror than Soviet citizens generally.[69]

In some respects, what happened to the Poles in the Eastern Borderlands in September 1939 can be viewed as a continuation of the Great Terror. The group that was targeted for blind retribution, because of their nationality and social status, and not on account of any specific wrongdoings, was the *de facto* Polish minority.

Thousands of Poles, for the most part civilians and ordinary soldiers, were executed or lynched in the latter part of that bloody month alone, not by the Soviet invaders, who had not yet arrived, but by their fellow citizens, often their immediate neighbors. The killings were often inspired by, and played into the hands of, the Soviet invaders, as was the case in the small village of Brzostowica Mała, in the Białystok district, about fifty kilometers east of the city of Białystok.

This is a little-known but particularly heinous crime, where neighbor-on-neighbor violence against an entire community—something that would escalate dramatically as the war progressed—was pioneered. As many as fifty Poles were tortured and butchered by a Jewish-led band of local pro-Soviet Jews and Belorussians on 20 September, *before* the arrival of the Red Army.

Armed with blades and axes, and led by a Jewish trader named Zusko Ajzik, the band entered the village and proceeded to drag people out of their houses screaming, and then cruelly massacred the entire Polish population in a paroxysm of violence. The victims included Count Antoni Wołkowicki and his wife Ludwika, his brother-in-law Zygmunt Woynicz-Sianożęcki, the county reeve and his secretary, the accountant, the mailman, and the local teacher.

The victims of this orgy of bloodshed were tortured, tied with barbed wire, pummeled with sticks, forced to swallow quicklime, thrown into a ditch, and buried alive. The paralyzed Countess Ludwika Wołkowicka was dragged to the execution site by her hair. The murder was ordered by Żak Motyl, the Jewish head of the revolutionary committee in Brzostowica Wielka, which was composed of Jews and Belorussians.

Not surprisingly, the culprits were never punished. On the contrary, the NKVD officers praised them for their "class-conscious" actions. Zusko Ajzik became the president of the local cooperative. Several

---

[69] Timothy Snyder, *Bloodlands: Europe Between Hitler and Stalin* (New York: Basic Books, 2010), 89, 103–4.

other members of the band were accepted into the militia. *The ethnic aspect of the crime, however, is undeniable: only members of the Polish minority perished at the hands of their non-Polish neighbors— Stalin's willing executioners.*[70] This was occupied Poland's first Jedwabne.

Nothing of the kind happened to Jews at the hands of the Poles parts of Poland occupied by the Germans in September 1939. As early as 6 September, the first Pole, a postman by the name of Jan Jakub Semik from Limanowa, a town in southern Poland, was executed by the Germans for trying to intervene on behalf of a group of nine Jews who had been arrested, brutally thrown into waiting cars, kicked, and insulted. His pleas that they were decent people fell on deaf ears. The Germans ordered Semik to get into one of the cars and then drove off in the direction of the Cieniawa woods in the village of Mordarka (southern Poland near Nowy Sącz), where they shot him along with the Jews.

The number of such cases multiplied by the hundreds once the Holocaust got underway in mid–1941, and the Germans imposed a collective death sentence on the family of anyone who defied German decrees not to help Jews.[71] None of their neighbors came forward to

---

[70] Krzysztof Jasiewicz, *Lista strat ziemiaństwa polskiego 1939–1945* [The Register of the Death Toll of the Polish Landed Nobility] (Warsaw: Pomost-Alfa, 1995), 927, 1136–37; Wierzbicki, *Polacy i Białorusini w zaborze sowieckim* [Poles and Belarussians in the Soviet Occupation Zone], 70–72; Szawłowski, *Wojna polsko-sowiecka 1939* [Polish-Soviet War of 1939] (1995, 1997), vol. 1, 370; Wojciech Wybranowski, "Musieli zginąć, bo byli Polakami" [They Were Poles, So They Had to Die], *Nasz Dziennik*, 4 September 2001; Wojciech Wybranowski, "Są pierwsi świadkowie" [The First Witnesses Have Surfaced], *Nasz Dziennik*, 8-9 September 2001; Wojciech Wybranowski, "Komuniści przyszli nocą" [The Communists Came at Night], *Nasz Dziennik*, 23 September 2001. Zusko Ajzik was reportedly executed by the Germans in June 1941 on the site of the massacre of his victims, the Wołkowickis.
[71] Szymon Datner, *Las Sprawiedliwych* [The Grove of the Righteous] (Warsaw: Książka i Wiedza, 1968), 87, 114; Władysław Bartoszewski and Zofia Lewin, eds., *Righteous Among Nations: How Poles Helped the Jews, 1939–1945* (London: Earlscourt Publications, 1969), 72. Despite negative social phenomena such as looting and pointing Jews out to the Germans, which some Jews also engaged in, there was a great deal of solidarity among Poles toward the Jewish population. The solidarity became less visible as German measures against Jews intensified, especially after the death sentence was imposed for any contact with and help extended to Jews, and fear of *everyone* became pervasive. On Polish solidarity with the Jews see Havi Ben-Sasson, "Polish-Jewish Relations during the Holocaust: A Changing Jewish Viewpoint," in Robert Cherry and Annamaria Orla-Bukowska, eds., *Rethinking Poles and Jews: Troubled Past, Brighter Future* (Lanham, Maryland: Rowman & Littlefield, 2007), 89–

defend the Poles massacred in Brzostowica Mała, even though the risk faced for performing such a deed was negligible, since the massacre was engineered and carried out by the locals.

In the long run, however, more significant than the lack of solidarity with the Polish minority in the Eastern Borderlands in the face of Soviet aggression was the impunity with which the culprits were treated. In some cases, they were even rewarded with plum positions in the "new order." It sent a clear message to the occupied population that

---

97. As that article shows, the initial objective portrayal of Poles in Holocaust accounts later gave way to negative stereotypes. Most Poles were appalled at the treatment the Germans meted out to Jews. General Johannes Blaskowitz, commander of the Eighth German Army during the September 1939 campaign and subsequently Commander-in-Chief of the Eastern Territories, wrote to Field Marshal Walter von Brauchitsch, the Commander-in-Chief of the German Army, in his report of 6 February 1940: "The acts of violence carried out in public against Jews are arousing in religious Poles [literally, "in the Polish population, which is fundamentally pious (or God-fearing)"] not only the deepest disgust but also a great sense of pity for the Jewish population." See Ernst Klee, Willi Dressen, and Volker Reiss, *'Those Were the Days': The Holocaust through the Eyes of the Perpetrators and Bystanders* (London: Hamish Hamilton, 1991), 4; Jeremy Noakes and Geoffrey Pridham eds., *Nazism 1919–1945: A History in Documents and Eyewitness Accounts,* vol. 2: *Foreign Policy, War and Racial Extermination* (New York: Schocken Books, 1988), 939. Similarly, in the Soviet-occupied zone, despite claims to the contrary, cases of Jews—mostly the middle-aged and elderly, but seldom the radicalized youth—warning their grateful Polish neighbors of impending arrests and deportations, intervening on their behalf with Soviet officials, and providing other assistance, sometimes for payment or in gratitude for past favours, were fairly frequent. Grateful Poles made a point of recording hundreds of such acts of kindness, which refutes the supposition that they only noticed negative things about Jews, and that unfavorable comments were merely a projection of this supposed unilateral attitude. For many such examples see Wierzbicki, *Polacy i Żydzi w zaborze sowieckim* [Poles and Jews in the Soviet Occupation Zone], 132–42, and Mark Paul, *Neighbors on the Eve of the Holocaust: Polish-Jewish Relations in Soviet-Occupied Eastern Poland, 1939–1941,* posted online at: www.glaukopis.pl/pdf/czytelnia/NeighborsEveOfTheHolocaust.pdf (footnotes 1138 and 1139). Jewish historians have failed to notice this phenomenon. After citing one example of Jews in Rożyszcze helping to free from an NKVD prison a Pole who had previously helped Jews, Dov Levin states "these cases were few and far between; they must be treated as exceptions in the shaky relations between the Jews and their non-Jewish neighbors." See Levin, *The Lesser of Two Evils,* 62. However, that author made no effort to canvass Polish sources that recorded such help.

those so inclined could act with impunity and benefit from their crimes. These events were thus a prelude to occurrences directly following the German invasion of the area in June 1941, when they were repeated with the players cast in different roles. Although often lethal, as under the Soviet occupation, they were relatively few in relation to the overall numbers of their respective ethnic groups.

The Polish Nationalists:
A Mainly Theoretical Anti-Jewishness

Wojciech Jerzy Muszyński

"Do you know how to define an anti-Semite?" So asked Professor Herbert Romerstein, the Jewish grandson of a Bund activist originally from Mir in the Mińsk region, and later from the Bronx in New York City.

"Well," the elderly expert on Nazi and Soviet propaganda explained to me, "it's a person who hates Jews more than is necessary!"

The professor was satirizing the character and rational motivations of the Polish nationalists' anti-Jewish program in the first half of the twentieth century. The program is a complex case study, and modern attempts to explain it utilizing the currently popular dichotomy of anti-Semitism vs. philo-Semitism have been less than satisfactory.

The usage of the term anti-Semitism in itself, compromised by the Nazi past and the German-perpetrated genocide, with reference to Polish nationalists, automatically paralyzes all discussion and serious scholarly inquiry. It is difficult to resist the impression that the goal here remains to perpetuate the equivalency between the Polish nationalists and the Nazis. Such a stance is indicative of simplistic moralizing, not serious scholarship.

Only if reliable research proved a similarity between the political conceptions of the National Socialist Party and the Polish nationalists, would such a comparison be justified. Moral judgment may only and exclusively be proclaimed on the basis of empirical evidence. Research surely ought to be *sine ira et studio*.

In this sense, and from the cultural point of view, the employment of the word "anti-Semitism" in regard to the *Endecja* (the leading nationalist political party in Poland at the time) is hardly relevant and potentially misleading. Its anti-Jewish stance, and the associated political program, were completely unrelated to the racist anti-Semitism of the German variety.

The current *calque* of "anti-Semitism" constitutes an insult, and a platform to express one's ideological sympathies. It is, simultaneously, a very convenient way to accuse anyone who in his or her research emphasizes the complexity of the historical context that conditioned the relationship of the Polish nationalists towards the Jewish minority. This phenomenon originates in the experience of the mass murders of Jews during the Second World War. Thus, the following question surfaces: following the Holocaust, is it possible to undertake research on such difficult topics as anti-Jewishness? We believe that it certainly is.

The Polish nationalist camp – as a political movement both in the newly independent Poland, and during the Second World War – is assigned the role of the antagonist in literature on Polish-Jewish relations. Leftist and liberal historians apply the rule of group responsibility and accuse nationalists of taking, generally speaking, an immoral stance towards the Jews.

The list of accusations is very long, ranging from condemning the nationalists for their anti-Jewish behavior during the interwar years, through the alleged fomenting of unrest and various riots, which took place during that time, to the assigning of moral (co)culpability for the extermination of the Jews during the German occupation. Among some of the most extreme ones are arguments that conditions created in pre-war Poland later became conducive to the extermination of the Jews by the Germans.[1] Claims are even voiced regarding alleged complicity in the genocide, as well as reaping the benefits thereof.

In this case, it appears that as more time passes since the end of the Second World War, the more so do various intellectual speculations gain in popularity. Proponents of the speculative version of history claim to explain simply and logically the complex problems of the time. On the one hand, this approach is a result of a specific quest for sensational material, guided by the drive to become the first to introduce some sort of a bold and shocking argument. On the other

---

[1] In the newest Polish as well as Western historiography there exists a tendency to view the interwar Polish-Jewish conflict in modern categories, which is lead by certain liberal-minded historians. See e.g.: Ronald Modras, *Kościół katolicki i antysemityzm w Polsce w latach 1933–1939* [The Catholic Church and Anti-Semitism in Poland in 1933-1939] (Kraków: Homini, 2004); Anna Landau-Czajka, *Syn będzie Lech... Asymilacja Żydów w Polsce międzywojennej* [Our Son's Name Shall be Lech: The Assimilation of Jews in Interwar Poland] (Warsaw: Neriton, 2006); Anna Landau-Czajka, *W jednym stali domu... Koncepcja rozwiązania kwestii żydowskiej w publicystyce polskiej lat 1933–1939* [They Stood in One House: The Conceptions of Solving the Jewish Question in Polish Punditry in 1933-1939] (Warsaw: Neriton, 1998). It is worth mentioning that even the accepted periodization can generate reservations. The year 1933, in light of Hitler's rise to office, created a definite caesura for Germans, but not for Poles and the Jews living in Poland.

hand, it is also a product of insufficient historical knowledge and superficial archival research.

However, the scholarly publications of mainly leftist-liberal historians seem to promote a less radical argument, according to which the negative attitude of Poles towards Jews during the Second World War was a result of anti-Jewish rhetoric popularized by the interwar Polish nationalist camp.[2] This negative influence is naturally defined in multiple ways: from reluctance, through an active denial of assistance, to the persecution of Jews, including murder.

To begin with, the question requiring the most consideration is why the Polish nationalist movement remains the only group currently charged with collective guilt for its negative attitude towards Jews before the war? Let us not forget that the Endeks (also known as NDs or *narodowcy*) were not alone in the anti-Jewish rhetoric during the 1930s. It found fertile ground also among various factions of Józef Piłsudski's followers, including the younger *inteligentsia* focused around Jerzy Giedroyć and his publications, *Bunt Młodych* [Revolt of the Youth] and *Polityka* [Politics];[3] among the *milieus* of *Jutro Pracy*

---

[2] Lately, Dr. Piotr Osęka has put forth such moralizing and ahistorical views at the IPN-organized conference "The Nationalist Camp – Facts and Myths" (Warsaw, 27 January 2011). He admitted that it was difficult to establish to what degree the National Democratic (ND) journalism in the 1930s could have influenced Poles to commit crimes against Jews or to collaborate with the Germans in the extermination of the Jews. He also acknowledged that the activists of the nationalist camp did not incite Poles to collaborate with the Germans. In his opinion, the culpability of the NDs did not lie in the fact that they "urged the 'szmalcowniks' on or encouraged the looting of leftover Jewish property," but that there were voices appearing among the NDs that "the Jewish problem in Poland was taken care of with Nazi hands." "Spór o antysemityzm endecji – dyskusja w IPN" [The Controversy over Endek Anti-Semitism: A Discussion at the IPN], *PAP*, 27 January 2011.

[3] One of the more interesting publications of this type was the brochure *Polska idea imperialna* [The Polish Imperial Idea] (Warsaw: 1938), the programmatic text of the *Polityka milieu*. The chapter pertaining to Jews contains many remarks similar in nature to the theses proposed by the SN and ONR, particularly: the fiasco of the assimilation of Jewish masses, as well as their lack of loyalty towards the interests of the Polish state. Included in it was a plan to curb "Jewish influence in Poland": "It is, based on the already mentioned examples, absolutely insufficient to exert commercial pressure on Jews through simple competition. Simple competition ought to be supported by the following set of directives: 1. *Numerus clausus* in higher schools and colleges, as well as the liberal professions. 2. Non-admission of Jews to public positions, especially any managerial ones. 3. The limiting of government contracts to Christian firms. It ought to be mentioned that in a great many of the cases there is a lack of sufficiently responsible Christian businesses, so much so in fact that this policy could only grow in concurrence with Polish domination of the economy. 4. Commercial policies to propel the peasant element, used to minimal expectations, towards commerce and industry and thus the most effective part of successful competition with Jewish businesses. 5. A legally

[Work of Tomorrow] and *Nowa Kadrowa* [The New Cadre]; and the political program of the Camp of National Unity, which ruled the country at the time.[4] Anti-Jewish themes were appearing in the center-right Christian Democratic press and the statements of the peasant-populist People's Party activists on many different levels.

These enunciations did not differ from the propaganda of the NDs, who were divided in their attitudes towards the Jews into moderates and radicals. Therefore, it would be incorrect to claim that Jewish themes equally dominated the headlines of all the prewar publications. When it comes to popular journalism, the modern-day reader would indeed be shocked by the sheer volume of sharply anti-Jewish propaganda. There were, nevertheless, other journals that published such content sporadically. In turn, some other publications effectively toned such messages down. Archival research offers the best illustration of this trend.

Whereas in the *Sztafeta* (journal of the Radical-Nationalist Camp [ONR]) Jews were mentioned often, and portrayed negatively – this was, in fact, one of the periodical's leading themes – while in the weekly *Prosto z Mostu* (Straight Talk or, literally "Right from the Bridge," which had informal links to the ONR *milieu*) it appeared less frequently and was characterized by much less antipathy. The case of the two flagship publications of the Nationalist Party was similar. In the newspaper *Warszawski Dziennik Narodowy* [Warsaw National Daily], the articles pertaining to Jews were incomparably more radical than in the parallel *Myśl Narodowa* [National Thought], a journal intended for the *inteligentsia*.

Even those pre-war pundits known for their sharp wit never crossed the line of condoning violence. While their tempers often flared in the already heated journalistic debates, it was still difficult to find anything

---

sanctioned permit for Christian firms to propagandize a list of these firms; prohibition of anonymous firms disguising Jewish owners; a ban on the changing of names etc. 6. The assignment of all political and commercial offices of importance to the state solely for native-born Poles, because only they can fully guarantee that they will show a high level of care for state interests." See: Rafał Habielski, *Dokąd nam iść wypada! Jerzy Giedroyć. Od „Buntu Młodych" do „Kultury"* [Where We Should Go: Jerzy Giedroyć – From the *Revolt of the Youth* to *Kultura*] (Warsaw: Biblioteka „Więzi," 2006), 182–184.

[4] Jacek Majchrowski, *Silni, zwarci, gotowi. Myśl polityczna Obozu Zjednoczenia Narodowego* [Strong, United, and Ready: The Political Thought of the Camp of National Unity] (Warsaw: PWN, 1985), 126–137.

remotely close to a call for a physical "settlement of scores" with the Jews, not to mention veiled suggestions of pogroms or mass murder.[5]

Comparisons with the Nazis

Nonetheless, certain historians persist in comparing the SN or the ONR with the German Nazis. In fact, a similar argument was employed against them by their political rivals before the war. The nationalists resisted these allegations, although initially Hitler and his National Socialism had not revealed their genocidal character at this point and, therefore, did not awaken equivocally pejorative connotations on the popular level. Thus, Jan Mosdorf, the leader of the Radical-Nationalist Camp, wrote:

> We are neither fascists nor Nazis chiefly because we are a purely Polish movement. We do not need foreign ideals. We do not consider ourselves fascists or Nazis also on account of their many faults, and even sins, which we do not wish to burden ourselves with. These are not models that we wish to emulate.[6]

It is worth remembering that Warsaw never experienced its equivalent, or *Kristallnacht*. This fact should serve to caution against comparing the political conditions in prewar Poland and Nazi Germany. Polish nationalism of the 1930s appeared as an oasis of serenity, not only in contrast to the Third Reich, but also other countries. For example, in Romania during the 1930s, the Iron Guard remained (like the NDs) in sharp and stark opposition to the government. Yet, political warfare was not limited solely to the journals, but fueled bloody unrest and pogroms with the participation of nationalists. Hitler's case notwithstanding, before the outbreak of the Second World War, a disproportionately larger amount of Jews suffered in the Soviet Union, under the rule of Lenin and Stalin, than in the Second Polish Republic, under Piłsudski and Rydz-Śmigły.

But were the NDs really capable of becoming the "allies" of the German National Socialists with regards to the "Jewish Question," as some leftist and liberal historians claim or imply? Could one really postulate such a simple dependence? Is not the conflating of German Nazism and Polish National Democracy an act of abusing and blatantly manipulating the historical facts?

---

[5] Andrzej Friszke, *O kształt niepodległej* [For the Shape of an Independent Poland] (Warsaw: Biblioteka „Więzi," 1989), 314.
[6] *Sztafeta*, 23 May 1934.

The nationalist camp in independent Poland consequentially opposed any political ties to Germany, regardless of its political system. Berlin's politics – seeking to create the necessary conditions to retrieve territories lost at Versailles, mostly at Poland's expense – significantly influenced this behavior.[7] The anti-German stance of the NDs waxed further upon Hitler's ascent to power and Germany's simultaneous resurgence on the international scene. Hitler's leadership cult in the Third Reich astonished the NDs and provoked comparisons with the Soviet regime.[8]

Still, this did not hinder the nationalists' initial interest in the growing dynamics of the NSDAP (Nazi Party) and its social influence. With time, these feelings gave way to apprehension regarding the militarism and imperialist slogans of the Nazis. The relationship was simple: as the significance of Hitler and his Germany grew, so did the criticism and animosity of the Polish nationalist press.[9]

When the outbreak of war in Europe became ultimately unavoidable, Polish nationalists declared themselves *en bloc* on the side of the French and British coalition and against the Germans. Such a choice was endorsed even by those Endeks, who had not disguised their skepticism of the liberal democratic system, which both Allied countries symbolized.

For the NDs, the possibility of an alliance with the Nazi Germans was inconceivable. Let us emphasize that they faced a choice and picked sides consciously, although some did so without much euphoria. They chose, using the language of the nationalist press of the 1930s, an alliance with "Western plutocracy," "the freemasons," "defenders of the Jews," "the rotting democratic-liberal system," and "the moneyed capitalist international."

Simultaneously, they stood against the anti-Communist bloc and the "young nationalist Europe," which – although dominated by Germany – comprised Italy, Hungary, and potentially Spain as well, which, as Catholic nations, were considered friendly to Poland. In April of 1939,

---

[7] This was widely discussed, among others, by Stanisław Kozicki. See: Maciej Marszał, *Włoski faszyzm i niemiecki narodowy socjalizm w poglądach ideologow Narodowej Demokracji 1926–1939* [Italian Fascism and German National Socialism in the Views of the Theorists of National Democracy, 1926-1939] (Łódź: Kolonia Limited, 2001), 79–118.

[8] Krzysztof Kawalec, *Narodowa Demokracja wobec faszyzmu 1922–1939* [National Democracy Vis-a-Vis Fascism, 1922-1939] (Warsaw: PIW, 1989), 187.

[9] Jędrzej Giertych, while reviewing Hermann Rauschning's book, called National Socialism a "movement that attained victory through falsehoods and deception, bringing terror, slavery and lawlessness." See "Rewolucja nihilizmu" [The Revolution of Nihilsm], *Polityka Narodowa*, no. 4–6, April – June 1939.

the SN chief, Kazimierz Kowalski said: "Finding ourselves in a war camp opposed to nationalist Spain or fascist Italy would be a real tragedy for us [...]. I have to conclude nonetheless, that at the present time the German danger is the most important issue. Those who will be fighting the Germans will be our allies, [and] those that will support the Germans will become our enemies."[10]

Contentions of National Democratic (*narodowcy*, or ND) ideological inspiration derived from German anti-Semitism thus appear quite unfounded and are not corroborated by any sources. The anti-Jewishness of the NDs was *sui generis*, having resulted from specific Polish conditions at the time. It was based on anti-Judaism and particular economic issues, as reactions to the weakness or even lack of a Christian middle class. Endek anti-Jewishness was unrelated to German anti-Semitic racism. Therefore, we shall utilize several concrete examples to recreate the interwar discourse in all its complexity. We will return to the war period in the latter section of this work. The relationship of the NDs to Nazism is illustrated succinctly by a quote from Jędrzej Giertych, one of the chief ideologues of the ND movement during the 1930s: "I would not be a Nazi, even if I were German."[11]

It is true that the nationalists molded anti-Jewish sentiment into powerful propaganda slogans. Nevertheless, this did not mean that by adopting a negative stance towards Jews they endeavored to copy German models. German National Socialism and Polish nationalism were separated by a veritable ideological fissure. The fact that both movements, in a seemingly comparable fashion, related negatively towards the Jews does not constitute proof of ideological kinship.

The NDs, who adhered to the notion that the nation represents a spiritual link fashioned by common history and tradition, categorically rejected the Nazi definition of the "union of blood and race." The latter they condemned as a materialistic interpretation alien to the Polish

---

[10] Kazimierz Kowalski, *Polska wobec Niemiec (Przemówienie Kazimierza Kowalskiego, prezesa Zarz[ądu] Gł[ównego] Str[onnictwa] Nar[odowego] wygłoszone na zjeździe działaczy politycznych Stronnictwa Narodowego w dniu 30 IV 1939 w Warszawie)* [Poland Vis-a-Vis Germany: A speech by Kazimierz Kowalski, the Chairman of the Main Board of the Nationalist Party given at the conference of SN political activists on 30 April 1939] (Warsaw: 1939), 13–14.

[11] Jędrzej Giertych, *Kajakiem po Niemczech. Listy z podróży* [Traveling Through Germany on a Kayak: Letters from a Trip] (Pelplin: 1937), 87. Giertych outlined his opinion of Nazism in a different book: "When I speak with a Nazi, a fascist, [...] I feel like I'm speaking with a person completely alien to me, a world view that indicates many similarities, but nonetheless as a whole, a worldview that is not mine". See Jędrzej Giertych, *Hiszpania bohaterska* [Heroic Spain] (Warsaw: 1937), 157.

spirit. "We are not racists – wrote Jędrzej Giertych in his book *O wyjście z kryzysu* [To Overcome the Crisis] in 1938 – [for] we believe that belonging to a nation is, above all, a spiritual fact [...]. We will never follow the intellectual roads that lead away from Catholic doctrine (such as Nazism)." Therefore, to recapitulate the ideological stance of the NDs towards Jews, one can firmly state that while anti-Jewishness was accepted and even propagated as a political, cultural, and economic (albeit not religious) stance, the Endeks never embraced anti-Semitism in its current, racist-exterminationist meaning and context.[12]

The Moderating Influence of Christianity

The elements that restrained the NDs from attempting to emulate Nazism were the visible anti-Christian and neo-pagan motives driving National Socialism, coupled with an invocation of mythology and old Gothic beliefs, all in a quite shoddy package.[13] Pundits associated with the nationalist Polish press remarked that Nazism constituted, in and of itself, a new type of German religion.[14] Meanwhile, the ideological *credo* of Polish nationalists was a linking of nationalism with Catholicism, encapsulated in a statement written by Dmowski: "Catholicism is not an addition to Polishness or a type of coloring, but

---

[12] Zygmunt Zieliński, *Polska dwudziestego wieku. Kościół – Naród – mniejszości* [Twentieth-Century Poland: The Church, the Nation, and the Minorities] (Lublin: KUL, 1998), 89. Prewar journalism demonstrated the nationalist use of "anti-Semitism" to refer to the relationship with the Jews, but this did not embody the racist context of today. See: Jan Dobraczyński, „Obowiązek antysemityzmu" [The Duty of Anti-Semitism], *Myśl Narodowa* 6 (1938); Fr. F. Błotnicki, „Chrześcijaństwo i antysemityzm" [Christianity and Anti-Semitism], *Myśl Narodowa* 9 (1937).
[13] See e.g.: M. Pawlikowski, „Nacjonalizm i katolicyzm" [Nationalism and Catholicism], *Głos* 1 (12 January 1936); "Hitler, Żydzi i katolicyzm" [Hitler, the Jews, and Catholicism], *Warszawski Dziennik Narodowy* 66 (1 August 1935); "Różnice i zbieżności" [Similarities and Differences], *Ibid.* 23 (24 January 1936); "Obóz narodowy w Polsce nie naśladuje hitleryzmu" [The Nationalist Camp in Poland is not Emulating Hitlerism], *Polska Narodowa* 2 (20 November 1936).
[14] Karol Stojanowski, *Genoteizm a przyszłość katolicyzmu w Polsce* [Genotheism and the Future of Catholicism in Poland], *Myśl Narodowa* 5 (2 February 1936); *Ibid.*, *Rasizm i genoteizm a przyszłość katolicyzmu w Polsce* [Racism and Genotheism and the Future of Genotheism in Poland], *Myśl Narodowa* 6 (9 February 1936). Compare: Bogumił Grott, *Nacjonalizm chrześcijański, Narodowo-katolicka formacja ideowa w II Rzeczypospolitej na tle porównawczym* [Christian Nationalism: The Catholic Nationalist Ideological Formation in Interwar Poland, A Comparative View] (Kraków: Ostoja, 1996), 25–32.

resides in its essence, and in a great measure constitutes its core."[15] Hence, especially following the publication of the 1937 encyclical of Pope Pius XI, *Mit brennender Sorge* (German: With Burning Anxiety), which condemned National Socialism and German policies under Hitler, the Endecja expressed no interest in racist conceptions based on the German model.[16]

Let us underscore that, regardless of the nationalists' perceptions of Catholicism in political categories, i.e. as a great universalistic idea consolidating the Polish nation, the nationalists were also ardently religious in their private lives:

> We are Catholics not only because Poland is Catholic, because even if it were Muslim, truth would never cease being truth, only access to it would be harder and more painful to attain. We are Catholics not only because Catholic doctrine manages hardships and [Catholic] discipline manages conflicts better, not because we are impressed by the hierarchical organization of the church (which has been victorious for centuries), and neither finally due to the Church safeguarding and passing on the legacy of everything in classical civilization that had been good and untainted, but because we believe that the Church has been founded by God himself.[17]

Such an approach had indubitable consequences during the war, and became part of the distance and reluctance defining the attitude of the Catholic NDs (*katoendecy*, as Jan Tomasz Gross prefers to derisively label them)[18] toward German anti-Semitic propaganda.

---

[15] Roman Dmowski, *Kościół, naród i państwo* [Church, Nation, and State] (Warsaw: 1927), 9.

[16] Bogumił Grott, *Katolicyzm w doktrynach ugrupowań narodowo-radykalnych do roku 1939* [Catholicism in the Doctrines of Radical-Nationalist Groups Up to 1939] (Kraków: Nakład Uniw. Jagiellońskiego, 1987), 97–104; idem, *Religia, Kościół, etyka w ideach i koncepcjach prawicy polskiej. Narodowa Demokracja*, (Kraków: Nomos, 1993).

[17] Jan Mosdorf, *Wczoraj i Jutro* [Yesterday and Tomorrow] (Biała Podlaska: ARTE, 2005), 170.

[18] Jan Tomasz Gross states: "by utilizing the term »Catho-NDs«, I think about attitudes, about the worldview. The Catholic Church did not affirm ND-ism in itself, but the prewar Church hierarchy for the most part was rather easily influenced by the NDs. The NDs are thus both a political as well as an intellectual unit. In the eyes of many Poles this was the reification of the national interest. Strengthened by nationalism and anti-Semitism, it was a terribly destructive force." "Dyskusja redakcyjna Żydzi, Polacy i „Katoendecja" [Editorial Discussion on Jews, Poles, and 'Catho-NDism'], *Mówią Wieki*, 8 April 2008. The American sociologist did not, however, share with his readers his reflections on what constituted this "destructiveness" of the NDs, since he had not done any research in that area – instead, he finds it comfortable to repeat well-worn arguments based on stereotypes.

The Sources of ND Anti-Jewishness

Polish nationalists always enjoyed pointing out that their anti-Jewish program was born long before anyone ever heard of Nazism. For them, the Jewish issue was not at the center of their political thought, but was instead considered from a practical perspective. Before the outbreak of the Second World War, there were 3.5 million Jews on Polish soil. This was therefore a numerical concern, not one of irrational hatred, eugenic prejudice, or fictitious "purity and unity of race."

One can thus conclude that NDs were not anti-Semites because they were not guided by irrational racist prejudice, even though some considered such an irrational attitude scientific, modern, and progressive at the time. They were anti-Jewish because they understood the position as pragmatically necessary to realize their vision of state modernization: Poland as a nation-state, functioning along the Western European model, with a strong middle class, modernized agriculture, and upward social mobility for members of the lower classes.[19]

In the writings of Roman Dmowski and his camp, in contrast to Nazi punditry in Germany, the generic Jew was not presented as an inhuman parasite, but as a human being like any "true Pole." The only difference was that the NDs treated the Jew as an unwelcome guest, an economic competitor, and a political opponent.[20] Hence, the demand for forced or voluntary emigration, as well as declarations of support for an independent Jewish state. The methods that were used against Jews by the Germans left the NDs outraged long before the Holocaust: "None of us will laud the perpetration of crimes against anyone. That means against Jews as well."[21]

The NDs were not concerned about nursing racial prejudice but, rather, about persuasively justifying their political and economic aims, which were rational from their point of view.[22] The main goal was to

---

[19] It was economic issues that would constitute the dominating motif of anti-Jewish nationalist action in the 1930s. See Andrzej Friszke, *O kształt niepodległej*, 309.
[20] Michał Andrzejczak, *Faszyzm włoski i hitleryzm w publicystyce Romana Dmowskiego w latach 1922–1939* [Italian Fascism and Hitlerism in Roman Dmowski's Writings, 1922-1939] (Wrocław: Nortom, 2010), 164 (footnote 139); Mieczysław Sobczak, *Stosunek Narodowej Demokracji do kwestii żydowskiej w Polsce w latach 1918–1939* [The Attitude of National Democracy to the Jewish Question in Poland, 1918-1939] (Wrocław: Wyd. Uniw. Ekonomicznego we Wrocławiu, 1998), 415.
[21] *Orędownik* 76 (1 April 1933).
[22] A. Friszke, *O kształt Niepodległej* [For the Shape of an Independent Poland], 309–310. The author stated that the 1930s saw a growth of "ideological anti-Semitism" among nationalists leading to a "Judeocentrism," i.e. a lens through which all political,

build the foundations of an economic boycott, which constituted an element of the struggle to create a Polish middle class focused on craftsmanship as well as medium and light commerce. The aim was thus to regain influence in Jewish-minority-dominated sectors of the economy, and to open more jobs for Poles, especially those leaving the overpopulated villages. The presence of the Jewish Diaspora, numbering over 3.5 million people, obviously interfered with these plans.

Eventually, the problem of what the NDs saw as insufficient Polish representation in the liberal professions arose and contributed to the arsenal of nationalist slogans. Polish lawyers, engineers, and doctors that were educated during the 1930s were to become the new intellectual elite of society. They were to push their Jewish competitors out of the market. The limiting of Jewish admission to Polish universities (*numerus clausus*) was to further this end. The institutions of higher learning – according to the nationalists – were intended to chiefly educate the Christian youth.

It is worth adding that these types of restrictions were not only a Polish specialty and comprised a disgraceful tactic even in countries commonly considered democratic.[23] Admittedly, during the mid-1930s

---

economic and cultural factors were considered primarily on the basis of competition with Jews. This opinion appears to be true only in the economic context. It was not the goal of nationalists to create an artificial, abstract ideology, but rather to implement the first economic postulate by all means available: a marginalization of the positions of Jews in commerce. Such was the primary goal of propagating the most prominent anti-Jewish papers at the time, such as Henryk Rolicki (Tadeusz Gluziński), *Zmierzch Izraela* [The End of Israel], (Warsaw: 1934); Jędrzej Giertych, *Tragizm losów Polski* [The Tragic Nature of Poland's Fate] (Pelplin: n.p., 1936); Fr. Stanisław Trzeciak, *Program światowej polityki żydowskiej (konspiracja i dekonspiracja)* [The Program of Jewish World Politics (The Conspiracy Unveiled)] (Warsaw: n.p.,1936); Stanisław Tworkowski, *Polska bez Żydów* [Poland Without Jews] (Warsaw: n.p., 1939); as well as a series of similar, less popular brochures and books. To further this type of propaganda the notorius brochure, *The Protocols of the Elders of Zion*, was also used. It was republished several times during the 1920s and 1930s, and its publishers vouched for its authenticity.

[23] *Numerus clausus* (Lat. Fixed number) – this restriction was applied in many European countries, such as: Hungary (where it was passed in the early 1920), Austria, the Baltic states (Estonia, Latvia, Lithuania), Czechoslovakia, Germany, Holland, Rumania, Britain, and Yugoslavia. See: Peter Tibor Nagy, "The Numerus Clausus in Inter-War Hungary: Pioneering European Antisemitism," *East European Jewish Affairs* 35, no. 1 (2005): 13–22. Between 1932 and 1938 the number of Jews attending the University of Kaunas dropped from 26.5 to 14.7%. Jewish students were forced to sit in different seats in lecture halls, and the total number decreased from 1,206 students in 1932 to 500 in 1939. Polish interwar restrictions, added unofficially as internal house rules, lasted for barely a decade, and therefore an incomparably shorter amount of time

the most radical nationalists pitched the slogan of *numerus nullus* – a complete ban on Jewish university students in Poland – but it was obvious that this idea was from its inception a utopian one.[24] Today one may bemoan that similar events took place. Such laws are generally considered unacceptable. Even so, in the majority of Polish universities, the proportion of Jewish students was never reduced to their percentage of the country's population.

Biological racism never gained much popularity in the Polish context. For the Polish nationalist, even the radical nationalist, there was no problem in accepting as a compatriot an individual with a Jewish, German, Russian, or any other background – so long as they willingly and consciously declared their accession to Polishness (*polskość*), and even more so if they supported the worldview of the NDs. According to Professor Wincenty Lutosławski, a philosopher connected to the NDs and a friend of Roman Dmowski, the decisive factor of belonging to the Polish nation was the spiritual connection with the community and the embracing of common goals.

Even language was a lesser priority, whereas ethnicity was entirely insignificant: "The Polish nation comprises Polonized Germans, Tatars, Armenians, Roma, and Jews, provided that they live for the common ideal of Poland. [...] A black man or an American Indian can also become a true Pole, if he accepts the spiritual heritage of the Polish nation contained in its literature, art, politics, [and] customs, and if he possesses a steadfast will to contribute to the development of the Poles' national being."[25]

Many such individuals could be found among the nationalists, including the leaders and theorists, if only to mention a few. Stanisław Piasecki, who was of Jewish origin, was one of the leading nationalist journalists during the 1930s. During the war, he helped organize the nationalist underground and was murdered by the Nazis in Palmiry in

---

than those for Jews, Blacks, Catholics and other "undesirables" in many universities in the US (Harvard, Yale, Columbia, Cornell) and Canada (McGill, University of Toronto, University of Manitoba). See Leonard Dinnerstein, *Anti-Semitism in America* (New York: Oxford University Press, 1994); Jerome Karabel, *The Chosen: The Hidden History of Admission and Exclusion at Harvard, Yale and Princeton* (Boston: Mariner, 2005). The policy of restricting the rights of blacks and other minorities to obtain education in the US continued until the 1960s.

[24] „Rezultaty walki młodzieży akademickiej o Numerus Nullus na uniwersytecie" [The Results of the University Youth's Struggle for the Numerus Clausus], *Wszechpolak*, 16 October 1938, vol. 21. The article was labeled: "Numerus Nullus – a new stage of war."

[25] Wincenty Lutosławski, *Posłannictwo polskiego narodu* [The Mission of the Polish Nation] (Warsaw: Rój, 1939), 23–24.

1941. Stanisław Stroński had a similar ethnic background. Similarly, Jan Mosdorf, Henryk Rossman, and many other activists of the ONR or the All-Polish Youth (*Młodzież Wszechpolska*), were descended from Polonized ethnically-German townspeople.

One could also find representatives of all ethnic groups among the nationalists, which pointed to the multicultural and collective tradition of the First Republic/Polish-Lithuanian Commonwealth, beginning with Tatars, Karaim Jews, and Armenians, and ending with Poleshuks and Ruthenians. If any of them wanted to become Poles, the nationalists would accept them without reservations.[26] The possibility of forced Polonization of national minorities was firmly rejected: "We abhor such methods, we weren't reared in Berlin."[27] Nor did the Endeks ever attempt to verify anyone's Polishness through genealogical research, with the aim of establishing the percentage of "pure Polish blood."

Meanwhile, this became an existential problem for many German citizens at the time. After the introduction of the Nuremberg laws in 1935, some Germans began to discover with horror that, for example, due to the "non-Aryan" origin of a grandfather they became second-class citizens. These were real human tragedies. In the case of German National Socialists, the acceptance of, for instance, a long Germanized Jew as a compatriot was impossible. For this reason alone the conflating of German Nazi and Polish nationalist political thought appears intellectually dishonest and even abusive. In fact, it may be considered libel.

Furthermore, the German version of biological racism, complete with its apotheosis of the "Germanic spirit" and the pseudoscientific research on Germanic racial superiority (*Herrenvolk*), was considered by the Polish nationalists not only as an intellectually primitive conception, but a seriously flawed one from the perspective of science as well. Professor Karol Stojanowski, a lecturer at the University of Poznań and a distinguished activist of the National Party, criticized Nazi theories from the anthropological point of view.[28] He argued that

---

[26] This corresponds with the opinion held by professor Zygmunt Zieliński (KUL), according to whom the deeper the assimilation of Jews, the less they sensed anti-Jewish sentiment. Zygmunt Zieliński, *Polska dwudziestego wieku* [Twentieth-Century Poland], 88.

[27] Cited in: Jacek Majchrowski, *Szkice z historii polskiej prawicy politycznej lat Drugiej Rzeczypospolitej* [An Outline of the History of the Polish Political Right During the Second Republic] (Kraków: Nakładem Uniw. Jagiellońskiego, 1986), 60.

[28] Marszał, *Włoski faszyzm i niemiecki*, 174–209; Albert S. Kotowski, *Narodowa demokracja wobec nazizmu i Trzeciej Rzeszy* [National Democracy Vis-a-Vis Nazism

the ideological racism of the NSDAP, regardless of its anti-Semitic dimension, was also characterized by an anti-Slavism already deeply rooted in the German mentality. All of this, including German national chauvinism, led to – in his opinion – a dangerous political phenomenon that transformed National Socialist Germany into a direct threat for its eastern neighbors, especially Poland.[29] This could have constituted another possible reason why the Endek press and political brochures simply did not utilize racist arguments against the Jews.

The Holocaust

The ultimate test for the Polish nationalists' stance towards the Nazis, their ideology, as well as the Jews, took place during the Second World War, during the German and Soviet occupations. An archival query undertaken by myself furnished a large amount of material, some of which I utilized in several articles and essays. The underground nationalist press was essentially the only source permitting one to follow how the nationalist position was shaped within a changing environment. This allows the scholar to verify whether the nationalists accepted the German anti-Semitic rhetoric to any degree, and finally, to gauge their attitude towards the extermination of Jews.

On the basis of the results of this query it is possible to conclude that, in comparison with the prewar period, the Jewish topic was much less present in the periodicals of the underground nationalist movement. The nationalists did not, however, cease taking an interest in the topic in the new socio-political conditions. Rather, it seems that they focused more on Polish issues, although this is not a rule. From the outset of the Nazi occupation, the Polish nationalists declared in their underground publications that they will not watch the German persecution of the Jewish populace with approval. Moreover, they made clear that the occupier would not obtain any assistance from them in repressing the Jews.

---

and the Third Reich] (Toruń: Adam Marszałek, 2006), 52–53; Piotr Grabowiec, „Działalność naukowa i polityczna Karola Stojanowskiego" [Karol Stojanowski's Scholarly and Political Activism] in Tomasz Sikorski and Adam Wątor, eds., *Narodowa Demokracja XIX–XXI wiek* [National Democracy From the Nineteenth to the Twenty-First Century] (Szczecin: Wydział Humanistycznego Uniwersytetu Szczecińskiego, 2008), 647–662.
[29] Karol Stojanowski, *Teorie nordyczne jako parawan imperializmu niemieckiego* [Nordic Theories as a Veil Disguising German Imperialism] (Poznań: n.p., 1932); *Ibid.*, Rasizm przeciw Słowiańszczyźnie [Racism Against Slavdom] (Poznań: n.p., 1934).

This approach to the "Jewish Question" was expressed in the nationalist press for the entire duration of the German occupation. One of the first testimonies to this effect was an informational piece in the weekly *Szaniec* [Rampart], an underground ONR publication, which discussed the unrest in Warsaw before Easter of 1940:

> Beginning with 26 March of this year, the occupiers are staging pogroms of Jews in Warsaw. Pogroms on a wider scale took place in the bazaars on the streets Stalowa, Ząbkowska, Hale Mirowskie, Krochmalna, at Kercel Square, and in the Old Town. Individual Jewish shops and apartments were looted in the entire city. The template was visible everywhere: the street rabble were transported in trucks to the place of the pogrom, where, under the direction of the *Volksdeutsche*, the ruffians began their dirty work in the presence of the police and German gendarmerie. The gendarmes on the street carefully dressed the injuries of the beaten and bleeding Jews. After filming the whole scene, the gangs were ushered back into cars and driven to further jobs.[30]

In this case, the nationalist press was most likely the first to unveil the German provocations – known as the "Easter Pogrom" in current historiography – but also stated that only the "street rabble" can participate in attacks on Jews organized by the enemy. It was widely believed, although rarely noted in writing, that Polish-Jewish relations were an internal Polish problem, and no help was desired from the occupier in its solution.

An announcement published by *Szaniec* a year later, on the subject of the German efforts to recruit Poles as guards in labor camps for Jews, provides testimony of this. The radical-nationalist periodical warned that any Polish participation in this initiative, as well as all help offered to the occupier in creating this formation (camp guards) would be considered treason.[31] That meant the death penalty.

From late 1941, the nationalist press, which often reported cases of German crimes, began to dedicate more space to the deportation and executions affecting the Jewish population.[32] Most of this information appeared in 1942, the apogee of the German extermination campaign, which began with the liquidation of ghettos in smaller towns. One of the most characteristic examples was the report from Lublin:

---

[30] *Szaniec*, no. 15, 9 April 1940.
[31] *Ibid.*, no. 8 (57), 1–15 March 1941.
[32] *Ibid.*, no. 4, 15 February 1942.

At the beginning of April, the Germans completely destroyed the ghetto. There were most recently around 45,000 Jews living in Lublin. With the help of Bolshevik volunteer regiments (former POWs), they murdered around 1,000 including women and children, while 5,000 were forcibly moved to the Majdan Tatarski suburb [...]. The rest were taken in unknown directions to the Eastern Borderlands. [...] About 3,000 were taken to Trawniki and placed in the hall of a defunct sugar factory. A couple of days later about 2,000 bodies were withdrawn and transported by train, presumably Jews poisoned by testing new weaponized gases.[33]

This was most likely the first underground publication informing of mass killings through the use of toxic gases.

Supplementing these reports of war crimes were statistical data to inform the reader about the scale of German genocide: "In 1940, the number of Jews living in Warsaw amounted to 460,000, but on 22 July 1942 it was around 400,000. This decrease is explained by the high death toll. Until 10 September [1942], about 250,000 were to be deported. Transports were usually to Treblinka. A series of local ghettos had been liquidated [...]. Generally, the number of Jews in the General Government, which had once been around 2 million, now fell to 1 million and 100 thousand."[34] The source of these statistics is difficult to establish but they appear to have nonetheless mirrored reality quite accurately.

Information about the fate of Jews in the German death camps was provided on multiple occasions: "Jews are deported to Majdanek in freight trains, *en masse* and on a daily basis. Only a small number of Jews managed to escape the transports. Jews are very well aware of what awaits them in the camps, but it is only a few that would prefer death at the hands of a guard rather than in a gas chamber."[35] The greatest death factory – KL Auschwitz – was not, by any means, forgotten: "In Oświęcim (Ger. *Auschwitz*), a branch of the Berlin Institute of Hygiene was installed in Block No. 10, where experiments are undertaken in the areas of castration, sterilization, and artificial insemination on 200 Jewish men and 25 Jewish women."[36]

Information on the annihilation of Jews was published mainly in concise form by mentioning facts and the number of victims. These were plentiful. For example, in *Szaniec* they constituted around 40 percent of the general information and references pertaining to Jews.

---

[33] *Ibid.*, no. 9 (83), 1 May 1942.
[34] *Na Zachodnim Szańcu* [On the Western Rampart], no. 5, 27 September 1942.
[35] *Polska Informacja Prasowa* [Polish Press Information], 14 May 1943.
[36] *Wielka Polska* [Great Poland], 19 June 1943.

There was no differentiation between suffering of Jews and that of Poles. Based on the cited examples one can confirm that the editors of Polish nationalist publications did not attempt to conceal the truth about the Holocaust. Rather, they were one of the first sources to inform Poles about the situation.

In spite of old anti-Jewish animosities, the rule of national egoism was not applied in this case. Such an approach would dictate that the underground press limit itself to the dissemination of information on specific issues concerning Poles exclusively, and, consequently, ambivalence towards Jewish suffering. Such a stance could have been easily justified *post facto*, by claiming, e.g., ignorance of Jewish extermination or the limited capacity of underground publications, or even the constant threat of exposure and the certain deaths of editors, printers, and distributors. Such was not the case, however. Thus, it cannot be alleged that the NDs were indifferent towards the Jewish tragedy, or satisfied with the developments. Accusations of this type, in light of the presented research, appear quite dishonest.

The tragedy of the Jewish community had a great influence on the nationalists. It is worth returning to the question whether the German racist ideology and anti-Semitic propaganda resonated with them. As demonstrated above, the underground press attempted to expose the methods utilized in 1940 by the occupying forces to awaken anti-Jewish hatred among the Polish population.

Another similar example was the pamphlet ironically entitled "Defenders of Christianity": "During the period of liquidating the smaller ghettoes in the Łódź region, the Germans always implemented the following ceremony: Jews were locked for two days in the local church, and after their deportation the defiled church was left wide open for the Polish population to see."[37] German anti-Semitism was regularly discredited and derided in all possible ways: "The methods of the German war against Jews are so revolting, that the Polish language lacks the words to stigmatize them. We are not responsible for the massacres of Jewish populations, and as much we would like to, we are unable to halt them."[38]

The radical opposition of the national press was caused by the criminal methods used by Germans against the Jews during the so-called Great Expulsion from the Warsaw Ghetto in 1942: "Let there be no doubt, for we must proclaim that the methods chosen by the Germans against the Jews are not only alien to us, but disgusting. They

---

[37] *Szaniec*, 16 January 1943.
[38] *Wielka Polska*, no. 11, 27 September 1942.

are irreconcilable with our conception of humanity, with our Catholic teachings, and our national tradition. In no possible manner would we even be capable of imitating the German methods, regardless of whom they affect. Neither would we apply such methods to the Jews."[39]

German war crimes were universally condemned, but the nationalist mindset still contained certain prewar anti-Jewish stereotypes. Nonetheless, they no longer exerted an influence on the moral evaluation of the Holocaust, which the nationalists did not justify, appreciate, or laud in any way: "Jews ought to be perceived with all requisite objectivity: one can – and must – see in them an enemy of our culture, our economic independence, our fully sovereign life – but at the same time, feel sympathy for the defenseless being suffocated in the gas chambers of Treblinka, bestially murdered by their coreligionists, and later the Ukrainians or Latvians."[40]

The opposition to the German genocide was accompanied by a condemnation of the participating collaborators. This concerned the foreign volunteer units in the German service, i.e. certain particularly zealous groups of mass-murderers comprised of Latvians, Ukrainians, and Lithuanians. The latter group was charged with shamelessly participating in the butchery that consumed the Jews in Lithuania, namely Kaunas and Wilno/Vilnius. The participation of the auxiliary Lithuanian units in persecuting the Poles had also not been forgotten:[41]

> Partisan Lithuanian bands [which were later transformed into police battalions] recruited from ex-Lithuanian military personnel in the Red Army, while chanting the slogan of combating Bolshevism, would attack local towns, pillage, and cut down Jews indiscriminately, or shoot them under the pretext of collaboration with Bolsheviks and local urban civil organizations (Poles). [...] At the present time, and according to verified data, the Kaunas and Wilno regions saw their Jewish populace completely annihilated. Not only are the men executed (shot) in groups, but also women, the elderly, and children. These operations are handled by Lithuanian military personnel with officers at the helm, while representatives of German forces take photos and make films. After the quick removal of Wilno Jews to the ghetto, which proved unable to accommodate such a number of people (over 50,000), everything except the belongings they were able to carry was confiscated, including baggage and transported belongings. In the course of a month, it became a recurring daily task to take a couple hundred people from the ghetto to the Ponary Hills and shoot them there. The Jewish populace in Vilnius is

---

[39] *Informator Narodowy* [The National Informer], 11 August 1942.
[40] *Walka* [Struggle], no. 19, 25 May 1944.
[41] *Polak* [The Pole], no. 3, 15 October 1942.

systematically extirpated; there will probably be only a small amount of specialists that will be permitted to work in the German army supply chain. Presently, there are barely 12,000 Jews left.[42]

Nationalists also watched with disgust the activities of the voluntary *Jüdischer Ordnungsdienst* (Jewish Ghetto Police), which not only helped the Germans keep order in the ghettos, but also persecuted residents and, in its last phase, helped organize the mass deportations to the death camps. Such acts were thus characterized: "[...] in the first phase, Germans did not occupy themselves directly with 'annihilation.' They were relieved by the so-called Jewish Police, whose numbers grew rapidly ... It uncovered, for example, hideouts that Germans would have never found!" The editorial section commented: "every one of us Poles believed that the behavior of the Jewish Police was characteristic of not only the 'police mindset,' but put simply – of the Jewish mindset."[43]

The Jewish collaborators of the police and the Gestapo were described with even greater animosity and contempt for denouncing their compatriots hiding "on the Aryan side," as well as Poles who assisted the escapees.[44] Here is an example from the countryside, as depicted in the underground press:

---

[42] *Szaniec*, no. 4 (78), 15 February 1942.

[43] *Walka*, no. 29, 31 July 1943.

[44] In February of 1944, Germans arrested a group of soldiers of the National Military Organization – Home Army as well as members of the All-Polish Youth in Warsaw. All of them were soon shot in Pawiak. The tragedy was caused by two Jewish female informants, agents of the Gestapo, who received help from the underground movement and managed to escape from the ghetto. Among the murdered was Zdzisław Chrzanowski, the younger brother of Professor Wiesław Chrzanowski. See: Wojciech Jerzy Muszyński and Jolanta Mysiakowska-Muszyńska, eds., *Lista strat działaczy obozu narodowego w latach 1939–1955. Słownik biograficzny* [A List of Losses Suffered by the Nationalist Camp in 1939-1955: A Biographical Dictionary], Vol. 1 (Warsaw: IPN, 2010). This was not an isolated incident, as proven by the following Home Army report from 1943: "Warsaw is being plagued by a group of Jewish blackmailers that are terrorizing rich Jews who are in hiding. For not informing the Gestapo, they demand significant sums of money. Members of this band claim that they are dedicating the money to helping poor Jews. The head of the band is some Jewish doctor. This gang also uses Aryan help. [...] The Germans utilize secret Jewish agents to persecute Jews, as well as find locally hidden individuals – many of these agents prowl particularly in the Kraków region. There have been a significant number of these agents on the loose in the Warsaw area, who work for the Gestapo at the risk of their life. Aside from searching for Polish organizations, particularly leftist ones as mentioned in this paper, their main objective is to find hidden Jewry and people of Jewish origin with the goal of handing them over to Germans." AAN file 228/17-8, p. 77.

On 3 March a strong unit of SS and gendarmerie encircled the village Zarzetka in Węgrów County. At the head of the invading Germans walked the well-known Jewish Communist, Rubin from Wołomin, who, after having escaped from the liquidation of the ghetto, hid in the region and often found help and safety in Zarzetka. The Jew Rubin fingered each person that hosted and helped Jews. From the indicated ones, 40 were shot on the spot and 140 arrested and deported. All livestock and food was taken, and the village burnt to the ground.[45]

It is worth considering whether the publication of such pieces of information exerted a negative impact on assistance provided to the Jews in general. It might possibly have had such an effect, although we should avoid overly exaggerating it. Those who provided aid helped, as a general rule, those whom they knew – their friends, or individuals which had been referred to them by their families or even acquaintances – thus, they did not have to fear treachery on the part of their guests. One should also remember that such incidents became the stuff of gossip in the countryside. Rather predictably, facts became overinflated or transformed entirely, thereby instilling fear. In critical situations these could definitely contribute to the refusal to assist a person in need.

Such information, published by the underground press, which the people under occupation trusted and regarded highly, was intended not only to contradict false gossip and its rationale. It also constituted a type of warning for the readers against underestimating strangers and their use in German entrapment operations. Furthermore, the main responsibility of the underground publishers was to warn the population against the occupiers' anti-Polish actions and their horrifying *modus operandi*. This included the truly diabolical ruse of employing Jewish agents against Polish benefactors.

In addition, the nationalist underground press also stigmatized ethnic Poles who blackmailed Jews, demanding a ransom for silence in the form of money or valuables. The nationalists similarly condemned informers who denounced Poles affiliated with the underground resistance. From the moral point of view, it was completely irrelevant whether the blackmailers and informers were ethnic Poles or members of a minority. Cases of *szmalcownictwo* (blackmail) and denunciations were regarded as a social pathology worse than the plague of

---

[45] *Walka*, no. 13, 7 March [sic! April] 1943.

alcoholism or prostitution.[46] The exploitation of the tragedy of human beings living in constant fear of death was treated not only as dishonorable, but also as behavior unbecoming of a Pole and Catholic.

An analysis of Polish nationalist underground publications indicates that the nationalists employed a dualistic approach towards Jews. On the one hand, they were concerned with concrete matters: German war crimes, the Holocaust, and sympathy for those being murdered in camps and ghettos. On the other hand, they addressed abstract matters as well.

Thus, there appeared essays outlining the attitude towards the activities of Jewish leaders in the United States and Great Britain, exaggerating the alleged influence of freemasonry and the "Jewish International," their anti-Polish attitude and ties to communism. Nationalist rhetoric displayed continuities with the prewar era in other ways as well, for they emphasized that "the Jews" adhered to their own distinctive political goals and national aims, which included separating themselves off from Polishness and resisting the process of assimilation, with only very few exceptions. Thus, according to the nationalists, the only possible and beneficial way for Poland to diffuse this Polish-Jewish conflict of interests would be a complete, or almost complete removal of this minority from Polish soil. However, they emphasized that this would be accomplished only after the victorious end to the war. The destination of such a well-planned mass exodus would have been the biblical homeland of the Jews: Palestine, or what would become Israel.[47]

Another argument for Jewish emigration was a supposed indifference towards Polish affairs, both before and during the war. Such statements appeared in the press after the wave of Jewish desertion from the ranks of the Polish Armed Forces in the West in early 1944. The editors, in a series of articles, vented their discontent. Desertion was considered cowardice and a further example of Jewish disloyalty to Poland, especially at a moment when the greatest collective effort was required in the struggle for freedom.

---

[46] "Regardless of whether the thieves and snitches are Poles, Belarusians, Jews, or Lithuanians, they will all be equally and mercilessly persecuted." *Aktualne wiadomości z Polski i ze świata* [Current News From Poland and the World], vol. 33, 3 September 1943. For more on blackmailers see: *Praca i Walka* [Work and Combat], no. 6 (23), 15 March 1944.

[47] "Wytyczne programowe ruchu narodowego w Polsce (program Stronnictwa Narodowego" [Guidelines for the Nationalist Movement in Poland (Political Program of the Nationalist Party)], 1945.

The editors were further aggravated as a result of the publicity attracted by the incident, the lenient verdicts of the Polish military tribunal, followed by an almost immediate amnesty for the defendants, as well as the fact that the Polish government was compelled to explain itself before Western public opinion.

One of the main reasons behind mentioning the movement's political distance towards the Jews was a conviction of the latter's particularly close relations with the Communist movement. This position, present in the ND publications of the 1920s and 1930s, entrenched itself further following the experience of the Soviet occupation in the Eastern Borderlands in 1939-1941.

And while it seems that collaboration was the work of a minority of Jews, chiefly the youth and the pro-Communist Jewish proletariat, for many Poles the Jewish militiaman with a red armband became a symbol of the Soviet regime in Wilno and Lwów.[48]

Articles depicting the Jews as staunch supporters of Poland's Sovietization appeared primarily at the beginning of the war, in 1940 – 1941, when the persecution of this minority had not reached its eventual genocidal dimension. They were also printed, but only sporadically, in later periods. The majority of such pieces described facts and events as witnessed by locals, which were to exemplify the alleged Jewish betrayal of Poland and collaboration in the Communist movement. They recounted such occurrences as the warm welcomes extended to the invading Red Army by some Jews, the construction of "victory arches," as well as tossing flowers onto Soviet tanks, and Jewish choirs singing the "International." For example, *Szaniec* published an account describing a young Jew who derided Poles on the day of the invasion: "Now what? Where's your Poland now? You wanted a Poland without Jews, and now you'll get Jews without Poland!"[49]

Certain articles cited examples testifying that Jews not only greeted, but even aided Soviet units militarily in taking the Eastern Borderlands, created a red militia, and took part in disarming and even murdering

---

[48] This was confirmed by a report from Col. Stefan Rowecki to Gen. Stanisław Sosabowski from 8 February 1940: "Hatred toward Bolsheviks produces a highly exacerbated peasant and lower middle class anger towards Jews, for the reason of the Soviet sympathies of the Jewish masses (contrary to Zionists and the Bundists), as well as numerous Jewish participation in the new Bolshevik administration and militia (i.e. police) [...]". "Raport o sytuacji w kraju" [Report on the Situation in Poland] in *Armia Krajowa w Dokumentach 1939-1945* [The Home Army in Documents] (Wrocław, Warsaw, and Kraków: Ossolineum, 1990), 1: 106.

[49] *Szaniec*, 1 January 1943.

Polish soldiers.⁵⁰ Even Jews incarcerated in Soviet prisons supposedly collaborated.⁵¹ They were associated with the terror aimed at the Polish population in these regions as well. According to the nationalist press, the Soviet occupation became a veritable paradise for the Jews, who became the invaders' closest collaborators. It was the Jews, it was claimed, who staffed the public offices while insulting Polish national sentiments with impunity at every step.⁵²

Even so, it is important to point out that the nationalists did not blame the Jews for every manifestation of collaboration with the Soviets. Hence, examples of ethnically Polish Soviet collaborators in Wilno and Lwów at the beginning of the war were also mentioned by the nationalist press. Even though opinions on Jewish collaboration reflected the historical reality to a large extent, they did not mirror it fully. Recent studies show that entire cross-sections of the Jewish population – especially private businessmen, religious and social activists, or ordinary shopkeepers – became victims of Soviet repression during 1940-1941.

The nationalist press rarely noticed this. Because the Jewish theme was not of primary interest, the nationalists limited themselves to relating general information while dedicating most space to Polish affairs. It is noteworthy that the overrepresentation of individuals of Jewish descent in the Soviet occupation structures was so extensive that it became noticeable not only for Polish nationalists, but also non-Communist Jews, who regarded this as a completely unnatural phenomenon.⁵³

In June 1941, the outbreak of the Soviet-German war rapidly ended the Soviet occupation of the Polish Eastern Borderlands, although only for a three-year period. Simultaneously, the image of the collaborating Jew disappeared along with Bolshevik rule. Nevertheless, some bitterness remained, along with the conviction of Jewish disloyalty towards Poland. Even so, subsequent exposure to German mass murders soon erased it to a considerable degree. The nationalists continued to adhere to the view that the Jews burned with a special sympathy for the Soviet Union and opposed Poland's existence as an

---

⁵⁰ *Walka*, no. 30, 25 July 1941.
⁵¹ *Ibid.*, no. 34, 29 August 1941.
⁵² *Ibid.*, no. 44, 7 November 1941.
⁵³ "90% of the administrators of our association were Jews. A similar situation existed in other associations and social cooperatives in the Lvov region, consisting of all branches of industry, production, and commerce." See Henryk Reiss, *Z deszczu pod rynnę... Wspomnienia polskiego Żyda* [From the Fire Into the Frying Pan: The Memoirs of a Polish Jew] (Warsaw: Wyd. Polonia, 1993), 41.

independent nation-state. Hence, for example, warnings that Polish Jews who had emigrated were drafting plans to regain their influence in postwar Poland.

The underground press focused primarily on current affairs. During 1942–1944, it presented concrete information about Jewish participation in criminal gangs operating in the countryside. Such bands, acting with impunity, were the plague of the Polish countryside. Both nationalist and Home Army partisan units stated that the destruction of this pathology is a primary objective that must be achieved at all costs. While analyzing this phenomenon, it was noted that many of these groups operated as Communist "partisans." Yet, instead of fighting the Germans and protecting locals, they instead oppressed and robbed them while avoiding contact with enemy forces. The description of these bands included Jewish participation therein and the criminal acts they committed.

Nonetheless, the Jewish role was not exaggerated, nor were the Jewish members of the bands portrayed as the sole culprits. An example of this was a note written in the weekly *Wielka Polska* [Great Poland], which included information from the locality, along with reports on robberies linked to the Communist underground: "The Święty Krzyż [i.e. Kielce] area is ravaged by the Lebioda and Lepierz bands, the latter consisting of some Bolshevik paratroopers and Jews. Aside from this, there also exist purely Jewish groups, which are the most ruthless in their robberies. Lepierz's band, aside from robbery, also rapes women."[54]

The entry of the Red Army in 1944/1945, and the subsequent establishment of a Communist puppet government (Polish Committee of National Liberation, or PKWN), created a new context for the Polish underground. Mass arrests and deportations of underground independentists to the Soviet interior, along with a simultaneous, purely instrumental favoritism shown to the Jews, were certainly recorded by the underground publications.

Paradoxically, articles with an anti-Jewish slant appeared rarely at this time. Although the nationalists acknowledged the role of some Jews in building the foundations of the Communist regime in Poland – in contrast to the first Soviet occupation – the topic was not as noticeable and overly exaggerated. Especially at the outset of the second Soviet occupation, in late 1944, the presence of Jews in the Communist army or the newly formed secret police (UB) was regularly overlooked. They were mentioned with a hint of distaste, but in a

---

[54] *Wielka Polska*, no. 18, 20 April 1943.

humoristic form free of hatred. It was widely believed that the establishment of a Communist regime was ultimately irrelevant, since this process was only a transient one. The nationalists expected that the Soviet occupation would end quickly and its agents would have to flee Poland just like German collaborators before them.

The national press clearly separated Jewish Communists/Soviet collaborators from the rest of the Jewish community in the country. Their attitude towards the vast majority of harmless Jews, who did not display any hostility towards the independence movement, was one of neutrality. The nationalist ire focused on Jews collaborating with the Soviets and local Communists, particularly UB employees, Polish Workers' Party activists, administrative officials, and propagandists. In this case, the animosity grew, especially since the international situation offered increasingly less hope of removing the Communists from power and liberating the country from Soviet domination. For example, in May 1945 it was reported that 150,000 Jews survived the German occupation. "The majority returned to commerce, and particularly the work of middlemen; the intelligentsia also returned to its jobs. *With these [Jews] we have no quarrel* [emphasis added]. Alongside them, however, there survived the Jew [who is an] eternal denouncer, accuser, and an avenger of real and perceived injustices."[55]

The attitude towards pro-Communist Jews was comparable to the nationalists' position vis-à-vis ethnic Poles or members of other minorities collaborating with the new occupiers. The only exception consisted in the fact that the nationalist underground press did not issue death threats to Jews, nor did it call for bloody revenge for crimes committed in UB torture chambers. The case was different in relation to both Communist and nationalist (UPA) Ukrainians. Wierzchowiny, a village in the Lublin area pacified by the National Armed Forces (NSZ), provides an example:[56]

---

[55] *Naród w walce* [Nation in Struggle], 30 May 1945.
[56] The issue of Wierzchowiny divides historians: the dominant perspective is that this pacification was, in its essence, an act of liquidating particular Communist activists. Whether over 200 people were murdered there, as propagandized by the Polish People's Republic, animates discussion to this day. This question cannot be decisively answered without an accurate exhumation of bodies. This event possess a very broad literary scholarship (chronologically): Maria Turlejska, „*Te pokolenia żałobami czarne...*" *Skazani na śmierć i ich sędziowie 1944–1954* [Those Generations Black With Mourning: Those Sentenced to Death and Their Judges, 1944-1954] (Warsaw: Niezależna Oficyna Wydawnicza, 1990); Leszek Żebrowski, „Działalność tzw. band pozorowanych jako metoda zwalczania podziemia niepodległościowego w latach 1944–1947" [The Activities of So-Called False Flag Bands as a Method of Combating the Underground, 1944-1947] in *Skryte oblicze systemu komunistycznego: U źródeł*

Wierzchowiny was one of the many examples of the Haydamak parasite, which, to the east of the Bug [River], murders Poles in the open, but on this side of the border joins the UB [secret police] or the PPR [i.e. the Communist Party] and liquidates Poles. They were punished for these crimes. Such shall be the fate of every traitor. Faced with an uncompromising war, we shall not shrink before radical measures. We not only claim responsibility for Wierzchowiny, but also prophesy numerous other "Dogs' Fields" for the Haydamaks. This is an answer to the mass murders taking place to the east of the Bug, targeting the defenseless Polish population.[57]

The propaganda aspect of a war with the Soviet occupation did not obscure the nationalists' assessment of the situation. They did not attempt to whitewash ethnic Poles or to burden Jews with the totality of the evil committed by Communism. In fact, as opposed to the situation in the Eastern Borderlands in 1939-1941, it was not Communist Jews but ethnic Poles who shouldered most of the responsibility for the Sovietization of Poland. In 1947, *Echo Bałtyckie* condemned the "puppet government of a group of traitors" and the fact that "a handful of traitors from Targowica are attempting to use Poles themselves to destroy us as an independent nation through any means at their disposal."[58]

---

zła... [The Hidden Face of the System: At the Root of the Evil ...], (Warsaw: Tow. im. Stanisława ze Skarbimierza, 1997); Grzegorz Motyka and Rafał Wnuk, *Pany i rezuny: współpraca AK-WiN i UPA 1945–1947* [Lords and Butchers: AK and UPA Cooperation in 1945-1947] (Warsaw: Volumen, 1997); Rafał Wnuk, „Wierzchowiny i Huta" in *Polska 1944/45–1989*, vol. 4, (Warsaw: PAN, 1999), 71–88; Krzysztof Komorowski, *Polityka i władza: konspiracja zbrojna ruchu narodowego 1939–1945* [Politics and Power: The Armed Underground of the Nationalist Movement] (Warsaw: Rytm, 2000); Mirosław Piotrowski, *Narodowe Siły Zbrojne na Lubelszczyźnie 1944–1947* [The National Armed Forces in the Lublin Region, 1944-1947] (Lublin: Tow. Naukowe KUL, 2009). Wierzchowiny has also been mentioned in journalistic texts, of which the most documented and popular are: Marcin Zaborski, „Proces 23" [The Trial of the 23", *Gazeta Polska*, 9 December 1993; *Ibid.*, "Zbrodnia nie popełniona przez NSZ" [A Crime Not Committed by the NSZ], *Gazeta Polska*, 15 September 1994; Piotr Lipiński, "Czerwone dalie," *Gazeta Wyborcza*, 10–11 February 1996; Janusz Wrona, *Wierzchowiny – zbrodnia rozpoznana* [Wierzchowny, A Crime Recognized], *Nasze słowo*, 8 October 1996; D. Goszczyński [pseudonym], "Zagadka Wierzchowin" [The Mystery of Wierzchowiny], *Nasza Polska*, 11 July 1996 (copy: "Szczerbiec" 1998, vol. 9, p. 61–65); A. G. Kister, "Wierzchowiny," *Nasza Polska*, 4 February 2003; Piotr Lipiński, *Ofiary niejasnego* [The Victims of the Unclear] (Warsaw: Prószyński i S-ka, 2004).
[57] *Szczerbiec*, 23 June 1945, no. 23. It was further written that the village of Wierzchowiny was a base of recruitment for Ukrainian collaborationists, including the 14 SS "Galizien" Division, and after the war the residents joined the ranks of the UB.
[58] *Echo Bałtyckie* [Baltic Echo], 6 April 1947.

The underground press employed great caution when discussing greater or lesser outbursts of anti-Jewish violence on Polish soil, such as the ones in Rzeszów, Kraków, and, eventually, in Kielce. They were viewed as Communist provocations aiming to smear the independence movement, thereby discrediting it in the eyes of Western public opinion. "The anti-Jewish incident, which occurred in Kraków in 1945 was inspired by the NKVD and quickly spun out of control – the population as well as the militia joined in *en masse*."[59] In a very similar fashion, the "Kielce Pogrom" was described as perpetrated not by Poles, but rather the Communist terror apparatus, i.e. the UB:

> We condemn the mass killings in Kielce. We condemn them all the more because they were the work of a group of people at the disposal of the "state" provocation apparatus. Today, there is no doubt that this killing was perpetrated by the security apparatus, whose goal was to tarnish our country's image abroad, thereby justifying the necessity of Russian intervention. The whole affair is obvious (*grubo jest szyta sprawa*).[60]

Not only the nationalists arrived at such conclusions. A similar point of view was adopted by publications tied to the underground Freedom and Independence Union (Zrzeszenie Wolność i Niezawisłość)[61] as well as many other anti-Communist organizations.

Through the evaluation of the wartime and postwar periods from the perspective of the relationship between Polish nationalists and Jews, one can argue that this theme, in comparison to the intensity of its exploitation before the war, was far from a priority for the underground. The exceptions to this rule consisted of reports on the mass murder of the Jews, which constituted an act of moral opposition to the crime in a situation wherein the Germans attempted to cover up its genocidal character. On the other hand, the nationalists were happy to point out that the Germans had not found Polish volunteers to assist them in the act of genocide:

---

[59] *Informacje polityczne* [Political Information], August 1945; „Kwestia żydowska" [The Jewish Question], *Ku wolności* [Onward to Fredom], March 1946.
[60] „Sprawa kielecka" [The Case of Kielce], *Strażnica kresowa* [The Frontier Guard Post], no. 40, 20 July 1946.
[61] "Bandyta Radkiewicz – przygotował prowokację kielecką" [The Bandit Radkiewicz – He Prepared the Kielce Provocation], [brochure, 1946]; *Orzeł biały* [White Eagle], no. 4–5, June-July 1946; *Niepodległość* [Independence], no. 10, July 1946; *Niepodległość* [Independence], no. 16, 12 September 1946, as well as no. 17 from 19 September 1946; *Do wiadomości wszystkich Polaków* [Informing All Poles], [brochure] October 1948.

In this current moment, a most difficult moment for the Jewish nation, a certain truth surfaces which debunks the great myth of Polish anti-Semitism, which had been constructed for decades, and with such destructive power against Poland. [...] Hitler found collaborators in all of Europe, except for Poland, where he found none despite his best efforts. The most radical elements in Poland protest in their illegal journals. Not one single group or association aided the anti-Jewish action in the slightest degree.[62]

Archival sources do not confirm the theories of certain liberal and leftist historians that the influence of Nazi anti-Semitic propaganda and the process of Jewish extermination reinforced the nationalists (or the Poles in general) in their aggressive stance towards this minority during the war. Such an assertion is as baseless as the contention about the support – or assent – granted by Polish nationalist groups towards the mass murder of the Jews.

In reality, there was no "anti-Semitic campaign" in clandestine nationalist periodicals of the time. What was noticeable, however, was a significant amount of confusion defining the approach towards the Jews. In addition to solid and verified information one can find stereotypes as well.[63] In comparing the prewar and wartime periods

---

[62] *Sprawy Narodu* [The Affairs of the Nation], no. 8/9, February-May 1944.

[63] After the war, the nationalists and their press played the role of the scapegoat. This was an alibi for all those that before the war, during, and shortly after, subscribed to various anti-Jewish sentiments. From about 1956, it was convenient to place the blame for the anti-Jewish past on the now defenseless NDs. In fact, in order to legitimize one's self in the ranks of the liberal, pro-Communist *milieu*, calling the NDs "Nazis" or National Socialists was a very easy path to take. It is a quite understandable and transparent political and propaganda move. It explains the essence of hatred towards the nationalists, and the process of a step-by-step attribution of a false image. Yet, it distorts the historical truth. Unjust and hurtful evaluations of the underground nationalist press and its relationship with Jews can be found in Kazimierz Iranek Osmęcki, *Kto ratuje jedno życie... Polacy i Żydzi 1939–1945* [Whoever Saves One Life: Poles and Jews, 1939-1945] (London: Orbis Books, 1968), 245–250, where the press of the NSZ is defined as "combating the Jews (*zwalczająca Żydów*)." Władysław Bartoszewski *reflexively* accused the nationalist Right of indifference or animosity towards Jewish martyrology (Władysław Bartoszewski and Zofia. Lewinówna, *Ten jest z ojczyzny mojej. Polacy z pomocą Żydom 1939–1945* [He is From My Fatherland: Poles Helping Jews, 1939-1945], (Kraków: Znak, 1969), 18). A similar viewpoint was voiced by Israel Gutman, *Żydzi warszawscy 1939–1943* [Warsaw Jews, 1939-1943] (Warsaw: Rytm, 1993), 536, 539–540. In turn, Paweł Szapiro, in his article "Prasa konspiracyjna jako źródło do dziejów stosunków polsko-żydowskich w latach II wojny światowej – uwagi, pytania, propozycje badawcze" [The Underground Press as a Source for the History of Polish-Jewish Relations During the Second World War], *Biuletyn Żydowskiego Instytutu Historycznego* 3–4 (1988): 205–206, believed that using the term "anti-Semitic" to describe the nationalist underground press was correct.

(including the Soviet occupation after 1944) one factor remains unchanged: the ND journals were free of racist elements or undertones.

Furthermore – like during the interwar years – the nationalist underground recognized a person of Jewish origin as a Pole, provided that the individual embraced Polishness voluntarily, assimilated into the culture, professed the Catholic faith, and displayed Polish patriotism, especially in the ranks of the nationalist movement. Such persons were not treated as outsiders, but as brothers-in-arms, and were promised recognition after the victorious war.

These were not idle declarations. One of the heroes of the underground was Szmul Ostwind, a veteran of the I Legionary Brigade, a police officer before the war. During the German occupation he was known as Stanisław Ostwind-Zuzga "Kropidło" and became involved with the National Military Organization (NOW) in the southern Podlasie region. As a member of the NSZ from 1942, and a major, he held the position of a district NSZ commander in Węgrów during both the Nazi and the second Soviet occupations. He was arrested by the UB on 3 January 1945, sentenced to death by a military tribunal, and killed on 4 February 1945.[64]

The nationalist press emphasized, however, that Poland had no room for those refusing to assimilate in full, are indifferent to the country's affairs, and refuse to sacrifice for her. This pertained to those Jews who resisted Polonization and remained faithful to their nation and religion, in addition to ethnic Germans, Lithuanians and Ukrainians, who refused to abandon their separatist goals and integral nationalism. Their disloyalty towards Poland during the war period – including the active undermining of the Polish Republic, collaboration with the enemy, voluntary service in the German and Soviet armies – caused the nationalists to view any further coexistence as impossible.

In this context, it is worth explaining that the postwar mass displacement of peoples organized by the Communist regime in Poland in cooperation with the USSR (e.g., mass deportations of arrested soldiers of the Home Army and NSZ to the USSR; the expulsions of Poles from the Eastern Borderlands after the Soviet annexation; but also the wave of Jewish emigration from post-Yalta Poland in 1946-

---

[64] Mariusz Bechta, *Między Bolszewią z Niemcami. Konspiracja polityczna i wojskowa Polskiego Obozu Narodowego na Podlasiu w latach 1939–1945* [Between the Bolsheviks and the Germans: The Political and Military Underground of the Polish Nationalist Camp in Podlasie in 1939-1945] (Warsaw: IPN, 2008), 519; Marek Gałęzowski and Richard Pipes, *Na wzór Berka Joselewicza. Żołnierze i oficerowie pochodzenia żydowskiego w legionach Polskich* [Emulating Berek Joselewicz: Soldiers and Officers of Jewish Descent in the Polish Legions] (Warsaw: IPN, 2010), 516.

1947; and the deportations of Ruthenians, Lemkos, and Ukrainians within Poland) differed greatly from similar solutions planned by the nationalists.

The postwar deportations were characterized by inhumane conditions, looting and violence, and even a lack of basic verification whether an individual forcibly deported was Polish. Thus, they resembled a chaotic ethnic cleansing campaign rather than a well-planned resettlement project. The underground nationalist press strongly protested against such a treatment of human beings, whether Polish or not.[65]

Conclusion

Thus, I have presented a general outline of the ND stance towards Jews and German racism during the 1930s and 1940s. Based on an analysis of periodicals and the political thought of the Nationalist Party and the Radical-Nationalist Camp, as well as other underground publications during the war period, one can conclude that their attitude was definitely neither racist nor an attempt to emulate Nazi ideology.

In addition, it is worth remembering that National Democracy was a large political movement. Thus, it may have been possible to see the sporadic appearance of statements representing other approaches to Nazism during the prewar period. However, their exceptionality confirms the general rule.

The nationalists were not consistent in their collective negative attitude towards the Jews, which their publications during the Holocaust demonstrate. Yet, they consistently rejected racism and any ideological affinities to it. Such a reaction was apparently the result of a strong Christian element present in the Polish nationalist mindset. This constituted a barrier deflecting many various ideological pathologies (totalitarianism, chauvinism, and eugenicism).

---

[65] "In Wilno, in which 134,000 terrorized residents signed up for repatriation west of the Bug River, half of whom had already managed to leave, Polish speech was nearly non-existent. The streets ring, by contrast, with Russian, Lithuanian, and Hebrew." "Z opowiadań 'repatrianta.' Trzecia okupacja bolszewicka w Wileńszczyźnie" [From the Memoirs of a "Repatriated" Person: The Third Bolshevik Occupation of the Wilno Region], *Biuletyn Wewnętrzny Kresowiaków*, no. 1, November 1945 in Marek Jan Chodakiewicz and Wojciech Jerzy Muszyński, eds., *„Żeby Polska była polska!". Antologi publicystyki konspiracyjnej podziemia narodowego, 1939-1950* [So That Poland Remains Polish! An Anthology of the Polish Nationalist Underground Press], 656.

The linking of Catholicism and nationalism, sometimes pejoratively referred to as "Catho-NDism," enabled Christian morality to ultimately prevail over national egoism. During the course of the war, this helped check extreme temptations to settle scores with minorities considered to be enemies. By contrast, in the case of Ukrainian nationalism, the Christian handbrake was missing, which led to butchery and pogroms of both Poles and Jews alike. The above demonstrates the impossibility of equating Polish nationalists and the German Nazis, but also the Ukrainian and Lithuanian integral nationalists, if only because the nationalism of the Endeks did not posses a genocidal dimension and never led to mass murder.

The moralizing of the Endecja's ideological enemies who, as historians, attempt to conceal their politically correct theories under the mask of "objectivity," are devoid of any significant intellectual value. After all, postmodernist theorizing cannot substitute for insightful research and historical analysis.

THE POLISH NATIONALISTS AND THE JEWS: EVERYDAY PRACTICE DURING THE GERMAN OCCUPATION, AND THE CASE OF THE NATIONAL ARMED FORCES (NSZ)

Sebastian Bojemski

(Translated by Paweł Styrna)

The National Armed Forces (*Narodowe Siły Zbrojne*, or NSZ) and the National Radical Camp (*Obóz Narodowo Radykalny*, ONR) remain a constant reference point in the vivid discussions of Polish-Jewish relations. Yet, until recently almost no concurrent research has been conducted on the topic of Jewish ties to the NSZ.[1] The objective of the query results presented in this chapter is to present a neglected feature of this armed formation and its political base.

At this juncture, it is too late to re-create fully the complex relations between the Polish nationalists and the Jews during the Second World War. Most witnesses were forced to remain silent for over half a century and have now passed away. For over five decades, former NSZ soldiers were persecuted and forbidden to defend themselves. Yet, they

---

[1] See Marek Jan Chodakiewicz, *Żydzi i Polacy 1918–1955. Współistnienie – Zagłada – Komunizm* [Jews and Poles, 1918-1955: Coexistence, the Holocaust, and Communism] (Warsaw: Fronda, 2000); Wojciech Jerzy Muszyński, *W walce o Wielką Polskę. Propaganda zaplecza politycznego Narodowych Sił Zbrojnych (1939–1945)* [The Struggle for Greater Poland: The Propaganda of the Political Base of the National Armed Forces (1939-1945)] (Warsaw: Rekonkwista, 2000), 283–325; *Ibid.*, „Konspiracyjna prasa narodowa a sprawa żydowska" [The Underground Polish Nationalist Press and the Jewish Question], *Fronda* 25/26 (2001); S. Brzozowski (Sebastian Bojemski), „NSZ a Żydzi" [The NSZ and the Jews], *Nowe Państwo* (2001); Sebastian Bojemski, „Sprawiedliwi wśród narodowców Polski" [Righteous Gentiles Amongst the Polish Nationalists], *Fronda* 25/26 (2001); Jan Żaryn, „Elity obozu narodowego wobec zagłady Żydów" [The Elites of the Polish Nationalist Camp Vis-à-vis the Shoah] in Andrzej Żbikowski, ed., *Polacy i Żydzi pod okupacją niemiecką 1939–1945. Studia i materiały* [Poles and Jews Under the German Occupation, 1939-1945: Studies and Materials] (Warsaw: IPN, 2006).

were accused of the most heinous acts, towards the Jews in particular. The latest research demonstrates the baseless nature of these charges. The results of detailed studies show the differences between theoretical anti-Jewish propaganda and practical reality. Moreover, this research clarifies the secondary and subordinate nature of the so-called Jewish Question in the propaganda and punditry released by the NSZ and its political patrons.

In a recent anthology of the nationalist underground press during the years 1939-1950, the editors of the selection, Marek Jan Chodakiewicz and Wojciech Jerzy Muszyński, offered the thesis that during the Second World War the nationalist underground – the Nationalist Party (*Stronnictwo Narodowe*); the Nationalist Radical Camp (*Obóz Narodowo-Radykalny*); the National Armed Forces; and the National Military Organization (*Narodowa Organizacja Wojskowa*) – did not treat the Jewish issue as a leitmotif: "We emphasize, however, that the so-called Jewish Question was treated rather marginally by the underground Endek press, especially in comparison with the prewar period."[2]

Admittedly, pieces dealing with the Jews were characterized by an equivocal tone. Yet, it is crucial to point out that the Endeks strongly and unreservedly opposed the Nazi policy of extermination, warning the Poles against participation in pogroms inspired by the occupier or otherwise taking part in the German-engineered operation. Their attitude was aptly characterized by Zofia Kossak-Szczucka, who wrote in her famous *Protest*:

> Thus, We, the Catholic Poles, speak out. Our feelings towards the Jews have not changed. We have not ceased to consider them as the political, economic, and ideological adversaries of Poland. Moreover, we realize that they hate us more than the Germans, [and] that they deem us responsible for their tragedy. The causes of this shall remain a mystery of the Jewish soul, yet this fact finds constant confirmation. Awareness of these feelings by no means absolves us of the duty to condemn the crime (*zbrodnia*).
>
> We do not wish to be the likes of Pontius Pilate. We do not have the opportunity to actively resist the German mass murder, nor can we prevent it or save anyone. Yet, we protest from the depths of our hearts, which are filled with mercy, indignation, and horror. God Himself demands that we

---

[2] Marek Jan Chodakiewicz and Wojciech Jerzy Muszyński, eds., „*Żeby Polska była polska!" Antologia publicystyki konspiracyjnej podziemia narodowego 1939–1950* ["So Poland Remains Polish!" An Anthology of the Polish Nationalist Underground Press, 1939-1950] (Warsaw: IPN, 2010), 87.

protest, for He is a God who forbade killing. The Christian conscience also demands it. Every creature known as a human being has a right to be loved by his fellow man. The blood of the innocents calls upon Heaven for revenge. Anyone who fails to support our protest is not a Catholic.[3]

In spite of a glaring ignorance on the part of most scholars of the NSZ's attitude towards the Jews, extreme claims are nevertheless put forth at every opportunity on the alleged participation of Polish nationalist military units in the extermination of the Jewish minority. This opinion is commonplace, especially among historians who follow the neo-Stalinist narrative.

In Poland, the mistake also surfaces during public debates on the NSZ. Marek J. Chodakiewicz's monograph on the history of Polish-Jewish relations during the period of 1918-1955 offers a more comprehensive treatment of assistance provided to the Jews by the Polish nationalists.[4]

Exemplary of scholarly dishonesty in this matter is a well-known publication authored by Israel Gutman and Shmuel Krakowski, *Unequal Victims: Poles and Jews During World War Two*, which charges the Polish underground of 120 murders of Jews. Yet, out of 26 concrete incidents, only *one* is pinned on the NSZ. Upon closer inspection, also based upon postwar Jewish documentation, it turns out that this crime also wasn't the work of the NSZ, but of the Germans.[5]

Reuben Ainsztein, in turn, writes about thousands of Jews, as well as Poles helping shelter them, who perished at the hands of NSZ units. One of the examples of the NSZ partisans' criminal activities was an armed engagement with a Communist People's Guard (*Gwardia Ludowa*) Ludwik Waryński "Lions" unit, commanded by Izrael Ajzenman, also known as Julian Kaniewski, "Julek," and "Chytry"

---

[3] Posted at: www.zydziwpolsce.edu.pl/biblioteka/zrodla/r3_5d.html.
[4] See. M.J. Chodakiewicz, *Żydzi i Polacy,* and particularly the following parts: *Żegota i inni: Uwarunkowania i ograniczenia pomocy* [Żegota and Others: The Conditions and Limitations Affecting Assistance] (302–307); *Uwarunkowania i ograniczenia pomocy* [Conditions and Limitations Affecting Assistance] (307–312); *Niepodległościowcy o Żydach* [The Independentists' View of the Jews] (315–327); *Podziemie „polskich antysemitów"* [An Underground of "Polish Anti-Semites"] (341–347); *Zbawcy* [The Rescuers] (426–432).
[5] According to Gutman and Krakowski, a massacre of a dozen or so Jews occurred in the village of Zakrzówek. The alleged perpetrators were NSZ soldiers. See Israel Gutman and Shmuel Krakowski, *Unequal Victims: Poles and Jews During World War Two* (New York: Holocaust Library, 1986), 217. Yet, postwar testimonies of Jewish survivors indicate that the crime was committed by the Germans. See Archiwum Państwowe [State Archive of] Lublin, Kraśnik district, collection 4, file 320.

["Sly One"]. "This activity resulted in the murdering of thousands of Jews then in hiding [...]."[6] The author then describes the alleged effects of Order "Special Action No. 1" (*Akcja Specjalna nr 1*), issued by NSZ commander Col. Ignacy Oziewicz "Czesław."

In reality, the order was concerned primarily with the liquidation of banditry and acquiring the means to continue the resistance. Moreover, the "Lions" unit – composed of ethnic Jews and led by a prewar criminal – was responsible for many crimes committed against Christian Poles. Its actions constituted an element of the Soviet plan to "cleanse the country of reaction" (*oczyszczanie terenu z reakcji*). Hence, this was quite simply a Communist outfit engaged in common banditry.[7]

Pinning anti-Jewish crimes on the NSZ was also possible because of provocations that took place during the war. Various criminal gangs masqueraded as independentist organizations to facilitate their activities. One such group, claiming to represent the "Executive of the National Armed Forces" (*Egzekutywa Narodowych Sił Zbrojnych*), mailed the following letter to the supervisor of a house on Daniłowska Street No. 32 in Warsaw on 13 September 1943:

> We wish to notify you that in the house under Your care there lives on the ground floor (smashed windows) a Jewess, who is visited by two Jews. [A]nd, on the first floor, there lives a Jewess who speaks Polish rather poorly. Because Bielany must be cleansed of the Jewish element, we call upon You to remove these people within seven days (counting from the date of the sending of this letter). Otherwise, a sentence shall be meted out, and You shall be punished as well (including possibly the death penalty).[8]

Information regarding provocations by this band was passed on by NSZ intelligence to the organization's District Command for the Warsaw Municipality. The intelligence department initiated an investigation, which established that no Jews had been hiding in the building in question, and that the whole case was of a criminal nature. The NSZ Headquarters were promptly notified. Eventually, the Deputy Chief of Staff of the NSZ, Lt. Col. Albin Walenty Rak "Lesiński,"

---

[6] Reuben Ainsztein, *Jewish Resistance in Nazi-Occupied Eastern Europe*, Vol. 1 (New York: Barnes & Noble Books, 1974), 406–407.

[7] After the war, Julian Ajzenman faced criminal charges before the Regional Military Court in Warsaw. For a comprehensive treatment of the AL-GL's "partisan" activities see the document collection by Marek Jan Chodakiewicz, Leszek Żebrowski, and Piotr Gontarczyk, eds., *Tajne oblicze GL-AL i PPR. Dokumenty* [The Secret Face of the GL-AL and the PPR: Documents], Vols. 1–3 (Warsaw: Burchard Edition, 1997–1999).

[8] AAN, NSZ dopływ [new acquisitions, uncatalogued]. 2008.

proposed to "notify the house owner that the NSZ never sent him any letters, and that someone was misappropriating the good name of the NSZ."[9]

No further information is extant regarding any consequences the above bandits may have suffered for impersonating NSZ soldiers. We may assume that the group would have been physically liquidated had NSZ intelligence succeeded in identifying them. This was, after all, the NSZ's approach to blackmailers (*szmalcownicy*). For instance, one Borys Pilnik was shot for blackmailing activities by Piotr Olędzki from the Lizard Union's (*Związek Jaszczurczy*) Liquidation Cell under the command of Sec. Lt. Tadeusz Siemiątkowski "Mazur."[10] The hit was ordered by the Underground Combat Command (*Kierownictwo Walki Podziemnej*), acting upon a court verdict issued by the Civilian Special Court (*Cywilny Sąd Specjalny*).[11]

Another unfounded myth is the claim, perpetuated by some historians, that the NSZ drafted proscription lists of individuals actively aiding Jews.[12] The Intelligence Service Center – acting in conjunction with, and upon the request of the Government Representation for the Nation (*Delegatura Rządu na Kraj*) – prepared lists of individuals suspected of left-wing extremism. Hence, Irena Sendlerowa, a distinguished activist of the "Żegota" Council to Aid Jews, but also a member of the Workers' Party of Polish Socialists (*Robotnicza Partia Polskich Socjalistów*), appeared on such a list. Thus, she was included as an RPPS member. Otherwise, her "Żegota" associates – such as the Nationalist Party's Jan Dobraczyński, or a prewar ONR "Falanga" activist,[13] Witold Rothenburg-Rościszewski, both of whom, like Sendlerowa, had been honored as Righteous Gentiles[14] – would have been blacklisted as well.

Gathering files on activists of the extreme Left was in accordance with the prewar practice of the Polish State Police as well as the Polish Army's intelligence and counterintelligence branches. In the underground these activities were continued by Home Army

---

[9] *Ibid.*
[10] See P. Olędzki's testimony in R. Sierchuła's collection.
[11] *Rzeczpospolita Polska*, 1943.
[12] See Tomasz Szarota, "Listy nienawiści" ["Lists of Hatred"], *Polityka* 44-2425 (2003), 70.
[13] Wojciech Jerzy Muszyński, „Sprawiedliwy z ONR 'Falanga'" ["A Righteous Gentile from the ONR 'Falanga'"], *Biuletyn Instytutu Pamięci Narodowej* 11 (2010): 97–101.
[14] See Yisrael Gutman, ed., *Księga Sprawiedliwych wśród Narodów Świata. Ratujący Żydów podczas Holocaustu. Polska* [The Book of Righteous Gentiles: Rescuers of Jews During the Holocaust, Poland] (Kraków: Yad Vashem, 2009), 126–127, 623–624, 646–647.

counterintelligence and the underground police, the State Security Corps. It must be strongly emphasized that inclusion on such a list was by no means equivalent to a death sentence.

In spite of the political enmity, NSZ soldiers assisted the exterminated Jews. Currently, court records constitute the best source in identifying these Righteous Gentiles among the ranks of this formation. The appendices to these court records include "morality testimonies" (*świadectwa moralności*, i.e. character references) offered by Jews. Yet, combing through these materials may prove quite tedious, for the Communist regime in Poland prosecuted tens of thousands of NSZ soldiers.

Nevertheless, the truth is slowly surfacing, even if "incidentally." Thus, we "incidentally" discovered in Marek J. Chodakiewicz's book, *The National Armed Forces: The "Tooth" Against Two Enemies,* that many Jews found shelter with families affiliated with the NSZ in Kraśnik County in southwestern Lublin Province.[15] In fact, we will find information about fifteen NSZ-affiliated families assisting Jews within the space of just two pages. Similar information may be gleaned from the veterans' published memoirs. Władysław Marcinkowski "Jaxa" a.k.a. "Szymkiewicz" – the commander-in-chief of the Lizard Union, and eventual Deputy Commander of the NSZ's Holy Cross Brigade (*Brygada Swiętokrzyska*) – relates that a Jew worked in his factory.[16] Similarly, the family of Władysław Kołaciński "Żbik" saved several Jews from certain death.[17]

The Polish Christian family which sheltered Bronisław Geremek, a future Foreign Minister in post-Communist Poland, was tied to the Kielce regional structures of the NSZ. Geremek recalled:

> I found my way into the home of a patriotic Polish family, which maintained numerous ties with the underground [...]. One day, when no one was home, a strongly built man knocked on the door. He claimed to be the house owners' cousin. I'm not sure if he had been previously aware of my existence. He belonged to the National Armed Forces. I talked to him for half an hour, until one of the owners returned home. He took out his weapon and played with it while rocking back and forth in his chair. He questioned me about where I came from and what I'm doing here. Never

---

[15] See M.J. Chodakiewicz, *Narodowe Siły Zbrojne. „Ząb". Przeciw dwu wrogom* [The National Armed Forces: "The Tooth" Against Two Enemies] (Warsaw: Fronda, 1999), 117–118.

[16] See W. Marcinkowski "Jaxa," *Wspomnienia 1934–1945* [Memoirs: 1934-1945] (Warsaw: Burchard, 1998), 108–109.

[17] See Władysław Kołaciński "Żbik," *Między młotem a swastyką* [Between the Hammer and the Sickle] (Warsaw: Wydawnictwo – Słowo Narodowe, 1990), 234-235.

before and never afterwards was I in such fear of my life as during that moment. Later, he came over rather often, but he never turned me in.[18]

It is impossible to state with any degree of certainty the percentage of trees planted in honor of Polish nationalists in Yad Vashem's Grove of Righteous Gentiles. After all, they might not even have revealed their political leanings to the Jews they were sheltering.

In this context, it may be worthwhile to mention the activities of Dr. Felicjan Loth, a duty physician at the infamous Pawiak Prison who helped the Jewish inmates. Loth had been a prewar ONR activist, a member of the nationalist radical underground during the war, and a likely member of the ONR's postwar "Poland" Executive Organization. In Anka Grupińska's book, *Ciągle po kole: Rozmowy z żołnierzami getta warszawskiego* [What Goes Around Comes Around: Conversations with the Soldiers of the Warsaw Ghetto], the Jewish Combat Organization's liaison, Adina Blady Szwajgier, recalled Dr. Loth in most positive terms:

> Felek Loth left behind a beautiful legacy. He spent almost the entire war at the Pawiak [Prison]. And we were well aware of his demeanor. [...] Felek, the prisoner-physician, never identified a Jew. [...] His father, Prof. Loth, had been a bestial (*zwierzęcy*) anti-Semite before the war [...]. And these people – Felek's parents – sheltered Jews in their own home.[19]

The case of Fathers Stanisław Trzeciak and Marceli Godlewski, two Roman Catholic priests associated with the nationalist movement, further confirm this phenomenon.[20] Ludwik Hirszfeld wrote the following about the rescue operation conducted by Fr. Godlewski, recognized as a Righteous Gentile in 2009:

---

[18] Piotr Bojarski, Włodzimierz Nowak, with Joanna Szczęsna, „Bronisław Geremek ucieka z getta. Chudy chłopak w czterech swetrach" ["Bronisław Geremek Escapes From the Ghetto: A Skinny Boy Wearing Four Sweaters"], *Gazeta Wyborcza: Duży Format*, 21 June 2008.
[19] Anka Grupińska *Ciągle po kole. Rozmowy z żołnierzami getta warszawskiego* [What Goes Around Comes Around: Conversations with Soldiers From the Warsaw Ghetto] (Warsaw: Twój Styl, 2000), 185.
[20] See Tomasz Szarota, *U progu Zagłady: Zajścia antyżydowskie i pogromy w okupowanej Europie* [On the Eve of the Holocaust: Anti-Jewish Incidents and Pogroms in Occupied Europe] (Warsaw: Sic!, 2000), 49; W.J. Muszyński, *Trzeciak Stanisław* in *Encyklopedia „Białych Plam"* [The Encyclopedia of Gaps] (Radom: PWE, 2006), Vol. XVII, 214; Karol Madaj and Małgorzata Żuławnik, *Proboszcz getta* [The Ghetto's Parson] (Warsaw: IPN, 2010).

Prelate Godlewski. Simply recalling his name moves me. [He represented] passion and love in one soul. Once [he was] a militant anti-Semite, as his words and writings testified. But when destiny brought him face to face with that depth of misery, he rejected his previous attitude and committed the immense fire in his priestly heart to the Jews.

When his beautiful, grey head appeared, so reminiscent of Piotr Skarga's as portrayed by Matejko, all heads bowed to him in love and humility. All of us, both young and old, loved him, and we tore him away for a brief conversation. And he was not greedy with his time. He taught the Catechism to the children, and he headed the city district's Caritas organization, ordering that soup be dispensed to the hungry, regardless of whether they were Christian or Jews.[21]

The commander of the Białystok and Northern Mazovian District, and a subsequent head of the part of the NSZ that refused to integrate with the AK, Col. Stanisław Nakoniecznikow "Kmicic," along with his family, sheltered the Glucks/Gołuchowskis and Julian Gojcherman/ Dobrowolski for the duration of the war.[22] In turn, the chief of the NSZ Forgery Bureau, Władysław Weker "Franciszek," provided false documents to a prewar cabaret host, Fryderyk Jarossy. The latter was sheltered by an NSZ intelligence officer, Irena Grynkiewicz "Lala." The above mentioned forgery bureau also employed an unidentified Jewish woman known only by her *nom de guerre* of "Niusia."[23] Thanks to the contacts of the NSZ intelligence chief Major Wiktor Gostomski "Nałęcz," who knew the Swiss consul, Jarossy was able to escape the General Gouvernement with a Swiss passport.[24]

The head of the NSZ Anti-Communist Department, Antoni Szperlich, claimed in his postwar deposition for the Communist secret police (UB) that he provided food for Zofia Krajtenkraft, the mother of the prewar General Secretary of Polish Radio and a ghetto inmate.[25] Janina Kossuth – a member of the nationalist underground, and a relative of the famous ONR activists, Jan, Julian, and Ryszard Sędek – can also boast of a tree in the Grove of Righteous Gentiles.[26]

---

[21] Ludwik Hirszfeld, *Historia jednego życia* [The Story of One Life] (Warsaw: PAX, 1957), 306–307.
[22] Nakoniecznikow family materials in Leszek Żebrowski's collection.
[23] See Józef Maria Cieśliński's letter to the author, dated 23 November 2000, in author's collection (further as J.M. Cieśliński's letter).
[24] Władysław Miłkowski, „Ocalenie Fryderyka Jarossy" [The Rescue of Fryderyk Jarossy], *Szaniec Chrobrego* 53 (220) (2001): 36–37.
[25] AIPN (Archives of the Institute of National Remembrance) 01251/138, Mf 2630, Antoni Szperlich's testimony, p. 153.
[26] See *Księga Sprawiedliwych* [The Book of the Righteous], 329-330.

Edward Marcin Kemnitz, the political chief of the ONR for the Warsaw Province, and his father sheltered a group of Jews in large bales of hay on the premises of their own estate. Moreover, the Rosenthal family and Leon Herzberg received false identity documents from the Kemnitzes. The Kemnitz family also subsidized the activities of "Żegota" and provided financial assistance for Jews in the Warsaw Ghetto. In his memoirs Kemnitz wrote:

> For completely humane reasons, i.e. on account of the suffering common to both Poles and Jews, our entire family, with our father taking the lead, joined in the assistance activities. We were not concerned about the danger which we faced. [...] In early 1943, before the Ghetto Uprising, I was asked to transport cases containing weaponry and ammunition, intended for the Jewish fighters, using our factory cart to a location near the ghetto, i.e. Elektoralna Street. [...] I also served as the intermediary facilitating two purchases of arms for the ghetto [...].[27]

In 1983 Kemnitz was awarded a medal as a Righteous Gentile.[28] Similarly, the survivors thanked the ONR-affiliated Olizar and Żaryn families from the Szeligi estate near Warsaw, as well as the family of the Catholic journalist Henryk Ryszewski.[29]

The younger members of the ONR also undertook such initiatives. For instance, Sławomir Modzelewski "Lanc," a Warsaw NSZ cadet officer and a prewar member of the ONR's School Groups, sheltered Jews with the help of his mother. "Lanc" and his mother received a Righteous Gentile diploma and medal from Yad Vashem.

Nationalist lawyers also participated in the rescue operations. For example, one of the initiators of the Secret Supreme Attorneys' Council

---

[27] Edward Marcin Kemnitz, *Wspomnienia z pracy politycznej i społecznej w latach 1923–1956* [Reminiscences From My Political and Social Work During the Years 1923-1956] (London: self-published, 1983), 72–74. Jews were also sheltered by Fr. Władysław Bayer (Bajer), most likely a cousin of ONR leader, Witold Bayer. See Władysław Bartoszewski and Zofia Lewinowna, *Ten jest z ojczyzny mojej. Polacy z pomocą Żydom 1939–1945* [He is From My Fatherland: Poles Aiding Jews, 1939-1945] (Kraków: Znak, 1969), 823–825.

[28] See *Księga Sprawiedliwych* [The Book of the Righteous], 290. In the ONR Kemnitz collaborated politically with the factory owner Smoleński, who during the Nazi occupation employed Jews in his enterprise in the Warsaw district of Praga. See Lawrence N. Powell, *Troubled Memory: Anne Levy, The Holocaust and David Duke's Louisiana* (Chapel Hill and London: University of North Carolina Press, 2000), 280–81.

[29] *Księga Sprawiedliwych* [The Book of the Righteous], 510–511, 633; Michał Grynberg, *Words To Outlive Us: Voices from the Warsaw Ghetto* (New York: Metropolitan Books, 2002), 364–69.

was Leon Nowodworski. Witold Bayer supported the establishment of district structures in Kraków and Lwów. One of the goals of this organization was to maintain high moral standards among attorneys, in addition to self-help, which included assisting Jewish attorneys. The last objective was by no means hampered by the fact that the leadership included ONR activists, such as: Dr. Juliusz Sas-Wisłocki and Władysław Babel from Kraków, and Roman Załucki from Lwów.[30]

Roman Blum, the head of the Kraków structures of the NSZ's civilian base, the National Civilian Service, is also awaiting commemoration. A prewar Nationalist Party activist, Blum was arrested in December 1943 for providing false documents to Jews. Blum was subsequently incarcerated in Gross-Rosen and Flossenburg, where he was shot in March 1945.[31]

Antoni Mokrzycki, the president of the Dentists' Association and an SN (Nationalist Party) member, was murdered by the Germans in the vicinity of Gęsia Street in Warsaw in July 1943 for assisting Jews. His sons, ONR members Jan and Stanisław, perished along with him. Mokrzycki's wife was deported to Auschwitz one month later.[32]

In turn, Jan Rutkowski from the Warsaw NSZ Infantry Cadet Officers' School smuggled bread into the ghetto near Bonifraterska Street.[33] Janina Kisiel-Konopacka "Janka Pistolet," the liaison between

---

[30] See Andrzej Kisza, Zdzisław Krzemiński, and Roman Łyczywek, *Historia adwokatury polskiej* [The History of the Polish Legal Profession] (Warsaw: M.C. Kwadrat, 1995), 140–166; Witold Bayer, *Samorząd adwokacki w dobie walki z okupacją hitlerowską* [Legal Corporations During the Struggle Against the Hitlerite Aggression], *Palestra*, No. 11 (1968); Wojciech Jerzy Muszyński, "Bayer Witold" in *Konspiracja i opór społeczny w Polsce 1944–1956. Słownik biograficzny* [The Underground and Social Resistance in Poland, 1944-1956], Vol. IV (Kraków, Warsaw, and Wrocław: IPN, 2010), 22–27; Sebastian Bojemski, *Witold Bayer. Zarys sylwetki działacza politycznego* [Witold Bayer: A Biographical Outline of a Political Activist], manuscript. In Lwów Jews found shelter with Dr. Kasperski, an SN activist, Wanda Wysocka, and an unidentified student who had been a prewar anti-Jewish activist. See: Jan Kot, *Chestnut Roulette: The Amazing Story of a Lvov Jewish Youth Who Triumphs Over Adversity, Outwtting the Nazis and Luftwaffe!* (Jerusalem: Mazo Publishers, 2008), 18, 79–81, 93–94, 145–47; Eliahu Yones, *Smoke in the Sand: The Jews of Lvov in the War Years 1939–1944* (Jerusalem and New York: Gefen Publishing House, 2004), 240; E.J. Feuerman, „Moi lwowscy profesorowie" [My Lwów Professors], *Zeszyty Historyczne* 117 (1996): 66.

[31] Waldemar Grabowski, *Polska tajna administracja cywilna 1940–1945* [The Secret Polish Civil Administration, 1939-1945] (Warsaw: IPN, 2003), 39; J. Żaryn, *Elity obozu*, 403.

[32] Ruta Pragier, *Żydzi czy Polacy* [Jews or Poles?] (Warsaw: Oficyna Wydawnicza, 1992), 80–81

[33] J. Rutkowski's letter to the author, dated 20 January 2000, in author's collection (further as J. Rutkowski's letter).

the Warsaw and Lublin NSZ, helped the Jews in the same manner.[34] The mother of Józef Maria Cieśliński "Mścisławski," the commander of the Special Action (AS) Platoon in Warsaw, sheltered a Jewish woman, who carried an illegal identity document issued to a Mrs. Burska, in her flat on Pius XI Street, Apartment No. 22.[35]

Feliks Pisarewski-Parry also received help from the Warsaw NSZ. During the fall of 1942 he was freed from Pawiak Prison by a diversionary unit of the NSZ Warsaw District, commanded by Capt. Piotr Zacharewicz "Zawadzki." He immediately joined the group. Parry participated in the unit's operations, preparing false documents, and planning the liberation of Pawiak prisoners. Even though some of Parry's prewar acquaintances had been ONR members, his membership in the NSZ made a powerful impression on him: "In spite of being an opponent of the ONR [...] I became an NSZ officer holding a relatively high post!"[36] Thanks to his NSZ contacts, he underwent a foreskin re-attachment operation. The procedure did not transpire without its entertaining moments:

> On the day following [the procedure] someone knocked as agreed upon, and an assistant [...] flew [sic!] into the room. It is now difficult to describe her entry. Golden locks of hair above her blue eyes, bare, curvy shoulders, breasts sharply visible through a batiste blouse, and legs like a dream! A true spring apparition! She looked at me expressively and, with Marlene Dietrichs's unsettling alto, uttered: 'We'll remove the stitches.' I understood and nodded, but my stupid friend ... did not. When her long, painted fingers unwrapped the patient's cold packs, his poor, loyal friend couldn't withstand it. The stitches popped. The assistant, at first embarrassed, or perhaps amused, quickly applied cold water and ice. After a few days new stitches ended this sad episode.[37]

Along with other NSZ soldiers, Parry helped the Jews:

> One day during the late spring someone knocked on our door. [...] There was a Jewish boy standing in the doorway. [He was] dirty, wet, and hungry. Both Piotr [Capt. 'Zawadzki'] and I had wet eyes, and probably [wet] hearts. The boy showed us a slip with the name of his new host family living on Filtrowa Street. We bathed and fed him, after which Piotr

---

[34] Barbara Otwinowska and Teresa Drzal, *Zawołać po imieniu. Księga kobiet – więźniów politycznych 1944–1958* [To Call by Name: A Book of Female Political Prisoners, 1944-1958], Vol. 1 (Nadarzyn: Vipart, 1999), 216.
[35] See J.M. Cieśliński's letter.
[36] Feliks Pisarewski-Parry *Orły i reszki* [Heads and Tails] (Warsaw: Iskry, 1984), 65.
[37] *Ibid.*, 67-68.

established contact with the Traczyks, for that was the surname of these brave people.[38]

Another NSZ officer of Jewish extraction was the commander of Węgrów County, subordinated to the Podlasie District No. XII, Mjr. Stanisław Ostwin-Zuzga "Kropidło." He was murdered not by the Nazis, but by the Communists in February 1945.[39] Within this structure, the Jews were also assisted by the district commander, Sec. Lt. Stanisław Miodoński "Sokół," and Capt. Jerzy Wojtkowski "Jerzy Drzazga," the head of Special Action units.[40]

Fragmentary information also survived regarding Staszek Kotok, a Jewish musician from Wilno, who received false documents from ONR affiliates and became a liaison. He traversed the country by train, under the cover of an itinerant beggar-musician, carrying secret orders and instructions for the underground.[41] All we know about Jerzy Lando was that he was an NSZ soldier.[42]

The Warsaw units of the NSZ also included individuals of Jewish descent, such as Stanisław Piotrowski "Stasiek" serving in the District Commander's protection platoon (*pluton osłonowy*), and an unidentified person in a group of the Auxiliary Military Womens' Service.[43] Zofia Lipmann, a Jewish woman, was also in charge of listening to foreign radio broadcasts for the propaganda purposes of the ONR-affiliated *Szaniec* [Rampart] periodical.[44] Witold and Natalia Borowski also sheltered a Jewish family. Borowski was an activist of the Youth of Great Poland and the Nationalist Party, an NSZ soldier, and an editor of the periodical *Wielka Polska (Great Poland)*. His wife served as the commander of the Auxiliary Military Womens' Service in Warsaw District No. 1 – South.[45]

---

[38] *Ibid.*, 84-85.
[39] Mariusz Bechta, *Między Bolszewią a Niemcami. Konspiracja polityczna i wojskowa Polskiego Obozu Narodowego na Podlasiu w latach 1939–1952* [Between the Bolsheviks and the Germans: The Political and Military Underground of the Polish Nationalist Movement in the Podlasie Region in 1939-1952] (Warszawa: RYTM, 2004), 519.
[40] *Ibid.*
[41] Severin Gabriel, *In the Ruins of Warsaw Streets* (Jerusalem and New York: Gefen, 2005), 46–47.
[42] Jerzy Lando, *Saved by My Face: A True Story of Courage and Escape in War-torn Poland* (Edinburgh and London: Mainstream, 2002), 184–208.
[43] See J. Rutkowski's letter; J.M. Cieśliński's letter.
[44] Jerzy Śmiechowski's testimony, author's collection.
[45] Wiesław Chrzanowski, *Pół wieku polityki, czyli rzecz o obronie czynnej* [Half a Century of Politics: On Active Defense] (Warsaw: Ad Astra, 1997), 88.

It is important to remember that German cruelty shocked even the most radical nationalists. The indignation expressed by a prewar nationalist from Zakopane, Dr. Franciszek Kowalski testifies to this: "Before the war I was an anti-Semite; only Hitler's bestiality towards the Jews changed me. I could never imagine that man is capable of falling so low as the Germans."[46]

Jan Mosdorf represented the most famous case of such a transformation. As an Auschwitz inmate, he heroically assisted his Jewish fellow prisoners. One former inmate, Wolf Gliksman, recalled: "Jan Mosdorf risked his life more than once by smuggling my letters, intended for a female relative, into the women's camp in Brzezinka [Birkenau]. [...] He worked in Birkenau and he frequently brought me vegetables, a piece of bread, or something to wear."

According to historian Philip Friedman:

> In the camp Mosdorf changed his attitude towards Jews. He shared the contents of some food packages he received from friends with the Jews. While working in the camp office, he warned the Jews several times about the impending selections for gassing.[47]

Due to his assistance to the Jews and participation in the camp underground, Mosdorf was denounced and shot. He was not the only high-ranking activist of the prewar ONR who risked his life to help the Jews.

While fighting the Germans, the famous Holy Cross Brigade captured the women's concentration camp in Holišov (a branch of KL Flossenbürg), liberating the inmates. The situation was extremely tragic. Had the Brigade's commander, Lt. Col. Antoni Dąbrowski "Bohun," not acted quickly, the women would have been burned alive. The NSZ thus liberated about 1,000 women, including 300 Jewesses.

This event would have passed unnoticed had Lt. Col. "Bohun" not written an article about it ("Polish Partisan Leader Recalls Liberating Holiszow") for *The Jewish Voice*.[48] He described his initial encounter with the female inmates in his Polish-language memoirs:

---

[46] Bartoszewski and Lewinówna, *Ten jest* [He is From My Fatherland], 92.
[47] Philip Friedman, *Their Brothers' Keepers* (New York: Crown Publishers, 1978), 114. The author also mentions nationalists who treated the Jews with empathy: Stanisław Piasecki, Adolf Nowaczyński, Witold Rudnicki, and Jerzy Czarkowski.
[48] Antoni Bohun-Dąbrowski, "Polish partisan leader recalls liberating Holiszow," *The Jewish Voice*, 19 June 1986, 14.

Suddenly, the Adjutant, Sec. Lt. Zygmunt, ran up to me, reporting that there were two barracks located on the left, both cordoned off with an electric, barbed-wire fence. The gate was locked with chains and locks. The barrack doors were closed as well. Emaciated faces looked out from small windows and we could hear loud calls for help. I immediately called for and ordered the camp commandant to turn off the electricity supply to the fence. In reply to my question about the reasons for the closing and isolating these two barracks, he said that, on the Führer's orders, all the female Jewish inmates have been locked inside. The buildings, along with the women, were to be doused with gasoline and burned to the ground as the American forces approached to within 20 kilometers of Holišov [...].

I wanted to go inside, but the macabre sight stopped me cold right at the entrance. From within the dark interior of the building there penetrated a horrible odor of human excrement mixed with the stench of rotting corpses. From these crevices there crawled out into the daylight the last surviving women crying tears of joy. They were so weak they couldn't stand. [...] Along with the liberated inmates, I experienced a sense of joy that was difficult to describe. I was proud and satisfied with my officers, NCOs, and soldiers who performed this mission well.[49]

There were Jews in the ranks of the Holy Cross Brigade as well, including private "Antoni" and private "Fryc," whose identities remain unknown, but whose ancestry was by no means kept secret within the unit. It is likely that two soldiers mentioned in a May 1945 order – privates Zeisler and Zimmerman – were also of Jewish extraction.[50]

Jewish NSZ soldiers also fought in greatest Polish battle of the Second World War, the Warsaw Uprising. They could be found in every sector of the insurrectionary front: on the barricades, fighting with weapons in hand; and in the rear, transporting the wounded or supplying food. The liberated inmates of the labor camp on Gęsia Street in the Varsovian district of Wola joined the auxiliary groups of the Motorized Flying Brigade (*Brygada Dyspozycyjna Zmotoryzowana*) in the Old Town. This information was gleaned from a report written in 1952 by Jan Machulski "Juliusz Gryf," an NSZ officer serving in the Old Town, while imprisoned in Wronki by the Communists. The

---

[49] Antoni Bohun-Dąbrowski, *Byłem dowódcą Brygady Świętokrzyskiej Narodowych Sił Zbrojnych* [I Was the Commander of the Holy Cross Brigade of the National Armed Forces] (Wrocław and Warsaw: Wers, 1989), 160.
[50] Czesław Brzoza, *Rozkazy Dzienne Brygady Świętokrzyskiej Narodowych Sił Zbrojnych 1944–1945* [The Daily Reports of the Holy Cross Brigade of the National Armed Forces, 1944-1945] (Kraków: Fundacja Centrum Dokumentacji Czynu Niepodległościowego, 2003), 388.

credibility of the information provided by Machulski appears quite high because it contains details that the UB could easily verify:

> Capt. Gozdawa [Lucjan Giżyński] undertook an unsuccessful prisoner-liberation operation targeting Pawiak Prison during the first days of the rising. The Germans managed to repulse this attack. The action did, however, result in the liberation of about 300 inmates held at the penal camp on Gęsia Street. These were the citizens – mainly or exclusively of Jewish nationality – of almost all of the European countries occupied by the Germans. Very few of them could speak a few words of Polish. All of them had reached the limits of their physical exhaustion and had only their striped prison clothing and footwear.
>
> After unsuccessful attempts to obtain help and care for these people from the AL high command, the head of the chancellery of Mjr. [Ferdynand Silny] 'Grad' [the commander of the Brigade's Reconnaissance Regiment], a Jew by the name of Józef Wojciechowski (false name; I do not know his real one) [Szymon Gottesman] turned to me, as the adjutant to [Lt. Col. Zygmunt] Reliszko [the commander of the NSZ Motorized Flying Brigade], with a request to take care of these people.
>
> After communicating with Reliszko in this matter, and convincing him that these people cannot be left without care in such a difficult situation, I conducted talks on this subject with a representative of relief efforts for Jews in Poland, Citizen 'Józef' (who, after the liberation, was the deputy chairman of the Central Committee of Jews in Poland, which I found out from this Józef Wojciechowski, whom I met in 1945 in Wrocław as a paper merchant and the owner of a paper goods workshop, who then resided at no. 46 or 48 on Gen. Świerczewski Street, i.e. former Ogrodowa Street) and his adjutant, Citizen 'Adam' (a lumber merchant from Złota Street by the name of Tarteltaub, or something similar).
>
> Thus, Citizen Józef agreed to provide us with any amount of money we required, but I did not accept the money. Instead, I solved the problem by integrating the Jews into the [NSZ Motorized Flying] Brigade upon their agreement.[51]

Perhaps the author was expecting a more lenient sentence by recalling the assistance he provided to the Jews during the Warsaw Uprising. He was already aware that his superior, Col. Reliszko, was freed precisely because of Jewish testimonies corroborating that he helped the Shoah victims.

---

[51] AIPN 00231/217, Jan Machulski's testimony, 1952, p. 67.

Jerzy Żmidygier-Konopka "Poręba," the son of Warsaw University Professor Żmidygier-Konopka, who was of Jewish origin, also fought in the ranks of a "Gozdawa" unit NSZ team headed by Sergeant Cadet Officer Tadeusz Niezabitowski "Lubicz." "Poręba" participated in many combat missions, including: the capture of the State Securities Production Facility (*Państwowa Wytwórnia Papierów Wartościowych*); an attack on the Gdański Railroad Station; and the taking of an anti-aircraft gun on Teatralny Square. He was awarded the *Virtuti Militari* and Cross of the Valiant medals. He was killed in combat on 25 August 1944 within the ruins of the Bank of Poland (*Bank Polski*).

Stanisław Pinkus "Panienka" also fought in Warsaw's Old Town district under the false identity of Franciszek Kubiak. Pinkus was a soldier of the National Military Organization's (NOW) "Gustaw" Battalion. He perished on 13 August 1944, along with his brothers-in-arms from the Scout Combat Liaison Platoon, as a result of a tank explosion.[52] He was not the only Jew fighting in the ranks of the NOW.

Quite often Jews belonging to NSZ units held positions of responsibility. Capt. Born-Bornstein, initially a member of the far-left Polish People's Army (*Polska Armia Ludowa*), headed the medical service of the insurrectionary "Chrobry II" grouping, a unit with an NSZ pedigree. Born-Bornstein later wrote in his memoirs: "The NSZ haunted [*prześladował*] me a long time to come. In 1945, Dr. Wiesenfeld (Ciosnowski), a laryngologist living at Ben Jehuda Street 100, and the nurse Kowalska, jointly signed and falsely denounced me [to the UB] as an alleged NSZ member [...]."[53]

Jews also served in a subunit of "Chrobry II" – a company commanded by Sec. Lt. Leonard Kancelarczyk "Jeremi" of the NSZ-ONR – which "Jeremi" organized in cooperation with other NSZ-ONR officers. Two Jewish Military Union officers, Marian Rozenstof and Henryk Gumiński, also fought and died in the ranks of its Storm Team "Baśka."[54] In addition, the company's canteen also fed a larger, unidentified group of Jews. Information on this subject is available in *Fraszka na szefa kompanii* [An Epigram for a Company Head]: "For

---

[52] Jerzy Świderski, *Dziennik harcerza powstańca batalionu NOW/AK „Gustaw"* [The Diary of a Scout Insurrectionist from the NOW/AK "Gustaw" Battalion] (Warsaw: Oficyna Wydawnictwo Łoś-Graf, 2004), 199; Barbara Engelking and Dariusz Libionka, *Żydzi w powstańczej Warszawie* [The Jews in Insurrectionary Warsaw] (Warsaw: Centrum Badań nad Zagładą Żydów, 2009), 104.
[53] Roman Born-Borstein, *Powstanie Warszawskie. Wspomnienia* [The Warsaw Uprising: Memoirs] (London: Oficyna Poetów i Malarzy, 1988), 77.
[54] See Chaim Lazar Litai, *Muranowska 7: The Warsaw Ghetto Rising* (Tel Aviv: Massada, 1966), 327.

my hard toil in a dark kitchen, [and] for feeding *a whole flock of Jews* [emphasis added], they awarded me only a Cross of Merit, instead of a *Virtuti Militari.*"[55] During the Uprising, Jewess Karolina Stefania Marek "Stefa" monitored the airwaves for the editorial board of *Żołnierz Starego Miast* [Old Town Soldier]. The editorial board's orderly was a Jew known only as "Adam." The "Warszawianka" Company's platoon commanded by Sec. Lt. Józef Maria Cieśliński included an unidentified Jew, "Ryksiarz."[56] Last but not least, Calel Perechodnik, the famous author of occupation-era memoirs, served in a company of "Chrobry II" headed by Lt. Mikołaj Kobyliński "Kos," whose unit originated in the Underground Army of the "Sword and Plow" Movement, which had joined the NSZ in July 1944.[57]

Thus, a detailed analysis reveals quite a few NSZ soldiers of Jewish ancestry. Their identities were acknowledged by their Christian brothers-in-arms, but their descent was not a source of antipathy.

Some Jews attempted to demonstrate their gratitude for the NSZ soldiers' heroic stance during the Holocaust by attempting to assist the formation's veterans detained in Communist prisons during the Stalinist period. It is difficult to establish the exact percentage of Jews rescued by NSZ veterans who repaid their debt in this manner. Even so, character references from Jews were extremely valuable on account of both the anti-Semitic connotations associated with the NSZ and the Polish nationalists, as well as the Jewish descent of a significant part of the leadership of the communist security apparatus.

Thus, Col. Zygmunt Reliszko "Kołodziejski" – the inspector of the NSZ-AK Western Zone – was released thanks to the assistance of Jews he rescued from the labor camp on Gęsia Street during the Warsaw Uprising. His deputy, Col. Jan Moraczewski "Król," spent only a year in secret police custody in Poznań thanks to aid provided to a Jew during a roundup in Częstochowa.[58] It is also quite possible that Aniela Steinsberg's written declaration that the ONR member Ostromęcki sheltered her niece also influenced the nature of his death sentence, which would be commuted:

---

[55] *Kilkorgu Jeremiaków kronika krótka* [A Short Chronicle of a Few Jeremiaks], 51. (copy in author's collection), manuscript.
[56] J.M. Cieśliński's letter to the author, 30 January 2000, in author's collection.
[57] See „Rozkaz dzienny nr 18" 1 batalionu zgrupowania „Chrobry II" z 4 IX 1944 r. ["Daily Order No. 18" for the 1st Battalion of the grouping "Chrobry II" dated 4 September 1944], CA MSWiA (The Central Archive of the Ministry of Internal Affairs and Administration), AK Collection, vol. 185, p. 17).
[58] See J. Moraczewski's testimony in author's collection.

> Upon learning that Mirosław Ostromęcki was sentenced to death, I feel duty-bound to inform the President-Citizen [Bolesław Bierut] of the following: I met Mirosław Ostromęcki during the fall of 1944 in Włochy near Warsaw. At the time, he assisted and sheltered my niece, Julia Berli, knowing well that she was of Jewish descent. He did this selflessly. I also know that during the same time he also helped other Jews. I declared my readiness to present these facts before the court, but I was never called upon.[59]

Cases of Polish nationalists assisted by formerly sheltered Jews were plentiful. During the trial against Jerzy Regulski – an ONR activist and NSZ soldier, currently a professor and specialist on local self-government – Natan Karwasser declared: "During the occupation, when I was hiding from the German criminals, I visited the Regulskis in Zarybie. They helped me as much as they could and helped me survive."[60] Jerzy's father, Janusz, was in the ONR's leadership. Other family members, including his mother, Halina, and his sister, Hanna, also worked for the NSZ.

Julian Tuwim, a poet of Jewish descent, personally interceded with Bolesław Bierut on behalf of two nationalists sentenced to death: Jerzy Kozarzewski "Konrad," a courier for the Holy Cross Brigade, and Mirosław Ostromęcki. In turn, the case file of a Kraków ONR activist, Jerzy Zakulski ("Rudolf," "Borejsza," "Czarny Mecenas") contains a notary-stamped declaration by Maria Bernstein (who later changed her surname to Błeszyńska):

> Jerzy Zakulski, who then resided, along with his father, the late Ludwik, in Kraków Podgórze on Św. Kinga Street No. 7, sheltered me in his flat after I snuck out of the ghetto at night, along with a three-year-old child, in addition to Jan Bahr's family, which lived at Długa Street No. 1/39. After a while, their relative, Zofia Józefa Strycharska, helped them find a safer hideout in Myślenice for my child and me, where we stayed until the end of the war. I am providing this testimony under oath because I wish to express my gratitude. They saved our lives by risking their own. I have only now learned of the charges and the verdict [death].[61]

---

[59] Copy in author's collection.
[60] Copy in author's collection. The Zarybie estate, in addition to sheltering Karwasser, also hosted Stefan Korboński, an activist of the peasant-populist People's Party (Stronnictwo Ludowe); and the head of Civil Combat (Walka Cywilna), Jerzy Iłłakowicz, an ONR activist; as well as Czesław Miłosz. See M. Wittelis, „Z cyklu Album z Podkową: Zarybie" ["From the Horseshoe Album Series: Zarybie"], *Podkowiański Magazyn kulturalny* 1 (8) (1995).
[61] Copy in author's collection.

The declaration was prepared on 23 June 1947 but it failed to help. The death sentence was carried out on 31 July.

While fleeing Communist-occupied Poland, NSZ officer Wiktor Roman Skiba received assistance from a Jewish man he saved during the Holocaust. The latter offered to help Skiba obtain decent employment.

> During the war Antek, an old schoolmate of Jewish descent, lived at Jacek's [the author's] house for two years. He never left the house during that time. Now he was a PPR [Polish Workers' Party, i.e. the Communists] member and the director of one of the largest industrial associations in the country.[62]

Julian Kamiński, a physician in Capt. Władysław Kołaciński "Żbik's" unit, also interceded on behalf of his fellow NSZ soldiers quite a few times:

> I am a 54-year-old physician who had practiced medicine in Przedbórz, in the County of Końskie, for twenty years. As a Jew I was held in the ghetto in Przedbórz until the action of 9 October 1942, when I escaped from the ghetto and hid in the villages. In late 1943 I managed to join a partisan unit in the area of Włoszczowa. I was accepted as the unit's physician. Only after serving in this unit did I learn that I am in an NSZ detachment.
>
> This unit was sometimes visited by Denkiewicz Bogusław, *nom de guerre* "Bolesław," a lieutenant whom I knew from the prewar years because he came to Przedbórz quite frequently. Although he knew I was a Jew, he nevertheless gave me the highest possible recommendation. The commander told me about this later and through his recommendation he contributed greatly to saving my life. [...] I am therefore addressing my impassioned plea to You, Mr. President, to pardon Lt. "Bolesław" who proved himself to be a real human being and saved my life, in spite of the Hitlerite darkness.[63]

Fr. Prof. Szczepan Sobalkowski "Andrzej Bobola," the chaplain of the Kielce District of the NSZ, sheltered and cared for a Jewish couple from Wieluń for the entire duration of the German occupation. As a result, he received a lighter sentence from a Communist court.[64] The verdict against Klemens Jędrzejczyk (part of the trial against the

---

[62] Wiktor Roman Skiba, *Na skibach świata* [On the Ridges of the World] (London: Veritas, 1979), 24–25.
[63] Julian Kamiński's letter to Bolesław Bierut, 10 May 1947, copy in Leszek Żebrowski's collection.
[64] Case file of Szczepan Sobalkowski, copy in Leszek Żebrowski's collection.

members of the Command of the NSZ District of Częstochowa-Silesia) includes the following sentence: "[He] assisted [...] the Jews whom he was sheltering and subsequently issued them with false identity papers."[65] Lejbko Goldman and Izaak Halber testified that Lt. Władysław Wyszczółkowski "Sęp" – the adjutant to the commander of the NSZ Podlasie District – sheltered the Jews and their possessions, in addition to providing them with false documents.[66] Partly as a result of this testimony the accused were eventually acquitted.

Baseless accusations of NSZ collaboration with the Germans levied by extremist circles compel the veterans to protest. In his book *On the Ridges of the World* Wiktor Roman Skiba "Jacek Wolański" – the commander of the Pruszków County structure of the NSZ's Warsaw Municipal District, and an ONR member – declared:

> I must emphasize firmly that, within the district in which I served during the entire occupation, I never encountered a single NSZ action aimed against the Jews, or any single manifestation of anti-Semitism on the part of the NSZ. I will say more [...]. In 1943 and 1944 my three-room apartment became the shelter for Jews, the lawyer Antoni L., along with his wife and young son. I knew him from our school days. After the war L. assumed a high post in the state administration.[67]

Other NSZ veterans spoke out in a similar spirit during a discussion about the formation in the liberal-left *Gazeta Wyborcza* [Electoral Gazette] during the years 1992-1993. One of the most emotional fragments of this debate was certainly Jerzy Kozarzewski's letter to the editors: "As a member of an independentist organization, I consider it an insult to be included in the ranks of the oppressors of the Polish Jews."[68] This statement is particularly important because Kozarzewski was sentenced by the Communists to death for independentist activities. Yet, Julian Tuwim saved his life.

Accusations generating controversy and disputes were also levied against the NSZ during moments of particular significance for Poles. On the fiftieth anniversary of the outbreak of the Warsaw Uprising (1994), Michał Cichy, a journalist writing for *Gazeta Wyborcza*, reviewed the memoirs of Calel Perechodnik, a Jewish insurrectionist fighting for an NSZ-AK-"MiP" unit. Cichy claimed that

---

[65] Case file of Klemens Jędrzejczyk, copy in Leszek Żebrowski's collection.
[66] Case file of Stanisław Jurczak and friends, copy in Leszek Żebrowski's collection.
[67] Skiba, *Na skibach* [On the Ridges], 52.
[68] Jerzy Kozarzewski, „W imię pojednania" ["In the Name of Reconciliation"] *Gazeta Wyborcza*, 26 March 1993.

"[Perechodnik] survived even the Warsaw Uprising, when the AK and NSZ slaughtered a plethora of survivors from the ghetto."[69] He supported his theory with an article entitled "Polacy – Żydzi: czarne karty Powstania" ["Poles and Jews: The Dark Side of the Uprising"], claiming that, among other things, the NSZ murdered several dozen Jews on Długa Street 25.[70]

Historian Andrzej Paczkowski defended the article – so offensive to the Uprising's participants – by arguing that "it is sad – but simultaneously natural – that, while writing the truth, one must explain one's good intentions." Włodzimierz Borodziej, a scholar associated with Warsaw University's Institute of History, took a similar approach: "Cichy's piece is important as a contribution to a better understanding of the history of Polish-Jewish relations, for we do not come to understand the past through declarations but through tedious, time-consuming research."[71]

Yet, the basis of the accusation was a claim by Bernard Mark, which was unsupported by any research, that "an NSZ unit from the Old Town murdered a group of thirty Jews on Długa Street 25. These Jews managed to survive during the entire span of the war and now came out in to the open, in hope of liberation, only to be liquidated by the bullets of the NSZ's soldiers."[72] Mark cited the testimonies of Gustawa Wilner, Tadeusz Sarnecki, and Barbara Temkin-Berman. The problem is that neither the testimony of Tadeusz Sarnecki, on deposit in the National Library of Poland, nor Barbara Temkin-Berman's memoir (published in 2000), contain such information.[73] Wilner's testimony is, in turn, inaccessible.

---

[69] Michał Cichy, „Wspomnienia umarłego" ["The Testimony of the Dead"], *Gazeta Wyborcza,* 15 December 1993.
[70] Michał Cichy, „Polacy – Żydzi: czarne karty Powstania" ["Poles and Jews: The Dark Side of the Uprising"], *Gazeta Wyborcza,* 29–30 January 1994.
[71] Compare Michał Cichy, „Polacy – Żydzi"; Tomasz Strzembosz, „Polacy–Żydzi. Czarna karta *Gazety Wyborczej*" ["Poles and Jews: The Dark Side of *The Electoral Gazette*], *Gazeta Wyborcza,* 5–6 February 1994, Andrzej Paczkowski, „Grzech mówienia prawdy?" ["The Sin of Telling the Truth?"], *Ibid.*; Włodzimierz Borodziej, „Wysoki stopień ryzyka" ["A High Degree of Risk"], *Ibid.*; Leszek Żebrowski, *Paszkwil Wyborczej* [Slander by the Electoral Gazette] (Warsaw: Burchard Edition, 1995).
[72] Bernard Mark, *Walka i zagłada warszawskiego getta* [The Struggle and Destruction of the Warsaw Ghetto] (Warsaw: Wydawnictwo Ministerstwa Obrony Narodowej, 1959), 468.
[73] Barbara Temkin-Berman, *Dziennik z podziemia* [A Diary from the Underground], comp. Anka Grupińska and Paweł Szapiro (Warsaw: Twój Styl, 2000).

Temkin-Berman's memoirs were published on the basis of a photocopy of the original, hand-written document in the archive of Kibutz Beit Lohamei Hagetaot. According to the publishers, the manuscript written directly after the war contains numerous indications of self-censorship. In his work on the Łódź Ghetto (published in 1988), Dr. Icchak (Henryk) Rubin went so far as to state:

> Human beings instinctively seek out the culprits of their misfortunes and they tend towards generalizations in their search. They utilize their imagination, supplementing the gaps with details from their personal experiences. Thus, the testimonies and memoirs are dominated by a tendency towards holistic descriptions of the situation in the ghetto. The character and content of these was decisively influenced by the time period during which they were written, i.e. the same political forces which established the nature and aims of scholarly research. The functionaries of the Jewish Committees, as Communist Party nominees, gathered these testimonies while indicating who was guilty and what the culprits deserved. Thus, almost all the testimonies contain identical assessments and their style and content are quite stereotypical. They appear as if they had been dictated. The authors wished to please the organizers of the testimony-gathering initiative. Quite often, they simply feared writing anything contrary to what they [the Jewish Committee representatives] suggested.[74]

The archives of the Jewish Historical Institute (ŻIH) also contain "corrected" testimonies. In this context, it may be worthwhile to quote the American historian John Armstrong:

> I asked the ŻIH Archive employee why this was the case. He intimated that purges and the correcting of testimonies took place during the Communist period. This fact does not necessarily negate the usefulness of the collection. Yet, I emphasize that it must be approached with exceptional caution.[75]

Meanwhile, Sarnecki mentioned the NSZ twice in his testimony:

> [We were in] the Press Headquarters of the Home Army's Warsaw-North Zone. All of us Old Town journalists gathered here, regardless of political

---

[74] Icchak (Henryk) Rubin, *Żydzi w Łodzi pod niemiecką okupacją, 1939-1945* [The Jews in Łódź Under the German Occupation] (London: Kontra, 1988), 38 in Marek Jan Chodakiewicz, *Kłopoty z kuracją szokową: wstrząsnąć sumieniami, czy wstrząsnąć nauką?* [Problems With Shock Therapy: Jolting the Conscience or Jolting Scholarship?], manuscript, English version available at www.glaukopis.pl.

[75] Chodakiewicz, *Kłopoty z kuracją ...* [Problems With Shock Therapy ...].

belief and party affiliation. I am convinced that all of us, not excepting the journalists from the National Armed Forces, now had only one thing in mind: the wall created by historical tradition, conscious political efforts, and the national temperament between most of society and those who, on account of their close ties to the Soviet Union and their activities in the East, are suddenly rising on the wave of the fortunes of war to the role of a decisive factor with the greatest prospects for the future.

A press conference in the office of the *Delegatura's* Information Department. The sense of launching the Warsaw Uprising is under debate: Someone asked: 'So what should be done?'

Several individuals answered in unison: 'Capitulate! We should capitulate ostentatiously to cast our horrible accusation directly into the world's face, [to emphasize] that the inability to assist us is a painful and undeserved disappointment for us.'

Another individual asked: 'An undeserved disappointment?'

A representative of the National Armed Forces replied: 'Oh yes! We are spilling our blood on the battlefields of France, Belgium, and Italy, and all we can expect in return is an excuse that it is too risky, dangerous, and far to help us. Is the Polish soldier fighting at Monte Cassino not placing his life on the line? Hence, are we not entitled to a sacrifice of at least some Allied blood?'

I posed the question: 'If we won't receive any help, or if it will arrive too late, is it not better to simply capitulate?'

The NSZ journalist once again yelled out [with disdain]: 'Let the capitulators go to the Germans with white rags on brush handles!'[76]

It therefore turns out that Tadeusz Sarnecki not only failed to mention any alleged massacre of Jews committed by an NSZ unit, but actually presented the organization's journalists in the most flattering light. It is particularly ironic that Calel Perechodnik, whose memoir served as the basis for an attack on NSZ and AK veterans, participated in the Warsaw Uprising as part of a unit originating in the Underground Army of the "Sword and Plow" Movement, a detachment which was eventually incorporated into the NSZ-AK.[77]

---

[76] Tadeusz Sarnecki/"Janusz Korwin" was a Party of Polish Democrats activist (*Stronnictwo Demokratów Polskich*) (BN, mf 58194, *Wspomnienia z Powstania Warszawskiego* [A Memoir From the Warsaw Uprising], 34).

[77] See „Rozkaz dzienny" [Daily Order], p. 136.

Thus, as the above examples indicate, Polish-Jewish relations are an intricately complex problem that resists reductionist clichés serving unscholarly ends. The participation of Jews in NSZ partisan and insurrectionary units is undeniable. Unquestionable is also the assistance provided by Polish nationalists from all factions and organizations to the Jews during the Holocaust. This once again demonstrates that antipathies vis-à-vis a nameless collective do not necessarily translate into negative relations between individual human beings. This is important to remember in the context of the recent debate on Polish-Jewish relations during the Second World War.

It is also worthwhile to pose a follow-up question: if the most theoretically anti-Jewish Polish political activists behaved as shown above, then what was the norm for the rest of Polish society during the Holocaust?[78]

---

[78] Both recent research and published memoirs broaden our knowledge of the involvement of individuals with nationalist views in assisting Jews during the Holocaust. In this context, it may be worthwhile to mention the following persons: Bojanowski, a landowner from an area near Warsaw (*Memorial Book of Tlumacz: The Life and Destruction of a Jewish Community*, comp. S. Blond (Tel Aviv: Tlumacz Society, 1976), cxlv); Edward Gołoś [*The Death Camp Treblinka: A Documentary*, comp. A. Donat (New York: 1979), 249]; Maria Dąbrowska, a teacher from Włodzimierz Wołyński, sheltered 18 Jews She was arrested and tortured by the Germans, and subsequently shot for refusing to divulge any names [W. Zajączkowski, *Martyrs of Charity*, part 1 (Washington, DC: St. Maximilian Kolbe Foundation, 1987), 269]; Ludwik Golecki from Parczew [B. Mandelkern and M. Czarnecki, *Escape from the Nazis* (Toronto: James Lorimer & Co., 1988), 24]; the Prokops from Lublin [D.-N. Cukierman, *A Guardian Angel: Memories of Lublin* (East Bentleigh, Victoria: E. Csaky, 1997), 153]; Jadwiga Bielecka from Warsaw [P.F. Dembowski, *Christians in the Warsaw Ghetto: An Epitaph for the Unremembered* (Notre Dame: University of Notre Dame Press, 2005), 107]; Walenty Beck of Żółkiew [C. Kramer and S. Glantz, *Clara's War: A Young Girl's True Story of Miraculous Survival under the Nazis* (London: Emblem, 2008), 65, 94]; Tadeusz Duchowski, an SN member [R.J. Berger, *Constructing a Collective Memory of the Holocaust: A Life History of Two Brothers' Survival* (Niwot, CO: University Press of Colorado, 1995), 52–53]; Maria Rościszowska, a Warsaw school principal [M. Zylberberg, *A Warsaw Diary, 1939–1945* (London: Vallentine Mitchell, 1969), 133]; Maria Zagałowa (*Wspomnienia z lat 1941-1959* [Memoirs from 1941-1959], BN, manuscript section 13023, pg. 23); Tadeusz Mikułowski, an activist of the nationalist-affiliated Association of High School and University Instructors (*Towarzystwo Nauczycieli Szkół Średnich i Wyższych*) (W. Bartoszewski, „Wszystko, co polskie, jest moje" ["All That is Polish is Mine"], *Rzeczpospolita*, 10 December 2004); Józef Witwicki and Ignacy Nowicki [Ryszard Juszkiewicz, *Losy Żydów mławskich w okresie II-ej wojny światowej* [The Fate of Mława Jews During the Second World War] (Mława: Towarzystwo Przyjaciół Ziemi Mławskiej, 1994), 117, 119].

Synopses of Chapters

Marek Jan Chodakiewicz, "Reflections: A New Work, but the Same Old Method"

Historian Marek Jan Chodakiewicz's chapter on "Reflections" is an anchor to scrutinize the deep flaws of Jan T. Gross's *Golden Harvest*. Chodakiewicz outlines conceptual problems that are elaborated upon by other scholars in the present volume. Next, in addition to contextualizing the events, Chodakiewicz focuses on Gross's methodology. He further exposes Gross's apparent inability or unwillingness to understand the universal human condition. Instead, the author of *Golden Harvest* indulges in ethnic stereotyping and outright racism against Christian Poles.

Gross attributes virtually any and all pathologies occurring in German-occupied Poland to the Polish ethnicity of the perpetrators. Simultaneously, he disregards similar or identical behavior among other ethnic groups, both in Poland during the Holocaust, and throughout the world during various periods of violent upheaval. Gross's selective use of evidence is another serious shortcoming as is his aversion to contextualizing. This allows the author to portray antisocial pathologies as social norms, while ignoring examples of heroic behavior and any evidence contrary to his thesis.

According to Chodakiewicz, the author of *Golden Harvest* adheres to post-modernism, an ideology that rests on the assumption that the truth is relative and subjective, and therefore cannot be approximated. This "truth," in turn, signifies that, at least in theory, one interpretation of history is as good as another. Since the ends justify the means, what matters is the alleged nobility of the objective, such as ushering in another utopia by seizing the moral high ground via putatively combating racism and anti-Semitism and fostering "tolerance" and "diversity."

In Gross's case, Chodakiewicz argues, the goal is to employ Poland in general, and the theme of Polish-Jewish relations in particular, as a vehicle to attack Christianity, tradition, patriotism, and other conservative values undergirding Western Civilization. Thus, rather than scholarship, *Golden Harvest* is yet another political salvo in the cultural war.

Peter Stachura, "Insults Instead of Facts: Notes on the Recent Debate on Poles and Jews"

Peter Stachura, a British historian of modern Poland and Germany, subjects Gross's methodology to further scholarly criticism. He argues that "Gross and traditional notions of sound, empirically-supported, objective scholarship – which aims to ascertain the true facts of historical circumstances, and to weigh these calmly in the interests of balance and clarity – are irreconcilable." Stachura then proceeds to bolster his reasoning with examples, focusing on Jewish property during the Holocaust.

One of Gross's main claims is that Christian Poles benefited from the redistribution of the wealth of the exterminated Jews while helping the Nazi Germans rob and murder them. Stachura deploys his knowledge of the Third Reich to demonstrate that the German system was designed to prevent such an eventuality. Thus, it was the Nazi state and its functionaries that reaped the fruits of the expropriation of the murdered Jews. Any transfers of wealth to Poles or, for that matter, members of any other European nationality (including voluntary collaborators and involuntary servants), were merely accidental "leaks" in an otherwise smoothly-functioning machinery of despoliation and death.

Moreover, Stachura adds, these hardly compensated for the severe economic blows the Germans inflicted upon the Poles. After all, Polish Christian property was subject to mass confiscation by the Third Reich as well, and any serious reconstruction of Holocaust-era Polish history cannot gloss over this fact. Gross's continuing distortions constitute grounds to classify him in the same league as the likes of David Irving, a Holocaust revisionist.

Piotr Gontarczyk, "'If the Facts Are Against Us, Too Bad for the Facts': On Jan Tomasz Gross's Scholarly Method in *Golden Harvest*"

Piotr Gontarczyk, an expert on Poland's Communist movement during and after the Second World War, investigates the apparent immunity to any scholarly criticism exhibited by Jan T. Gross and his followers. In particular, he interrogates the Grossian/neo-Stalinist assertion that individual ethnic Poles who robbed, harassed, and even murdered Jews during the Holocaust did not constitute the dregs of Polish society, but rather a representative cross-section of a degenerate, greedy, and deeply anti-Semitic society.

The traditional, logocentric, and empirical methods of reconstructing the past, Gontarczyk argues, lie outside of Gross's field of interest. All too often, he appears to employ the attitude that "if the facts are against us, too bad for the facts" in crafting his narrative. In fact, in his attempts to bask in the spotlight, the author of *Golden Harvest* refuses to reject any method of falsifying the historical reality. The methods Gross employs have been lifted from the realm of pop-culture, where the aim is to shock, insult, and utilize scandals to gain the greatest publicity possible.

Teresa Preker, "The Attitude of the Polish Population Towards Jewish Escapees from the Treblinka, Sobibór, and Bełżec Death Camps in Light of Jewish and Polish Testimonies"

The late Teresa Preker, a Righteous Gentile and Polish liberal historian, offers a much-needed, if posthumous, corrective to Gross's portrayal of the ethnic Polish population in the vicinity of the Treblinka death camp.

In *Golden Harvest,* the local peasantry is depicted as consisting solely of degenerates collaborating and prostituting themselves with the Ukrainian SS guards manning the camp. As a result, the nearby villages benefited from an alleged injection of Jewish wealth. Yet, this is an incomplete reconstruction of events on the microscale, according to Preker. Gross failed to pay attention to Preker's research which had been published almost 20 years before.

Preker scrutinized dozens of testimonies of Jewish escapees from Treblinka, Sobibór, and Bełżec, and the local Polish denizens. Unlike Gross, Preker subjects all of her sources – both Jewish and Polish – to a critical analysis. Her findings indicate a wide array of Polish reactions toward the predicament of the Jewish fugitives. Some villagers sheltered the escapees, while others provided food, transportation, or directions. Others turned them away. Some indeed robbed the Jews, but those crimes were carried out mainly by criminal bands roaming the countryside. The robbers often posed as representatives of the Home Army, or some other resistance outfit, which undoubtedly fed claims that the Polish independentist underground attacked or even killed Jews. The primary motive behind the robberies was not anti-Semitism, but avarice.

In addition, the main factor responsible for the refusal to shelter or assist the escapees was fear of Nazi repression, not hatred of the Jews. Furthermore, refusals, robberies, and other unpleasant experiences are often strongly emphasized in the testimonies of the escapees. Ordinary, haphazard, assistance, on the other hand, was treated as "normal" and, therefore, unworthy of mentioning.

Mark Paul, "The Rescue of Jewish Escapees from the Treblinka Death Camp"

The essay by independent Canadian scholar Mark Paul supplements Teresa Preker's article with additional testimonies of Jewish escapees from Treblinka, who received assistance from the local Polish peasantry. Paul's research supports Preker's earlier findings but directly contradicts the Grossian school's narrative of the callous, anti-Semitic perfidy of the Polish Catholic peasantry. In fact, the rural folk provided a great deal of help to the Jewish escapees, consisting mostly of temporary shelter or food. Overwhelmingly, Jews who turned to the Poles for help received some form of assistance. A number managed to find long-term shelter – an endeavor fraught with many dangers – with the local farmers.

While Jews were occasionally robbed, cases of murder or denouncement to the Germans were actually rather rare, and indeed, active and passive protection of the Jews was the norm in the Polish countryside. In addition, Paul documents cases of Jewish disbelief at the prospect of mass murder by the Nazis. Moreover, he discovered that Jews charged with sorting the clothing and removing the golden teeth of Treblinka victims buried some of the valuables on the premises of the camp. It was this "treasure" that was later sought by local grave robbers.

Paweł Styrna, "Tale of Two Hamlets: The Cases of Wólka-Okrąglik and Gniewczyna"

Jan T. Gross insists upon converting single cases or incidents into general, all-Polish norms, and Paweł Styrna, a scholar at the Institute of World Politics, shows how the Princeton sociologist accomplishes it. In *Golden Harvest*, Gross focuses on two localities in occupied Poland. The first is Wólka-Okrąglik, a village adjacent to the Treblinka death camp. Its residents allegedly collaborated and prostituted themselves *en masse* with Ukrainian SS-men guarding the camp. As a result, Gross claims, they benefited handsomely from the Holocaust. In the hamlet of Gniewczyna in southern Poland, a gang of influential local thugs tortured a group of eighteen Jews, raping the women, and robbing everyone. Afterwards, the perpetrators denounced them to the Germans, who promptly arrived and executed all the Jews, following a hearty breakfast with the criminals.

Thus, Gross arrives at a conclusion that paints the "statistical Pole" of the Holocaust era in the most unflattering light possible. But were the examples he selected at all representative of the norm? Paweł Styrna's research on the two villages suggests a negative answer to this question.

A diversity of behavioral patterns manifested itself both in the two hamlets and throughout the occupied Polish lands. Pathologies were neither the sole, nor the dominant Polish responses to the war. Yet, such occurrences should not surprise researchers, given the effects of wartime trauma and demoralization on both civilians and military personnel. Last but not least, Styrna asks scholars to ponder whether, and to what degree, the Polish-speaking peasants perpetrating atrocities on the Jews can be considered nationally-conscious Poles.

Ryszard Tyndorf, "Collective Rescue Efforts by Poles on Behalf of Jews in the German-Occupied Polish Countryside"

Research on the rescue efforts of Jews by the Christian Poles is surprisingly still in its infancy. Only recently has Yad Vashem published two volumes dedicated to 5,333 Polish rescuers recognized as Righteous Gentiles by the end of the year 2000. As of January 1, 2011, the distinction of "Righteous Among the Nations" has been granted to 6,266 Poles, who form the single largest national group honored by that institution.

The vast majority of Poles who extended assistance to Jews have not received any recognition, and in many cases their Jewish benefactors have since died or severed contact with them. It is difficult to estimate the number of Poles who sheltered or—much more often—assisted Jews in other ways.

Polish historian Teresa Preker, herself a Righteous Gentile, estimated their number could run as high as 300,000. However, this may be a conservative estimate. It is also apparent that it took the silent support of many additional hundreds of thousands of Poles, in defiance of German decrees that made punishable by death all forms of assistance to Jews, for the rescue efforts to succeed.

The toll in human sacrifice that Poles paid for this rescue effort is staggering. Research conducted by Poland's Institute of National Remembrance, which is still ongoing, has confirmed more than one thousand documented cases in which Poles—women, children, and men, often entire families—were executed, burned alive, or perished in prisons and concentration camps for helping Jews. Most of these acts of Nazi terror occurred in the countryside where the majority of Jews survived.

Bethany M. Pałuk, "Looting as a Case Against Racial Determinism"

In *Golden Harvest*, looting is characterized as a phenomenon uniquely restricted to Christian ethnic Poles. This amounts to not only a distortion of history, but also an assault on common sense. As Bethany M. Pałuk demonstrates, even the most cursory glance at the history of the Second World War will reveal that looting was indeed a universal and worldwide phenomenon during that terrible conflagration, as is always the case in times of armed conflict, civil strife, and social decomposition. No ethnic group or social stratum has managed to remain immune. Thus, during the Second World War in occupied Poland, it was not only ethnic Poles who happened to loot the scraps of Jewish property left behind by the Germans. In fact, as Pałuk's research indicates, cases of Jewish-on-Jewish looting occurred as well, in addition to incidents of Poles and other Christians being looted by Jews. She cites a telling example of rich Jews looting hogs from foreign companies in the city of Lublin during a German bombing raid in September 1939. Pałuk also illustrates her point with similar examples from other events and cultures. Such facts illustrate the deeply-flawed nature of Gross's revisionist opinions.

Fr. Waldemar Chrostowski, "Moral Dilemmas in Turbulent Times"

Nowadays it is quite easy to judge the morality of individuals and groups in bygone times. The choices made by the perpetrators who killed, the collaborators who assisted them, and the onlookers who stood by passively during the Holocaust, quite correctly and understandably, continue to elicit outrage, shock, and soul-searching. We often wonder why relatively so few righteous heroes appeared actively to resist evil.

Such reflections are usually accompanied by an unconscious assumption that had we lived during the Holocaust, then we certainly would have displayed far greater courage than our ancestors. After all, we are not anti-Semites, racists, or murderers. Unfortunately, such noble sentiments suffer from one serious flaw. Namely, they ignore completely the historical context in which the extermination of European Jewry occurred. Especially in the case of German-occupied Poland, factors such as wartime traumatization, Nazi terror, and the mass murder of Christian Poles – occurring parallel to the *Shoah* – are missing from the equation.

Before proceeding to judge our predecessors we would do well to study the historical dilemmas and moral choices they faced. There are limits to condemning our forefathers and distancing ourselves from them. We cannot say for certain how we would have behaved in light of similar circumstances. Those calling upon us to examine our collective conscience do not have the benefit of such knowledge either. Perhaps it is even possible that they haven't bothered to ponder this problematic ethical question, or have chosen not to do so.

Barbara Gorczycka-Muszyńska, "Whose Tenements? A Legal Analysis of the Status of Former Jewish Property in Light of Postwar Polish Law"

Barbara Gorczycka-Muszyńska, a retired Polish judge, examines the theory that Polish citizens enriched themselves at the cost of Holocaust victims by appropriating their property. The theory, she concludes, fails to stand up to scrutiny. During the Nazi occupation these properties (usually referred to as "post-Jewish" properties in the legal parlance of the Nazis and Communists) were confiscated by the Third Reich. Any violations of this newly-Germanized property, by Poles or members of any other non-German ethnicity, were punishable by imprisonment in a concentration camp or death. The common practice of the occupiers in relation to the appropriated valuables and real estate was to utilize and protect them from theft or perceived misappropriation by the undesirables. After the war, these properties came under the province of the Communist state apparatus in Soviet-occupied Poland. In part, some of the properties were regained by former owners or their legal representatives. The properties of those former proprietors who failed to claim their properties, or were unable to do so (usually because they had been murdered) before 1948, were nationalized. Afterwards, as the Communist regime began to further consolidate its control over the country and its economy, even briefly restored properties were once again confiscated.

Tomasz Sommer, "Jan T. Gross's Methodology in *Golden Harvest* From the Perspective of Sociology"

Many professional historians, including those sympathetic to Gross, have pointed out serious flaws in his historical methodology. Gross's supporters usually answer this charge by emphasizing that he was trained as a sociologist, not as a historian. Yet, sociologist Tomasz Sommer argues that the author of *Golden Harvest* fails to adhere to the basic canons of the discipline even in his own field of expertise. Gross's employment of a photograph of alleged Treblinka-area "treasure" hunters is a case in point. Lacking exact information as to the circumstances in which the picture was taken and ignoring information that refutes his premise, Gross nevertheless utilizes it as a kind of compass, allowing him to treat the testimonies and events he presents as facts. The photograph serves as a metaphor of sorts, an embodiment of his thesis. This could be somewhat justifiable as a literary or dramatic device, but is far removed from any scholarly method. Accordingly, Gross's book may be treated as a more or less successful work of literature, not as a methodologically-supported reconstruction of real events. Thus, the conclusion appears justified that Gross's usage of the photograph is unscholarly and therefore academically unethical.

John Radziłowski, "The Neo-Stalinist Discourse in Polish Historical Studies in the United States"

According to historian John Radziłowski, the works of Jan Tomasz Gross and his supporters may be classified as the neo-Stalinist school of historiography. This is not to argue that these scholars are necessarily admirers of Joseph Stalin or Communist sympathizers.

Rather, it may be demonstrated that their approach to Polish history parallels closely the assumptions and propaganda themes of the original school of Stalinist historiography.

Following the imposition of Soviet communism on Poland after the Second World War, the new cadres of Marxist intellectuals sought to create the "new man" in Poland by completely rewriting the nation's history. The essential elements of their interpretation consisted of an intensely negative attitude towards Poland's past; hostility toward Christianity in general, and Polish Catholicism in particular; and enmity toward Polish "nationalism," patriotism, and traditions. Moreover, they levied accusations of anti-Semitism and collaboration with the Nazis against their political enemies, which included essentially all non-Communists, i.e. the vast majority of the nation. The Catholic Church and the independentist underground were the main targets of such charges.

After the fall of communism and the opening of some Communist archives, a neo-Stalinist school of Polish historiography emerged. To a striking degree, its claims echo those of the postwar Stalinists proper. One of the most salient features of this school is the weaponization of accusations of anti-Semitism. Another is the perpetuation of a black legend of Polish history. The history of modern Poland, in particular, is portrayed as a nefarious exercise in chauvinistic "nationalism" and deadly anti-Semitism.

Communism, on the other hand, appears in an ostensibly neutral or even slightly positive light, and its crimes are either relativized or glossed over. In fact, the neo-Stalinist school also pushes Nazi atrocities and terror deep into the background when the goal is to emphasize the real or alleged crimes of certain ethnic Poles during the Holocaust.

All of this is accompanied by a highly biased and greatly selective approach to evidence. In other words, only those materials which support the neo-Stalinists' thesis are deployed. After all, what matters is not approximating any objective truth but achieving an ideological goal – a "new," completely transformed Polish-speaking man. Regardless of the intentions, such a methodology cannot be classified as scholarship. In addition, the neo-Stalinist discourse places obstacles in the path of Polish-Jewish reconciliation.

Mark Paul, "Poles and Jews in Poland's Eastern Borderlands in September 1939"

In some respects, what happened to the Poles in the Eastern Borderlands in September 1939 can be viewed as a continuation of Stalin's Great Terror. The group that was targeted for blind retribution, because of its nationality and social status, and not on account of any specific wrongdoings, was the *de facto* Polish minority.

Thousands of Poles, for the most part civilians and ordinary soldiers, were executed or lynched in the latter part of that bloody month alone, not by the Soviet invaders, who had not yet arrived, but by their fellow citizens, often their immediate neighbors. The killings were often inspired by, and played into the hands of, the Soviet invaders, as was the case in the small village of Brzostowica Mała, in the Białystok district, about fifty kilometers east of the city of Białystok. This is a little-known but particularly heinous crime, where neighbor-on-neighbor violence against an entire community—something that would escalate dramatically as the war progressed—was pioneered. As many as fifty Poles were tortured and butchered by a Jewish-led band of local pro-Soviet Jews and Belarusians on 20 September, *before* the arrival of the Red Army.

In the long run, however, more significant than the lack of solidarity with the Polish minority in the Eastern Borderlands in the face of Soviet aggression was the impunity with which the culprits were treated. In some cases, they were even rewarded with plum positions in the "new order." Such treatment sent a clear message to the occupied population that those so inclined could act with impunity and benefit from their crimes. These events were thus a prelude to occurrences directly following the German invasion of the area in June 1941, when they were repeated with the players cast in different roles. Although often lethal, as under the Soviet occupation, they were relatively few in relation to the overall numbers of their respective ethnic groups.

Wojciech Jerzy Muszyński, "A Mainly Theoretical Anti-Jewishness"

The Polish nationalists (also known as the National Democrats, NDs, *Endecja*, or *narodowcy*) have often been compared with the German Nazis. Undoubtedly, the paramount reason for this was the *Endecja's* anti-Jewish program. Yet, historian Wojciech Jerzy Muszyński explains that the comparison is fundamentally flawed. The two movements – Polish National Democracy and German National Socialism – were essentially incompatible and irreconcilable.

The *Endecja* was a *sui generis* political movement specific to Poland and firmly grounded in Christianity. As a nationalist movement, it arose in response to a particular need, namely Polish attempts to rebuild an independent state during an era when Poland was partitioned between three foreign powers: Germany, Russia, and Austria-Hungary. Furthermore, the birth of the *Endecja* in partitioned Poland predated the rise of Nazism in Germany by about thirty years. Its program was not an emulation of the NSDAP's.

The Nazis were a revolutionary, neo-pagan movement, while the Endeks were conservative democrats and, from the 1920s forward, increasingly Catholic. Their anti-Jewishness was not of the German Nazis' racist-exterminationist variety. Rather, it was an old fashioned conservative one. It was based on political, cultural, and economic factors. It was not absolute, and was limited by the *Endecja's* Christian conservative character. This allowed the Polish nationalists to write openly about the ongoing extermination of the Jews during the Holocaust, which they overwhelmingly condemned as a violation of the tenets of Christianity. In addition, quite a few *Endeks* actively aided Jews, in spite of distrust towards the Jews as a group. Yet, neo-Stalinists continue to equate the nationalists and the Nazis, which Muszyński considers an unfortunate symptom of the post-modernist politicization of historiography.

Sebastian Bojemski, "The Polish Nationalists and the Jews: Everyday Practice During the German Occupation, and the Case of the National Armed Forces (NSZ)"

The National Armed Forces (*Narodowe Siły Zbrojne: NSZ*) were one of the main independentist underground resistance organizations under the Nazi and Soviet occupations. Politically, the NSZ was an armed emanation of the Polish nationalist movement.

The main accusations traditionally levied against the NSZ were that this formation killed Jews and collaborated with the Nazis. Both have their origins in Communist propaganda to delegitimize them as a moral force, thus providing the pretext for their extermination to pave the way for Poland's Sovietization. As historian Sebastian Bojemski demonstrates, both accusations are also baseless in light of the available historical evidence.

Polish-Jewish relations during the Second World War constituted an extremely complex phenomenon. The participation of Jews in NSZ partisan and insurrectionary units is as undeniable as the assistance Jews received from nationalists of various orientations and organizations during the Holocaust. The conclusion is that, once again, antipathies harbored against certain abstract groups need not translate into, and effect, relations between human beings. It is essential to keep this in mind in light of the ongoing debate on the history of Polish-Jewish relations during the Second World War. It is also worthwhile to ask the following question: If the most anti-Jewish Polish political activists behaved in such a manner, then what was the norm for the rest of Polish society?

About the Authors

Sebastian Bojemski is a graduate of Warsaw University's Institute of History.

Marek Jan Chodakiewicz is Professor of History and the current holder of the Kościuszko Chair of Polish Studies at the Institute of World Politics (IWP) in Washington, DC. From 2005-2010, he served as a Presidential Appointee on the United States Holocaust Memorial Council, which operates the United States Holocaust Memorial Museum, the country's national institution for the documentation, study and interpretation of Holocaust history and a memorial to the millions of human beings murdered during the Holocaust.

Fr. Waldemar Chrostowski is a Roman Catholic clergyman, theologian, Bible scholar, and a professor at the Cardinal Stefan Wyszyński University in Warsaw. A champion of Polish-Jewish dialogue, he formerly served as a director of the Polish Council of Christians and Jews.

Piotr Gontarczyk is a historian with a PhD from Warsaw University's Department of Journalism and Political Sciences, and a researcher affiliated with the IPN Bureau of Public Education.

Barbara Gorczycka-Muszyńska is a Polish attorney and a retired judge.

Wojciech Jerzy Muszyński holds a PhD in history and works as a researcher at the Institute of National Memory (*Instytut Pamięci Narodowej*) in Warsaw. Dr. Muszyński is the editor-in-chief of the scholarly historical quarterly *Glaukopis*.

Bethany M. Pałuk is a doctoral student of modern Polish history. She lives in the United States.

Mark Paul is an independent Canadian scholar.

Teresa Preker was a soldier of the underground Home Army and a member of the Council to Aid Jews ("Żegota"). A leading scholar of the Holocaust in Poland, she was recognized by the Yad Vashem Institute as a Righteous Gentile. She passed away in 1998.

John Radziłowski is Professor of History at the University of Alaska Southeast and a researcher affiliated with the Piast Institute in Hamtramck, Michigan.

Tomasz Sommer holds a doctorate in sociology. He is the co-owner and editor-in-chief of the Polish-based conservative-libertarian weekly *Najwyższy CZAS!* [High Time!]. Dr. Sommer is the Vice-President of a free-market think-tank, the Globalization Institute (*Instytut Globalizacji*).

Peter D. Stachura is the director of the Research Center for Modern Polish History and Professor Emeritus of Modern European History at the University of Stirling in Scotland.

Paweł Styrna earned a Master's degree in modern European history – with concurrent specializations in modern Polish and Soviet history – from the University of Illinois at Chicago. He is currently studying international relations at the Institute of World Politics in Washington, DC.

Ryszard Tyndorf is an attorney and an independent researcher of modern Polish history.

INDEX OF GEOGRAPHIC NAMES

Antolin, 53

Antopol, 272

Auschwitz, 12, 42, 53, 64, 78, 82, 108, 149, 244-245, 268, 312, 337, 339

Bełżec, 21, 47, 51, 97-104, 112, 115-118, 171, 184, 236, 351

Borysław, 72

Brześć

Brest Litovsk, 286

Brzostowica Mała, 34, 292, 294, 362

Brzostowica Wielka, 34, 293

Chicago, 170, 205

Chrzanów, 47

Dereczyn, 273-274, 280, 282

Drohiczyn Poleski, 274

Dubno, 191, 274

Ebensee, 212

Gniewczyna, 138, 142, 149, 150-153, 353

Godziszów, 53

Grodno, 54, 261, 271-275

Holišov (Holiszów), 337-338

Janów Poleski, 274

Japan, 28

Jasiorówka, 130

Jedwabne, 25, 33-35, 38, 64, 81, 83, 92-95, 176, 243-245, 253, 290-293

Kielce, 87-89, 123, 167, 232, 245, 254, 320, 322-323, 332, 345

Kobryń, 212, 288

Kraśnik, 27, 39, 40-41, 43, 45-56, 172, 198, 329, 332

Łódź, 98, 122, 158, 160-161, 166, 185, 212, 226, 268, 302, 313, 348

Łosice, 123, 158

Lublin, 37, 39, 42, 57, 88, 91, 107, 121, 165, 171-174, 183, 196-197, 208, 231, 272-273, 304, 311, 321, 329, 332, 337, 350, 358

Luboml, 286-288

Lwów, 72, 99, 149, 169, 185, 192, 261, 318, 336

Majdanek, 39, 42, 312

Maliszewa, 145

Mordarka, 293

Ostrowiec Świętokrzyski, 209

Paulinów, 34, 134-135, 147

Przemyśl, 183, 208, 268, 272

Radomyśl, 61

Rzeszów, 89, 170-171, 279, 322

Sobibór, 21, 98-100, 102, 106-107, 111, 113, 116, 171-172, 179, 355

Thessalonika, 213

Treblinka, 16, 21-24, 27, 34, 70-77, 85, 92, 98-136, 142-148, 172, 179, 180-182, 234, 238, 312, 314, 350, 355-357, 360

Urzędów, 43, 46, 172

Vaihingen an der Enz, 213

Warsaw, 26-27, 31, 38, 40, 51, 82, 86, 92, 101-102, 106, 110, 131-139, 144, 152, 160-171, 178, 181, 186, 185, 187, 189, 191, 203, 213, 227, 232, 279, 306-307, 316, 318-319, 337, 340, 342-349, 351-356, 365

Wierzchowiny, 321-322

Wólka-Okrąglik, 32, 70, 124, 139, 142, 144-145, 147, 149-150, 153, 356-357

Zakrzówek, 42, 46, 61, 329

Zelwa, 274, 281, 283, 286

Złoczów, 72, 188, 192, 212

INDEX OF PROPER NAMES

Ainsztein, Reuben, 188, 329-330

Ajzenman, Izrael, 329

Arad, Yitzhak, 118-119, 131

Armstrong, John, 348

Auerbach, Rachel, 76

Bauer, Yehuda, 192-193, 263, 269-270, 272, 282, 286, 288, 290

Blaskowitz, Johannes (Gen.), 197, 294

Blum, Roman, 336

Borodziej, Włodzimierz, 347

Bouthoul, Gaston, 239

Browning, Christopher, 30, 244

Chodakiewicz, Marek Jan, 15, 21, 26-27, 29, 33, 38-39, 41, 60, 64, 89, 141-142, 151, 198, 207, 243, 253, 290, 326-330, 332, 348, 353-354, 365

Cichy, Michał, 346-347

Connelly, John, 244-245, 249, 254

Cukierman, Icchak, 148

Dąbrowska, Maria, 94, 350

Dąbrowski, Antoni ("Bohun"), 336

Dmowski, Roman, 303, 305, 307

Donat, Aleksander, 98, 112

Eisler, Jerzy, 95

Engel, David, 241

Engelking-Boni, Barbara, 35, 86

Gać, Stanisław, 87-88

Geremek, Bronisław, 331-332

Giedroyć, Jerzy, 95, 296-297

Giertych, Jędrzej, 302-303, 306

Głuchowski, Piotr, 23, 70, 234

Godlewski, Marceli, 333

Godlewski, Wacław, 82

Goldhagen, Daniel Jonah, 30, 249

Gontarczyk, Piotr, 15, 24, 27, 70, 73, 80, 88-89, 142, 330, 355, 365

Górski, Józef, 142, 147

Grabowski, Jan, 35-36, 65, 79, 86, 89, 253

Grabski, August, 95

Gramsci, Antonio, 248

Greiser, Arthur, 66-67, 195

Grossman, Vasilii, 142, 146-147

Grupińska, Anka, 333, 347

Grynkiewicz, Irena ("Lala"), 334

Gutman, Israel, 130, 154, 324, 329

Herbert, Zbigniew, 250, 254

Hirszfeld, Ludwik, 158, 333-334

Iwaszkiewicz, Jarosław, 94

Jakubson, Dawid, 283

John Paul II, 221, 249

Karski, Jan, 259

Kemnitz, Edward Marcin, 335

Kenney, Padraic, 254

Kiełbasa, Stanisław ("Dziadek"), 55

Kołaciński, Władysław ("Żbik"), 332

Korboński, Stefan, 93-94, 344

Korczyński, Grzegorz, 27, 88

Kossak-Szczucka, Zofia, 328

Kowalski, Marcin, 23, 70, 234

Kozarzewski, Jerzy, 344, 346

Krakowski, Shmuel, 329

Krivoshein, Semen, 288

Królikowski, Jerzy, 103, 109, 114, 143

Kurtyka, Janusz, 35, 96

Lando, Jerzy, 338

Lehmann, Rosa, 250, 253

Levin, Dov, 263, 272-273, 294

Lipmann, Zofia, 338

Loth, Felicjan, 333

Lutosławski, Wincenty, 308

Machcewicz, Paweł, 81, 95, 290

Madajczyk, Czesław, 61

Majewski, Michał, 24, 73, 125

Marcinkowski, Władysław ("Jaxa"), 332

Markiel, Tadeusz, 149-152

Michlic, Joanna, 253, 290

Mokrzycki, Antoni, 336

Mosdorf, Jan, 301, 305, 308, 339

Musiał, Bogdan, 72, 82, 95

Nakonicznikow, Stanisław ("Kmicic"), 334

Nowak, Jerzy Robert, 94, 212, 278

Ostwin-Zuzga, Stanisław ("Kropidło"), 338

Oziewicz, Ignacy ("Czesław"), 330

Paczkowski, Andrzej, 347

Paul, Mark, 16, 17, 33-34, 54, 117, 147, 154, 259, 270, 294, 356, 362, 365

Paulsson, Gunnar S., 49, 155-156, 183-184, 245

Perechodnik, Calel, 209, 343, 346-347, 349

Petelewicz, Jakub, 87-88

Piasecki, Stanisław, 308, 339

Piłsudski, Józef, 299, 301

Pius XI, 220, 304

Pius XII, 31, 220

Pogonowski, Iwo, 26

Preker, Teresa, 6, 16, 21, 98, 355-356, 358, 365

Reszka, Paweł, 24, 73, 125

Ringelblum, Emanuel, 65, 80-81, 90, 160, 164, 208, 212, 272

Romerstein, Herbert, 294

Rossman, Henryk, 308

Rydz-Śmigły, Edward, 301

Sarnecki, Tadeusz, 347-349

Sendler, Irena, 331

Sereny, Gitta, 124, 142, 144-145

Skibińska, Alina, 65, 87-88

Śmietanka-Kruszelnicki, Ryszard, 95

Snyder, Timothy, 244, 260, 269, 291-292

Spychaj/Sobczyński, Władysław, 89

Spychalski, Marian, 87

Stalin, Joseph, 12-13, 29, 148, 225, 237, 244, 246, 259-260, 282, 286, 291-293, 301, 361-362

Stroński, Stanisław, 308

Strzembosz, Tomasz, 83, 95, 247, 268, 275, 277, 279, 347

Styron, William, 252

Szaynok, Bożena, 75, 95

Thompson, Ewa, 29

Trunk, Isaiah, 46, 131, 192, 209

Trzeciak, Stanisław, 306, 333

Tuwim, Julian, 346

Wróbel, Piotr, 253

Ząbecki, Franciszek, 101, 108, 108, 114, 124, 131, 134, 144-146

Żbikowski, Andrzej, 65, 140, 142, 176, 192, 208, 212, 260, 272, 327

Żebrowski, Leszek, 27, 37, 77, 89, 125, 321, 330, 334, 345-347

Zinn, Howard, 249

About Leopolis Press

Leopolis Press was founded in 2000 by the late Adam B. Ulam, Gurney Professor of History and Political Science, and Director of the Russian Research Center at Harvard University.

Professor Ulam created the Leopolis imprint during his final illness, in order to publish his 20th and last book, *Understanding the Cold War: A Historian's Personal Reflections*.

Leopolis was the medieval Latin name for Lwów, the Polish city where Adam Ulam was born and lived for seventeen years. The city, whose Latin name means "Lion City," had the lion as its emblem.

In late 2002, Leopolis Press began collaboration with the Kościuszko Chair at the Miller Center of Public Affairs, at the University of Virginia. The purpose was to publish a collection of scholarly papers on the transition of Poland to a temporary European democracy.

Named after the great Polish-American general of the American Revolution, the Kościuszko Chair moved to the Institute of World Politics (IWP), a graduate school of national security and international affairs, in 2008.

In 2011, Professor Ulam's widow, Molly Ulam, placed Leopolis Press into the custody of the Kościuszko Chair at IWP. At that time, Leopolis Press assumed the heraldic device of the Kościuszko Chair as its logo: a circular red, white and blue Kościuszko scytheman's cap and crossed scythes, adapted from the symbol of the American-founded Kościuszko Air Squadron that assisted Poland during the victorious war against the Soviets in 1920, and the US and British-backed 303 "Kościuszko" Polish Fighter Squadron of the Polish Government in Exile to fight the Nazis in World War II.

Readers may follow the activities of the Kościuszko Chair and discussions of Leopolis Press publications at leopolispress.com.

www.ingramcontent.com/pod-product-compliance
Lightning Source LLC
Chambersburg PA
CBHW071618170426
43195CB00038B/1408